The Study of Children in Religions

The Study of
Children in Religions

A Methods Handbook

Edited by Susan B. Ridgely

NEW YORK UNIVERSITY PRESS
New York and London

NEW YORK UNIVERSITY PRESS
New York and London
www.nyupress.org

References to Internet websites (URLs) were accurate at the time of writing.
Neither the author nor New York University Press is responsible for URLs
that may have expired or changed since the manuscript was prepared.

Library of Congress Cataloging-in-Publication Data

The Study of Children in Religions : a methods handbook /
edited by Susan B. Ridgely.
p. cm.
Includes bibliographical references and index.
ISBN 978-0-8147-7646-9 (cl : alk. paper) —
ISBN 978-0-8147-7746-6 (ebook) —
ISBN 978-0-8147-7747-3 (ebook)
1. Children—Religious life. I. Ridgely, Susan B. (Susan Bales)
BL625.5.S78   2011
200.83—dc23   2011024715

New York University Press books are printed on acid-free paper,
and their binding materials are chosen for strength and durability.
We strive to use environmentally responsible suppliers and materials
to the greatest extent possible in publishing our books.

Manufactured in the United States of America

10 9 8 7 6 5 4 3 2 1

Contents

Foreword

———— PIA CHRISTENSEN ————————————————

Already, when opening this book and reading through the first pages, you, the reader, will realize that you are holding a book of great importance. I warmly welcome the book and its effort to create a firmer foundation for an area of scholarship that has hitherto been relatively neglected. It brings together two research traditions: the study of religion and the study of children and childhood as understood from the perspectives of children themselves. The volume opens a space in which children's own perspectives on spirituality, religious beliefs, and religious practices are positioned as central to their social identities, everyday lives, and social relationships.

The Study of Children in Religions: A Methods Handbook is published at a time of intense international tension and debate, in which the role of religion and faith in contemporary societies is at the fore. This is a remarkable development when one remembers that only a decade or two ago, in European countries at least, society was seen as being in the midst of a long and durable wave of secularization. Religion was seen to have a fading importance in many societies, of interest only as sets of beliefs held by minority communities. More recently, however, it has become clear that what we see is an upsurge in religious pluralism and a greater diversity of religious and faith traditions in most societies. This development has also underpinned a new interest in children and spirituality and the call for understanding the role of religion in children's lives and education (Jackson and McKenna 2005).

During the twentieth century the right of children and young people to belong to and practice their preferred religion has been constituted as an important part of childhood politics, especially after the UN General Assembly accepted the Convention on the Rights of the Child (CRC) in 1989. The CRC posed a challenge to values, identities, and the position conventionally ascribed to children and, along with that challenge, issued a wider call for cooperation, knowledge exchange, and joint action among professionals, policy makers, and academic scholars. Across the world children began to experience the effects of changed patterns of household formation and dissolution, transnational migration, increasing economic inequality, and more socially differentiated spatial patterns in cities. Children began to have access to many sources of information and values, which further broadened their socialization. The mass media, consumerism, and public services constituted children as individuals who had to construct their personal and social identities from a diversity of ideas, beliefs, and values, often expressed through the availability of new products. As these trends have occurred, new social and cultural spaces for children are emerging, but so are new demands and political dilemmas. Indeed, some European countries are debating women's public performance of faith, with legislation pending that would reduce their right to dress in accordance with their religious practices and to perform as ordained priests. In other parts of the world, religious tensions are at the heart of armed conflicts, entailing physical harm and attacks on civil society in the form of prejudice, discrimination, and the infringement of human rights.

At the same time, since the early 1990s notions of children and childhood have been theoretically expanded and elaborated. A renewed Childhood Studies emerged as a distinct multi- and interdisciplinary field of study in its own right. The achievements of this new field have been many. They include giving children conceptual autonomy and, accordingly, granting their voices and agency important recognition. This book asserts that such notions of children's social agency need to encompass children as moral, spiritual, and religious agents. As children's perspectives become visible in religious studies, the richness of their expressions of spirituality and their role in the creation and recreation of new and traditional religious practices is being revealed. Children are not only the products of passive socialization by schools, families, and communities but also the products of peer interaction and active community engagement. At the same time, religion can be recognized as a way to open oneself to compassion for and mindfulness about the world at large and one's own place within it through practices such as meditation, ritual, and prayer. These practices enable social and cultural connection as well as conveying key values and ways of living with others. Importantly, I envision that the study of children and religion will help to take the focus away from the intense scrutiny of the "ills" of youth culture and youth risk practices, such as are displayed in alcohol consumption, smoking, and early sexual debut, and support a renewed concern with young people's values, morals, and ethics. This study enables us to ask about the role of spirituality and faith in young people's everyday lives, whether these are embedded in religion or in a sense of shared humanity and environmental concern.

This handbook is therefore an important resource for future methodological practice and debate in the fields of religious studies and childhood studies. It will be useful to both students and experienced researchers in the field, for it provides important insight into an international field of inquiry by presenting case studies conducted by scholars from around the world who are working in the areas of childhood studies and religious studies.

The volume encourages researchers to engage with broad theoretical and methodological questions, thus inviting readers to explore such questions in the specific context of their own work. Throughout their explorations, I would encourage scholars to avoid any artificial boundary-in-principle between children and adults in the study of religion.

I have elsewhere suggested that the participation of children in research emphasizes the dialogical qualities and the potential, in my own case, of ethnography to reveal research relations over time (Christensen 2004). The dialogical approach is not only fruitful but, I would argue, fundamental to research that wishes to build on children's active participation and engage with the complexity of their everyday lives and relationships. Research with children that builds on children's active participation and wishes to engage with the complexity of children's relationships will need to investigate key cultural ideas, such as the categories used to describe generations and life-course stages. This investigation requires researchers to explore, clarify, and critically question their own preconceptions. Contributors to this book emphasize that scholars of religion wishing to study children's perspectives and practices must first engage with the way they define "the child." This reasserts the fundamental anthropological question "what is a human?" by inviting reflections on the questions "what is a child?" and "what is an adult?" (Christensen 2004). Related to this is another question that this volume addresses: in research with children, what is the best way of handling the often taken-for-granted distinction between adult and child (Christensen and James 2008)? Researchers tend to position themselves in relation to a general notion of what an adult is, assuming that this notion is somehow commonly shared across social and cultural settings. I suggest, however, that researchers of children and religion need a careful working out of the various "versions" or representations of "what an adult is" and "what a child is" in the everyday interactions of particular settings such as at school, in places of worship, and in children's interactions with faith leaders, parents, and community leaders.

By raising this question, the book echoes the need to question the essentialism with which the studies of children and religion have both been conventionally suffused. It does this, for example, by questioning the rather passive role usually granted to children in studies of children's socialization into faith beliefs. We are also reminded that the primacy given to age may tend to occlude other equally important aspects of children's identities, such as gender, ethnicity, religious afffiliation, socioeconomic status, and cultural and political identity (Christensen and James 2008).

Research *with* children has not only grown in volume over the past two decades but, in doing so, has also generated a more engaged discussion of the particular methodological and ethical issues that this raises for researchers. This volume contributes to the field by drawing attention to research with children across a range of different religious contexts and exploring different aspects of the research process. It provides a comprehensive discussion of the methodological and theoretical approaches of central concern to researchers within religious studies and within childhood studies—and these are of interest more widely to the human and social sciences. It represents a rich collection of contributions from authors with a wide range of disciplinary backgrounds, research practices, and theoretical perspectives. In my own writing I have often advocated the importance of seeing research with children as essentially a dialogical enterprise—that is, as a practical engagement with local cultural practices of communication. Thus, by observing children's language use, their conceptual meanings, and their actions, the researcher is able to piece together a picture of the social interactions and the connections among people. At the same time, the researcher will be able to engage with the differences constituted in the field between and among children and adults. This form of engagement includes an appreciation of how different contexts, for example the school, the church, the home, and the street, constitute a set of positions from which children and adults "speak."

This volume contributes to a wider concern with taking children in all age groups seriously and communicating with them in ways that put children's views about their own spirituality and religious practices at the center of the investigation. In this volume the contributors genuinely and sincerely engage with understanding children's experiences, and their aim is to situate these perspectives and practices in the context of the reality of the children's and young people's lives. As research partners, children and young people are keen to know that their experiences may create change and help other children. For some children and young people it is crucial for their participation that adults (especially those in authority) hear their views so that they will perhaps come to better understand children or, indeed, contribute to changing their lives. In my view this handbook makes such a contribution not only to the field of children and religion but also to a wider need to understand children in different religious contexts around the world.

Acknowledgments

Putting together this volume has been one of the most rewarding experiences of my academic career. It put me in touch with wonderful scholars who have a great passion for bringing childhood studies into the mainstream of American academia. Many scholars offered support for this work, including Robert Orsi, who has been an important conversation partner and continually challenges me to think more critically about the interaction of children and religion. In the early stages of this project, Myra Bluebond-Langer also offered tremendous support and suggestions for highlighting the key features of child-centered studies. I owe an incredible debt of gratitude to Jennifer Hammer at New York University Press and to the anonymous reviewers of this volume, particularly those who offered insights on the introduction.

The preparation of this book has taken many months, and throughout the course of this project, a number of the contributors have dealt with sickness, fires, and various other life transitions. Yet, each met deadlines despite these life challenges. Even when my own life dictated that contributors readjust their schedules to accommodate the birth of my son, each author did so with enthusiasm. I wish to thank them all for their continued commitment to the volume.

Throughout the project I have been reminded again about the value of good friends, family, and colleagues. Ideas for the book were refined during talks with Lynn Neal, Thomas Tweed, Jim Feldman, Jodi Eichler-Levine, Stephanie Spehar, and my other colleagues at the University of Wisconsin–Oshkosh. Helen Kinsella's careful eye for argument also improved the volume, while her friendship made the completion of the project enriching. As always, I found unwavering support from my parents and sisters. This project began when I became pregnant with my daughter, Millie, and ended in the early weeks of the life of my son, Andersen. They are constant reminders of how necessary this work is. My husband, Steve, was my frequent consultant throughout the project. He enriched the volume, and our lives, with his insights and humor. Finally, this book is dedicated to my grandfather, John F. Bales II, in honor of his 100th birthday. He has been a role model for me in many ways, particularly for his ability to connect with people of all ages and backgrounds with honesty, dignity, and generosity.

Introduction

SUSAN B. RIDGELY

In much of religious studies scholarship, as in most religious practice, children appear primarily as reflections of adult concerns about the present or as projections of adult concerns for the future. Until recently, the absence of children's voices in religion—and the widely shared assumptions about childhood that inform this absence—led many scholars to view children as uncritically following the beliefs of their parents. Scholars assumed that adults are the sole creators and promoters of religious traditions and beliefs, overlooking any roles that children play in the creation or modification of religion as they respond to adult efforts to nurture their faith. Guided by theories from childhood studies, however, scholars have begun to appreciate the benefits of a child-centered perspective that can reveal the complex ways in which children can both negotiate and transform their faiths. When making this shift, scholars must, as historian Harry Hendrick reminds us, "be aware that we are studying people—with voices, concerns, and interpretations of their own—not ideas or concepts."[1] Studying children, rather than the *idea* of "the child," raises questions that researchers interested in adult issues often overlook. This volume assists those interested in religion and young people in their efforts to understand children, in all their fullness, as they participate in and work to create their own faith communities and sacred practices. The contributors offer concrete suggestions for creating methodologies that allow scholars to study adult discourses about children and the ways in which the words and actions of those same children reflect, interrupt, and challenge these discourses. Scholars interested in children and religion who want to explore the idea of childhood autonomy in religious studies, and to think critically about what we currently know about children and religion, should find much to learn in this volume.

Religious studies scholar Robert Orsi and others questioned whether adults can ever truly achieve child-centeredness in their work or access children's thoughts about religion because of the complicated ways in which children's voices are influenced by and intertwined with the adults around them (including adult researchers), the marketplace, and their peers.[2] He is correct in focusing attention on the very real obstacles to accessing children's points of view given the power difference between adult researchers and their young subjects, the ways in which children are socialized, and the distance that exists between adulthood and childhood. As scholars we can never fully identify the experience of childhood religion, for children, like adults, live in a network of relationships that inform, and sometimes even dictate, their interpretations of the world around them. The point of child-centered research, then, is not to gain access to the *Truth* of childhood religious experience (since, as Buddhist studies scholar Robert A. Sharf's essay on [adult] experience reminds us, that doesn't exist and is always a projection), but to begin listening to its subjects and their perceptions, needs, and hopes.[3] The fact that children exist within these relational networks—as all individuals do—does not diminish their participation in religious traditions, nor does it diminish what we can learn from making our best attempt to understand how children build their own unique interpretations of religion, both in conversation with the adults in their lives and among themselves.

If, because of these complexities, we choose to focus on adult influence to the exclusion of children's perceptions of reality, children remain passive reflections of adult desires and fears. To gain a more accurate picture of communal religious life, however, children must be recognized as substantive beings with particular concerns of their own, concerns that agree with, diverge from, and challenge what adults have taught them. Although the pedophilia crisis in the Catholic Church may be an extreme example, what Orsi warned in his article about this crisis can be applied to the study of religion generally as well as to children's agency within religious institutions. Orsi writes that we must "find ways of making children more authentically and autonomously present in the contemporary Christian context and . . . [to] protect their autonomy rather than putting in place safeguards that only serve to locate children ever more completely under absolute adult authority and protection."[4] Orsi's theory of childhood autonomy will only be instantiated by actual practice. If children are going to have some control over their religious lives, they need first to be given the right to speak about them.

Children and Religion

Most of the research exploring the intersection between age and religion is found in psychology, theology, sociology, or specific subfields of religious studies, particularly in studies on new religious movements (NRMs). In 1990, psychologist Robert Coles published *The Spiritual Life of Children*, which analyzed conversations he had had with children of many faiths during his research for his *Children of Crisis* series.[5] This work, along with a growing interest in children across the academy, spurred a number of articles and conferences, including *The Church and Childhood,* an edited volume that resulted from the 1993 Ecclesiastical History Conference. Further, it may have helped to make scholars already interested in children and childhood, such as anthropologist Charlotte E. Hardman, coeditor with Susan J. Palmer of *Children in New Religions* (1999), aware of the need for work on young people in religious studies. It was, however, in sociology where the first fruits of a consistent focus on children and religion were seen. Here, a small group of researchers developed a sustained interested in how young people understood their religious practices, as well as how adults remembered the religion of their childhood. Robert Wuthnow's *Growing Up Religious* (1999) and Christian Smith's *National Study of Youth and Religion* (2001-2010) sparked work on children and religion in sociology.[6] By 2000, increased interest in children across academia, along with these early works in sociology and on NRMs, led to the first panel on children and religion at the American Academy of Religion (AAR). Simultaneously, revolutionary studies like Marcia Bunge's *Child in Christian Thought* appeared in theology (2001), and Robert Orsi convened a series of conferences on the study of children's religion, culminating in an unpublished report sponsored by the Lilly Endowment entitled "Mapping the Ground of Children's Religion" (2001). Those meetings and that report have served in large part as the inspiration for the approach taken in this volume. By 2003, increased interest in nurturing children in their faith prompted developmental psychologist Chris Boyatzis to convene the first meeting on religious and spiritual development and Marcia Bunge and her colleagues to create the AAR Childhood Studies and Religion consultation. Scholarship spurred by these efforts provided many insightful and stimulating ideas, but it still did not challenge the prevailing adultist perspective in the field or offer the tools with which scholars might critique this perspective.

After 2000, studies highlighted young people as primary objects of study in interesting ways, but almost none incorporated the insights and agency of the children in a sustained way. Scholarship was about children rather than being informed by them. Adult assumptions and concerns about children, their religious formation, and their safety, rather than children's own perspectives, also inflect recent articles and books that center on children in religious traditions. The 2009 groundbreaking works *Children and Childhood in World Religions* and *Children and Childhood in American Religions* use almost exclusively adult-generated materials (and adult-centered perspectives in the analysis of these materials) to present new and important information about how religious traditions view children, parental responsibilities, and the resources available to nurture children's faith.[7] Although these studies on the religious formation of children in various traditions illuminate much about these faiths and offer an invaluable resource to scholars, they only tell a portion of the story. To understand what religious practice means to children, we would do well to follow the lead of childhood studies scholarship, balancing our investigations of adult ideas about children and childhood with those of children's thoughts about their own beliefs and practices.

Childhood Studies and Religion

Traditionally, the work conducted in childhood studies, both in the United States and in Europe, has centered on children in schools, courthouses, streets, shopping centers, and almost everywhere else except churches, synagogues, temples, and other places of religious engagement. For instance, substantial volumes such as *The Children's Culture Reader* (1998) and *An Introduction to Childhood Studies* (2004) make no significant references to religion.[8] That does not mean that this absence has gone unnoticed. Most of the major organizations concerned with children and childhood do have a few religious studies scholars involved in their programs, but their contributions are often overshadowed by the great numbers of scholars from other fields, with other interests, who contribute to the listservs, choose themes for conferences, and lead seminars. We hope that this volume will create a scholarly community within which those interested in children and religion can begin to collaborate, building from and expanding on the interdisciplinary research of those who have had a much stronger voice in childhood studies.

Building on the scholarship of childhood studies across the academy, this volume draws on research from a variety of fields, including sociology, theology, developmental psychology, and religious studies. This interdisciplinary collection provides an initial set of case studies that offer assistance in developing procedures to access young people's perceptions of their religious experiences. Hearing children speak for themselves carries the risk of undermining many of our assumptions about young people and childhood (such as childhood innocence), but then it is these very assumptions that should be critically evaluated. With children reconceived as political actors and stakeholders in their religious communities, all stand to gain a fuller understanding of the role of children in religious life and the role of religion in children's lives. Policymakers, for instance, may hear the opinions of the now largely silent constituency most directly impacted by some of their decisions, and children themselves would have an opportunity to become fuller participants in discussions about their best interests, their religious practices, and their theology. To be successful, such an approach would require scholars to use children's own definitions of the sacred and of faith community, not those offered to them by adults. It is this approach that this volume illustrates.

Who Is "the Child" in This Volume?

The Study of Children in Religions: A Methods Handbook developed out of the intersection of these two distinct bodies of work: religious studies—with its focus on the role of faith in communities—and childhood studies—with its emphasis on children's capabilities (rather than their limitations) and its child-centered modes of analysis. From this child-centered perspective, defining who is a child becomes much more complex than it first appears from a legal perspective. Does this term refer simply to a range of ages, such as everyone under eighteen, sixteen, or thirteen? Or do we measure a child by a particular level of maturity and insight? Contributor Chris Boyatzis deemphasizes age as the sole determinant; instead, contributors to this volume and the children who are its subject offer a range of answers to this question. For many young people, the definition of "child" is contextual. A nine-year-old consultant once explained to me that a child "is someone who doesn't know anything." Therefore, before First Communion she was, in her view, a child in the Catholic Church. After she experienced the taste of the consecrated host and learned the gestures that accompanied the Eucharist, she felt that she had left the realm of childhood within the context of the church, even if she and her classmates were still considered children in other aspects of their identities. Similarly, the "hidden children" of World War II (the Jewish children in the Netherlands who were sent to live with Christian families) interviewed by Diane Wolf still thought of themselves in certain contexts as children, although many of them were well over eighty years old. For these children, childhood was not a time of innocence, as many adults idealize it to be, but a time of uncertainty and upheaval. Thus, while in general this methodological handbook includes studies of children between the ages of three and eighteen, the range of ages often defined as childhood, it also illustrates how the intersection of age and maturity, as well as age and political and social circumstances, help to constitute who is identified as a child. The contributions presented here demonstrate that context, more than age or maturity, is often the most significant factor in age classification, whether the classification is done by children or adults.

This volume consists of seventeen chapters of interdisciplinary approaches that offer practical guidance for fruitfully engaging in child-centered work. The scope of methods used in the volume includes ethnography, survey data, literary analysis, archival research, and studies of a diversity of faiths and cultural moments. Matching the breadth of methods is the range of particular historical periods and specific communities discussed, from early American Protestantism, Cheyenne encounters with Christians in the late 1800s, African American Christianity of the 1920s, and American Hare Krishnas in the 1970s to contemporary religious practice among Muslims in Bosnia and Catholics in the United States. In conducting this work, we discovered that mapping this complicated interplay of children's perspectives with those of their teachers, parents, biographers, peers, and the market deepened our understandings of children, their individual religious practices, and their interactions within their religious communities.

A Child-Centered Perspective on History and Theory

This interdisciplinary approach revealed five areas of methodological overlap. The first of these five areas focused on a child-centered perspective on history and theory. Many scholars from across the academy have turned to developmental psychology for insights into integrating children (as subjects and objects) in their research. In his chapter, for instance, Chris Boyatzis reads his interactions with children, in both the clinical and the educational setting, in terms of the findings of early stage-theory developmental psychologists such as Jean Piaget and Lev Vygotszky. Although these stage theories are still used by many churches and educational institutions, Boyatzis's contribution challenges the starting point of these theories that view children primarily in relationship to their incipient adulthood, stressing what we might learn from new efforts to "reconcile the very complex tension between thinking of children as full-fledged 'beings' or young and immature 'becomings.'"

Sarah Pike's chapter on adolescence also highlights how using a child-centered perspective when researching histories and theories of childhood forces us to reconsider what we think we know about young people. Here, Pike offers a nuanced historical investigation into so-called teenage rebellion, particularly with respect to the hybrid religious identities that teens create. Priscilla Alderson's contribution closes this section by reading seminal texts in sociology from a child-centered perspective to discover what they reveal about children as rights holders. Alderson's piece builds a framework for respectfully engaging with children that is important for researchers working in all time periods.

Using Ethnography to Talk with Contemporary Children

The chapters in the second section offer suggestions on how to negotiate power differences between child subjects and adult researchers. They also offer strategies for scholars to disentangle adult instructions and interpretations from children's own individual perceptions built on these teachings and other data, and from the researchers' own involvement.

For these authors, the challenge of accessing contemporary children's points of view begins with writing a successful institutional review board (IRB) proposal. By blending the theoretical and the practical, Cindy Dell Clark provides valuable strategies for writing an IRB proposal that honors children's rights and satisfies institutional concerns about work with human subjects. As Clark discusses ways to integrate child-centered protocols into one's research, she also offers creative suggestions to help scholars translate their projects into the language of the IRB, thus overcoming one of the most frequently cited obstacles to doing research with children.

My chapter on ethnography builds on Clark's. I offer specific examples of how scholars can allow children to shape the research project and how (somewhat ironically) fulfilling IRB requirements can constitute one step toward creating an environment in which the children, rather than researchers, take the lead. E. Burke Rochford's ethnographic work explores how Hare Krishna boys created their own definitions of insider and outsider that both affirm their parents' teachings and also maintained the flexibility to allow him—a nonmember, a scholar—to be a part of their community of International Society of Krishna Consciousness. He demonstrates how children can make scholars aware of shifting norms and values within religious communities. In "Playing with Fire (and Water, Earth, and Air)," Zohreh Kermani offers an intriguing study of pagan children, using many of the ethnographic methods that Rochford and I discuss, to analyze another role that boundaries play in children's religious lives. Kermani's chapter considers the complex intersection of pagan parents' teachings about enchantment with the children's own interpretations of their religious experiences. She provides helpful suggestions for other researchers struggling to analyze children's interpretations in ways that respect adult influence as well as recognize how children's perceptions also reflect the child's own concerns and interests. Finally, Kristy

Nabhan-Warren's chapter examines adult-child interactions with a focus on how researchers can use a child-centered perspective to enter adolescent communities. Her work with Latino teen gang members in Phoenix emphasizes that to understand young people's religious interpretations scholars must embrace teens' religious creativity, rather than measuring their understandings against an established norm.

Studying Children in Schools

While these chapters all examine children within their religious communities, the third section focuses on research methods for working with contemporary children within the site most commonly associated with children: schools. As the three contributions in this section demonstrate, schools are the primary site of children's activity and the area of the tightest adult control and influence. Sally Anderson begins by examining school, in this case a Jewish school in Denmark, as a place for rehearsing the child's future roles in the "real world," a world that adults and many children agree exists somewhere other than in school. Having set up the school as a place of preparation, practice, and play, Anderson raises important issues for researchers working within this institution; for example, how does this understanding that school is a place to practice for real life influence the answers young people give in interviews, on surveys, or through other forms of data collection about the religious events they participate in there? Jennifer Beste's chapter on Catholic children's participation in the Catechesis of the Good Shepherd picks up on school as a place of rehearsal as she examines the interaction between students and teachers as they prepare for First Reconciliation.

Ruqayya Khan offers scholars a nonethnographic way to explore children's religious worlds with her in-depth analysis of her experiences developing surveys with Bosnian Muslim high school students. Comparing the results from this chapter with Smith's survey of teens in the United States shows how the results from adult-constructed surveys, like Smith's, might be complemented by the findings from similar child-centered instruments.

Using Adult-Generated Material about Children

The fourth section of the volume deals directly with the methodological issues involved in reading adult-authored assessments of children and documents about children from a child-centered perspective. Discovering ways to analyze the religious experiences of children during various historical periods can be a daunting task because it is often assumed that children left little or no trace in the historical record.

These scholars uncover previously ignored sources of children's interpretations of their religious practice and demonstrate how even adult-authored texts and toys for children reveal something about the lives of young people when analyzed from a child-centered perspective. Rebecca Sachs Norris invites readers into "The Battle for the Toy Box" as she examines contemporary religiously themed toys, games, and dolls. She argues that despite the fact that these items are created by adults and marketed, in many respects, to parents rather than to children, they reveal important information about the material children are able to employ. In her reexamination of children's Puritan literature, Philippa Koch rereads these stories using only the information about theology and society that children of the period would have possessed. Although the children's voices were not literally audible in this study, by adopting the children's perspective Koch is able to effectively argue for a more hopeful vision of Puritan childhood than found in other scholarly work. The careful analysis done in these chapters also reminds all scholars trying to engage in child-centered research that child's play is never separate from the adult world.

Even those scholars who have discovered children's perspectives within common sources soon come to realize that working through the layers of adult influence presents a difficult challenge. While many historians have used the African American–owned *Chicago Defender* in research on black America, Moira Hinderer is the first to use "Defender Jr.," the paper's children's column, as a means of accessing children's interpretations of their religious experiences. She uses these columns, particularly the children's letters to the editor, in conjunction with diaries, memoirs, and the broader historical context, to examine religious life for newly arrived young migrants to Chicago during the Great Migration. Hinderer's case study demonstrates the value and the limitations of these materials, as well as ways of effectively navigating a bricolage of sources.

Similarly, through a close child-centered reading of the adult-authored historical texts about "Minnie," a Cheyenne girl who was kidnapped at the massacre of Sand Creek in 1864, Ann Braude explores narratives written about historical children across their lifetimes, reading through adult political posturing about what is in the best interest of the child to access some elements of the child's own interests. Interestingly, Braude's work also highlights one of the limitations of ethnography—its lack of longitudinal data. Like Braude's efforts to sketch Minnie from stories and reports about her,

Amy Holmes-Tagchungdarpa's chapter explores how scholars can engage in child-centered analyses of biographies, particularly those written about spiritually adept children. These authors demonstrate how to adjust for (or remain aware of) the many filters through which the child's voice must pass before it makes it into the historical record. All of the authors in this section discover new meanings hitherto hidden when sources were interpreted from the adult perspective.

A childhood remembered also exists in this space between the actual and the imagined, the remembered and the memorialized. Using memory as a primary source in child-centered research on the recent past explicates the interconnection between the child and the adult in yet another distinct way. Diane Wolf's piece on the "hidden children" of World War II offers keen insights into how memories reveal the emotional texture of situations from childhood, even if the chronological facts and details of the events become blurred. Further, her analysis, along with Braude's, cautions scholars to recognize the limits of children's abilities to influence the world around them even as scholars seek to find and honor young people's perspectives on, and agency in, their religious lives.

Themes Revealed through Child-Centered Methodologies

In attempting to view lived religion from children's points of view, the contributions to this volume highlight three major themes that cut across these methodologies: (1) the interconnectedness of children's religious lives with those of adults; (2) the materiality of children's religious experiences as it is expressed in embodied practices, fears, clothing, and toys; and (3) the pragmatism that children use to create their own dynamic, hybrid religious worlds.

As the volume demonstrates, children, like adults, are never absolutely autonomous beings, regardless of age. When working with adults, researchers often overlook the ways in which adults' thoughts are also shaped by their social networks and religious traditions. With children, however, the layers of adult interconnectedness and societal oversight of children with which the researcher must contend makes manifest children's dependency rather than their agency. Children are guarded by the state, as seen in Clark's chapter on the IRB, and they are also monitored by parents, school officials, and religious leaders. Nabhan-Warren and I both discuss the role of adults as gatekeepers and the intersubjectivity of children's religious lives.

Once entering the field or the archives, many of the contributions attend to children's relationships with the adults in their community as well as to the researcher, and to the way adult efforts to pass on their traditions influence children's perceptions of their religious practices. Kermani's chapter on pagan children, like Rochford's and Beste's contributions, highlights the complex ways in which adult input, itself informed by the tradition and the community, and children's own experiences come together to create children's interpretations of religious events and community beliefs. In so doing, these chapters illuminate the constructed nature of religious traditions as they are made and remade in conversations between adults and children. As Amy Holmes-Tagchungdarpa states in her chapter analyzing biographies of a Tibetan Buddhist child believed to be the incarnation of a religious master, "the child's words and actions can never be fully separated from communal perceptions and definitions of them."

The complexity of accessing historical children's voices stems from researchers' dependence on scant archival sources on children as well as the dense layers of adult influence and political desires that are intertwined with the children's lives in these materials. Holmes-Tagchungdarpa's chapter, for example, emphasizes that in biography children's lives are often written to satisfy the needs of adults and the expectations of their religious community. Similarly, Koch's chapter on Puritan children's literature sifts through the desires that both the adult authors and contemporary scholars have invested in this material to offer a convincing reading of this literature as a source of hope and help, rather than as yet another indication of the abuses of Puritan childhood. These chapters on both contemporary and historical children emphasize that new discoveries can be made when researchers carefully identify the networks within which children's interpretations of their religious lives are created and attempt to see those lives (and hear those stories) from the children's perspective. Given the interconnectedness of children and adults as well as children and their peer groups, more work needs to be done on how children and adults build religious worlds and interpretations together, as well as the influence that siblings and peers have on each others' perceptions of religion.

The Materiality of Children's Religious Expressions

Children's religious experience is often made manifest through an embodied practice wherein the joys, pains, and traumas of life are expressed through theologically meaningful movement, celebrations, clothing, and body art. This emphasis on materiality, as Chris Boyatzis argues, should not be taken as evidence that young people cannot and do not think abstractly and deeply about their beliefs. Nor should it be taken as a rejection of their parents' beliefs, as Pike explains. Rather, their choice of materials, and their presentation of those materials, carry particular meanings, which often build on, and personalize, adult expressions of faith. Boyatzis studies parent-child conversations about faith, attending to the way children both influence parents' thinking on religion and are influenced by it.

Thus, this turn to the material does not inherently limit children's abilities to concrete modes of thinking the way early stage theories of development did. Instead, it pushes scholars to take children's religious practice seriously. Anderson's contribution on Seders in Jewish schools highlights the need for parents to teach children the motions, words, tastes, and dress to make religious ritual complete. The schooltime rites Anderson discusses carry with them the sense of being just for practice, from the perspective of both the students and the educators. Thus, the meaning given to the symbolism and practice of each ritual depends to a large degree on context.

As children learn the significance of religious movements and clothing, they then can use them for their own purposes. One of Wolf's subjects, looking back over her time as a hidden Jewish child in Amsterdam during World War II, remembered her (former) Jewish identity being woven into her *shabbos* dress, a dress her new Christian mother destroyed ostensibly to protect her. While clothing seemed important for many children, Kristy Nabhan-Warren's consultants embody their Latino Catholic identity through their body art. Just as these contemporary young people used religion to give meaning to their lives on the margins of American society, so too did the African American children who settled in the ghettos of Chicago during the Great Migration, discussed by Hinderer. From the perspective of the young people themselves, as Hinderer argues, movies and music added to their religious lives and gave them a moment of relief from poverty, rather than put their faith at risk, as many adults of the time period—parents, ministers, reporters, and researchers—surmised.

The children in these chapters who are dealing directly with violence, death, and war undermine essentialist assumptions about exactly who children are, just as they overturn assumptions about where proper religion can be found. Analyzing the lives of these young people highlights how the belief in children as innocent or in childhood as a carefree moment is an adult projection rather than a reality. More research into children's material religion and visual culture in the forms of play, dress, art, and music will help to deconstruct adult assumptions that blind scholars from seeing children as people in their own right. Once laid bare, we add to our understanding of how religious meanings are made and sustained for all members of faith communities.

Further, other children in this volume seem to place more emphasis on religion as an expression of joy than on religion as an expression of fear. The pagan young people with whom Kermani worked appeared to revel in the enchanted worlds to which adults introduced them. Similarly, the young people who attended the Catechesis of the Good Shepherd classes Beste observed, although fearful of their first reconciliation, spoke more about happiness and joy than fright. Norris's examination of the marketplace also emphasizes adult hopes that their children will find religion both meaningful and fun. Centering children's interpretations of religion, which are often built from stories and guided play, will help to further detail religion's role in bringing joy to its practitioners as well as in helping them mediate sadness.

In giving equal, if not greater, weight to material expressions of religion over the theological aspects of it, the religion of young people has a dynamic quality to it that appears to be less pronounced in adult lived religion.[9] Sometimes, contrary to adult desires, children do more than imitate the older generations' practices. Children sort through the networks of support and influence in their lives to find meaningful ways to express their religious beliefs and develop practices that synthesize adult teachings with their own interpretations and needs.

Children's Religion as Dynamic Pragmatism

As they find ways to imbue their worlds with religious meaning, children are neither imitators nor wholesale innovators; rather, they build upon what they know satisfies, reaching within and across traditions, time periods, and adult classifications as their needs dictate. A number of the contributors in this volume stress that children often take a pragmatic approach to religion: to fulfill needs that their inherited tradition cannot, they develop hybrid traditions that include elements of their inherited faith that have proven efficacious as well as practices and images that they learn from friends, the media, and the marketplace.[10] Pike's chapter, for example, offers a nuanced investigation into teenage rebellion, particularly with respect to inherited religious affiliation and current teen practice. Similarly, Nabhan-Warren argues that working with teens requires shedding "preconceived notions . . . of religion (good/bad, real/unreal) and similar dichotomizations of youth (good/bad, normal/deviant)" so that scholars may enter into the religious worlds of teenagers, who often make their own definitions of what is sacred and what is profane. This kind of religious mixing, which often tends to blur the secular and the sacred (at least as they are defined by adults), is not new; as mentioned earlier, it can also be seen in Hinderer's chapter. In fact, young people not yet steeped in an institutional heritage, existing in that betwixt-and-between place in their lives, and who have exposure to more possibilities for religious beliefs and practices than their parents may have an affinity for this kind of hybridity.

Attending to this kind of pragmatic religious mixing and the way it emerges from within dense networks of influence from peers, parents, pastors, and the marketplace opens many new avenues for research. For instance, following the strands of youth religious practice might push child-centered scholars to move beyond denominational boundaries. For many children, classification as "Protestant," "Hindu," Buddhist," or "Catholic" might be the least salient part of their identity. Instead, the key element of their faith may be a focus on coping with suffering, practicing yoga, or working for peace. Many of these practices are shared with other youths rooted in different inherited faith traditions, and that too becomes a crucial element in their faith. To understand the choices that facilitated these interconnections, scholars need to do all they can to view these worlds as the children do, to respect the decisions the children make, to learn the meanings that the children give their religious symbols and practices, and to take those meanings seriously.

Children are more than just vessels for adult concerns for the future of their faiths; children have a place within their religious worlds in their own right. Centering children reminds us of the significance of age and experience as an analytical category, encourages us to turn to other methods and sources that might deepen our understanding of children's perspectives on their religious lives, and compels us to reexamine existing sources using a new child-centered lens. The contributors highlight the ways in which young people both influence the religious communities in which they are raised and form new hybrid religious groups and practices that have yet to be studied in detail. These efforts have the potential to enrich our understandings of religious practice throughout the world as we gain a greater insight into children's religious lives both in formally recognized religious institutions and within their own personally constructed religious communities.

1. Harry Hendrick, "The Child as a Social Actor in Historical Sources: Problems of Identification and Interpretation," in *Research with Children: Perspectives and Practices*, edited by Alison James and Pia Christensen (Routledge: New York, 2008), 41.

2. Robert Orsi, "Mapping the Ground of Children's Religion: A Beginning" (unpublished manuscript, 2001),

3. Robert A. Sharf, "Experience," in Mark C. Taylor's *Critical Terms in Religious Studies* (Chicago: University of Chicago Press, 1998), 94-116.

4. Robert Orsi, "A Crisis about the Theology of Children," *Harvard Divinity School Bulletin* 6 November 2007: http://www.hds.harvard.edu/news/bulletin/articles/orsi.html.

5. Coles, *The Spiritual Life of Children* (Boston: Houghton Mifflin, 1990) and Coles, *Children in Crisis* (Boston: Atlantic-Little, Brown, 1978), *The Moral Life of Children* (Boston: Atlantic Monthly Press, 1986), and *The Political Life of Children* (Boston: Atlantic Monthly Press, 1986).

6. For more on the National Study of Youth and Religion see http://www.youthandreligion.org/research/.

7. Don S. Browning and Bonnie J. Miller-McLemore, eds., *Children and Childhood in American Religions* (New Brunswick, NJ: Rutgers University Press, 2009); Don S. Browning and Marcia J. Bunge, eds., *Children and Childhood in World Religions* (New Brunswick, NJ: Rutgers University Press, 2009).

8. Henry Jenkins, ed., *The Children's Culture Reader* (New York: New York University Press, 1998) and Mary Jane Kehily, ed., *An Introduction to Childhood Studies* (New York: Open University Press, 2004). For more on the exclusion of religion from childhood studies see Bonnie J. Miller-McLemore and Don S. Browning's introduction to *Children and Childhood in American Religion* (New Brunswick, NJ: Rutgers University Press, 2009), 7-8.

9. Although in other fields, such as developmental psychology, the differentiation of the spiritual from the religious has led to some interesting findings, on this issue I agree with Robert Orsi, who argues that the roots of the distinction between the spiritual and the religious can be found in an anti-Catholic rhetoric—and, further, that today the spiritual is preferred over the institutional because it is believed to be beyond the taint of politics, history, and the human. However, from the perspective of religious studies, all religion is the product of human hands as they respond to their own social and political time period. Thus, throughout the volume I use the term "religion" almost exclusively. Robert Orsi, "When 2 + 2 = Five, or the Quest for an Abundant Empiricism," *Spiritus: A Journal of Christian Spirituality* 6 no.1 (Spring 2006): 113-21.

10. My use of the term "pragmatic" is informed by the work of Richard Rorty and Jeffery Stout. For a more in-depth discussion, see, for instance, Rorty, *Philosophy and the Mirror of Nature* (Princeton, NJ: Princeton University Press, 1979) and Stout, *Democracy and Tradition* (Princeton, NJ: Princeton University Press, 2003).

A Childist Approach
to Theory and History

Agency, Voice, and Maturity in Children's Religious and Spiritual Development

CHRIS BOYATZIS

When my youngest daughter was about eight years old, at bedtime one night she said to her mother, "At this age, should I believe in God or not? Not that I'm mad at him, I just don't really believe." Her mother asked calmly, "What does that mean?" My daughter responded, "Well, I just . . . don't believe that he exists. I believe in Jesus and Mary and stuff, but not God." Referring to Jesus, she then said, "I believe that even when he's a baby, he's grown up, too. When he's little he knows that he's big." Trying to clarify our daughter's thoughts, my wife said, "You don't know if the 'big' God exists," to which our daughter shouted, "Yeah, right! Yes, that's what I believe in. Not God . . . right now I don't really believe in someone who's big enough to be everywhere at the same time." The discussion then waned and drifted toward other topics—pajamas and teeth brushing—and after several minutes, our daughter rushed to and leapt atop our bed with her arms full of books, happily announcing, "I got all my God books!"

Has a developmental-psychological approach to religious and spiritual development effectively incorporated a "children's-studies" essence? That is, has the developmental-psychological study of children's religious and spiritual development recognized children, like the one mentioned above with her arms full of "God books," as active beings with voice and agency? Has the field of developmental psychology considered children as individuals rather than as members of a particular age group within an age-based stage theory (the likes of which have dominated developmental psychology through its history)? It is possible, perhaps likely, that the theoretical embrace of cognitive-developmentalism as the dominant framework within developmental psychology has caused a kind of pigeonholing of children into particular categories and classes as thinkers and thereby has concomitantly neglected their individuality. Related to "maturity" is the complex issue of competence.

Developmental psychology has varied in its presumptions about children's competence—in general or within specific domains—ranging from, in some eras, viewing the infant and young child as rather incompetent to, at other times, considering them surprisingly competent.

Before attempting to answer these questions in depth, I will first circumscribe our topic and provide some definitions. My use of the term "child" is meant to be narrower than a traditional United Nations Convention on the Rights of the Child definition, which includes anyone up to the age of eighteen. Here I am considering *younger* children, focusing on an age range anywhere from toddlerhood through middle childhood. A practical reason for this truncation is this chapter's brevity, but a deeper conceptual reason is that a focus on younger children makes it easier to explore issues of voice and agency and maturity, primarily because young children are viewed by adults and society as having distinctly *less* voice, agency, maturity, and competence than older youth.

Maturity is one of the cornerstones of developmental theory, as it is the telos toward which growth moves. The corollary to this, of course, is the starting presumption that children are immature. There is a serious tension within children's studies between viewing the child as competent and viewing the child as incompetent. When young, children are small, not very coordinated, and lacking in reason and common sense. They get lost or distracted easily, make a mess at meals, cry a lot, choose the worst times to be fussy, relieve themselves in their pants, and insert digits into orifices. How can we see them as competent beings, with voices worth listening to?

One danger of this conceptualization is that, in terms of children's religious and spiritual growth, children are viewed merely as "spiritual becomings" rather than spiritual "beings." As eminent children's-studies scholar Alison James (2004) and other writers have argued, age is a dangerous proxy for maturity. This is especially evident in discussions of children's religious or spiritual maturity. In contrast to the assumptions of many developmental psychologists, anyone who has spent time around children in a house of worship or in a faith formation class or in Sunday School knows that age holds at best a tenuous link to spiritual insight or energy or maturity. The wizened silver-headed person down the pew might suffer from hardening of religious attitudes whereas children often startle us with their insights.

I recall my year as a religious teacher at a private Episcopal school in Virginia, where I led weekly brief lessons to separate groups of three-year-olds, four-year-olds, and five-year-olds. I left that school every week having learned something genuine from one of the four-year-olds, whom I'll call

Ethan. I came to refer to him as "my little theologian," and I saw that he not only had more insight on most issues than his classmates but perhaps had even more insight than I. During my lesson on the Good Samaritan, I used an anecdote from personal experience to help make the lesson more concrete and memorable. I told them that I had recently been in a coffee shop in nearby Washington, D.C., and was approached by an unkempt homeless woman. I admitted to the children exactly what I had done when she approached me—I ignored her, as if she were invisible. I had some discomfort sharing this story, but they deserved the truth. About two months later, I was in the bathroom washing my hands when little Ethan entered the bathroom and pulled up a footstool to reach the knobs to wash his own hands. Staring straight into the mirror and without turning toward me, Ethan quietly said, "Dr. Chris, why didn't you help that woman that time? That time a woman asked you, why didn't you help her?" It dawned on me that he was referring to my anecdote from the Good Samaritan lesson. So I told him, honestly, that I sort of froze and ignored her, and that I knew even then that it was the wrong thing to do.

Now, there are several aspects of this incident that are noteworthy. Surely one is that Ethan, my little theologian, actually recalled my story months later, a sign of genuine learning that all teachers hope for. I'd like to think that another significant aspect of this exchange is what Ethan seemed to forget or overlook, which was the epilogue of my anecdote that I had shared with the class—that I felt so bad about ignoring the woman that I later went out and found her down the street and gave her some money. But what matters here is that this preschool-aged boy—egocentric by Piagetian presumptions, merely preconventionally moral by Kohlberg's, deficient on various metrics of psychological maturity—recognized the moral inconsistency depicted by a significant adult. In his question to me, putatively his "religion teacher," this little boy held me accountable—in postmodern parlance, he spoke truth to power.

This dynamic of a young boy's challenge to our implicit power differential is not within the purview of a developmental-psychology approach. His moral astuteness is not easily accounted for within its theories. Listening to the child's voice helps me, as a developmental psychologist, recognize blind spots in our approaches to children. This anecdote also highlights children's maturity vis-à-vis contexts of authority in children's lives (in this case, a private preschool but in a broader sense the moral accountability of religion itself). Anyone who has spent enough time in churches and congregations knows that children occasionally witness outright moral failure by adults as well as more frequent duplicity, hypocrisy, and lack of authenticity. A common instance in their own experience is the confirmation ritual, used in many traditions to mark a youth as committed to the faith. Of course, what matters to these traditions is that the child is now old enough to have reason and make an informed, "mature" decision to accept the teachings of the faith. It may be especially disturbing to the youths involved, then, that so many seem pressured into going through the confirmation motions, and if they feel that they are not ready to do so often silence themselves so as not to cause trouble in the congregation or disappoint their parents. If we are concerned about children's agency and voice and choice of action in the pursuit of their identity (Meacham 2004), then this inauthentic form of confirmation will teach the child many lessons, most of which are problematic.

A child-centered approach would investigate these kinds of issues in children's lives—their perception and experience of hypocrisy and moral shortcomings in the adults and putative moral teachers around them. Surely adults wrestle with these painful facts of life, and we should learn whether and how children do so. The methodological approach would have to be genuine and probing enough to get to the heart of the matter. This means that standard approaches used by developmental psychologists—structured tasks, semistructured interviews—may not suffice. What is needed is a genuine qualitative approach that entails patient, careful listening to children while speaking with them in extended conversations. The researcher might heed Coles's suggestion (Coles 1990) to think of such exchanges with children as *conversations* rather than interviews.

The Developmental-Psychological Study of Religious and Spiritual Development

The field of children's religious and spiritual development has blossomed in the past decade, after long neglect. A review of the PsycINFO database of all the psychology literature from 1996 to 2002 found that only about half of 1 percent of all the papers published on child development had anything to do with religion or religious development (Boyatzis 2003a). Fortunately, there has been much progress. For example, more than half the dissertations ever done on children and spirituality have appeared since 2000, and at the other end of the scholarly pipeline, many edited volumes of high-level scholarship have appeared. One of the most prominent was *The Handbook of Spiritual Development in Childhood and Adolescence* (Roehlkepartain, King, Wagener, and Benson 2005). In addition, other edited volumes have explored children's religious and spiritual development (e.g., Allen 2008; Dowling and Scarlett 2006; Ratcliff 2004). The past decade has seen a spate of special issues on child and adolescent religion and spirituality: *Review of Religious Research* (Boyatzis 2003b), *Applied Developmental Science* (King and Boyatzis 2004), *The International Journal for the Psychology of Religion* (Boyatzis 2006), and *New Directions for Youth Development* (Benson, Roehlkepartain, and Hong 2008). Finally, proof that religious development is moving toward the mainstream is that the most recent edition of the prestigious *Handbook of Child Psychology*, the "bible" in child development scholarship, has an entire chapter on religious and spiritual development (Oser, Scarlett, and Bucher 2006). In contrast, the *Handbook*'s prior edition, in 1998, had, among its thousands of pages, a mere three subject-index references to religion and spirituality.

We will focus here on the attempts to include children's spirituality within developmental psychology, by necessity omitting several fields that have much to say about children's religious development, including children's theology (e.g., Miller-McLemore 2003), religious education (e.g., Westerhoff 2000), and others. First, though, it is necessary to contextualize the term "religion," which has been used by developmental psychologists in a couple of ways. First, it has been used to refer to a *context* of development—it is a social setting for development rather than a domain or process. A second meaning has been the development of what I call religious cognition—that is, how children think about and understand what religions care about: God, prayer, the afterlife, and so on. In line with the first definition, developmentalists are inclined to view religion as a traditional, organized institution with shared beliefs, rituals, creeds, sacraments, and so forth that are enacted and expressed within a community; in this view, children's religious development pertains to their engagement with or growth within these organized, traditional faith contexts. This would create a vast array of topics for developmentalists to study. However, the irony is that social scientists working from a developmental-psychological perspective have largely failed to actually assess (a) what happens to and within such religious contexts and (b) how children are affected by it. In the words of scholars who have examined these matters, religious institutions remain as "unexamined crucibles" for children's spiritual or religious growth (Roehlkepartain and Patel 2005). There are important exceptions to this state of affairs, such as ethnographer Susan B. Ridgely's (2005) superb ethnographic study of Roman Catholic children's experiences and interpretations of First Communion, or the study by religious-development scholar Joyce Mercer and colleagues (Mercer, Matthews, and Walz 2004) of children's experiences within their congregations and houses of worship. But these works may not even count as "exceptions" because such ethnographic works as those just mentioned have not been done by psychologists. This fact only reinforces the conclusion that a developmental-psychological approach is not capturing the child's religious or spiritual growth or experience, inside or outside religious contexts.

One key experience within organized religion is ritual; some religions are sacramental and all have rituals. These mechanisms are essential to provide the child with a sense of connectedness to the sacred transcendent and to the faith community around him or her. Despite the centrality of rituals to world religions, it is true, as Ridgely (2005) has argued, that we know virtually nothing about how *children* understand and experience them. This paucity of knowledge only reinforces the pervasive adultocentric account of children. An antidote would be research that would close the apparent chasm between what *adults* think children understand and know and what children actually believe and understand. A child-centered methodology would investigate children's experience of many rituals. Among the questions such scholarship would investigate include the following. How do Jewish children make sense of the mourning ritual of sitting *shiva* or of leaving an empty chair for Elijah at the Passover seder? What is the experience of Roman Catholic children as they pray to a statue of the Virgin Mary? How are Muslim children transformed by the *hajj* to Mecca? If developmentalists were to study these kinds of questions, our field's efforts would correspond to what world religions actually care about, and our knowledge of children's religious growth would become more valid and complete.

While the preceding comments are meant to underscore the need to study children's experience of religious rituals in religious contexts, children also engage in religious rituals outside of formal contexts. Consider this anecdote from a colleague of mine. As a young Roman Catholic child, she would cut out small circles of Wonder bread and compress them into flat discs to "play communion" with her younger sisters. Acting as the priest, she gave the "communion wafers" to her siblings along with grape juice as the eucharistic blood of Christ (the juice served in gaudy wine glasses to highlight the specialness of the ritual). Decades later, this woman recalls that her parents commended her religious play, saying it proved she was "taking religion seriously." This ritualistic play with siblings or peers probably occurs more often than developmentalists realize (in part because such play may transpire in private child-only settings). A developmental approach needs to study children's ritual as children understand and experience it, within and outside of organized religion. It would seem helpful to scholars if their methodologies for studying such experience would derive not only from their own creativity but also from children's input, as children may know best when and where such activity transpires and, of course, what it means.

Children's Religious Cognition

As noted above, a second use of "religion" refers to the growth of competence in a domain concerned with religious issues. In developmental psychology this approach would really focus on what we can call "religious cognition," mainly because inquiry into the way children think about religion fits squarely into the dominant paradigm of cognitive-developmentalism. The ascendance of cognitive psychology in the 1950s and 1960s ushered in studies relying on Piagetian-type semistructured interviews of children's concepts of prayer (Long, Elkind, and Spilka 1967), God (Heller 1986), and religion more generally (Elkind 1970; Goldman 1964). These studies revealed fascinating developmental trends in the way children think about these topics across childhood, but scholars were too eager to map out this religious cognition in terms of distinct "stages" of religious thought. In brief, religious cognition seemed to progress from "concrete" thinking about religion (e.g., God is an anthropomorphized old man; Protestants and Jews are different because Jewish people "wear little hats on their heads") to more abstract understanding. The scholars in this field generated stages of religious cognition that often paralleled closely those of Piaget's dominant stage model of cognitive growth.

As developmental psychologists Carl Johnson and Chris Boyatzis (2005) explained, more contemporary scholarship has evolved from the earlier simplistic characterizations, using new theories of cognitive development that emphasize children's intuitive and domain-specific knowledge (Boyer 1994). These ideas emphasize the "counterintuitive" nature of religious figures or processes (e.g., they violate ordinary expectations, as in the case of omniscient or eternal spiritual beings) and posit that counterintuitive beliefs function as part of the child's implicit theory of mind, which provides children with fixed qualities to apply to religious figures (e.g., "My supernatural God thinks and feels and worries [like all beings with minds do]."). Some cognitive-developmentalists (Evans 2000) have argued that young children seem prepared to be theists. For example, when children (even those from nonreligious families) offer explanations of the origins of things (e.g., dinosaurs), they reveal a propensity toward teleological and creationist explanations.

Another revision in cognitive-developmentalism is that children and adults are viewed as not so radically different in their thinking. This is a major advance in our understanding of children's religious cognition. Instead of the Piaget-inspired linear march from childhood's irrational magical thinking to the older child's and adult's rational logical thinking, developmentalists now assert that multiple thought processes coexist in children's and adults' minds (Subbotsky 1993). As developmental psychologist Jacqui Woolley (2000) claimed, "Children's minds are not inherently one way or another—not inherently magical nor inherently rational" (pp. 126-27). Children and adults alike can use magical thinking, enact superstitions, and wrestle with the boundaries between the real and the imagined. Both children and adults integrate natural and supernatural qualities in their gods. This characterization of children's religious cognition is somewhat consonant with a children's-studies perspective because it recognizes that a plethora of thought processes can inhabit the child's mind at any time instead of a singular epistemology tightly yoked to chronological age.

While the methodologies scientists use are often ingenious, they frequently reflect traditional assumptions. Presumably, developmentalists' current depictions of children as religious beings, or at least as religious thinkers, will undergo even more dramatic revision as we use more time-consuming qualitative methods that plumb children's individual thinking more deeply. As famed psychiatrist and author Robert Coles (1990) would regularly tell the children whom he was interviewing, it was his job to be a listener and to learn from them. It may strike most developmentalists as a radical proposition to have children enter the process of designing the methodologies that will be used to understand them. I can envision "focus groups" with children of various ages being convened to discuss what the researcher hopes to learn and children's suggestions for how best to acquire such knowledge. This process could entail interview methods or other procedures that the researcher alone might not generate. Because all scholars are captives of their discipline's norms, this expansion of methodology through an unorthodox subversion of epistemological power may bear sweet fruit for developmentalists' knowledge of children's spiritual and religious lives.

The Dangers of Developmental Theory

One of the most famous theoretical frameworks used to understand children's spiritual growth is James Fowler's (1981) impressive work, *Stages of Faith*, a book that synthesized the stage-development theories of Piaget, Erikson, and Kohlberg to create a theoretical framework for the way faith emerges and develops across childhood and the lifespan. The fact that Fowler's great book and theory emphasize the way people think about faith, and the way their thinking about faith is tied very tightly to chronological age, reflects the Piagetian zeitgeist and the hegemony of Piagetian cognitive-developmentalism in that era. Of course, Fowler's book was not merely theoretical, as it used data from structured interviews with hundreds of subjects. Fowler's theory illustrates more broadly how stage theories constrain our understanding of the varieties of religious development, in part because stage theories fail to account for the dramatic variability between and within individuals at any given age.

Fowler's (1981) stage theory of faith emphasizes modal stages that are closely linked to particular chronological age ranges. Fowler's own data prove that *variability* of faith orientation is quite common within a single age. Fowler's study shows that fully 72 percent of children in middle childhood possessed the "age-appropriate" stage of mythic-literal faith, with the remaining 28 percent representing a substantial minority that doesn't "fit." Further, in that very age group, the children interviewed scored in *four* different stages or combined adjacent stages. In the subsequent early-adolescence stage of synthetic-conventional faith, only 50 percent of teens scored in this stage, and in this early-adolescent sample the youth scored in *five* different stages or substages. (The variability is even greater at older ages.) My point in sharing these data is to encourage us to question our veneration of stage theories that lump into tidy chrono-boxes the messy, abundant diversity of children's spirituality.

There are at least two major problematic consequences of this excessive faith in stage theory. The first is that our theories can distort the reality of children's spiritual and religious development. Our knowledge and ways of understanding children and youth are then in error, at least in part, when we take theory from what it can be, a helpful guide, to some dangerous monolithic instantiation of empirical truth. The second serious consequence of theory worship is that our actual work with children in applied settings may be misguided. If the adults working with children use their age as a proxy for their maturity and view them as reducible to a label from some stage theory, it is rather more likely that the children's individuality, maturity, and competence will be misjudged, resulting in educational and faith-formation programming and shared activities that may be less than optimal for the individual children involved (not to mention the tradition—offensive to me—in many congregations of excluding children from formal worship because their religious or behavioral immaturity makes them less than eligible for full inclusion in the worship and sacraments of the faith).

How Do Parents and Children Discuss
Religious and Spiritual Issues?

Perhaps parents know from experience that children engage them in serious discussions about faith, and these discussions can be crucial "engines" in
children's—and parents'—spiritual and religious development. Such conversations are rich contexts for religious socialization and may be a mechanism
through which parents and children co-construct spiritual meaning (Boyatzis 2004). Recent studies have examined such communication and reveal
how developmentalists have incorporated children's voice and agency in
their study of children's religiosity. While the field in general has yet to make
adequate room for children's agency, some scholars of family interaction have
posited what are, to me, necessary new models of child-adult interaction that
challenge antiquated views of children as passive recipients of parental input.
The social relational framework (Kuczynski 2003) posits that children manifest agency through their ongoing interactions with adults, in which adults
and children influence and shape each other's understanding and meaning in
bidirectional and reciprocal processes. These dynamics can strike many different chords, including conflict, contradiction, and ambiguity, and the relationship can maintain an asymmetry in power, but the essence of this view of
agency is the child's active and interdependent role in shaping his or her own
experience and growth as well as others'.

One study of Christian families (Boyatzis and Janicki 2003) with children ages three to twelve asked parents to complete a religious-conversation
diary for two weeks as well as to complete survey measures on the topics,
frequency, setting, and processes of such conversations. Diary entries were
recorded close to three times per week on average, a frequency corroborated
by survey data from parents. The different methods were chosen intentionally to learn how the different tools would reveal different insights. Surveys are notoriously inadequate for capturing children's voice and agency,
whereas diaries (written by parents) may come a bit closer, even if they present their own constraints. Content analyses of diaries revealed that children
were active participants in conservations about religion and spirituality—
they initiated and terminated about half of conversations, spoke as much
as parents did, and frequently asked questions and offered their own views.
They revealed children's power of negation, their ability to resist certain topics or lines of reasoning by parents. The diary data confirmed that children
are active participants and that in many families a "bidirectional reciprocal"
style is more prominent than a unilateral dynamic. These findings refute the

venerable terminology and presumption in the religious-socialization literature of "transmission," imputing little agency and voice to the child and only
a tabula-rasa capacity to be formed.

Other studies have supported the characterization of the family as a complicated multiplicity of influences. Family scholars David Dollahite and J. Y.
Thatcher (2003) studied parents and teens in religious Jewish, Christian, and
Muslim families. Through surveys and interviews, the subjects described
how parents tried to shape youths' religiosity (e.g., ensuring worship attendance, praying with children). In interviews, parents and adolescents cited
conversations more frequently than any other method of influence, and the
teenagers rated conversations as the most important means for growth of
faith. Two discourse styles in families emerged. One was a "youth-centered"
style emphasizing adolescents' spiritual needs, and the other was a "parent-
centered" style emphasizing parents talking rather than listening and not
taking adolescents' views as priorities. The youth-centered model is akin
to the bidirectional dynamic, and it was described not only by adolescents
but also by parents as yielding more positive experiences. This style probably creates (and reflects) a more open family milieu in which parents can
influence children and children can influence parents. This latter dynamic
has been sorely neglected in the social-science literature, due to the long-
standing presumption of parentàchild influence as the only causal arrow.

In many conversations, the parents' goal is to transmit information to
their children. In this case, the child is often viewed as ignorant, in need of
the parent as a teacher. Indeed, diary analyses in Boyatzis and Janicki (2003)
suggest that children sometimes ask questions that require factual answers.
But if we view children as spiritually competent and mature, we are more
ready to recognize what is also true, that children possess complex ideas
about spiritual and religious concepts, ask questions that provoke parents'
reflection, and draw religious meaning from symbols and actions around
them (Coles 1990; Hay and Nye 1998; Wuthnow 1999). As Coles has stated,
beginning at surprisingly early ages children ask the very metaphysical and
existential questions that philosophers, theologians, and less cerebral types
have been asking for millennia. Coles describes children as "spiritual pilgrims." Indeed, we might say that children are but a short version of *homo
poeta*, "man the meaning maker." With these metaphors in mind, parents
may see themselves as fellow pilgrims on a spiritual journey toward meaning.

In this bidirectional reciprocity, parents try to cultivate rather than
indoctrinate their child's views. Children speak often, initiate and termi-
nate conversations, express their doubts, show frustration when they fail to

understand, and struggle with epistemological complexities. In this open-communication milieu, parents and children challenge each other, point out logical discrepancies or attitudinal hypocrisies, and help each other grow. Here is a conversation, from Boyatzis (2004, pp. 184-85), that illustrates these features; the family involved is my own and the child here is my youngest daughter, then age six. The child initiates the conversation and asks many questions, and gets annoyed at times and insistent at others. The parents and child both actively shape the conversation and draw each other's views out. While finishing dinner, her mother (M) was nearby reading and I (F) was casually reading aloud the Ten Commandments from the Bible to the child (C) and her older sister.

C: Did God have a wife? A baby? A son?

F: He had a baby boy—Jesus.

C: But does God have a wife? (*sounding troubled*) If God wants Jesus to be born, he can't have eggs. Only baby ducks do! If God wanted Jesus to come, he couldn't cuz there was no wife around.

M: An angel came around, Gabriel, and said to Mary, "Would you be Jesus' mommy?" So God put Jesus in Mary's tummy, and God was taking care of Jesus in Mary's tummy.

C: He would actually come out with a cross on his forehead.

M: Why?

C: Because he's special.

M: Special, why?

C: Cuz everybody really loves him, and thinks he's special. But God is so big. How could he fit in Mary's tummy? All squished up?

M: Because God wanted to be with us. That's why God came as Jesus, to see what it's like to be a person. God's not (*in deep authoritarian voice*) "I'm a God above everyone," but lives with the people. Do all these things—get sick, play—to know what it's like to be a person.

C: God looks like—he has a big, like, thingie, like a trident, except it's not a trident, a stick like gold with a green thing. God is holding that now, a red and sort of dark green and a gold jewel that's his hat. The costume he's wearing matches his hat. (*Pauses for several seconds . . . then in exasperated tone*) Can we change the subject?

M: Sure.

C: (*indignantly*) Cuz I know a lot about God, and you told me things I already knew.

(*All is quiet for about five seconds, everyone else reading silently . . .*)

c: Mom, does God have a house? Does he read books?

m: I don't think so. I'm not sure.

c: Is God a girl or man?

m: I think both.

c: How can one side be a girl and the other side a man? (*Sounding excited . . .*) I know—sometimes God does boy things and sometimes girl things. (*Pauses several seconds . . .*) I think God is a girl.

m: You may be right.

f: Why do you think God is a girl?

c: I don't know. Girls might think God is a girl, and boys might think he's a boy. (*Exasperated . . .*) Can we change the subject, fast-forward to another thing.

m: OK.

This verbatim example illustrates many features of a reciprocal communication style in which the child has obvious agency and voice. It also indicates that the analysis of natural, spontaneous, parent-child conversations is an informative and valuable arena for study.

Different Forms of Children's Agency

From a theoretical and practical perspective, there is a risk to imputing to children too much agency or maturity or competence. To continue the above topic of parent-child conversation about religion (see Boyatzis 2004), we can envision some families that uphold the child as such a young sage that the parents would be reluctant to teach, mentor, share, or guide their spiritual prodigy. This could be tantamount to a form of parental-spiritual permissiveness that borders on the indulgent, a style that is known to have many undesirable outcomes for children. We also would expect that some families possess a distinct "parent-as-mentor, child-as-apprentice" asymmetrical role structure. In other families, there may be more fluidity and sharing between these roles so that power and knowledge is more symmetrical; at the very least they are understood to be inherent in parents and children alike. In other families the child may be viewed as something of a "spiritual savant." Many cultural groups view children as spiritual beings, as "spiritual emissaries" from the "other side" of an ancestral spirit realm. In some cultures, parents—especially African American, Caribbean, and African—describe their young children as "old souls" or as having "come here to teach me something" (Mattis et al. 2005). It is likely that some families may use only one of these modes consistently whereas other families may display more flexibility at different times due to spiritual maturation in parent and/or child. It would behoove developmental psychologists to study families very closely, with interview and naturalistic observation and video- and audiotaping methods, to learn about the nature of these types of parent-child relationships regarding spiritual discourse. Such inquiry would help illuminate the negotiation between parents and children of voice, agency, and power.

Conclusion

We have discussed several aspects of a developmental-psychological approach to children's religious development with attention to the way children's agency, voice, maturity, and competence are understood within that approach. Has this approach sufficiently attended to these qualities in children? The simple answer is no, a resounding no. The dominance of cognitive-developmentalism and stage theory has impeded our understanding of religious and spiritual growth and subsequently our ability to impute to children agency, voice, and maturity. Not all is lost, however, as we have also examined some changes and advances in our understanding of children; we focused mainly on recent views of children as thinkers and as active participants in family interaction and communication about religious issues. Throughout, we have considered suggestions of how to move forward methodologically to better understand children's agency, voice, and maturity. Doing so will help us better reconcile the very complex tension between thinking of children as full-fledged "beings" or young and immature "becomings."

Religion and Youth in American Culture

SARAH PIKE

One night, Maia, a budding environmentalist, and her high school boyfriend climbed over the fence of a housing development in southern California that was being built on a site where desert tortoises lived. The teen saboteurs put Karo syrup and tampons into the gas tanks of bulldozers on the construction site and pulled up survey stakes. Maia felt exhilarated when they left the site and marked that night as the moment of her conversion, a "tipping point" after which she was committed to radical environmental activism for several years. Looking back, she saw this period of her life as one of spiritual seeking, as she blended the moral values of her upbringing among Jehovah's Witnesses with contemporary neopagan and environmentalist views of the natural world as sacred.[1]

For many Americans, Maia's actions constitute "ecoterrorism," while for others, she might be seen as a poster child for youthful resistance to suburban sprawl. Her actions, like those of other young radical activists that I have interviewed, are labeled as amoral and antisocial.[2] In media and law enforcement accounts of radical activism, young activists in particular (and the majority of those branded "ecoterrorists" first became involved in illegal actions while still in high school) are seen as dangerous because of their perceived absence of morality.

Instead of lacking a system of values, Maia, like other teenage activists, had a sense of herself as a spiritual person with high moral standards. She grew up in a family of Jehovah's Witnesses in a small town in southern California, but as an adolescent began questioning her family's religious beliefs. Her parents did not own a television and encouraged her to read books and play outside, where she came to feel a sense of closeness with desert creatures, even digging holes for them that she filled with water. While in high school she became a radical environmentalist, engaging in civil disobedience throughout her young adult years, including tree sits and road blockades. While still in high school, she was troubled by what she saw happening around her, as more and more tract homes were built in the open spaces she had enjoyed as a child. She recalls developing a powerful but undefined religious identity that combined her belief that other creatures are sacred beings with an ethics of right and wrong that she inherited from her parents. Like Maia, many young activists draw from a variety of ethical and religious beliefs, as well as experiences in nature and in youth culture, to create new identities and moral commitments. When their new identities challenge the social norms around them, such teenagers are often demonized.

In the United States since at least the 1950s, rebellious teenagers have often been blamed for a litany of social ills.[3] Americans' ambivalence toward young activists—terrorists or heroes—mirrors a general cultural unease about teenagers, who are seen as dangerous and threatening on the one hand and bearers of a future vision of society on the other. The demonizing of radical activists as terrorists follows a more general pattern of what cultural critic Henry Giroux calls "strategies of scapegoating and commodifying" youth that have taken on distinctive features since the rise of the teenager after World War II.[4] As professor of education Nancy Lesko sees it in her study of the cultural construction of adolescence, "Adolescence became a social space in which progress or degeneration was visualized, embodied, measured, and affirmed."[5] Since young people are so often imagined as degenerate and lacking moral values, it is ironic that there have been so few studies of their religious and spiritual lives. The actions of radical activists and other demonized youth cannot be fully understood without giving attention to their moral and religious worlds.

Although a handful of scholars in recent years have explored teenage spirituality through surveys and interviews, religious studies scholars on the whole tend to disregard the religious worlds of adolescents, while most research on youth culture pays little or no attention to religious beliefs and practices.[6] Religious studies scholars can and should learn from research on youth culture and at the same time draw attention to the silence around young people's lives in the field of religious studies and the absence of religion in studies of youth cultures. Adolescence is a time of crucial importance to the formation of religious identity. Even teenagers who are unaffiliated with religious institutions make moral commitments and think about and live out relationships with spiritual beings.[7]

In the following pages, I want to explore some themes that emerge from the literature on youth that are particularly relevant to the relationship between religion and the study of adolescents: the representation of teenagers as dark and demonic; assumptions that teenagers are in a liminal phase of life and thus prone to conversion; the cultural geography of adolescent spaces; and the construction of multiple and mobile identities in adolescence.[8] These aspects of youth culture and religious experience shape teenagers' everyday lives and have evolved over the past century as "youth" has taken on its own momentum.

Youth Culture in the West

Since at least the mid-twentieth century, binary oppositions have characterized representations of American teenagers; they are imagined as powerful advocates for social change or delinquent troublemakers. "Fear of young people sells," sociologist Karen Sternheimer observes in her study, *Kids These Days*.[9] Cultural critic Charles Acland argues that adolescents fulfilled a unique role in late-twentieth-century American culture as they became transgressive *others* who were secretly revered: "Youth sits strangely in hegemony. It is feared, it is desired, it holds promise, it is wasted."[10] Most Americans are familiar with dark and threatening stereotypes of teenagers who are criminal, suspicious, and out of control: terrorists, school shooters, Goths, gangbangers. But adolescents' lived experiences complicate these kinds of stereotypes, even as the stereotypes endure and take on a life of their own in the news and entertainment media.

Media constructions of evil and deviant adolescents often bear little resemblance to the realities of American teenagers' lives. Sociologist Mike Males argues in *The Scapegoat Generation* that rumors of adolescent criminality and fears about adolescent violence in the 1980s did not match research findings that rates of teenage suicide and drug overdose, two of many possible examples, actually declined from the 1970s to the 1980s; teenagers were far safer than they used to be, Males concluded.[11] Sternheimer demonstrates that American schools became safer during the 1990s and 2000s, even though adults perceived them as more dangerous.[12] Because teenagers in the 1980s were the healthiest and best educated ever, "experiencing long-term declines in all problem behaviors," according to Males, "[i]t was a singularly odd time for professionals, authorities, and the media to suddenly proclaim an 'epidemic' of youth crises. Considerable evidence has been amassed that agency and industry self-interest, not the true conditions of teenagers, were the real motivators."[13] For this reason, stories and stereotypes of dangerous and troubled teenagers tend to reveal more about the theological and social concerns of adults than anything useful concerning the lives of teenagers.

Although adolescents have been viewed suspiciously in other eras, since the mid-twentieth century, with the rise of the concept of the teenager as inhabiting a separate phase of life with its own clothing styles and entertainment choices, scapegoating of teenagers has intensified. In the United States at the end of World War II, teenage culture became increasingly removed from adult supervision and adolescents were seen and saw themselves as what journalist Patricia Hersch calls "a tribe apart."[14] From the 1950s on, young people gradually became separate from and mysterious to adults. Psychologist Elliott Currie laments the pervasive view he finds among adults in the 1990s that teenagers were "fundamentally different creatures . . . in effect aliens who had mysteriously landed among us."[15] Distancing teenagers from adults and younger children consigns them to a special and separate world. As a *Newsweek* cover story on "The Secret Life of Teens" proclaimed, "Sex, Drugs and Rock Have Worried Parents for Decades, but Now the Net, Videogames, and No-Holds-Barred Music Are Creating New Worlds That Many Adults Can't Enter."[16] As this story suggests, the explosion of electronic technologies in the 1990s seemed to further distance adults from a separate and secluded youth culture.

Many decades of constructing the teenager as a threat contribute to the persistence of scapegoating teens as deviants and delinquents in American culture at the beginning of the twenty-first century. The term "juvenile delinquents" was coined in the 1810s, a foreshadowing of what would become a difficult assumption to shake: that youth gathering in groups posed a threat to the social order.[17] By the late nineteenth century, industrialization brought about significant changes to young people's lives, as increasing numbers of them enrolled in schools and populated cities. Rapidly expanding urban populations resulted in the view that cities were places for youth disconnected from family ties to gather. Adult Americans responded vigorously to what they perceived to be the threat of unbounded and undisciplined youth. They developed institutions to "actively corral American youth" into the newly industrialized society, particularly through high schools, settlement houses, and sanatoriums. According to historian Beth Bailey, "sociosexual" fears in particular led middle-class Americans "to redefine youth as a period demanding special institutions and protections" because young people were imagined to be at the mercy of uncontrollable urges.[18] Youth organizations emerged in the early twentieth century as part of an ongoing campaign by religious leaders and other adults to socialize young men and women, and especially to protect them from themselves. To take just two important examples, the YMCA grew rapidly in cities at the end of the nineteenth century and the Boy Scouts of America was founded in 1910.[19]

Both of these organizations were intended to cut across class and color lines and religious denominations. What had been a designation for middle-class youth—"adolescence"—began to include the working class as well. In many communities, especially in cities, young people began to have more in common with each other than with adults of their own gender, class, and race.[20]

It was American high schools at the end of the nineteenth century and the beginning of the twentieth, as historian William J. Reese has shown, that were mainly responsible for the rise of the teenager as a class of its own, even though educators and politicians who created the schools had other goals in mind.[21] High schools began as agents of socialization: "the high school was designed as an assimilation machine from the very beginning," according to journalist Jon Savage, and the number of high schools increased more than 750 percent between 1880 and 1900.[22] By the 1920s, American high school enrollment was at an all-time high and teenagers were seen as "the vanguard of the consumer revolution."[23]

First the Depression and then World War II helped to further ensure that teenagers became a powerful social force that was increasingly removed from parental control. During the Depression, American high school enrollment expanded in order to keep teenagers out of the workforce.[24] By 1940, high school had become the norm for young Americans, with twice as many students enrolled as in 1930.[25] World War II had an even greater impact, as the social and political meaning of adolescence changed throughout the West during the 1940s. In the United States, for instance, pre–army age men were encouraged to be fully employed and became economically important as both producers and consumers. At this time, teenagers were increasingly visible as workers and by the end of the war were seen as harbingers of a new age, the "Age of the Teen."[26] Journalist Jon Savage aptly sums up the beginning of this new "teen age" at the end of World War II when he explains that two months after *Vogue* magazine declared the coming of a new teenage revolution, the United States dropped the atom bomb on Hiroshima and Nagasaki: "The Allies won the war at exactly the moment that America's latest product was coming off the production line."[27] This "product," the teenage consumer, was being researched and developed during the same decades that the United States was becoming a global power and promoting capitalism around the world. As historian Oded Heilbronner puts it, after World War II there was a significant shift "from a culture *for* youth to a culture *of* youth."[28] As further evidence of this shift, sociologist Talcott Parsons coined the term "youth culture" in a 1942 article; the magazine *Seventeen*, aimed at teen girls, was launched in 1944; and in 1945

Vogue magazine heralded a "teen-age revolution."[29] As these examples suggest, since the 1940s, youth culture has been inextricably tied to capitalism even when it has resisted and coopted the market.[30]

Adult concern and teen empowerment both increased in post–World War II America, as youth culture, initiated first by high school and then by marketing executives, took hold. The 1950s saw the greatest growth in a self-contained teenage culture, including more African American and working-class adolescents, as a generation of American kids came to be "identified as a market in their own right."[31] By 1957, for example, the youth market was worth over $30 billion a year.[32] According to historian Grace Palladino's history of teenagers, with the baby boom, youth definitively displaced age as the source of power in America.[33] Historian Eric Hobsbawm claims that during the 1950s and 1960s, youth had come to be seen as an end in itself, not simply a stage of development towards adulthood.[34] Hobsbawm identified two of the factors contributing to the special status of youth culture in the West during the second half of the twentieth century: "First, 'youth' was not seen as a preparatory stage of adulthood but, in some sense, as the final stage of full human development. . . . The second novelty of the youth culture . . . : it was or became dominant in the 'developed market economies.'"[35] Teenagers were often viewed suspiciously because they were increasingly outside of adult control and inhabiting their own spaces, just as they had been for decades earlier, but now they had financial clout. The cultural and economic power of youth culture in the industrialized West, then, is responsible, at least in part, for the tendency to blame adolescents for social problems and to construct them as a threat to social order.

Adolescence as Liminality

Because adolescents are no longer children but not yet adults, their religious commitments are usually not fully formed. As psychologist Jeffrey Arnett explains it, the process of defining their worldviews, which begins in childhood, "intensifies during adolescence."[36] In his classic study of adolescence, psychologist G. Stanley Hall argued that youth *must* feel emotion, that adolescence is "the age of sentiment and religion."[37] Conversion can clearly play an important role in the process of exploring religious worldviews, as teenagers take what is given them and make it their own within the constraints of gender, race, class, and other limitations.

As adolescence came to be seen as a separate world unto itself, it was increasingly recognized as a liminal phase between child and adult identities.

Giroux argued in 1994 that young people are "condemned to wander within and between multiple borders and spaces marked by excess, otherness and difference. This is a world in which old certainties are ruptured and meaning becomes more contingent, less indebted to the dictates of reverence and established truth."[38] Many of the discourses about threatening youth identify teenagers as quintessential liminal or boundary figures. Lesko suggests that adolescents occupy positions in "*border zones* between the imagined end points of adult and child, male and female, sexual and asexual, rational and emotional, civilized and savage, and productive and unproductive."[39] Although teenagers think abstractly and multidimensionally because of "the yielding of the certainty of childhood," they are not yet seen as fully formed adults.[40] They are thought to be both vulnerable *and* potentially powerful because of their transitional status.

Why is it that Maia and other teenagers who undergo various kinds of conversions to religious and social movements are, as Maia put it to me, "ready to have their brains molded"? Psychologist Susan Harter observes that "the volatility of the self" characterizes adolescence because it is a time when individuals are experimenting with and integrating multiple concepts of the self.[41] As William James saw it, "the seeker of his truest, deepest self must review the list carefully, and pick out the one on which to stake his salvation."[42] Like Maia, many adolescents reach a tipping point when they begin questioning the religious views of their parents and experimenting with other religious practices or rejecting religion altogether.

Because American teenagers form a separate and economically powerful youth culture and are in the process of shaping their identities, they have often been seen as and have placed themselves in the position of converts to social and religious movements, such as Wicca and environmentalism. And so adolescents have long been the targets of aggressive proselytizing. For instance, young adults were active during the revivals of the Great Awakening (1730s) when the majority of those who converted were young men and women, a third of them in their teens. Moreover, three out of four converts in nineteenth-century revivals were young women.[43] Early New England Puritan theologian Jonathan Edwards (1703-1758), for instance, was particularly concerned about the salvation of young adults.[44] In fact, historian Steven Mintz observes that the Puritans' projection of their hopes and fears on the young is one of their lasting legacies.[45] From the Salem witchcraft outbreak of 1692 to the "satanic panic" of the 1980s when unsubstantiated rumors about Satan-worshiping teenagers spread around the United States, in American religious history adolescents have been seen as spiritually at risk.[46]

In the 1970s, this dynamic was evident when young adults were treated as victims of "cults," because new religious movements attracted a generation of youth interested in spiritual experimentation. Most young converts (typically between the ages of eighteen and twenty-three when they joined) left these movements over time and came to see religious experimentation as a phase in their lives.[47] These cases suggest that conversion to social and religious movements during teenage years often does not result in permanent commitments. As psychiatrist Saul Levine argues in response to fears about "cults," many young people undergo "radical departures" as a way to more decisively separate from their families, using the group or movement as a way to develop a unique identity.[48] For many young people, then, participation in religious and social movements is simply part of growing up, of trying on new identities to see what works.

Yet from the 1970s anticult movement through the 1980s satanism scare, fears about teenagers' attraction to alternative religious practices persisted. The vulnerable adolescent became a potent symbol in the 1980s, especially for a growing conservative evangelical Protestant movement. Conservative Christian publications about the dangers confronting adolescents and the threat they posed to others flourished from the 1980s into the twenty-first century.[49] Novels by conservative evangelical writers like Roger Elwood's *The Christening* (1986) and Frank Peretti's *Piercing the Darkness* (1988) foregrounded dangerous youth and urged parents to work vigilantly at keeping teenagers within the Christian flock. Conservative Christian fears about secular culture focused around teenagers, and the evangelical youth movement was one of the most significant responses to these fears. This movement is visible at large-scale Christian music festivals and rock concerts, "Hell Houses," and weekly youth group meetings in local churches.[50] For instance, in 2000, the estimated number of Christian music festivals attended by more than five thousand youth was five, but in 2005 it was thirty-five, and the growth of congregants in Mars Hill Church, a youth-led conservative church in Seattle, from 1998 to 2005, was from 150 to 3,500.[51] According to historian Eileen Luhr, during the 1990s, Protestant evangelicals "romanticized the revolutionary potential of youth rebellion," as they built a hugely successful youth movement that appropriated consumer culture and attracted large numbers of teenagers across North America.[52]

At the end of the twentieth century, when young adults converted to new religious trends such as Wicca and evangelical megachurches and to social movements such as radical environmentalism, they reflected broader cultural trends. At the same time, they changed the shape of these movements, often challenging popular assumptions about youth religiosity. For instance, while researching Christian youth movements, journalist Andrew Beaujon was surprised by the incongruous appearance of punks adorned with multiple piercings and mohawks who were spouting pro-life slogans.[53] From a different youth cultural context, a popular underground hard-core punk band of the early 1990s called Vegan Reich and fronted by Muslim singer/songwriter Sean Muttaqi, a vegan and animal rights advocate, also urged teenage followers to adopt pro-life views. What these examples have in common is that they emerged from specific youth cultural spaces, in these cases concerts and music festivals that stood apart from and yet in relation to adult Muslim and Christian worlds.

The Sacred Geography of Adolescents

Adolescents' lived experiences are expressed through and shaped by the places and spaces where they live and play. What happens to them in traditional religious settings may be less important than what they experience at rock concerts, music festivals, and other spaces in which they negotiate their identities in social contexts with their peers. Adolescents also move through real and virtual space and time, inhabiting parks and malls, seeking out places away from adult supervision where they can perform identities for other youth, their primary audience. They claim spaces outside themselves in new ways, often extending the self outwards into streets, parks, shopping centers, and virtual communities like MySpace while, at the same time, their sense of self is shaped by experiences in these places. In contrast to these outward expressions of identity, during adolescence there is also an interiorization of the world, as the internal state of the self and of emotions becomes heightened. As psychologist Susan Harter puts it, there is a shift away from concrete descriptions of the exterior world that are typical during childhood "to more abstract self-portraits that describe one's psychological interior in adolescence."[54]

Even micro-spaces that adolescents inhabit become extensions of their identities, as anthropologist Gerry Bloustien demonstrates in her study of teenage girls' self-making, especially bedrooms and secret places that teens fill with "the products of the imagination." Hilary, one of the girls with whom Bloustien worked, used a video camera provided by Bloustien to film a space she created under her house that she called the "Lost Forest" and filled with "candles, wall hangings, soft cushions and a book entitled *Wizard's Spells.*"[55] Teenagers like Hilary create identities and develop their own styles, gestures, and relationships with family and friends and with consumer culture in a sacred geography that also includes virtual spaces.

Teenagers look to the Internet for secrecy, privacy, belonging, and community, although Internet spaces can be intruded upon and patrolled by adults. At the end of the 1990s, when participation in online communities was less widespread, adolescents spent large amounts of time in a world unfamiliar to most of their parents and teachers. After the 1999 Columbine school shootings, in which two ostracized high school students gunned down twelve of their classmates before killing themselves, religious communities, parents, and schools worried about what teens were doing on the Internet and blamed video games for teenage violence.[56] As one reporter put it in a post-Columbine report, "the new teen wave is bigger, richer, better-educated and healthier than any other in history. But there's a dark side. . . ."[57] Parents' and other adults' suspicions about young people gathering outside their control were strengthened by the advent of the Internet.

At the same time, teen witches and teen born-again Christians, to give two prominent examples, were using the Internet to discover and share new religious identities.[58] Most of the teenage witches sociologists Helen Berger and Douglas Ezzy interviewed found their religion through books and on the Internet. As Berger and Ezzy observe, "the Internet may be the most important form of mediated community for the young Witches," and this trend seems likely to be true for other teenagers joining religions or experimenting with identities that are different from those of their parents.[59] When Mormon author Stephanie Meyer's novel *Twilight* (2005) and the subsequent books and Twilight films acquired a huge following among teenage girls, they too found a community on the Internet; for example, some MySpace sites include guidelines for treating the Twilight books like bibles.[60] In cases like this, when teenagers express, share, create, and subvert religious idioms and identities on the Internet, they are carving out important features in their sacred landscapes.

The natural world of parks and woods, like the Internet, offers spaces in which it is easier to avoid adult surveillance than at school or at home, and for this reason teenagers' moral commitments may also be shaped and changed by experiences in nature, either alone in relation to trees, creeks, and animals, or in the company of friends. Stephen Kellert of Yale's School of Forestry and Environmental Studies, one of the few scholars who has done substantial research on children and nature, argues that there are several phases of childhood attachment to nature but that it is ages thirteen to seventeen when ecological and moral values become increasingly important.[61] Some teenagers experience nature as sacred, or talk with or encounter spiritual beings in trees, as my interviews with neopagans demonstrate.[62] Jeff

Luers, a radical environmentalist who spent eleven years in prison for setting fire to SUVs at a car dealership, told me that he started talking to trees when he was a neopagan teenager. Two years before the arson, when he was nineteen, Luers found himself alone in Oregon's Willamette Forest while participating in a campaign to save an old-growth forest of Douglas fir, western hemlock, and red cedar: "Standing before them is a humbling experience . . . like standing before a God or Goddess," he explained in "How I Became an Eco-Warrior," an essay he wrote in prison.[63] Places to be alone become important to many adolescents, as landscape architect Patsy Eubanks Owens discovered in her research on teenagers' preferences for "natural and undeveloped landscapes" that helped them "put things in perspective."[64]

Meaningful life experiences in nature may also include important others, such as adult mentors and teen friends. Environmental studies scholar Tori Derr suggests that for many teenagers, important places are increasingly identified as *socially* significant rather than appreciated for their inherent beauty or wildness. In fact, it seems that attachments to places during adolescence are often formed *because* of the social experiences that occur in them rather than from any sense of their inherent worth. According to Derr, places in which significant experiences occur with friends and family are more likely to become meaningful and then integrated into self-identity.[65]

For adolescents, then, places may be valued for different reasons than they are for children and adults. Both being alone *and* hanging out with friends become central to adolescents' developing sense of self in important, and even sacred, landscapes. How they negotiate and experience the relationships among spaces such as mosques and churches, their own rooms, the natural world, and teenage hangouts has been little studied, and yet clearly the geography of adolescence is an important feature of youth culture and religiosity.

Multiple and Mobile Identities

As they move through natural and cultural landscapes, adolescents create moral systems and modes of behavior and styles, bending and blending those available in popular culture, the media, their families, and their communities. Maia, the radical environmentalist, rejected her parents' religion, and yet she found that her Jehovah's Witness upbringing gave her an advantage when she went door to door canvassing for environmental causes. She also credited her parents with instilling in her a clear sense of right and wrong. Most observers might assume that "tree huggers" camping in the woods and chanting environmentalist slogans at loggers have nothing in common with Bible-toting Witnesses, but our assumptions that teenagers who reject the organized religions of their parents slough off their pasts so easily is often mistaken. Bloustien blames scholars' tendency to identify separate rebellious youth cultures for the overemphasis on the separateness of youth: "It is only because youth groupings are viewed as separate units that the continuous link between youth behavior, styles and values and their parent cultures . . . has been overlooked."[66] Stereotypes of young rebels often obscure the ways in which apparently "deviant" teenagers carry on their parents' legacies at the same time that they are bringing something new into being.

Teenagers challenge oversimplifications of youth as a separate class when they sift through elements of their parents' lives, rejecting some and holding onto others. They also experience belonging to a youth culture differently along the lines of gender and ethnicity. For example, Bloustien argues in her study of Australian and American teenagers that young women's experiences may be as fundamentally different from young men's as young adults' lives are from their parents. If most early cultural studies scholars associated with the work of the Birmingham Centre for Contemporary Cultural Studies (CCCS) identified resistant and subversive youth, these were often white males; punk women and punk men of color, for instance, experienced their subcultural identities differently.[67] For teenagers raised in ethnic or religious minorities, making over their heritage in their own way may be particularly important. Journalist Michael Muhammad Knight, who converted from Catholicism to Islam when he was sixteen, published a novel about Muslim punks—*The Taqwacores*—in 2005. According to the book's cover, its story includes "Umar, the straight-edge Sunni; Rabeya, the buraq-clad riot grrl; Jehangir, the dope-smoking mohawk-wearing Sufi (who plays rooftop calls-to-prayer on his electric guitar)—and their collective articulation of a heresy-friendly, pluralist Islam. Full of punk references (real and invented) and enough Arabic phrases to fully deck out your skateboard."[68] The work of Knight in uncovering Muslim-American youth culture is rife with examples of teenagers negotiating their identities in reference to American popular culture as well as the religious traditions of their families.

Pakistani Americans Shajehan Khan and Basin Usmani, who founded the Kominas, a Muslim punk band, participated in a "taqwacore" tour organized by Knight in 2007.The Kominas and other Muslim punk bands have attracted second-generation immigrants who do not feel they belong in American culture or in their families. Khan describes his own discomfort as a teenager growing up in Massachusetts: "Why are my parents so weird? Why is my culture so weird? I hope I don't smell like curry when I leave the house."[69] As the Kominas' music spread on the Internet and in underground clubs, fans responded in kind: one fan e-mailed them, "Relief only just begins to emphatically stress what I felt realizing your [sic] Pakistani and have a Mohawk too."[70] These hybrid religious identities are symbolically enacted and theatrically performed, challenging stereotypes of Muslim Americans. Cultural studies scholar Dick Hebdige argues that "the politics of youth culture is a politics of gesture, symbol, and metaphor."[71] Hybrid styles such as those that blend punk and Islam become a new kind of religious politics of gesture among young people. Like Maia's Jehovah's Witnesses–informed environmentalist identity, their hybrid identities are not easily located in terms of institutional belonging.

By the end of the twentieth century, the proportion of young people identifying with a particular religious tradition had declined, as had high school students' weekly attendance at religious services.[72] But scholars have yet to sufficiently explore what this means in terms of the way adolescents live their beliefs in daily life outside of religious institutions. As Lynn Schofield Clark points out in *From Angels to Aliens: Teenagers, the Media, and the Supernatural* (2003), at the end of the twentieth century teenagers were drawn to spirituality and the supernatural (angels and aliens, for example) even when they did not regularly attend religious services. Nondenominational Christian music festivals like the popular summer festival Cornerstone and solitary teenage witches on the Internet are other examples of hard-to-quantify teenage religiosity.[73] The experiences of teenagers like Maia reveal the limitations of statistics about declining teenage religiosity and call into question the trope of troubled and dangerous youth.

Like the Kominas, who "shred stereotypes," Maia rejected conflicting loyalties. She credits her Witness parents for her sense of moral commitment, and yet her radical actions reveal her passion for protecting nonhuman species. As Maia developed her own belief system in her teenage years, she drew from her experiences growing up in a Jehovah's Witness family, contemporary paganism, deep ecology, and Buddhism. Her changing religious identity and activist commitment exemplify the ways in which the spiritual lives of teenagers serve as prime examples of trends on the American religious landscape: the spread of religious meaning making outside of religious institutions; the personalization of identities within traditional religions; and the emergence of new religious phenomena, such as neopagan environmentalism, music festivals, and Muslim American punk rock tours. When scholars turn their attention to changing and shifting religious identities during adolescence, it becomes clear that adolescence is not an island situated apart from adult worlds and that demonizing teenagers does not further our understanding of the important issues in their lives. In fact, adolescents' stories express the ways in which they play with and blend multiple religious and cultural beliefs and practices in creative ways in their daily lives, as they move across the boundaries of various cultural and geographic sites.

NOTES

1. I have changed her name and a few identifying details.

2. "FBI: Eco-Terrorism Remains No. 1 Domestic Terror Threat," Fox News, Monday, March 31, 2008, http://www.foxnews.com/story/0,2933,343768,00.html, accessed 3/29/10.

3. As historian of childhood Steven Mintz observes in *Huck's Raft: A History of American Childhood* (Cambridge, MA: Harvard University Press, 2004), "children have long served as a lightning rod for America's anxieties about society as a whole" (340).

4. Henry A. Giroux, *Channel Surfing: Race Talk and the Destruction of Today's Youth* (New York: St. Martin's, 1997), 2.

5. Nancy Lesko, *Act Your Age! A Cultural Construction of Adolescence* (New York: Routledge Farmer, 2001), 35.

6. For recent studies of religious teenagers see Christian Smith with Melissa Lundquist Denton, *Soul-Searching: The Religious and Spiritual Lives of American Teenagers* (Oxford: Oxford University Press, 2005), Mark D. Regnerus, *Forbidden Fruit: Sex and Religion in the Lives of American Teenagers* (New York: Oxford University Press, 2007), and historian Eileen Luhr, *Witnessing Suburbia: Conservatives and Christian Youth Culture* (Berkeley: University of California Press, 2009).

7. Lynn Schofield Clark, *From Angels to Aliens: Teenagers, the Media, and the Supernatural* (New York: Oxford University Press, 2003), 5.

8. Although I use "teenager," "adolescent," and "youth" interchangeably, my focus is on 13-19-year-olds. The tropes of dangerous, threatening, liminal youth tend to be attached to these ages. Jeffrey Jenson Arnett has critiqued the category "youth" in *Emerging Adulthood: The Winding Road from the Late Teens through the Twenties* (New York: Oxford University Press, 2004).

9. Sternheimer, *Kids These Days: Facts and Fictions about Today's Youth* (Lanham, MD: Rowman & Littlefield, 2006), 2.

10. Acland, *Youth, Murder, Spectacle: The Cultural Politics of "Youth in Crisis"* (Boulder, CO: Westview Press, 1994), 145.

11. Mike A. Males, *The Scapegoat Generation: America's War on Adolescents* (Monroe, ME: Common Courage Press, 1996.

12. Sternheimer, 12.

13. Males, 29.

14. Patricia Hersch, *A Tribe Apart: A Journey into the Heart of American Adolescence* (New York: Ballantine Books, 1999).

15. *The Road to Whatever: Middle-Class Culture and the Crisis of Adolescence* (New York: Picador, 2005), 4.

16. Devin Gordon, Anne Underwood, Tara Weingarten and Ana Figueroa, "The Secret Life of Teens: Sex, Drugs, and Rock Have Worried Parents for Decades, but Now the Net, Videogames, and No-Holds-Barred Music Are Creating New Worlds That Many Adults Can't Enter," May 10, 1999, http://www.newsweek.com/id/88252/page/1.

17. Savage, *Teenage: The Creation of Youth Culture* (New York: Viking, 2007), 9.

18. Beth L. Bailey, *From Front Porch to Back Seat: Courtship in Twentieth-Century America* (Baltimore: Johns Hopkins University Press, 1988), 9.

19. Mintz, 89.

20. Modell and Goodman, 97-99.

21. *The Origins of the American High School* (New Haven, CT: Yale University Press, 1995).

22. Savage, *Teenage: The Creation of Youth Culture* (New York: Viking, 2007), 69. The quotation is on p. 99.

23. America's "youth obsession" turned to the dark side in 1924 with the Leopold and Loeb case, in which two wealthy young men, Nathan Leopold (nineteen years old) and Richard Loeb (eighteen), murdered a fourteen-year-old boy in cold blood. It seemed to observers of the time that "the consumer society was creating its own monsters" (Savage, 200).

24. Mintz, 246.

25. Savage, 363. According to Savage, in 1940, 75 percent of 14-17-year-olds were enrolled in high school.

26. Ibid., 453.

27. Ibid., 465.

28. Oded Heilbronner, "From a Culture *for* Youth to a Culture *of* Youth: Recent Trends in the Historiography of Western Youth Cultures," *Contemporary European History* 17 (2008), 577.

29. Savage, 448-62.

30. Rob Latham, *Consuming Youth: Vampires, Cyborgs, and the Culture of Consumption* (Chicago: University of Chicago Press, 2002).

31. Latham, 42. According to Latham, "Contemporary American youth culture can profitably be studied in terms of a dialectic of exploitation and empowerment rooted in youth's practices of consumption" (4).

32. Latham, 42.

33. Palladino, *Teenagers: An American History* (New York: Basic Books, 1996).

34. Cited in Heilbronner, 588.

35. Pp. 325-27.

36. Arnett, 166.

37. Quoted in Savage, 71.

38. Quoted in *Rethinking Youth*, ed. Johanna Wyn and Rob White (Melbourne, Australia: Allen & Unwin, 1997), 20.

39. Lesko, 50.

40. Daniel Keating, "Adolescent Thinking," in *At the Threshold: The Developing Adolescent*, ed. Shirley S. Feldman and Glen R. Elliott (Cambridge, MA: Harvard University Press, 1990), 64.

41. Susan Harter, "Self and Identity Development," in Feldman and Elliott, 376.

42. William James quoted in Harter, 376.

43. Mintz, 29.

44. Gary Wills, "God in the Hands of Angry Sinners," *New York Review of Books*, April 8, 2004, http://www.nybooks.com/issues/2004/apr/08/.

45. Mintz, 31.

46. Carol Karlsen, *The Devil in the Shape of a Woman* and Mary Beth Norton, *In the Devil's Snare: The Salem Witchcraft Crisis of 1692* (New York: Knopf, 2002).

47. Saul Levine, *Radical Departures: Desperate Detours to Growing Up* (Orlando, FL: Harcourt Brace Jovanovich, 1984).

48. Typically, according to Levine, the "departer" moves away from the group when it has outlived its usefulness for this purpose. See also Stuart A. Wright, "The Dynamics of Movement Membership: Joining and Leaving NRMs," pp.187-210 in David G. Bromley (ed.), *Teaching New Religious Movements* (New York: Oxford University Press, 1997), 195.

49. Sarah M. Pike, "Dark Teens and Born-Again Martyrs: Captivity Narratives after Columbine," *Journal of the American Academy of Religion* 77 (September 2009), 647-79.

50. See for instance, Andrew Beaujon, *Body Piercing Saved My Life: Inside the Phenomenon of Christian Rock* (Cambridge, MA: Da Capo Press, 2007) and Jason Bivins's discussion of Hell Houses in *Religion of Fear: The Politics of Horror in Conservative Evangelicalism* (New York: Oxford University Press, 2008).

51. Lauren Sandler, *Righteous: Dispatches from the Evangelical Youth Movement* (New York: Viking, 2006).

52. Luhr, 7.

53. Beaujon, 187-216.

54. Harter, 355.

55. Gerry Bloustien, *Girl Making: A Cross-Cultural Ethnography on the Process of Growing up Female* (New York: Berghahn Books, 2003),123.

56. Gordon et al.

57. John Leland, "The Secret Life of Teens," in *Newsweek*, May 10, 1999, p. 45. Also see my discussion in Pike.

58. See Pike.

59. *Teenage Witches: Magical Youth and the Search for the Self* (New Brunswick, NJ: Rutgers University Press, 2007), 43.

60. "Twilight: the Black and Red Bible," http://blackandredbible.ning.com/, accessed April 23, 2010.

61. *Building for Life: Designing and Understanding the Human-Nature Connection* (Washington, DC: Island Press, 2005), 71.

62. Sarah M. Pike, *Earthly Bodies, Magical Selves: Contemporary Pagans and the Search for Community* (Berkeley: University of California Press, 2001), 155-81.

63. Jeffrey Luers, "How I Became an Eco-Warrior," Fall 2003, http://freefreenow.org/index.html, accessed October 2, 2006.

64. "Natural Landscapes, Gathering Places, and Prospect Refuges: Characteristics of Outdoor Places Valued by Teens," *Children's Environment Quarterly* 5 (Summer 1988): 18. A study of British teens actually found the opposite to be true, in part because parents kept setting rules and limits on their access to natural places (see Hugh Matthews and Faith Tucker, "On the Other Side of the Tracks: The Psychogeographies and Everyday Lives of Rural Teenagers in the UK," in *Children and Their Environments: Learning, Using, and Designing Spaces*, ed. Christopher Spencer and Mark Blades [Cambridge: Cambridge University Press, 2006], 161-75).

65. Tori Derr, "'Sometimes Birds Sound Like Fish': Perspectives on Children's Place Experiences," in Spencer and Blades, 112.

66. Bloustien, 211.

67. Angela McRobbie, *Feminism and Youth Culture* (Basingstoke: Macmillan, 1990). The Birmingham Centre for Contemporary Cultural Studies was founded in 1964 and became nearly synonymous with the study of youth subcultures, especially subcultures of style and music. Many cultural studies scholars interpreted youth subcultural belonging as youthful resistance to hegemonic culture, such as government and mainstream media, which constrained and subordinated the English working class.

68. AK Press website, http://www.akpress.org/2009/items/taqwacores, accessed June 16, 2008.

69. Omar Sacirbey, "The Clash: Punk Meets Islam in a Local Band That Shreds Stereotypes," *Boston Globe,* April 18, 2006, http://www.aarweb.org/programs/awards/journalism_awards/winners/2007sacirbey.pdf.

70. Ibid.

71. Dick Hebdige, "Posing . . . Threats, Striking . . . Poses: Youth, Surveillance, and Display" Vol. 11/12 No 37/38 (Madison: University of Wisconsin Press, 1982/1983), 86.

72. Clark, 5.

73. See Andrew Beaujon, *Body Piercing,* and Helen Berger and Douglas Ezzy, *Teenage Witches: Magical Youth and the Search for the Self* (New Brunswick, NJ: Rutgers University Press, 2007).

3

Children's Rights in Research about Religion and Spirituality

PRISCILLA ALDERSON

An erudite theologian suspected of being a heretic was asked
by a journalist, "Do you believe in God?" He replied cautiously,
"I can answer you but the answer is complex and I can promise you that you will not understand my answer. Do you want
me to go ahead?" "Certainly," said the journalist. "All right. The
answer is yes."

Barraclough 1999: 929

The theologian's replies raise questions for research about religion
and spirituality. How can we explore complexity within children's and adults'
seemingly simple, transparent religious beliefs? In secular societies, how can
we conduct convincing research about spirituality as the "sense of connections between the individual and the surrounding world" (Lundskow 2008:
3) and between humans and other species experienced in terms of mystery
and awe, generosity and gratitude (Beck 1992)? Spirituality may involve transcendence and intimations of holiness (Zinnbower et al. 1997). It may be the
expression of "our deepest selves" (Roof 1993) and our search for connectedness and meaning (Benson et al. 2003: 205-6).

"Factual" scientific empiricism, which accepts only data that can be
sensed and tested, dominates much social research, including research about
religion. Fundamentalists, both religious and atheistic, share starkly literal
readings of sacred texts and concepts such as "deity" and are eager to prove
or disprove the "truth." Given this empirical emphasis, are there authentic
and respectful ways to research the way children experience religion and
spirituality beyond the physical and social domains? And are we confined
to trying to observe and describe religious behaviors and reported beliefs
objectively, meaning without judgment? This chapter will review children's
rights in ethical research and then consider key questions about religion and
spirituality raised by founding sociologists. I will then address approaches in

current research, followed by some ideas on ways forward in rights-respecting research about children and religion.

Research about children tends to concentrate on small-scale, personal approaches separated from "adult," global, political concerns. Yet children and religion can only be understood within wider "adult" or whole societies, beyond the separate bubble called childhood, which is the changing sets of beliefs or theories about what children are and should be like, in contrast to real living children. This chapter therefore also connects research methods with the theories that inform them, theories being definitions and meanings, explanations, and hidden assumptions. Theories shape the whole nature and process of the way researchers select and manage their methods, questions, samples, data, findings, and conclusions.

Theories of religion and childhood that are hidden and taken for granted within a society can be obvious to outsiders. For example, Nancy Sheper-Hughes (1992) showed how very poor women in Brazil, forbidden to use contraceptives by the Roman Catholic Church, managed to feed most of their many children by denying food to some of their babies and treating them as "angel children" who wanted to die. Priests supplied the coffins and local children would bury the babies. Aravind Adiga (2010) showed how the precarious survival of slum children in Indian cities is further complicated when adults decide to assist or abuse them depending on whether they are Muslim or Hindu, and so to justify adult cruelty as moral and religious. When facing the greatest spiritual challenge, a slow death, children in an Illinois cancer ward talked among themselves about dying, but submitted to their parents' denial and ignoring of their hints, and to extremely aggressive and painful, yet futile, treatments. In this study, the researcher, Myra Bluebond-Langner (1978: 232), asked Jeffrey, aged six years, "Why do you always yell at your mother?" He replied, "Then she won't miss me when I've gone." His mother replied, "Jeffrey yells at me because he knows I can't take it. He yells so I have an excuse for leaving," raising questions about who was the most informed and mature person, the mother or the child. Bluebond-Langner (1978: 254) said she directed her rage about the children's suffering and loss at "this country for its priorities on spending [and on] a God I am not quite sure exists, but who deserves to be blamed just the same."

The examples illustrate challenges to children's embodied welfare, survival, and spiritual rights when, like many adults, they are theorized as not real people; when they suffer not only within global economic systems of extreme poverty but also as a result of certain costly, excessive medical treatments; and when religion is invoked to justify abuse. Although Bluebond-

Langner long ago vividly conveyed the profound understanding that young children can attain during life-threatening experiences, this is still widely denied. For example, it took us over two years gradually to convince a leading bioethics center that our similar findings were generalizable and therefore worth publishing and were not simply about exceptional "outliers" (Alderson et al. 2006). Rights-respecting research about children and religion therefore begins by seeing children, like adults, as fully human members of both local and global societies.

Children as Rights Holders

It is widely held that rights holders are mature and rational adult persons. However, other chapters in this book illustrate that children can be mature and rational in matters of religion (see also, for example, Roehlkepartain et al. 2005). This suggests that they can qualify as rights holders too. Rights are not clearly correlated with age or competence or maturity, as demonstrated when irrational and dangerous adults retain their rights. Some moral philosophers have asserted that children's rights to freedom of expression and religion are ill conceived because they "jeopardize the family as an institution" (Brighouse 2002: 9) and because infants lack agency and are like people in a coma or with severe Alzheimer's (Griffin 2002). However, children's early courage and commitment to their faith was shown, for example, by Quaker children in Reading, England. After the 1662 Quaker Act was passed, all Quakers over age sixteen were imprisoned and their meeting house was locked. Yet, despite being harassed and beaten, the children continued to hold silent meeting in the street (Westhill Friends 2010). Paul Connolly's sociology team (Connolly et al. 2002) found that three-year-olds in Northern Ireland were aware of cultural and political differences between Roman Catholic and Protestant Christian names and flags.

The inclusive view of inalienable rights from birth has religious origins in beliefs about God-given respect for the sacred in human nature (Woodiwiss 2005). The 1776 American Declaration of Independence states that "all men are created equal" and that "they are endowed by their Creator with certain inalienable rights." The United Nations Convention on the Rights of the Child (UNCRC 1989) attests that "recognition of the inherent dignity and of the equal and inalienable rights of all members of the human family is the foundation of freedom, justice and peace in the world." The UNCRC has been ratified by 193 (of 195) states, a strong international treaty. The UNCRC's forty-two main articles can broadly be divided into provision rights ("to a standard of living adequate for the child's physical, mental, spiritual, moral and social development" [Article 27] and to education and health care); protection rights (from abuse, neglect, discrimination, and cruel and degrading treatment and exploitation); "participation" rights, or modified forms of adult autonomy (right to life, right to form and express views though not to make decisions, freedoms of information and expression, of privacy and family life, of association and peaceful assembly, of thought, of conscience, and of religion). Freedom of religion, for example, assures every child's right to be welcomed into and nurtured in his or her family and community religion, from the religious ceremonies after birth onwards, without fear of discrimination or persecution. Like adult rights, child rights are qualified and not absolute. They must avoid harm to others and must respect public health, order, and morals, with extra protections for children's safety, best interests, and family life.

Rights-respecting and ethical research aims to ask worthwhile questions, to engage with valid theories and methods, and to be well designed, conducted, and reported (Alderson and Morrow 2010). Through every stage of a project, from first plans to final dissemination, researchers need to strive to balance their probing investigation and analysis with respect for children's rights to be heard "in all matters affecting the child" (UNCRC Article 12), and also with respect for children's rights to protection from harm, exploitation, and undue invasion of their privacy. This involves avoiding overintrusive questions and critical or dismissive comments that could humiliate children during data collection, analysis, and reporting. It also involves not overprotecting children to the extent of silencing and excluding them from research and from the potential to inform policy, practice, and public opinion and debate. Respect can be especially vital when one is researching such intimate and sensitive topics as spirituality and religion, which relate, as noted earlier, both to personal micro-concerns and also to political and economic macro-concerns, which affect children's basic rights to life, survival, and well-being. Children may be embarrassed to speak about private thoughts and, for example, about living in a violent area where it is hard to practice their religion.

Children tend to be doubly excluded from the "adult" research world. First, specialists in politics, economics, trade, work, law, theology, ethics, rights, and ecology seldom mention children although, now and in the future, many present matters will affect children more and over a longer time than they affect adults. Second, research about children tends to be limited to psycho-social inquiry into their education, care, play, development, and personal experiences. The social study of childhood has raised awareness of children's considerable capacities and agency, and shown how they are far more like adults than has been traditionally assumed (James and Prout 1997; Alderson 2008). Yet, paradoxically, childhood research still also often misleadingly confines children into separate, apolitical spaces fairly isolated from the above "adult" matters, such as the present global economic and housing crises. Yet the immense effects include debts being left for younger generations to repay. And when a home is repossessed, children may also lose their neighborhood, school, friends, and place of worship along with the congregation.

In another separation, research reports about children and religion tend to be in specialist literature and not in generic collections (such as James and Prout 1997; Franklin 2001; Lewis et al. 2004; Christensen and James 2008; Percy-Smith and Thomas 2010). One British collection of twenty-five papers about youth work was unusual in including a paper on religion—but only one. However, more youth workers are employed by the Church of England than by all the other institutions, and the paper concluded,

> The flawed assumption that secularism is neutral has led to a culture where faith-based work is progressively inhibited . . . particularly with the rising fear of religious extremism and, to a lesser extent, of organized religion in general. Secularism is communicated and imposed on a daily basis through the media, school, youth work and other role models, whereas evangelistic Christian youth work faces increasing opposition to its message. (Clayton and Stanton 2008: 117)

Researchers might examine young people's views on the seeming paradox of "rising fear . . . of organized religion" in Britain, where church and state are so intertwined, versus strong support for organized religion in the United States, where church and state are officially separate.

So far, this chapter has suggested that in order to understand children's and young people's own experiences and views about religion, researchers need to relate to them as real human beings, and not as undeveloped pre-beings. Respect for children includes paying attention to their rights through the selection of research topics, theories, and methods, as well as to influences on children and their religion exerted by politics, economics, and other "adult" matters beyond a supposed separate "world of childhood."

Questions from the Sociology of Religion, 1820-1920

Earlier sociologists traced powerful connections between religion and the rest of life, raising vital questions for research with people of all ages. Connected to the root word for ties ("ligation"), religion denotes both potentially negative restrictive bonds and also positive, enabling human ties and webs of relationships; each version of religion gives active form to spirituality. This section draws on Robert Nisbet's history of the sociology of religion. Nisbet considered that sociology is the only social science to examine the way religio-sacred myth, ritual, and sacrament inform secular life (1967: 221-63). Sociology perceives human nature and society as intrinsically moral, instead of assuming that secular, economic, utilitarian, self-interested, and competitive doctrines are "the essential and sufficing pillars of social analysis" (1967: 221). Nineteenth-century European sociologists, although they were mainly atheists, regarded religion as an integral foundation of society, implanting a deep sense of unity and promoting both social order and individual thought. Alexis de Tocqueville saw in religion the source of human conceptions of meaning and order, and of duty and true human nature, promoting wisdom and virtue as safeguards from paralyzing fear, disorder, and tyranny. Emile Durkheim traced to religion the historical origins of human intellect, language, philosophy, and science, concepts of time and space, and the sacred bonds of the social contract. Contrasting the sacred with the profane and secular, Durkheim explored how religions can deepen shared experiences of joy and sorrow and moral values, and can thereby defuse divisive individualism and anomie.

Max Weber (1978) also raised questions about differences between religious and secular values. He regarded the original charismatic religious leaders (for example, Buddha and Christ) as revolutionary, antitradition, and antiwealth. Yet their teachings quickly became routinized by their successors into dogma, ritual, law, and hierarchy, transforming their initial ideas on love, justice, and equity into the opposing values of acquiring wealth and power. Weber analyzed how large social changes depend on many influences. including people's deep values, motives, and meanings—their religion. He explored capitalism's religious origins in the sixteenth century. Work, wealth, and profit have always been tolerated and enjoyed as well as being morally challenged, but gradually they have become "ethically compelling and morally sovereign" (Nisbet 1967: 259). God's calling (vocation) and blessing are now strongly associated with prosperity and wealth. Georg Simmel understood human behaviors and relationships through piety: "the strange mixture of selfless devotion and desire, of humility and elation, of sensual immediacy and spiritual abstraction" beyond sheer egoism, "an emotion of the soul" that includes faith "in the power, the merit, the irresistibility and goodness of the other" (Simmel 1908/1959: 23, 33). The founding sociologists generally aligned spirituality with mature manhood. However, their histories of "primitive" religions, in which religion precedes and forms, rather than grows out of, later social and intellectual developments, suggest an innate spirituality in everyone, including children.

Nisbet (1967: 229-31) identified four basic perspectives among founding sociologists who saw religion as

- an indispensable, integrating, unifying, social force—its communal bonds necessary to social order and its sacred values necessary to moral consensus beyond secular reason and interest;
- a key to understanding and explaining historical and social change and their context in human values and motives;
- a sacred mystery involving rites and hierarchy that lend meaning, symbol, and power to secular concepts of community, family and individuality, status, authority, and society;
- a sense of divine majesty and sacred imperatives, originally fundamental to the first development of human thought and belief, of language and loyalty.

Current political, economic, and ecological crises raise these kinds of spiritual concerns, in formal religious teaching and in broader questions of ethics, values, piety, and charismatic leadership in troubling times. One example relating to all these questions occurred during spring 2010, when oil deep-mined by BP (formerly British Petroleum) gushed into the Gulf of Mexico. How does the disaster challenge the rights of present and future societies to obtain fuel at such high cost to the environment and surrounding neighborhoods? How might religious concepts of a sacred creation, human solidarity, and the heritage bequeathed to younger generations contribute to the mainly economic and engineering debates?

The founding sociologists' questions, their methods of analysis, and their profound conclusions are valuable in today's research about children and religion. The questions and research areas include the following. How can we best care now for present and future generations, children and adults, and for the planet and other species? What part can or should religion and ideas of the sacred play in today's global decisions? How far can "religion" be stretched to describe any shared passion, however secular, such as sport or consumerism? How do children and young people experience and discuss these kinds of questions of religion and spirituality, the good person and the good society?

Contemporary Research

This section considers how researchers can share respect, trust, and rapport with children who have devout beliefs that the researcher may or may not share. Dismissive relativism rejects accounts of faith, which by definition cannot be verified by scientific methods. Should researchers treat children's accounts as personal constructions, when it is irrelevant whether they are true or false? The philosopher Roger Trigg's view could apply to any kind of genuine faith. He asks, "Is Christianity true?" If sociologists say they do not deal with matters of truth and belief in religion or science, Trigg considers that they fail "to take seriously the fact that to the person holding it, the most important aspect is that *it is true* [and] ignoring [their truth] can appear tantamount to assuming their falsity" (Trigg 1985: 36; emphasis in original). Varying approaches to religion in contemporary research address the question of respecting children's (and adults') rights in terms of taking their beliefs seriously. They include mythos, children's views, education and therapy, nonjudgmentalism, and dialectical critical realism.

Mythos

The theologian Karen Armstrong (2009) analyzed how original beliefs perceived the sacred and God not as fact but as meaning, and religion as practical experiential knowledge. In all the major religions, people read sacred texts for mythos: to make sense of creation, suffering, life, and death, and to learn how to practice justice, peace, compassion, altruism, and solidarity. Today, texts are read more for logos: literal, factual, scientific realism. "Belief," though etymologically connected to "love" and commitment, altered into a checklist of opinions. By analyzing a tradition's mythos, however, researchers can explore the transcendent meaning and relevance the faith has to each participant. So when children talk about their faith, their views cannot be tested empirically but may be taken as valid in the context and meaning of their own experiences and relationships. In complex, sensitive research that can transcend literal meanings, Karen Winter's (2010) methods are helpful. They avoid potentially intimidating eye-to-eye contact. The researcher sits next to the child and the two talk while the child uses craft materials to decorate a small cardboard box with images of the self on the outside and of "wishes and feelings" on the inside.

Children's Views

Some of the founding sociologists' questions may sound too complex for research with children. Yet during discussions about these topics, sometimes linked to drama, music, art, or natural settings, even young children refer in their own terms to concepts of charisma or piety and wonder in their lives (Roehlkepartain et al. 2005). Children's discussions about religion show their efforts to make moral and spiritual sense of their puzzling, contradictory worlds. Harriet, when aged five years and attending a Church of England school, commented, "Christians believe that Jesus was born in Bethlehem" (personal communication). She neatly conveyed the uneasy relativism in current relationships among state, church, and school, and among parents, children, and teachers of all faiths and none. Amy, aged nine, and Robbie, aged six, while awaiting visits from both Father Christmas and the Tooth Fairy, discussed Prometheus's theft of fire from the gods (personal communication 2009). They implicitly relied on concepts of truth in both mythos and literal logos when trying to order the plethora of pantheons children now encounter:

> ROBBIE: I don't believe in gods. . . . I believe in Egyptian gods 'cos they were real people, they put animal heads on them.
> AMY: I'm not sure I really believe in Jesus. Maybe he was born a baby. He was accidentally caught up in something. He was loved, so maybe people say he will live forever and be son of God. Nobody's really sure, but something has to be true. He's so famous and everybody's believed in it for thousands of years, but it was 2,000 years ago and no one is left to tell the proper truth.
> *[Discussion of how the world started.]*
> ROBBIE: What I think how the world started is I think a long time ago . . . there was just one planet and soon a comet or something hit it, then it turned into loads of planets and they called them names after the gods they think are true. I don't really know. . . . I think people and our planet will be extinct soon and maybe the world will start again. [Talk of litter and felling too many trees.]

Asked for their views about angels, other young children showed the same thoughtful piecing together of many disparate fragments of information and disciplines ranging from philosophy, theology, and the paranormal to physics and engineering.

> "I like angels because they have wings and they're magic and the angel made them back alive again. Well, he was like a spirit." "They make wishes come true." "The angels' wings are made of a sort of material; it's got to be a light material otherwise they wouldn't fly." "Don't forget it's all by air power." "Angels live in heaven with God, they live in clouds." "I believe that when you die you become an angel and you live in heaven with God." "Nobody's ever even seen an angel and we like to know they could be real but it's good to know that it's always going to be a mystery." "Angels send messages from God to earth . . . like the world should be peaceful, people should be polite and respect others." (French et al. 2007)

Comparison with earlier accounts shows how faithfully children reflect their time and place, and the importance of understanding their diverse accounts in broad contexts. In the past, very young Christian children memorized prayers and Bible verses and confessed their sins. George Monkford recalled being ten years old in 1836. After stealing apples and stopping at the alehouse to hear singing he remembered, "O the guilt and fear I felt. . . . I kept repeating the Lord's prayer . . . to keep the devil (as I thought) from grasping me . . . the dread of hell and punishment of my sin often made me cry out, 'Do save me: do pardon me and I will lead a new life'" (Rosen 1994: 93).

Although there are many studies of children's own views gathered through ethnographies and semistructured interviews, I did not find any in research about religion. Rather than abstracted discussions and questionnaires, for example, on the meaning of God, it could be more rewarding to explore with children the lived spiritual dimensions in their lives, and their unique insights, especially during adversity: serious illness or armed conflict, forced migration, or poverty (for example, Katz 2004; Beah 2007). Spiritual questions about their faith in God and in human goodness could be woven into such research. For example, secular research about child asylum seekers has spiritual overtones. The sociologists (Pinson et al. 2010) found that British children from around seven years became horrified when young immigrants, who had become their school friends, were imprisoned or were due to be deported back to violent countries from which they had escaped. The British children, with their teachers and parents, mounted vigorous and sometimes successful protests. The researchers identified their growing political awareness and agency with a questioning of assumed values, such as confidence in British justice, and with "the politics of compassion," solidarity, and empathy with their peers.

Research for Education and Therapy

Psychologists Donald Ratcliff and Rebecca Nye (2006) intended to increase understanding, recognition, and nurturing of children's spirituality in all aspects of their lives, including effective treatments for "negative spirituality" in youth crime and violence. They aimed to strengthen agreed qualitative and quantitative, longitudinal, and international methods of research about spirituality with children of all ages. They were cautious about Piagetian stages and the risks of misrepresenting spirituality's complexity, depth, and fluidity. They worried that teaching *about* God might displace experience *of* God, and they believed that "children are more than potential, are whole persons now . . . deeply spiritual both in their day-to-day lives as well as in those moments of connectedness to Transcendence" (2006: 481). This implies that spirituality is innate, although it might unfold or deepen or emerge through fuller and more articulate consciousness. However, they were also concerned with "scientific rigor," clear definitions, measurements, and comparisons of incremental (developing rather than present) spirituality, and they aimed to generalize from, predict, and evaluate children's responses in different contexts. There are unresolved tensions between the authors' interpretive and more positivist approaches. Questionnaires for statistical analysis can hardly capture complex, ambiguous replies, of the kind quoted at the beginning of this chapter. And as the children quoted earlier illustrate, their responses may reflect what they have been told rather than some universal age-based spiritual development.

Nonjudgmentalism

Some researchers aim to be value free. The sociologist George Lundskow (2008) considers that religion is not primarily about objective, observable, measurable truth, but is rather derived from emotion and experience. Lundskow aims to examine contingent, constructed meanings impartially, and to see how religious beliefs and mores reflect, reinforce, and explain social mores. He explores what religions mean to the devout, although he gives some extreme examples that challenge his neutral stand (2008: 372, 393) of faiths that deny their founding values and propound autonomy and choice in spirituality as if it is a commodity. One example, from Smith and Denton (2005: 143), is that most North American young people today say that faith is important to them. However, they tend to see religion in terms of "moralistic therapeutic deism . . . profoundly individualistic. . . . [They presume] autonomous, individual self-direction to be a universal norm and life goal . . . an invisible and pervasive doxa . . . unrecognized, unquestioned." Individuals freely call on God for help when they desire it, as they would employ commercial products or services, and as freely they ignore God at other times. They also ignore other people's interests, without commitment or self-sacrifice or any sense of community.

Another example (Lundskow 2008: 391-95) is evangelical megachurches, where many congregations are poor and Black. The leaders collect millions of dollars from them, use tax avoidance schemes, and translate Christianity into simple misleading messages in such a way as to present Jesus as a business entrepreneur and profits as God's blessing. The leaders pressure congregations into supporting Republican policies, which especially favor inequality, while lobbying and donating vast funds to Republican politicians. The most disadvantaged groups are most likely to vote against state-aided health care and against higher taxes for the rich (Reynolds 2005), and one-third of them believe they will live to see the apocalyptic end of the world (Hochschild 2005). Such a meeting of religious, political, and economic beliefs fits Weber's view that secular societies disenchant religion. The beliefs powerfully affect young people directly and indirectly. The worship of wealth demands that richer children spend billions of dollars each year, while very low-paid child workers produce many of the goods. The system has to be fed by growing demand, fueled by advertising when hundreds of slogans, brands, and logos particularly target children daily, deeply influencing their moral beliefs, values, and aspirations (Klein 2000; Beder 2009). Meanwhile, global trade, investment and speculation, property bubbles, mining, and logging all leave great economic and ecological debts for decades ahead, which younger generations will have to repay, and raise religious questions about respect for justice and the environment. Lundskow's veto on judging how moral and authentic religious sects are could be overriden by assessing the sects not against arbitrary standards but on how they set examples and teach children to honor or violate their faith's founding precepts reviewed earlier.

Some organized religions' close associations with extreme greed, oppression, or violence can make religion-related value judgments seem especially suspect and "unscientific." Yet to describe oppressive religions without judgment can appear to condone them. Dialectical critical realism (DCR) denies that nonjudgmental objectivity is possible and argues that facts and values are inseparable, recognizing moral values at the heart of all human life (Bhaskar 2008). DCR also separates the reality of independent *being* (children, churches) from *knowing* (how we perceive and interpret reality) and examines how we tend to collapse being into knowing, things into thoughts, real, living, capable children into stereotypes of childhood. The philosopher Roy Bhaskar (2008: 291-92) argues that in the writer's and reader's sincere searching together for truth and meaning, on which research depends, freedom and truth are conditions of one another, and therefore honest communication implies shared commitment to the (sacred) ideals of human solidarity and universal human flourishing. DCR understands complex social life such as children and religion beyond child/ adult, body/spirit dichotomies, on four interacting planes altogether: physical bodies and environment; interpersonal relationships, emotions, and values; structures and institutions; and inner personality (flourishing, spiritual awareness of transcendence) (2008: 160). The four planes offer rich methods of analysis of children's religions.

Douglas Porpora's (2001) DCR research analyzed contemporary self-interested attitudes toward God, divorced from any communal relationships or loyalties or shared respect for rights and justice. Such self-obsession develops, he argues, into either extreme individualist greed or fanatical dogmatic submission. Porpora contends that everyone needs (true) religion to validate moral meaning in life and in social justice, to guide thought and action, and to mediate between individuals and society within a cosmic vision. Porpora considers that being, meaning, and morality all coincide, and today's worship of corporate profit dominates us all, turning even our souls into commodities. He cites the Hindu concept *avisya*, which refers to the phenomenon of superficial concerns obscuring deeper meaning in life. "As long as we are free to buy as much as we want of whatever we want at the lowest price, we are happy. We cease to notice that the real choices—what is made by whom, where and how—are no longer up to us" (Porpora 2001: 309). While infinite consumption exhausts the finite planet, DCR argues that we have to recognize alternatives, their absence, and their potential, and a major question for research is how religions foster or challenge consumerist convictions, especially in younger generations.

Ways Forward

The founding sociologists emphasized interdependence between religions and their social, political, economic, and natural world contexts. Their concerns are still highly relevant today in research about children and religion. The founders favored methods of describing, understanding, and explaining rather than measuring data. To do justice to valid, ethical, and complex research with children about religion and to respect their rights as real persons can involve using DCR approaches, which acknowledge the way rights and spirituality are integral to all human concerns, actions, and relationships. Religious values of the sacred and of solidarity have a lasting being and reality, as well as transient interpretations and practices. Researchers who share time and experiences with children on their terms are more likely to understand their views and explanations than researchers who use fairly fast, formal, standardized methods and questions.

Present social, economic, and ecological crises indicate pressing needs for adults and children to research and work and learn together interdependently in an effort to deal with these crises, in rights-respecting partnerships that draw on religious traditions and spiritual reserves.

This chapter has reviewed approaches that can help to deepen our understanding of children's religion and spirituality. The approaches include ways to use rights-respecting research methods and theories, to see children as real persons, and to connect their lives to "adult worlds" by analyzing how politics, economics, and other social structures intersect with religion. The approaches also draw on the profound insights of earlier sociologists and philosophers. Besides attending to the meaning in children's own accounts, researchers need to examine secular influences on today's faiths and religious education, and to assess these against the founding precepts that religions tend to share.

— II —

Using Ethnography to Talk
with Contemporary Children

4

Navigating the Institutional Review Board (IRB) for Child-Directed Qualitative Research

CINDY DELL CLARK

Above my desk, I have a quotation pinned to the wall, words attributed to the late, great singer Pearl Bailey. Bailey once shared this point of wisdom: "What the world needs now is more love and less paperwork." Bureaucratic reviews (such as tax returns, tenure applications, grant requests, and institutional reviews of research protocols) generally involve abundant forms to complete. An Institutional Review Board (IRB) application would seem to go astray of Pearl's advice. Yet, in order to do ethically certified research with children, I have learned to make an exception. Research on children's views is worth some red tape.

I am probably not alone in accepting the trade-off. Children have become more frequent participants in qualitative inquiry lately, including for religious and spiritual research (e.g., Bales 2005; Coles 1990; Csordas 2009; Haight 1998; Peshkin 1988; Williams and Lindsey 2005). The work of child-centered qualitative researchers with kids has used a range of methods, from ethnography to photography (Samuels 2004; Williams 2009), to give greater voice to the young. Each time a scholar has studied children's beliefs or knowledge or doings, clearance by an Institutional Review Board (IRB) presumably has preceded the fieldwork, as required by the researcher's academic institution. Each IRB has the official charge of ensuring the protection of human subjects and the privacy of their divulged information. In this chapter we delve into the process of gaining IRB approval when devising a qualitative study centered on children. I will draw from my experience with studying religious festival (Clark 1995), as well as health-related studies with kids (Clark 2003). I will present examples from medical and health research because such studies carry readily apparent moral implications, and because IRBs and literature on IRBs are especially oriented to health-related investigations. Biomedical research has tended to influence the evolution of American IRBs, in line with the fact that IRBs were fundamentally organized as a response to medical research gone astray. Let me share how this happened.

IRB: Then and Now

The IRB was born out of ethical necessity, in response to medical malfeasance. After World War II, in the United States and elsewhere, institutionalized children were given troublesome medical treatments under the guise of research. For instance, a study infected children with hepatitis and administered a drug known to have harmful side effects for the liver (Ross 2006). Children in America were infected or inoculated with dysentery, herpes, and polio (Grodin and Glantz 1994). In 1983, after government bodies uncovered the abuses in the United States, regulations for research were enacted at a federal level by the Department of Health and Human Services. Influential to this day is the so-called Common Rule, shared principles of federal agencies that govern the conduct of American IRBs. Implicit in the regulations and guidelines that were instituted was an emphasis on adult responsibility to protect children (Clark 2010). Adults, not children, comprised the IRB panels, including the lay members. By and large, IRB panels came to reflect a mature and narrow group: disproportionately white, male, well-educated, higher-income adults (Burke 2005). Given the generational composition of IRBs, protectionist adult definitions of risk and harm to children became the routine considerations. Children, not regarded to be of the legal age to consent to a study, have been asked to assent (a more minor acquiescence), while the primary consent comes from a parent or legal guardian (Ferraro, Orvedal, and Plaud 1998). Adults' choices are privileged in IRB rules even when the child is facing imminent mortality and the research may add pronounced discomfort or strain to life's end (Bluebond-Langner, DeCicco, and Belasco 2005).

Recently, weight has been thrown behind the argument that in many circumstances children are competent to fully consent to research in their own right. Childhood studies scholar Priscilla Alderson and her colleagues (2006), for instance, make the claim that diabetic children, who often manage their own disease through an understanding of the nature and purposes of treatment, are capable of informed consent in research. Five-year-olds they studied were trusted everyday with decisions and initiatives, such as doing a blood test on their own or deciding the amount of sweet foods they could eat at a party. From four years of age, children comprehended the principles and standards for controlling diabetes, and made choices applying this comprehension. Children thus operate competently, in the situation of diabetes, in conditions of high risk and potential adversity. This raises questions regarding assumptions that children's capacities for consent are in every context age-limited. Treating children with fairness and respect may require recognizing their capacities, rather than regarding them as inevitably fully reliant on adults. Protection of children can have the problematic side effect of silencing and marginalizing them (Bradley 2007).

If I were to devise an ideal system of ethical review, it would accommodate children's perspectives and competencies, while also weighing adults' responsibilities. Insight into parental concern is worth some scrutiny (Gordon, Yamokoski, and Kodish 2006). Parents, I have learned, can embrace research uneasily. In a discourse analysis of 140 naturally occurring parent-doctor conversations about children's research participation, Elisa Gordon detected that parents of leukemia patients, despite signing off on formal consent, spoke of biomedical research intentions with mistrust. This was made clear by the recurrence (in comments made by parents to physicians) of a negative metaphor: that of the guinea pig. The guinea pig metaphor served as a symbolic reference for the depersonalizing and disempowering status of a son or daughter in a medical experiment. The humanist critique of medicine's empiricist zeal is now fairly common (Kuipers 1989). Parents seemed to seize upon the guinea pig metaphor as a vivid, symbolic reference encapsulating their misgivings about experiments. Included under the guinea pig notion were (1) the impersonal way in which randomization trumps personalized treatment; (2) the demeaning sense that one's child (known as a "guinea pig") may be compromised in favor of the build-up of the medical profession's expertise; and (3) a lack of predictability about the impact of interventions on a child's well-being. Other aspects of a "guinea pig" comparison were (4) not wanting a child to be singled out for experimental rather than tried and true forms of treatment; and (5) wanting clear empowerment for a son or daughter to personally withdraw, without any taint of implied or perceived pressure by physicians. Ironically, the rule-bound uniformity that often drives IRB decisions (played out through depersonalized, objective standards) may inhibit parents' trust. To a large extent, parents indicate that a child's personhood is trumped during an impersonal experiment, rendering the child somewhat objectified. Experimental inquiry symbolically transforms a pediatric patient into a "guinea pig" with disadvantageous power relations and lessened dignity, parents say. Informed consent processes and sign-off may not stave off a subtle leeriness by mothers and fathers, since a sense of wariness and dehumanization may be inherent in positivist, "objective" methods.

So we see that the experimental method, with its emphasis on "objectivity" and "control," can cause parents to be guarded. On the other hand, qualitative research (less laced with positivist objectivity) lacks the experiment's depersonalization, a good thing to parents. Done properly, qualitative research is a more flexible path of investigation in which study participants have a shaping imprint on the inquiry's direction (Pritchard 2002). Qualitative researchers, in principle, surrender to the informant, rather than the other way around. This turns upside down the "guinea pig" conditions of experiments. Still, to the degree that IRBs are relatively less familiar with child-participatory or child-focused qualitative methods (versus quantitative ones), the advantages are less appreciated by typical IRB reviewers. Sparing the young person from randomized, fixed, impersonal handling, and instead paying attention to and adjusting for personal concerns is beneficial to research participants. This is reason enough to convince the IRB of the qualitative approach and its potency in consoling and empowering informants. A qualitative research protocol is not fixed, but responsive, and thereby adds to trust. Preparing a protocol for review may require specifying a range of options to be used during inquiry, to allow for a contingent sort of participation, rather than a rigid, unvarying, or uniform approach (Pritchard 2002).

Here's the bad news. IRBs, in recent years, have not fully succeeded in their mission to protect human subjects. For example, in a landmark 2001 decision of a Maryland court, a quantitative study design (approved by the Johns Hopkins University IRB) was cited for its mistreatment of vulnerable young subjects, by exposing some participants to lead paint without giving all the children an equal benefit of reduction of exposure (Beh 2002). It was researchers who were held responsible, and the IRB was cited directly for breach of duties. In another study overseen by the Johns Hopkins IRB in 2001, a healthy volunteer lost her life after a substance was administered in a manner unapproved by the FDA. Nor is Johns Hopkins the only prominent research institution at which IRB procedures have recently gone awry; a University of Pennsylvania gene therapy experiment led to the premature death of an eighteen-year-old subject (Beh 2002), in a case that involved failure to stop the research protocol when mortality rates rose. The University of Pennsylvania case was also tied to a conflict of interest in light of the commercial connections of the investigators.

These meltdowns show, of course, that the oversight duties of the IRB are consequential and not just empty ritual. To say that an IRB is mainly concerned with risk management for the institution's benefit (over and above the benefit to people) brushes over the substantive responsibility the IRB has to protect people of all ages. Real harm is a possibility in studies, even at prestigious institutions with long research records. Vigilance about ethics—no matter the required time and paperwork needed—is nothing to brush off.

Dealing with the IRB

The first time I dealt with a university IRB was my first day at a professorial job in a United States public university. Prior to that day, I had reflected on ethical matters over a two-decade, full-time career as an applied qualitative researcher. Applied qualitative research, in contrast to academic studies, rarely requires a formalistic, written ethical review, in line with the fact that applied work is usually not funded by federal sources specifying formal IRB clearance. As a scholarly newcomer, I was eager to engage the IRB process. Even before teaching a class, I checked the IRB website and went about seeking IRB approval for my first study as a faculty member. As at most universities, a significant amount of formal, standardized paperwork was involved. The IRB asked for twenty-one copies of all paperwork! My university, like most, required a training course (on-line) followed by a readily mastered test on "research with human subjects." (This on-line training and test is also required of research assistants or others working on the investigation.) Having passed the online course, I was then eligible to submit a study protocol, that is, the application that fully documents the study's steps and built-in ethical considerations. In the health or medical arena, IRBs devote 56 percent of their staff time to administrating, reviewing, and approving potential protocols (Sugarman et. al 2005). As a new faculty member, I certainly did not have 56 percent of my time available for an IRB application! Still, this did not deter me from patiently preparing the documents, eager as I was to get started on an inquiry with children about the felt meaning of cigarette smoking. With the confidence of an old pro turned scholar-novice, I finished, signed, sealed, and delivered my first protocol, a careful and clear documentation of a plan for interviewing young smokers. I was confident that this caring project, meant to get a kids'-eye view of tobacco smoking as a tool of understanding and intervention (Clark 1998), would pass muster with the IRB. It didn't. The IRB said I could not do the study I wanted to do, and that my plan to give children privacy about their participation in a study of cigarette smoking was inappropriate. The IRB wanted full parental disclosure as part of each child's recruitment, including telling the parent about the child's smoking, effectively eliminating confidentiality for the children. (Early tobacco smoking is not routinely divulged to parents by youth in everyday life.) Children's rights and perspectives were important priorities for my research approach, since children's views and experiences about smoking were the very point of the intended work. But in many American institutions of review, children's agency is not a paramount priority. In my IRB, reviewers sided with conventional power relations, in other words, parental dominion over children. The IRB articulated familiar construals of parents as protectors of children, at the expense of children's autonomy and privacy.

Currently, there is emergent skepticism by child-directed qualitative researchers about prevailing assumptions that adults are exclusively correct about children's welfare (Alderson, Sutcliffe, and Curtis 2006; Clark 2010). Honoring kids' confidences can be at odds with IRB emphasis on parental prerogative and protectiveness. A better balance needs to be struck between children's and parent's concerns.

While the IRB has the final word on how risks and benefits figure into a research study for the protection of children, a wide-angle lens reveals complexities, pluralisms, and contrasts. The juxtaposition of children's and parental interests poses an ethical conundrum. Learning children's own meanings requires research in which kids can be heard, unfiltered by elders. I believed (and still do) that the best way to learn how to intervene (and protect) children in the area of youth smoking was by fully understanding kids' direct experiences and significations. At present, IRBs in America emphasize parental protectionism and control, seen by adults on the IRB as mechanisms to reduce harm to kids. Children's agency is not overriding.

I took the disappointment in stride. I turned to other areas of research instead of smoking and was able to gain approval for subsequent studies, without feeling the sting of another IRB rejection. In the course of presenting later protocols, I was able to incorporate some practices that were child friendly, such as the manner by which research was explained to children and the way assent was obtained.

I also had a fruitful relationship later with the IRB at a large regional hospital, a collaborating partner in a study. (If a study is collaborative across institutions, all IRBs review that study, with the researcher seeking a consensus protocol.) I noticed that my university IRB made decisions a bit differently from the hospital IRB. Relatively speaking, the university IRB seemed to toe the line in their procedures in an almost mechanical or abstracted way. They "went by the book." Perhaps not surprisingly, the hospital was relatively more pragmatic in discerning the ethical impact of a study, in the context of practice.

Religious topics also raise impactful ethical issues, although not necessarily issues in which IRB evaluators are widely conversant. The wise investigator may need to "translate" for an IRB how issues of faith or spirituality can be viewed through the IRB lens. Predominant in the way IRBs frame things would be the risks and benefits of a given study. Tricky issues may be entailed. Could the risks to parents differ from the risks to children, when parents want to know what children say they believe, yet might punish a belief they don't approve? Since parents' views of a child's religiosity may be in tension with a child's own inclinations, the issues of privacy and autonomous consent by kids may become important issues. All the while, investigators tangling with these complexities will need to "translate" their child-relevant goals into the understood terms and priorities of IRB panelists.

In a way, dealing with the IRB is a kind of diplomacy: making sure that requests are framed and placed in a guise comprehensible, meaningful, and respectful to the IRB. Like an astute ambassador, a researcher learns from experience how her plans will be seen from the IRB's vantage point. With the translational fluency of a diplomat, a scholar can reason on behalf of a child-directed study with professionals who generally lack expertise about qualitative, or religion-related, or child-directed inquiry. Becoming such a "diplomat" engenders an ability to negotiate views of adults and children across interpretively distinct lines. The good news is that the implicated translational skills (Burke 2005) can be used in other contexts. Should a scholar seek to apply for grant funding, sabbatical privileges, publication opportunities, and the like, the capacity to diplomatically translate (learned from IRB interactions) can also enhance other sorts of overtures.

Philosopher Ivor Pritchard (2002) has drawn a clever comparison between the IRB and a troll, that is, the folkloric character that stood before a bridge and blocked the way of those wanting to pass by—demanding a toll for the right of passage. Pritchard (2002: 7) wrote,

> Trolls block the way—exacting tolls, asking questions, slowing things down, demanding to be appeased. IRB trolls exact their toll in the currency of time and effort needed to assemble IRB submissions, respond to IRB requests, and work through whatever modifications on which the IRB insists. IRBs' appetite for paper seems voracious.

But "trolls" can be approached and often convinced of allowing passage, if one bears in mind the need for translating one's own direction and rationale into the trolls' worldview. The skills of translation, across religious and generational boundaries, are ones that qualitative researchers of children and religion, of course, incorporate at multiple points in inquiry: in doing fieldwork, in reporting results, as well as in conceptualizing research. At all these points adults visit children's worlds—possibly children of other faiths—and channel the meanings of one generation (or faith) for others. Bridging IRB gaps of signification can be accomplished by such facility—by getting to know the IRB and relating its frameworks of meaning to children's needs and preferences.

Plans and Protocols

Just as you would consult documentation and instructions when completing a tax return or college application, careful attention must be paid to the procedures, forms, guidelines, and requests provided by your institution's IRB. (Many such documents are placed on the IRB's web pages.) Seek out this information and study it. If you are doing an inquiry on illness and religion, you will need to complete a test on the federal HIPAA rules, which deal with medical privacy. HIPAA rules would require an additional sign-off during informed consent.

In preparing your protocol for a qualitative study of children, you may detect that the IRB's expectations are tipped towards quantitative research procedures, not qualitative research. But don't be deterred. It is simply that the biomedical origins of IRBs have left an institutional legacy of quantitative more than qualitative research leanings. This requires, as mentioned before, translational skill. Explain in your protocol the methodological underpinnings of your qualitative study step by step, writing as if to address a person unfamiliar with the methods. Openly take account of risks and benefits. In your protocol, acknowledge that you are aware of children's vulnerability and are taking steps to assert protection, even if you also aim to treat children as having competence and agency. In a study of American mythical figures (Santa, the Easter Bunny, and the Tooth Fairy—Clark 1995) I wrote in the protocol how activities such as drawing were devised to protect children from finding out from the research process that these figures were "unreal" (an adult ontological premise, but not a child's). In other words, the questioning intended to tread carefully so as not to directly challenge the child's belief, which would be considered taboo in most of U.S. society. In a study I undertook of chronic illness (Clark 2003), the research plan again let children take the lead, a way of protecting children from being directly "taught" negative ideas (pain, mortality, suffocation, etc.) by the interview process; instead, children shared their own accounts about the illness experience, in part through taking and explaining photos. Here a child-centered practice that privileged open-ended sharing by the child could be framed as protective, a priority issue for the IRB.

Ensuring that children retain a position of power in research can be done, with the right features of study design. Professors of education Freeman and Mathison (2009) recommend that a research protocol actively involve children at every step. This could start with the way one assesses risks and benefits of the study, a central aspect of a protocol. My study of Halloween (Clark 2005) recognized in the protocol that some children aged seven and younger had pronounced fears of Halloween symbols (skeletons, gravestones, mummies, or other tokens of death). As a counter to such fears, interviews were planned so that children took the initiative from the outset—through showing and telling how Halloween was celebrated at home or making drawings, rather than directly raising anxiety-provoking cues about Halloween's dark side. The September 11 attacks occurred just prior to the last phase of my Halloween fieldwork in 2001. But since children's anxieties were taken into good account in the protocol, I was able to manage the unexpected source of trauma well.

As a general practice, carefully consider children's views as relevant to the whole research process (Goodenough 2007). Freeman and Mathison (2009) even recommend that children be central to determining what the sample selection criteria will be, that is, what categories of children would be relevant to include in the inquiry.

Kon (2006) has argued that children be given initiative during the assent procedure. Kon emphasized that explanations of research should focus on what children understand and relate to, adding that assent can be documented differently with children of differing ages. With children under ten, I have found, oral explanation is quite feasible (in conversation with the child), ideally with give and take that provides feedback about children's comprehension or need for clarification. In oral assent, the exchange can be documented through tape recording, verifying not only the researcher's words but also how well a child understands. A visual communication approach can also be employed, such as through an activity board. Nurse Lucy Bray (2007) used a visual activity board (with moveable pieces) that included text descriptions of these topics: confidentiality, assent, tape recording, lack of right or wrong answers, the researcher's role, and parental presence. Thirty picture pieces (with Velcro connectors) could be matched according to each topic's explanation, thereby accomplishing a multisensory, active "matching" approach to each child's briefing prior to assent.

The sort of exchange that occurs in the assent process, since it takes place at the outset of a session, sets the stage and establishes a tone for how freely the child will speak throughout the interview. A passive process in which the child has a subordinate position (and the adult dispenses all the explanations) does not set up conditions for a fully child-empowered conversation. So active forms of assent potentially benefit the fuller interview process.

Involving children actively in child-friendly ways (e.g., photos or drawings or matching pictures) contrasts with expecting children to submit to adult ways of communicating. For assent purposes, it is best to avoid showing kids under twelve documents that put them off through unfamiliar vocabulary and lengthy reading. Adult authority can easily seep into an exchange between adult and child; expecting a child to be more literate than he or she is is a way of expecting the child to be more "mature" than he or she is. This is intimidating, rather than empowering. It does not bode very well if the goal is to open children's perspectives and experiences.

In the protocol, the researcher will need to plan for maintaining anonymity and confidentiality—including from parents, teachers, or church leaders. I have studied kids with diabetes who have admitted to "cheating" on their diabetic diet on isolated occasions, information they did not wish their parents to know. Secrets, transgressions, or doubts are also apt to arise when children are asked about religion or spirituality. Apart from the crucial responsibility to report child abuse mentioned by the child, a high priority should be placed on preserving a child's privacy.

IRBs' federally given guidelines require inclusion. This prohibits discriminating so that some groups of children are excluded unnecessarily from a study. If a religious minority is singled out for interest in a study, the protocol should explain the basis for not including other groups.

Another area to plan for is the treatment of data and reporting. Even if a study has gone smoothly, problems can develop when it is time to make public what has been learned. As part of a study in which kids drew pictures, I assured children that what they shared was private. Preparing a book about the study for final printing, the publisher asked me if some of the children's drawings could be included in the volume. I contacted the children who made the drawings and obtained written permission of both child and parent to print their drawings anonymously in the book. Some of the children volunteered that they would like their names to appear, an age-appropriate sign of pride and mastery. Still, I declined the children's request for disclosing their identity, which was not signed off on by all the kids. Another issue I considered was the long shelf life of a book, such that children's names might appear for their entire lives. A study of religion that will remain in libraries for decades (or more) has to account for the disclosure of identity that will remain public long term, on into maturity. The child at the time of the research may want a drawing or quotation to appear with his name, but could the child feel differently as an adolescent, or as an adult? What if a conversion or change of heart occurs over that time? A compromise adopted by some researchers is to ask all children to actively choose a pseudonym to be used in publication (Alderson, Sutcliffe, and Curtis 2006). This is a procedure to specify in the protocol, a procedure with a known track record that could be documented for the IRB.

Should a study include randomization into control group and treatment groups, the randomization process can be geared for children's active involvement, as I have done. I took to the field an envelope of index cards, each with a number designation of a group (control = 1, treatment A = 2, treatment B = 3, etc.). I invited each child to close his or her eyes and reach into the envelope and pull out a card with a number on it, thereby selecting "what group you'll be in" in the study. The participatory drawing of numbers ensures that a child knows the investigator did not impose his group assignment (as in "guinea pig" conditions) but rather that this selection is triggered by the child, and, incidentally, in an engaging way the children seem to enjoy.

There is some debate about whether children should receive remuneration for their help in a study. Some feel that cash remuneration is a kind of coercion. This seems a double standard, since adults regularly receive payment for research participation, and children's contributions are not worthless. In research by Stephen J. Bagley, William W. Reynolds, and Robert M. Nelson (2007), it was found that "wage-payment" in research is appropriate. Such a payment serves as compensation to children age nine and older, acknowledging (but not coercing) their contribution of time and effort. For younger children, the authors claim, the value of money is not completely understood, which preempts the possibility that money will be a true means of coercion. This study may be evidence to cite in a protocol for the IRB, should you wish to use a cash remuneration to acknowledge the value of children's effort.

Your protocol should cover the planned steps in the study, communicating a rationale and ethical commentary for each step. It should also specify how participants in the study will be briefed about the results of the study. When a report has been published about a study I conducted, I sent the book or an article summary to families, and asked parents to share the material with their child. Other interesting projects, especially with teens or tweens, have involved children directly in reporting on the project. This might involve a community appearance, a video, or another chance for kids to give voice to their own responses, assuming that the public nature of their disclosure is part of the agreement prior to the research.

Indeed, involving children as active participants or co-investigators for a study is an approach now in considerable use by nongovernmental organizations. This trend correlated with passage of the UN Convention on the Rights of the Child, a document stipulating that children should have a voice in matters that affect them (Clark and Percy-Smith 2006). In one such project, children gave input on city planning—such as issues of traffic, use of space, and places kids could gather (Francis and Lorenzo 2005). Participation projects give children the role of decision making and consulting as a project unfolds. Despite the documented value of participation studies, adult hegemony sometimes stands in the way of implementing such a project (West 2007). Adults in a community have asserted that grownups should retain their authority, and that the power hierarchy should remain intact while children take a secondary, dependent role. Still, one could argue that children's participation in research is a way of fulfilling the IRB directive for research to include all human groups fully (i.e, all age groups). Overall, carrying out participation research (like ethnography itself) presents an anomaly to an IRB system that favors structure over flexibility. IRBs may find the relationships in participation research unpredictable or too unruly. IRB documentation has to allow for a range of responses and treatments toward the child participants, while being frank about the multiple directions that might be opened by inquiry in which children lead or colead.

Beliefs and Reflection

It is hard to imagine a subject matter more thoroughly entwined with human existence than belief, especially religious belief. Children's connection to religiosity and spirituality has long intrigued educators and scholars. Bronson Alcott (1991/1836-37), the American friend to Ralph Waldo Emerson and Henry David Thoreau, viewed children as preordained with spiritual acumen. Alcott carried out dialogues with children about religious matters in questions and answers that presaged qualitative research.

The ethics surrounding studies of children and religion hold particular challenges, perhaps in part because moral values are tied to the very subject of scrutiny. It would be worthwhile to know, for example, if religion exaggerates (by its own sense of authority) the issues of authority and hierarchy already inherent in the situation of adults conducting inquiry with kids (Post 2005). Do adults, as moral authorities and ontological arbiters, resist the upside-down process of empowering children to describe their beliefs freely and unjudged? In authoritative settings such as church or Sunday school, will children be inclined talk freely? Will children in a religious context sense pronounced superordinate pressure in the assent process? In reporting and discussing results, will denigration of young believers creep into the discourse on findings? (Letting interviewees or informants examine what is said about them, prior to publication, is a common step to prevent demeaning interpretation, and might be a safeguard for proper treatment of kids' expressed understandings about what they find sacred.)

Many would agree that a needed approach in children's inquiry, particularly when religion is the subject, is reflexivity on the part of the researcher, the sort of self-reflection and self-study that makes for a better understanding of the self-involved and subjective knowing process. Reflexivity is a way of recognizing how bias (in an adult studying kids) colors a researcher's perspective (Hufford 1995). No matter how much an adult scholar might wish to empathize with a child's beliefs, he or she still carries accumulated lifelong ideas within a taken-for-granted worldview, which may lead to discounting or missing a child's differing ontological assumptions.

The call to reflect upon one's own processes of knowing seems to be far afield from the "objective" and singularly structured expectations generally favored by positivists and the IRB. Reflexivity recognizes a complex and multivocal knowledge process. IRBs, with a more reductionist bent borrowed from biomedicine, accentuate singularity in knowledge. This is a distinction to appreciate, when dealing diplomatically with the IRB.

Children are capable both of actively making sense of religion and of impacting others in religious matters. The trick in being a researcher of children and religion is not to lose sight of children's distinctive, fully active constructions of meaning. Such autonomy in matters of faith is nothing new to experts on religion and spirituality. Scholars of religion are generally facile with ambivalent, multivoiced ways of knowing, and with layered, personally and socially intricate meaning making. IRB clearance, devoted as it generally is to empiricist standards and standardized yardsticks, involves something of an approach apart. Success at study approval is, in the end, a matter of honoring the traditions and beliefs of one group (the IRB), while not betraying one's own intricate intellectual stand. Although that may be challenging, scholars of religion have a major advantage. They already navigate, with grace and acumen, a plural reality from faith to faith and voice to voice.

5

"Maybe the Picture Will Tell You"

Methods for Hearing Children's
Perspectives on Religion

SUSAN B. RIDGELY

As I sat with John and Sarah, parents of seven children, in their farmhouse, discussing the stereotypes of conservative Christian families, their eldest daughter, nine-year-old Gwynn, sat down beside me. She listened quietly until I asked her father what key principles of Christianity he tried to teach his children, both through his missionary work and at home. He replied, "Along with being good and loving, [God] is deserving of our lives. And just the whole fact, at least as we believe it, he created the world and created us." Here Gwynn jumped in, "At least as we believe it? Didn't that happen?" For Gwynn, who was home schooled and whose father heads a mission organization, her father's move to display tolerance in an interview opened a new space of uncertainty, or even cultural relativity, in the conversation. She knew, as I did not, that her father did not speak that way when I, the researcher, was not around. Through this conversation both Gwynn and I gained new insights on how her parents tried to nurture a strong, devout Christian family. Through Gwynn's interruption, I learned that her father, although prepared for opposing viewpoints in his discussions as a missionary, taught Gwynn and her siblings without doubt or question that God created the world and that they were to make him the center of their lives.

When I began doing research with children, I worried that they would not be perceptive enough on their own to say anything of consequence. After all, at the churches I visited, the children always seemed to spend their time coloring, not paying attention to what was going on around them. I also worried that the children would only parrot what their parents said, as so many scholars and parents had warned me. Perhaps this fear that children did not or could not develop understandings of their own has contributed to the general lack of children's voices in the study of religion that is outlined in this volume's introduction. Children like Gwynn and others I talked with in my study of children's interpretations of First Communion,[1] however, showed me that young people do think for themselves and they do question their parents. Interviewing children alone and with their parents demonstrated that children do attend to the world in which they live and, as they do, they develop their own expectations and insights about that world. I believe that as a religious-studies scholar I have much to glean about the everyday rituals and practices of religion from some of its key participants: children. By allowing children to tell their stories themselves, I can gain a broader view of lived religion, going beyond traditional research methods and sources that use clergy, handbooks, catechisms, or other adult-generated media to discover how these adult-generated materials and the children's own desires come together to create distinctive interpretations of rituals and beliefs.

Further, children's insights about their religion and their families often differ significantly from the views of their parents.[2] To say that children have learned the lessons of scripture taught to them by their clergy and their parents does not mean that these children subscribe to the beliefs they have been taught or doctrines they have memorized. Religious-studies scholar Ruel Tyson and others, for instance, argue that "[g]estures are pivotal for they are at once public and personal. They are articulations of tacit beliefs and explicit feelings."[3] However, it remains true that the children in the churches that I worked with may have enacted the gestures of the Eucharist because of family pressure and obligation rather than their own belief. The only way for researchers to determine if the lessons learned by the children are those the adults intended to teach is to ask the children directly. Therefore, it is important to take the insights of all participants—men, women, boys, girls—into consideration to gain a greater understanding of religion as it is truly lived.

With this network of influences and pressures on children in mind, I endeavored to develop a methodology that would enable me to do research *with* the children rather than on them or about them. In this chapter, I outline my efforts to perform child-centered ethnographic work in both Catholic parishes and evangelical Christian homes and churches. I observed, participated in, and interviewed children about both formal rituals, such as First Communion, and informal rituals, such as vacation Bible school and AWANA (an Evangelical Christian youth program in which children earn prizes for memorizing Bible verses, playing games, and doing devotions). Rather than present a formula for researchers to follow, I propose a variety of methodological tools meant to help create a productive environment in which to interview children. It is my hope that future researchers will be able to adapt these methodologies to their own unique research settings. In developing these tools, I was guided by two foundational principles: allowing children to shape the research and creating an environment in which I made it clear that I was there to learn the children's perspective on their religious tradition, a subject in which they are the experts and I am the novice. My goal then is to develop a relationship with the children that allows them to show me how they express their beliefs and find meaning in the practices taught to them, rather than simply to address what I believe are the most salient issues in their religious communities. Of course, everything that I learn from my young consultants will be filtered through our relationship, but such is the case with all ethnographic work. Thus, my hope in creating a methodology is to be as transparent as possible in my interactions with the children and as open as I can be to what they have to teach me as I engage in fieldwork as well as in the analysis of the data I collect. At each stage, I strive to view each issue using only the knowledge and interpretive tools available to the children.

Allowing Children to Shape the Research

As I searched for ways to facilitate the children's participation in my research, I found that it was necessary to help them overcome their own perceptions of themselves as children, just as I worked continually through my own perceptions about them. Children, and well-intentioned researchers like me, often internalize the common assumptions about young peoples' supposedly inherent limitations, natural spirituality, and innocence. These assumptions are expressed to children through rules or more subtle inferences that remind them that they cannot participate in public (adult) discussions: children, for instance are continually reminded that they will "understand when they are older."[4] By meeting adult expectations—acting carefree and disinterested in serious issues, at least when the adults are around—children unwittingly reinforce the adult view, both to themselves and to the grownups around them, that children have few, if any, unique or worthwhile opinions on abstract topics such as life, death, and religion.[5] As a result, both children and adults often agree that young people are not important actors in the world beyond the home and the schoolyard, "the adult world." Given these beginning assumptions, to create a setting in which my young consultants could tell me their thoughts and feelings I had to develop a relationship with the children that was not built on the foundation of their need for protection or instruction from me.[6] To make this shift in our relationship work, however, I had to agree with the children that they did, in fact, know more than I about their religion.

While there will always be a power differential between researcher and consultant, I found that it can be mediated with some effort, and with a constant awareness on my part of my assumptions about the children's capabilities. From my experience, the most important step in mediating this power differential was to relinquish much of the control of the project to the children in an effort to create an environment in which I could learn from them. In doing so I unwittingly was the "least adult possible" from the children's perspective.[7] I did not come into the room in either the parishes or the AWANA meetings asking to be treated like their teachers or addressed like their teachers (although some children did address me in that way), nor did I pretend to be the seven-year-old that I was not. Sociologist William Corsaro and other researchers have characterized the young consultants' perceptions of them as "big kids," or "Big Bill" in Corsaro's case. For Corsaro, the children put him in the in-between category of "Big Bill" because of his inability to speak adultlike Italian.[8] In my case, the children knew that I was not just a "big kid," given my height and the way I interacted with their parents and teachers. As with Corsaro, however, the children did not place me fully in the adult category because I lacked too much knowledge to be a "real" adult. For me, never having received the Eucharist (when working with the Catholic children) and having no Bible verses stored away in my memory (when talking with the evangelical children) put me in a similar nonadult, in-between category. Researchers might also achieve this result by simply being open with the children about what they can teach adults and being honest about their own lack of knowledge. The children's realization that they knew more than I seemed to automatically disrupt the usual relationship between children and adults. I began my research project knowing that I had much to learn from the children; it was essential for me to demonstrate my lack of knowledge to my young consultants in order to gain their trust and acceptance.

Along with permitting the children to see my ineptness (what it seemed the children saw as my "un-adultness"), I had a different rapport with the children than did the other adults around them: I did not have a stake in their faith development. Telling me how they felt about their experiences in AWANA or expressing to me whether they believed what they were being taught in church had no repercussions from their teachers, parents, or clergy. Since I was not concerned with whether or not they had memorized a particular verse correctly or learned to cross themselves, I was able to just sit with the children, play with them, spend time with them, and listen. In an attempt to ensure that my study reflected the young participants' interests and not my own, I entered their classes and groups without a set plan or schedule for my research. As the children wrestled with the ideas that they were being taught at home, in church, or in school, I listened, without rushing to correct them.

If the goal of my child-centered research is to get the children to talk about their deeply held beliefs and to understand what they are saying, then I must spend significant amounts of time with them developing a common base of understanding. Only as we got to know each other and the children learned more about my research did I begin to participate more directly in the children's religious activities. Along with allowing the children to adjust to me and to decide if they were interested in talking to me, this time spent together had another important function. The successes in my research have come from the time I spent learning what the children learned, listening to the questions they asked, and watching how they interacted with each other before developing my research agenda. The children's goals and concerns, at least as they expressed them in class, in church, or within my earshot in the hallway, were reflected in my questions and interactions with them. Right away the children knew that they had been heard and were being taken seriously.

Thus, I let my understanding of how these particular children were viewing their religious participation guide my research, building a common vocabulary with them over time to examine their religious upbringing from their point of view.[9] The time researchers need to spend building this common vocabulary with the children may vary according to the issues the adults are exploring with the children and the researcher's knowledge of the community. The time spent learning the ways of the children's congregation, which is both separate from and intertwined with the adult congregation at different moments, need only be the time necessary to learn the children's concerns and the vocabulary they use to express those concerns. Once one has a common vocabulary with the children, then one can use that vocabulary to demonstrate to the children that they are being heard and to develop questions that are relevant to the young people and, therefore, worthy of answering.[10] Further, this understanding of the children's perspective can also be used to guide the researcher's interpretation of these answers once the interview is complete.

Attending classes, rehearsals, game nights, services, and masses with the children gave me a broad understanding of the many building blocks the children had to construct their interpretations of their religion. For example, had I only interviewed the children in the Catholic parishes after they received their First Communion, I would have heard little about their anxieties regarding the taste of the wine and the host. As Ryan said in an interview with me nine months after his First Communion, "I'm starting to get used to the taste [of the wine] now."[11] Had I not participated in the First Communion preparations with the children, I would have been offered comments like Ryan's about the taste of the wine only well after the sacrament in my post-Communion interviews, without any sort of context. I would have missed the intense concerns the children had about their abilities to perform the gestures of the ritual, or their change in focus from themselves to their parish as evidenced in their pre- and post-Communion pictures (figures 5.1 and 5.2). When taken alone, the post-Communion comments of the children about the taste of the wine and the palatability of the host, for example, may be the kind of interpretations that lead adult researchers to believe that children are incapable of truly understanding this rite. When these comments are placed in the context of the entire event and not just the end result, however, these remarks regarding taste serve to enhance the children's analysis of the event. From the children's perspective, the wine became a symbol of adulthood.

As Melissa stated in our pre-Communion interview, "I'm too young to drink real wine."[12] Similarly, as they practiced receiving Communion during class time, some of the children worried aloud about getting drunk or what it really meant for kids to be drinking alcohol.[13] While these concerns may seem cute from an adult perspective, the wink-and-smile response of adults toward children's worries reflects the perspective of someone who thinks of wine in terms of Chablis or merlot, not as a taboo. However, when I permitted myself to let go of my knowledge of varietals, I was able to build my interpretation of what wine meant to the children by using only the information available to them as they built their understandings.

To begin to hear what the children said about their experiences with the wine and the host, I had to maintain my child-centered approach to my research as I analyzed and wrote about my interviews with the children and the fieldwork that helped me to understand the interpretations that the young people shared. Remaining in a child-centered mindset once I left "the field," however, is not the norm. While transcripts are full of children's views, as childhood-studies scholars Pia Christensen and Alison James note, they are "generally analyzed and interpreted in terms of more abstract questions, which as a rule, reflect the beliefs and priorities of the researchers, rather than the children."[14] As I worked to put the children's priorities before mine, it became clear that the host, far from being a bland piece of bread, seemed to be the receptacle of the children's thoughts about transubstantiation. A child's comment that the host tasted like cardboard, when taken out of con-

Figure 5.1. Maureen's pre-Communion drawing.

Figure 5.2. Maureen's post-Communion drawing

text, might be viewed as another example of a "the cute things kids say" moment. However, when put in the context of the great degree of anticipation that the child had about how *consecrated* bread would taste, the comment might be understood to express unfulfilled expectations and tremendous disappointment that Jesus' body did not taste like something more delicious and magical—these children approached transubstantiation as a sensual rather than an intellectual experience.[15] This analysis of children and transubstantiation raises important questions; the children's questions serve to challenge the traditional understanding of religion.

Recognizing Children's Expertise about Their Religious Perspectives and Practices

To reach this point of shared conversation, where if I tried I could begin to see an event from something similar to the children's perspective, I first needed to be granted institutional approval to work with human subjects from the Institutional Review Board. The IRB requirements of informed consent seem to be, perhaps, the biggest hurdle for scholars who are interested in working directly with children. I have not had difficulty getting my research studies passed by review boards at various institutions, perhaps because I did not work with kids who had been labeled "at risk"; I got consent forms from all the parents; I talked only to children who volunteered; I had the children sign an assent form; and I reiterated repeatedly the child's ability to opt out of the research.

Many researchers wonder whether asking children to sign an assent form is even worth the effort, since they could never fully understand the implications of their participation in a research project. I am among a number of child-centered researchers who believe that getting the children's assent is essential. This process ensures that the research has attempted to help the children understand the project in which they are participating, gives the children a chance to ask questions, and demonstrates to the children that the researcher takes them seriously. I believe that the special category in which some scholars place children has much more to do with the scholars' presuppositions—in particular, the assumption that adults are competent and children are incompetent—than with the children's capacity for understanding the consequences of their participation in a research project. I believe that no consultants, adults or children, can be fully informed about what their participation in a project might mean for them in the future; that does not mean that researchers should not make every effort to explain the project and its implications. As Alderson has stated, "Children do not have to be perfect to qualify as competent, that is, reasonably informed and wise."[16] As a researcher, I make multiple ongoing efforts to do everything possible to try to ensure that the children are "reasonably informed." After all, we do not expect perfection from adults. The process of using assent forms served to alert the participants of all ages in my study that I was a child-centered researcher, offering me great insight into my consultants' concerns about the project and, perhaps more importantly, offering my consultants a view as to how I perceived them.

If my young consultants did not realize that their desires and interests took precedence over mine in our interactions, I hoped that letting them choose the place for our interview would tell them that I was following their lead and increase their sense of comfort and control. Most of the children seemed to have a place in mind, whether it was lying down in the religious education building's annex, sitting at a table in the hallway outside of faith formation class, meeting at an Arby's, or, in the case of teenagers, talking in the car on the way to church. For those children whom I met outside of church time, a trip to the fast-food restaurant offered a neutral, fun setting, and a treat for the consultants in exchange for their time. When I interviewed the children at church or at home, I gave them cookies to thank them for their time (cookies I made sure they did not have to share with parents or siblings).

Once we had settled on a place for the interview, I would set up my tape recorder as I verbally explained my project to the child again. Then I handed him or her an assent form to sign. I instructed the children more formally about how I would use what they taught me about First Communion, AWANA, or evangelicalism to write something that would help to show children's thoughts about their own faith development and experiences with organized religion. Through this interaction I hoped that the children would see that I saw them as partners and teachers in this project.

The walk to our interview site, or the time we spent ordering, usually gave me the first hints of how the children felt about speaking with me and how comfortable they felt in their church. Some children began talking with me as soon as we left the classroom or the gym where they attended AWANA and immediately led me to where they would feel most relaxed; others discussed their plans for the day or the week as we walked down the hall but were reluctant to choose a site to talk; still others demonstrated that they viewed this project as mine alone, as they quietly allowed me to search out a place for our conversation. For these quieter children, asking open-ended questions that reflected their expressed interests during game time at AWANA or in moments of discussion during faith formation became all the more important. As sociologist Jacqueline Scott has demonstrated, children can provide reliable answers to questions that are relevant to their lives, particularly when they are allowed to answer a question with "I don't know" and when the researcher is careful not to suggest that there was a correct answer to her questions.[17]

For teens and preteens this open-ended approach seemed to be as important as it was for the smaller children, as was the decision to allow the consultants to choose the spot for the interview. Although my work focused primarily on younger children, I had some success getting tweens and teens to talk more freely in the car as I drove them to church picnics, youth groups, or other events that the children had hoped to go to but that did not fit into their parents' schedules. In the car we were not sitting awkwardly facing each other and we had a common purpose—to get to a particular event that is of significant interest to my consultants. The event then became a natural starting point and we let the conversation flow from there.

Of course, when interviewing children or adults, conversation does not always flow. In my work with the First Communicants, I followed the lead of psychiatrist Robert Coles by using drawings to create a common visual vocabulary, offering the children another medium through which to express their understandings of the sacrament.[18] For most of the children, their favorite part of faith formation class was their art projects, which gave me some reassurance that they felt at ease, at least to some extent, with drawing. Using the knowledge that they learned in school, at home, and in faith formation classes, many of the children created pictures in response to my request that they "draw me a picture of First Communion." I hoped that this open-ended request might give them an opportunity to depict the most important aspect of the sacrament or the liturgy to them. For those who had not yet received the Eucharist, I hoped their images might reveal their expectations of the ritual. Although I could have included a number of different elements, such as play, in the interviews, I chose art because it offered the children another way to represent how they felt and what they valued with no significant input from me other than what our conversation may have lead them to imagine.

The crayons and the blank sheet of paper allowed the children to sketch out the topics of our conversation in a way that would permit us to analyze together the images that they drew. I was very careful to let the children tell me what the picture meant, bringing them into the analysis, rather than waiting until I was back in the office to explore the image's hidden meanings. Although I might have told a different story than my young consultants did, it was their interpretation of events I was interested in, not mine. Of course, I had final say about what would be included in the project and how it was presented, although the children did see the final text. So as I wrote I tried to be conscious of highlighting the children's voices and letting their interpretations guide the analysis and the organization of the book. Still, I am sure there were points in the interviewing and the writing process in which I failed to hear the children, in which my scholarly voice undermined those of the children. I hoped, though, that being conscious of my desire to put the children (not myself or the adults who nurtured them) at the center of my study helped me to look for methods that would allow them to feel comfortable and confident enough to share their understandings of their religious practice while simultaneously reminding me of my own research goals.

The drawing method seemed to work well for children like Christy, who in the process of a ten-minute interview described what she had drawn and then got quiet. When I asked her if there was anything else she thought I should know about First Communion, she replied, "I don't know, but maybe the picture will tell you."[19] With her help, it already had. Other children were quite comfortable talking even before they began drawing. Maureen and Melissa, for instance, told me about their friends, family, and waking up early Sunday mornings, as well as about First Communion. Although they all volunteered to talk, some children were much more reserved and anxious when we were sitting together than others. Christopher, for instance, could not remember his birthday when we first started talking. As we settled into our conversation, his sentences became longer and his anxiety seemed to lessen. Still, he twisted his fingers under the table as he explained why First Communion was important.[20] Clearly, to reach out to children like Christopher I needed to have more than one research technique available to me.

Although I eschewed the idea of using toys and dolls in my work with the First Communicants, for the children attending AWANA meetings the research was not focused on a single event, making it much more difficult to find a common theme for a drawing. Instead, I found that using the little toys that the children received as part of their participation in AWANA helped to facilitate conversation. Five-year-old George, for example, a terrific reader, was always ahead of the rest of his class in memorizing Bible verses. During this free time, he occupied himself by playing games under the table and commenting on the teacher's efforts to keep him in line. Although he was quite verbal at AWANA, when we met for a one-on-one conversation in the summer, he was much less interested in talking. We began the interview with a little bit of chatting about his summer, but his ready answer to all my questions quickly became, "I don't know." Since he often claimed not to know things that he had thought a great deal about in AWANA, I searched for another point of connection. Having just finished vacation Bible school, he had some of his Bible Memory Buddies with him, so I asked him about one of the characters he was holding: the little blue guy in the shape of a drop of water on the surfboard. "Oh, that's Dewed," George replied. "He reminds us that God is everywhere, even if you can't see him, just like water is everywhere in your body, even though you can't see it."[21] From there the conversation got a little easier, since our discussion was back safely in George's territory. Using Dewed, Electra, and the other Bible Memory Buddies was effective because they were George's toys and they had come from the workshop we were discussing. He felt comfortable with the toys and they worked as focal points around which his memories could form. I don't think that toys or dolls that I brought with me, which would not have had a clear connection to his experiences, would have had the same positive effect. Here again, I think the project's success came from working with what was familiar to the consultant, using toys that were relevant to the children and were capable of providing me with a familiar and comfortable framework for our discussion.

As I came to trust and respect children more, I was more comfortable with interviewing children together and doing intergenerational interviews. That is to say, I became more comfortable handing control over to my consultants. In intergenerational interviews, children and parents often end up interviewing each other, asking questions that I never would have thought to ask. Charlotte and her mother, for example, had an extended exchange about the various means of discipline used in their household, which ended in her mother agreeing that Charlotte should have some choice in whether she went to church. While I had long felt that children would be more candid and forthcoming if their parents were not in the room, the interview with Gwynn and her parents called that into question. In these multigenerational interviews, the children revealed their knowledge of serious topics and family dynamics of which their parents often assumed they were blissfully unaware. As the children demonstrated their knowledge and their interest, they shifted their position from someone who is seen and not heard to someone with important opinions to express and questions to ask. As Stewart Hoover, Lynn Schofield Clark, and Diane Alters found in their work on family and the media, the children often had their own questions that my interview allowed them to ask of their parents.[22] Moreover, the children also proved to be good checks on whether their parents' answers were reflecting the family ideology or whether they were just saying what they thought I wanted to hear—a concern generally voiced most strongly when one is working with children. The children here are questioners, not simply sponges soaking up what their parents, older siblings, or teachers tell them.

Maybe someday soon I will be brave enough to finally step aside in my research to a greater degree to do what Pricilla Alderson and others in childhood studies have done and train the children in research skills so they themselves can be the interviewers and the fieldworkers.[23] For now, though, simply allowing the children to speak on their own behalf would be a great step forward in religious studies. Including children's voices in the study of religion will continually shift the conversation to new areas of focus, areas that are generally overlooked because they are often embodied, sometimes fun, and usually not part of the official script for worship. Without a full understanding of these rituals from all points of view, however, scholars miss their meaning, not just for the children but for the adults who support them as well.

NOTES

1. See Susan Ridgely Bales, *When I Was a Child: Children's Interpretations of First Communion* (Chapel Hill: University of North Carolina Press, 2005).

2. As sociologist Jacqueline Scott argued, "It is essential to collect information from children themselves concerning their present experiences and their future aspirations. We cannot rely on parents, teachers, and other adults to accurately portray the situation for children." Jacqueline Scott, "Children as Respondents: The Challenge for Quantitative Methods" in *Research with Children: Perspectives and Practices*, 2nd edition, edited by Pia Christensen and Alison James (New York: Routledge Press, 2008), 87.

3. Ruel Tyson, "Introduction: Method and Spirit; Studying Diversity of Gestures in Religion" in *Diversities of Gifts: Field Studies in Southern Religion*, edited by Ruel W. Tyson, James L. Peacock, and Daniel W. Patterson (Chicago: University of Illinois Press, 1988), 4.

4. For more on the removal of children from public spaces and its consequence for children's lives see Jens Qvoturp, ed., *Studies in Modern Childhood: Society, Agency, and Culture* and Steven Mintz, *Huck's Raft: A History of American Childhood*.

5. For more on how children internalize adult understandings of children and try to live up to them, see Myra Bluebond-Langner's excellent study, *The Private Worlds of Dying Children* (Princeton, NJ: Princeton University Press, 1978) and my own work, Bales, *When I Was a Child*, 10-11, 116-17.

6. For more on how a researcher's assumptions about children affect research design see E. Kay Tisdall, John M. Davis, and Michael Gallagher's introduction to *Researching with Children and Young People: Research Design, Methods, and Analysis*, edited by E. Kay Tisdall, John M. Davis, and Michael Gallagher (Washington, DC: Sage Press, 2009), 4-5; and William A. Corsaro, *The Sociology of Childhood* (Thousand Oaks, CA: Pine Forage Press, 1997), 118-19.

7. For more on the notion of becoming "the least adult" when working with children see Tisdall, Davis, and Gallagher, 7

8. For more on Corsaro's methodology see his 2003 work, *We're Friends, Right? Inside Kids' Culture* (Washington, DC: Joseph Henry Press, 2003), 7-35.

9. I began doing interviews with the children anywhere from three months to one year after first meeting them. The time varied according to how comfortable the children felt with me and how well I felt I was able to understand what they saw as significant enough to be discussed in an interview.

10. For more on the importance of making interview questions and practices relevant to children see, for example, Alison James and Pia Christensen, "Researching Children and Childhood Cultures of Communication" in *Researching with Children: Perspectives and Practices*, edited by Alison James and Pia Christensen (New York: Routledge, 2008), 8; and Scott, "Children as Respondents," 88-90.

11. Eight-year-old boy, interviewed by the author, Durham, NC, 15 February 1998.

12. Melissa, interviewed by the author, Burlington, NC, 8 April 2001, quoted in Bales, *When I Was a Child*, 100.

13. Fieldnotes, Blessed Sacrament Catholic Church, 22 April 2001.

14. James and Christensen, "Researching Children and Childhood Cultures of Communications," 13.

15. For more on this discussion of taste see Bales, *When I Was a Child*, 92-102.

16. Priscilla Alderson, "Researching Children's Rights to Integrity," in *Children's Childhoods: Observed and Experienced*, ed. Barry Mayall (London: Flamer Press, 1994), 60.

17. Jacqueline Scott, "Children as Respondents," 88, 96.

18. Building on earlier psychological work with children by Anna Freud and others, Coles uses drawings as sources in all of his work with children. He discusses his methodology most fully in *Children of Crisis: A Study of Courage and Fear* (1967) and *Their Eyes Meeting the World: The Drawings and Paintings of Children*, edited by Margaret Sartor.

19. Christy, eight-year-old Latina, interviewed by the author, Burlington, NC, 1 April 2001.

20. Christopher, eight-year-old Anglo, interviewed by the author, Burlington, NC, 1 April 2001.

21. George, five-year-old boy, interview with the author, Madison, WI, 29 July 2008.

22. Stewart M. Hoover, Lynn Schofield Clark, and Diane F. Alters, *Media, Home, and Family* (New York: Routledge, 2004).

23. Priscilla Alderson, "Children as Researchers: Participation Rights and Research Methods" in *Researching with Children*, 276-90.

6

Boundary and Identity Work among
Hare Krishna Children

E. BURKE ROCHFORD JR.

Religious culture is vital to the success of new religious movements, given their oppositional stance toward the larger society (Rochford 2007a; Stark 1996). Without a supportive religious culture, alternative religions lack the foundation for sustaining a vibrant community of the faithful. As the noted sociologist Ann Swindler (1986) suggests, a stable culture allows belief and everyday experience to become aligned and thereby produces "settled lives." Part of the cultural work required of new religions involves establishing group boundaries to deflect the ongoing challenge of mainstream culture. These boundaries also facilitate the construction of oppositional religious identities, perhaps especially so for children growing up in unconventional religious worlds.

This chapter considers issues of culture, group boundaries, and identity among young children growing up in the International Society for Krishna Consciousness (ISKCON), more commonly known as the Hare Krishna movement,[1] in order to understand the challenges as well as the rewards associated with studying children in contexts where a researcher must cross religious boundaries. Such boundaries represent "objectified forms of social differences" that reveal patterns of social exclusion and group membership (Lamont and Molnar 2002:168). For ethnographers of religion, negotiating these boundaries represents a significant part of immersing oneself in the field. Researching children provides a unique opportunity to learn about the interpretive dimensions of boundary work. We will look specifically at children in ISKCON's Los Angeles *gurukula* (boarding school), where I conducted research in 1979 and 1980. At the time, children aged five and older were living separately from their parents in the *gurukula* (see Rochford 2007a).[2] Part of my research involved taking boys between the ages of six and eight to the beach, or to a nearby park for afternoon outings. I also accompanied them on a number of occasions when they distributed religious literature in neighborhoods around Los Angeles. As the boys and I participated in these contexts together we served as "worldview guides," helping each other to negotiate the boundaries and related identity markers that distinguished insiders from outsiders.

Empirically, we will consider two types of boundary work. The first involves efforts by the boys to make sense of and shape my identity in light of my ambiguous status as both an insider and an outsider to ISKCON. Identity work on their part involved strategies of boundary bridging meant to establish my identity as a devotee and thus part of their community The second entails interactions between the boys and members of the general public that represent boundary-crossing and boundary-maintenance situations distinguishing a Krishna identity from those of outsiders. Such events are critically important to forming the collective identities of children growing up in unconventional religions.

Religious Culture, Group Boundaries, and Identity

Being radical enterprises that challenge conventional values and social institutions, new religions face the world-building task of establishing religious cultures that remain more or less removed from mainstream influences (Rochford 2007a; Rochford and Bailey 2006). New religions thus seek to build structures of integration and separation meant to preserve the purity of the religious tradition and the way of life it sanctions. These structures promote group solidarity and identity by distinguishing "virtuous" insiders from the "evils" associated with the outside world. From an insider's perspective, what is "true," "moral," and "good" exists within the religious enclave; outside there exists "darkness," "pollution," and "danger" (Sivan 1995: 18). It is for this reason that alternative religions tend to favor collective forms of social organization such as communalism. As the sociologist Kai Erickson argues, group boundaries create and sustain cultural space removed from the hegemonic influences of the conventional world.

> [T]his means that communities are boundary maintaining: each has a specific territory in the world as a whole, not only in the sense that it occupies a defined region of geographical space but also in the sense that it takes over a particular niche in what might be called cultural space and develops its own "ethos" or "way" within that compass. Both of these dimensions of group space, the geographical and the cultural, set the community apart as a special place and provide an important point of reference for its members. (1966: 9-10)

From its earliest days, ISKCON's exclusive communal structure insulated members from many of the influences of the outside society. Group boundaries were controlled by way of both formal and informal sanctions. When I first began studying the movement in Los Angeles in 1975, for example, it was considered scandalous for a devotee to take up residence even one block away from the community's communal boundary. It was generally understood that such a move signaled a desire to engage in forbidden material activities and to avoid one's collective responsibilities to the devotee community. For children, communal boundaries proved of equal importance, as seen in the following incident described in 1980 by a devotee mother.

> V: One of the karmie [nondevotee] kids who lives down the street stole the bike of one of the younger kids in the [devotee] community. So the older boys went up the street looking for the bike. Of course they only went as far as Regent Ave.
>
> EBR: Why only that far?
>
> V: That's as far as they go.
>
> EBR: You mean they won't go past Regent?
>
> V: Yeah, it's not a rule or anything but the kids understand that's the limit.
>
> EBR: So what are the boundaries for the kids?
>
> V: Venice Blvd. to about where the BBT [Bhaktivedanta Book Trust] is and around the corner on Watseka to Regent. The kids don't go any farther than that. The older kids ride their bikes up Watseka to Regent and back but never around the block. They know to stay in the community.

Communalism thus imposes physical constraints on the space both adults and children can legitimately explore (Kanter 1972). But the affirmation of group boundaries can also take more symbolic forms. Note, for example, how some ISKCON mothers in Los Angeles instructed devotee children about nondevotees (karmies) on outings to the beach.

> The kids continually ask about the things they find on the beach. A common question is for a kid to pick up a beer bottle and ask, "What's this?" Or seeing non-devotees smoking cigarettes the kids ask, "What is that?" The mothers almost always say, "That's a beer bottle, karmies drink beer but we are devotees; devotees don't drink alcohol like the karmies." The kids just come to understand that they are different from everyone else.[3]

Although it is well understood that sects and new religions police their borders to minimize contacts that might challenge the beliefs and lifestyle of adherents, there are other circumstances in which members—adults and children alike—find reason to bridge differences that exist between insiders and outsiders through acts of inclusion. This may be particularly true in cases where members seek to maintain meaningful relationships with friends and/or family outside the group. It was just such a relationship that emerged between the devotee boys and me during my months of fieldwork in the Los Angeles *gurukula*. As our relationship developed over time, both they and I worked at finding common ground in an effort to give legitimacy to our developing friendship. Yet, as we will see, the only meaningful framework they possessed was ISKCON and Krishna Consciousness and thus inclusion centered on bringing me under the umbrella of being a devotee despite my ongoing commitments to the conventional world. Our roles reversed, however, when the boys and I ventured beyond the physical boundaries of the devotee community and the boys faced opposition because of their identities as Hare Krishna members. In these situations, I sought to instruct and support them in an effort to alleviate the distress they sometimes felt. As this implies, we worked to preserve the well-being of the other in the face of real or potential opposition and thus collaborated in what amounted to a politics of inclusion.[4]

Researcher and Researched: Boundary Bridging and the Politics of Inclusion

Researching alternative religions is fraught with difficulties, not least of which is gaining entry and developing rapport (Bromley and Carter 2001). My experiences researching the Hare Krishna have involved a variety of difficulties in this regard (see Rochford 1985, 1992, 2000, 2001). Yet in researching the boys in the *gurukula* I often experienced "gestures of inclusion" (Warner 1997: 220), especially after we formed a meaningful relationship. In essence, the cultural and religious differences that separated us gave way to efforts at boundary bridging. Initial curiosity and questioning about who I was turned into efforts on the boys' part to teach me the ropes of being a devotee and thus a legitimate part of their lives.

Right from the beginning I became a source of considerable interest to the nine boys in the ashram. On my first day, as we waited to go to the beach, one of the boys ran up to me with a piece of metal shaped like a fishing hook. It even had a jagged edge on the inside. Without thinking I replied, "It looks like a fishing hook to me." As soon as the words came out of my mouth I realized I was inviting further questioning because ISKCON members do not eat meat, including fish. Another boy standing nearby immediately asked, "Do you go fishing?" I responded that I didn't any longer but had when I was young. He then asked, "Do you eat fish?" After I responded that I didn't, he then inquired, "Are you a vegetarian?" With this I walked over and sat on the ground next to him and said, "Unlike you I grew up in a family that ate meat. When I was your age I ate meat. I didn't have the good fortune of growing up in a devotee family like you." On several other occasions that day I was asked by one of the boys if I was a devotee. Others wanted to know if I was becoming a devotee, aware that I was not wearing devotee clothing and thus was perhaps new to the community. Uncomfortable with this line of questioning, I didn't answer directly, saying only that I had been coming to the temple for a number of years. None of the boys chose to press the issue further.

Two weeks later another issue arose that again raised questions about my identity. It also yielded the first of many gestures of inclusion the boys directed towards me. The issue related to whether I wore *tilack* (sacred clay that devotees mark their noses and other parts of their bodies with each day). Because the boys had been in the water at the beach, the *tilack* had washed off the noses of a number of them. In unison they asked me if they still had *tilack* on their noses. I inspected each one and gave my assessment. Noticing that I didn't have any *tilack* on, one of the boys asked, "Do you wear *tilack*?" Before I could respond another boy interjected, "Maybe he only puts it on his body, not on his nose." Knowing that I didn't live in the community, the young boy was suggesting that I didn't need to wear *tilack* on my nose because it would only invite questions from nondevotees about my identity. Rather than challenge my devotee status because of my failure to wear *tilack*, he assumed instead that living outside of ISKCON left me with little choice but to hide my devotee identity from people likely to be unfavorable toward the Hare Krishna. Over the weeks and months to follow, the nature of my identity remained a topic and the boys continued to instruct me in the strategies of being a devotee while living and working in the conventional world, as can be seen in the following interaction.

K: "Bhakta Burke, are you going to shave your beard?"
EBR: "No time soon. I like my beard."
S (sitting to my right and running his fingers through my long hair): "Are you going to shave your head?"
EBR: "No."

U: "How come you don't have any beads?" (This as he grabs my shirt to check my neck for any beads that may be hiding beneath.)

Before I can respond another boy asks, "Do you work?"

EBR: "Sure."

U: "You should get beads that unscrew."

EBR: "That do what?"

U: "You can take them off because they unscrew." Turning to the boy on his left he says, "Show Bhakta Burke." He then grabs one of the strings of beads on his neck and unscrews the latch until they come off.

EBR: "Oh, I see."

U: "See, they come off. You can take them off if you have to for work."

A few minutes later while we waited for the vehicle to take us to the park, one of the boys turned to an adult devotee and said, "Bhakta Burke is going to start wearing beads and *tilack*."

EBR (feeling uneasy): "Well, he is trying to convince me to do so anyway. Nobody else has been able to."

With this the adult devotee smiled and said, "These children have a strange potency about them."

After being reminded on several occasions by the boys to purchase neck beads that unscrew, I finally did so. I purchased them one day at the community store just prior to showing up at the boys' ashram for lunch. When I entered the ashram one of the boys immediately saw my beads and cried out for all to hear, "Bhakta Burke, you got neck beads. Neck beads. You got neck beads. Bhakta Burke has neck beads." With this, all the boys excitedly came running to see my new beads. Clearly, my decision to wear neck beads represented a major turning point in my relationship with the boys, but as the following interaction a few weeks later reveals, they continued to worry about my commitments.

I came into the ashram and sat down for lunch with the boys before leaving for our afternoon outing. I sat next to Nemi, who looked at me intently before leaning over and quietly asking, "Bhakta Burke, where are you neck beads?"

Reaching under my shirt collar I pulled them out and said, "Right here."

Nemi asked, "Were you trying to hide them?"

I responded, "No. I don't like it when they pull tight around my neck so I keep them loose."

While my appearance was a major concern for the boys, there were other identity-related issues that emerged. One afternoon five of the boys and I were walking to pottery class on the other side of the community when I noticed a number of adult devotees standing on the sidewalk in front of the green apartment building across from the temple. As we came closer, I could see that the guru for the Los Angeles community was speaking with them. I kept walking until suddenly I realized that all the boys had dropped to the ground to pay their obeisances to the guru, Ramesvara Swami. I stopped to wait on the boys when I heard Subal say with some urgency, "It's Srila Ramesvara, pay your obeisances." The tone of his voice made it clear that he was giving an order rather than making a request. I immediately knelt down and bowed my head to the ground. When I got up I felt somewhat embarrassed. I never looked at Ramesvara or the others gathered around him as I quickly got up and kept walking with the boys. I then asked Subal, "Why must I pay obeisances?" He responded, "You must, he is the guru. You have to pay your obeisances to the guru." I asked, "Suppose I didn't?" He explained, "That would be an offense. Sooo offensive." I then thanked him for keeping me from being offensive.

One afternoon as the boys and I again waited for the teacher to drive us to the park, one of them turned to me and out of the blue asked, "Bhakta Burke, do you drink?" His question disarmed me momentarily, as I knew he was asking if I drank alcohol. Taken off guard by his question, I tried to fudge my answer somewhat, responding, "Not normally but sometimes at the university I go to parties and drink a beer with other students." The young devotee turned away with a concerned look on his face. A few minutes later, he turned to the boy sitting next to him and reported, "Bhakta Burke drinks." Not understanding the meaning of what was being said, the boy replied, "I drink a lot of water too." This elicited, "No, no, Bhakta Burke drinks alcohol! He goes to parties at his school and the karmies make him drink beer. He doesn't want to but they make him." The image I have now as I think about this exchange is that the karmies were somehow pouring beer down my throat while I protested all the while.

As the above interactions suggest, the boys wanted and perhaps needed to see me as a devotee like themselves. Their efforts had less to do with converting a wayward soul to Krishna Consciousness than with legitimating the meaningful relationship that we shared. As the anthropologist David Kertzer (1988: 76) argues, "Solidarity is produced by people acting together not by people thinking together." Given the importance they placed on our relationship, the boys taught me practical ways to be a devotee in the world (i.e., beads that can be taken off and on) and the importance of paying my respects to religious authority (i.e., bowing in the presence of the guru) so that my devotee status, and thus my standing in the community, would not be challenged. Finally, when my behavior raised potentially serious questions about my identity (i.e., consuming alcohol) the "karmies" were blamed, thus exonerating me from any culpability. By bridging rather than accentuating differences, the boys sought to keep me a legitimate part of their world as it simply wasn't within their imagination to think that a nondevotee (a karmie) could be worthy of their friendship and respect.

Boundary Crossing, Exclusion, and Collective Identity

New religions often face opposition because of their world-transforming objectives (Rochford and Bailey 2006). Opposition may come in the form of organized countermovements or, often, as diffuse "moral panics" by publics concerned about the supposed threats such groups represent. Clearly, the media is a central player in the drama that unfolds, and anticult groups often use the press to further their goals, including inciting public concern and opposition to new religions (Richardson and Introvigne 2007). Opposition fuels a dualistic attitude (i.e., "us" versus "them") not only among new religious adherents but for opponents and interested bystander publics as well. This dualism produces a politics of exclusion whereby all parties to the conflict attempt to preserve their mundane prejudices.

Exclusionary boundary work was commonplace on those occasions when the boys made contact with members of the general public. Some of these interactions were essentially staged events, such as when the boys distributed the movement's religious literature to nondevotees in public locations. In other cases, naturally occurring interactions brought group boundaries and identities into the foreground, as occurred one afternoon at Venice Beach.

As we walked onto the beach three nondevotee boys approached us with interest. Given that the devotee boys all had shaved heads and the teacher was dressed in a *dhoti*, it was obvious that as a group we were different from others on the beach that day. At first I paid little attention to the nondevotee youths as I walked down to the water with two of the boys who were anxious to swim. As I looked over my shoulder a few minutes later, however, I could see there was a standoff of sorts between the two groups of boys. After the teacher walked down to the water I decided to check on what was going on. By now the nondevotee boys were sitting on a water pipe high above the beach. I noticed immediately that two of them had bottles, one of whom was filling his with sand. As I came closer I could hear the nondevotees yelling comments like, "Fuck you. You're assholes." I sat down next to the six devotee boys and asked what was going on. "Why are they hassling you?" The oldest of the group said, "They are troublemakers." While no one spoke or responded to the hostile comments, everyone looked intently at the nondevotee boys. In hopes of getting a response, the nondevotee youths held the sand-filled bottles over their heads in a threatening manner. One of the older devotee boys came over to me and stated, "I understand these karmies. When they point that (middle) finger at you you just say, 'Same to you.'" Suddenly, one of the nondevotee youths threw several bottles and cans toward us, yelling "fuck you" as he did. None of the items came close to us, however. Again, the devotee boys remained silent but intensely focused on what was happening before them. Having failed to receive the response he was looking for, the nondevotee boy then smashed the bottom of a bottle over a railing. He waved the broken bottle menacingly in our direction. For the first time I could see tension growing in the boys' faces. At this point the teacher walked toward us, aware that something was going on. After getting a briefing from the boys, the teacher decided to sneak up on the nondevotee youths as they sat on the water pipe. As he climbed the wall to get up on the pipe the nondevotee boys jumped to the sand below and started running full speed. Two of the older devotee boys immediately chased after them. They stopped only when the teacher yelled at them to do so. When the boys returned one of them stated with some delight, "They were scared." The other said, "We almost caught them." I then responded, "Let's not let these [nondevotee] boys interfere with us having fun." A few minutes later, after things had settled down, a lifeguard approached us and several of the boys ran to tell him what had happened. Later, I saw the lifeguard on the boardwalk talking to the nondevotee troublemakers.

As we drove back to the ISKCON community the boys continued talking about the incident on the beach when suddenly the teacher asked,

"What do all these people walking along the street have in common?"
Nemi: "They are living in *Maya* [illusion]. They don't chant Hare Krishna."
Another boy responded, "They are eating meat, having illicit sex, and gambling."

Teacher: "No. They have not heard about Krishna. So at the time of death they will not know to chant Krishna's name." He then asked the boys, "What do you do at the time of death?"

In unison the boys responded, "Chant Hare Krishna."

As we approached Ocean Blvd. one of the boys said out loud, "These karmies are living in so much nonsense." Looking out of the window I saw clothing and other merchandise hanging in the shop windows as young people in bathing suits walked to and from the beach.

On several occasions we broke our normal afternoon routine and distributed books to members of the public instead. These outings often started off with excitement as the boys enjoyed competing with one another to see who could distribute the most books or get the most in donations, even though the teacher always instructed them to give the books away. But initial excitement often turned into disappointment given the responses the boys received from the nondevotees they approached. Their mounting distress often led me to intervene on their behalf.[5]

One afternoon when the boys were chanting and distributing literature at the park along the coastline in Santa Monica, one of them approached an older woman sitting on a bench. He offered her a *Back to Godhead* magazine, to which she replied, "No. I don't need that. Do you know Jesus Christ?" The boy said, "yes," and the woman responded, "He is coming soon you know." Another boy, Harinama, who had joined the conversation, agreed, "Yes, that's true," whereupon Jiva said, "I don't think that's true." The woman responded, "I'll go home and pray for you then." Harinama handed her the magazine and explained, "This is how we pray for you." Without responding the woman walked away. Jiva then came over to me and said that the woman had tried to trick him: "She knows that Jesus isn't coming." I responded that many Christians in fact believe that Jesus will return and are awaiting his arrival. He asked, "They really believe he is coming to earth?" and I responded, "Yes."

Another day we traveled to a Latino neighborhood to distribute religious texts printed in Spanish. This proved an especially difficult outing as the boys encountered numerous challenging remarks in addition to the more typical disinterest. Two of the boys knocked on an apartment door as I stood a few feet away.

HN: "Would you like to have this book?"

W (looking at HN carefully as if trying to understand what this person is): "Get out of here."

HN: "The book is free."

W: "I don't care. Get out of here."

J: "Why don't you want it, it's free?"

W: "Do you think I am crazy?"

J: "But it is about Krishna."

W: "Hare Krishna is crazy."

With this I immediately told the boys, "Let's go."

As we walked the boys recounted what had happened. One of them said, "Did you hear her say that Hare Krishna is crazy?"

EBR: "You boys have to understand that a lot of these people don't know about the Hare Krishna."

J: "They know about Krishna; they are just too demonic."

EBR: "Maybe but all they know about the Hare Krishna is from what they read in the newspaper. They have no real appreciation for Krishna Consciousness."

As we returned to the van after an hour of going door to door, the teacher and I quietly discussed how frustrated a number of the boys were. Many people closed their apartment doors in the boys' faces, or made rude and upsetting remarks, like the woman above. On one occasion an apartment manager threatened to call the police if we didn't leave the premises. Several of the boys complained, "People don't want them [books]. We shouldn't do it if they don't want them." Others felt embarrassed or timid about distributing the books and lingered behind to avoid having to knock on an apartment door. After getting everyone in the van the teacher announced, "Everyone listen to me. Everybody be quiet. Now how did you feel about that?" One of the boys said, "They didn't want the books." The teacher explained, "Can you see how agitated the karmies are? They are so involved in material life that they can't even appreciate our trying to bring them some spiritual knowledge. We should be so happy that we have the opportunity to pursue spiritual life."

Interactions such as those reported here made palpable for all involved the wall of separation that existed between the religious world of ISKCON and the culture of conventional American society. While these interactions were often painful for the boys, they nonetheless served as exemplars that elevated the devotee way of life above a karmie world devoid of spiritual understanding. Grasping this insight represented a critical part of the socialization process, for it helped shape the boys' identities as Krishna devotees and members of ISKCON.

Conclusion

Because new religions present broad challenges to mainstream values and institutions, sustaining an oppositional religious culture is vital to their long-term success (Lofland 1987; Rochford 2007a; Rochford and Bailey 2006; Stark 1996). This is especially true as family life expands and children must be socialized into the group's religious world. Given the deviant and often radical character of new religions, socialization into them involves more than learning the religious beliefs and practices that define the group; it also demands that children learn to navigate the boundaries that separate believers from the larger society. As we have seen, Hare Krishna children engaged in boundary work that involved both exclusion and inclusion as their identities as Krishna devotees and ISKCON members took shape. Critically, boundaries symbolically embody conceptual distinctions that define and categorize people, objects, and practices (Lamont and Molnar 2002: 168).

Children are especially useful in studying group boundaries and related boundary work precisely because their individual and collective identities are actively under construction. What adults blindly accept as taken-for-granted knowledge, children experience as curiosities and riddles worthy of their conscious attention. For this reason, children are worthy worldview guides for investigators studying new or unknown religious worlds. Moreover, as this case study suggests, children can serve as barometers of social change, mapping shifts in social boundaries that distinguish the religious group from the outside society.

NOTES

1. ISKCON's historical roots are traced to Bengal, India, in the sixteenth century. The Krishna Consciousness practiced by ISKCON members is part of the Krishna *bhakti* movement of Caitanya Mahaprabhu (1486-1533). A distinctive feature of the Gaudiya Vaisnava tradition to which ISKCON belongs is that Caitanya is believed to be an incarnation of Krishna. The movement was brought to the United States in 1965 by A. C. Bhaktivedanta Swami Prabhupada, or Srila Prabhupada, as he is called by his disciples and followers. ISKCON was incorporated as a religious organization in New York City in 1966 and is dedicated to spreading Krishna Consciousness, with communities and preaching centers throughout the world. The aim of the Krishna devotee is to become self-realized by chanting Hare Krishna and living an austere lifestyle that requires avoiding meat, intoxicants, illicit sex, and gambling. While young Westerners were drawn to the movement in the 1960s and 1970s, today the largest portion of ISKCON's North American and Western European membership is comprised of immigrant Indian-Hindus and their families (see Rochford 2007a:

181-200). For a discussion of the movement's growth and development in North America, see Rochford 1985, 2006, 2007a; Rochford and Bailey 2006; Shinn 1987; and Squarcini and Fizzotti 2004.

2. Traditionally, the ashram-based *gurukula* served as the institution responsible for enculturating ISKCON's children—that is, transferring the movement's spiritual and material culture to the next generation. To ensure successful cultural transmission the *gurukula* was structured to maximize boundary maintenance by limiting cross-cultural exchange between young devotees and the surrounding conventional culture. Although academic subjects were taught in the *gurukula*, its primary purpose was to teach children sense control and practices of renunciation because they were deemed essential to self-realization in Krishna Consciousness. Children attended the *gurukula* on a year-round basis, with occasional vacations to visit with parents. In Los Angeles, six to ten children of similar age and sex resided in ashrams. An adult teacher lived in the ashram, supervising the children and tending to their daily needs. In the mid-1980s, the ashram-based *gurukula* system disbanded in North America for financial reasons and because of growing awareness that some of ISKCON's children had been abused (see Rochford 2007a).

3. When I began my research on ISKCON, in 1975, it was common to hear devotees refer to outsiders as "demons." Such a dramatic term effectively reified communal boundaries. As devotee involvements with the outside society began to increase in the late 1970s, "karmie" became the preferred term. Although still boundary affirming, "karmie" held far fewer pejorative connotations than "demon." By the mid-1980s, "karmie" largely fell out of favor, being replaced by "nondevotee" as involvements in the outside society increased substantially for adults and children alike (Rochford 2000, 2007a).

4. It is important to note that the research reported on here occurred during a transitional period for ISKCON. By the late 1970s, a handful of adults in the Los Angeles community were working jobs outside of the movement and a growing number of older children were transitioning into the public middle school because ISKCON lacked a system of secondary education. Given these changes, group boundaries were being redrawn, something the boys in the ashram had an uncanny awareness of.

5. I found myself tutoring the boys in hopes of alleviating some of the distress they felt when their attempts were rejected. For example, the younger boys typically offered a book to the person contacted without comment. Not surprisingly, few were willing to take the book, fearing they would be obligated to purchase it or to make a donation. After one woman seemed confused and hesitant I broke into the interaction saying, "The book is free and is for your pleasure. We aren't asking for a donation, only that you enjoy reading the book." With this the woman took the book and we left. I told the two boys as we walked to the next apartment door, "You have to tell them right away that the book is free. If they don't understand that they probably won't take it. So tell them it is free and that you hope they will enjoy reading it."

7

Playing with Fire
(and Water, Earth, and Air)

Ritual Fluency and Improvisation among
Contemporary Pagan Children

ZOHREH KERMANI

Despite children's omission from a significant portion of the anthropological record, it is often the case that ethnographic methods can provide access to information by and about children that might be otherwise overlooked or inaccessible. Anthropologist Lawrence Hirschfield's provocatively titled article, "Why Don't Anthropologists Like Children?" contends, "Mainstream anthropology has marginalized children because it has marginalized the two things that children do especially well: children are strikingly adept at acquiring adult culture and, less obviously, adept at creating their own cultures."[1] Among contemporary American Pagans—and, indeed, among children in new religious movements in general—this marginalization is exacerbated by socialization and participation in a minority religion; children become, essentially, the edges of the periphery. Studying the ways in which Pagan children acquire adult culture—culture that has been improvised, for the most part, by the first-generation converts who parent them—can provide insights into the aspects of Pagan religious belief and morality that are reinforced among parents and children. Research of this sort has the potential to increase understanding of contemporary Pagan practice and to enhance the study of this new religion. Beyond providing data regarding the practices of adult new religious practitioners, however, child-centered ethnographic research can offer insight into the ways in which the magical and supernatural are not just understood, but also integrated and manipulated in daily Pagan life. Pagan parents offer their children a world filled with magical presences and supernatural events, and children use the raw materials of this magical world—stories, songs, rituals, costumes—to improvise and construct the religious worlds of their childhoods.

1. Methodological Issues: "Weren't You a Pagan Child?"

This chapter draws upon fieldwork conducted among contemporary American Pagan families in Massachusetts, New Hampshire, and Texas. This case study emerges from participant-observation and ethnographic interviews conducted with the families of Spiral Winds Coven at the semiannual Council of Magickal Arts festivals in central Texas. These gatherings take place in conjunction with the Beltane and Samhain holidays (April/May and October), and are generally attended by about fourteen hundred local Pagans—primarily adults, although many families attend, and the gatherings offer activities and events for children and teenagers. I attended four CMA festivals during 2006 and 2007, and camped with the Spiral Winds families each time. The children in the coven at the time my fieldwork began were two sets of siblings, ranging in age from five to eleven years old.[2] The children were generally quite receptive to the idea that I was trying to learn about what it was like to be a Pagan child and about the activities and conversations within their families. Some of the children expressed excitement at the prospect of their words and experiences appearing (albeit pseudonymously) in "a real book." Many children were particularly enamored of the digital voice recorder and microphone I used during our ethnographic interviews, often asking to hear pieces of our recorded conversations played back to them or borrowing the equipment to record conversations with one another. I once found a portion of a recorded interview with one Pagan parent to be untranscribable due to the muffled, distorted, and (unfortunately) inaudible murmurings of her six-year-old daughter surreptitiously mumbling a series of complaints directly into my recorder.

In the disarming way children sometimes have of crossing boundaries, the children's interest in the physical facts of the ethnographic study—my role as observer and quasi-adult, the artificial construction of the interviews, and the material objects of the methodology—sometimes dovetailed with the study itself. One six-year-old boy, Rowan, studied my microphone intently and asked, "Who's inside here listening?" Before I could respond, his mother answered, "Maybe the recorder fairy. Fairies have been known to occupy appliances." Spreading his fingers to gauge the size of the microphone, Rowan mused, "So this is how tall a fairy is. It flies around in here, and it flies up through here and pokes through. Hi, fairy!" Rowan agreed to answer questions about his participation in SpiralScouts activities, but insisted that he be allowed to "tell the fairy" his responses.[3] Rowan reimagined our conversation in a way that placed it within the realm of the magical, such that my presence, our conversation, and the tools of my study became elements of this enchanted world.

Not every child I encountered was entirely enthusiastic about his or her role as an informant; some expressed uncertainty about my ongoing presence at their events, and about the study as a whole. One first-grader asked me suspiciously, "Why do you need to know all this? Weren't you a Pagan child, too?" My explanation—that I was neither a Pagan child nor a Pagan adult, but was interested to learn more about her experiences—was met with the polite, indulgent smile that children reserve for the hopelessly naïve. For every child who greeted me enthusiastically at a SpiralScouts meeting as a "SpiralScouts Friend" or "that reporter," another eyed me warily from across the room and wondered aloud why I was at a SpiralScouts meeting unaccompanied by a child. This aspect of my presence was a particularly popular topic of discussion among some of the children at fieldwork sites, as they attempted to determine my role at these events. I was not a SpiralScouts leader; leaders wore green polo shirts and braided neck cords, and I was not in uniform. I was not a SpiralScouts parent; parents arrived with children and spent craft and snack times talking among themselves, while I arrived alone, talked to everyone, and scribbled in notebooks. And, despite my being relatively short for an adult, there was no mistaking me for a child. My presence challenged strict categories of "adult" (in these situations, equivalent to "parent") and "child."

Childhood studies scholar Pia Christensen's work has addressed this "distinctive role of the fieldworker and the research relationships that are developed during fieldwork." Christensen suggests, "[R]esearchers need to pay critical attention to the question, 'what is an adult?' when carrying out their work."[4] Among contemporary Pagans, the categories of "adulthood" and "childhood" are already ambiguous and troubled; contemporary Paganism idealizes a spiritual gravity and maturity in children at the same time that it encourages an exaggerated naïveté among adults. The role of the researcher is particularly complicated by this ambiguity, and by the fluidity of the category of "Pagan" itself. Almost all of the Pagan adults in this study were first-generation converts whose experience and familiarity with their new religion varied widely. In addition, the religion itself encourages improvisation and spontaneity in a way that often turns "observers" of rituals into impromptu participant-observers. In fact, one of my earliest ethnographic experiences of Pagan ritual involved being asked to cast the ritual circle.[5] This experience was not anomalous; in fact, it laid the foundation for my research among Pagan families. Fieldwork with Pagan children offered a particularly ambiguous experience, and I frequently found myself called upon by children to assist during an improvised ritual or regarded as the "authority" (by virtue of being the closest adult) on some matter of Pagan belief or practice.

Feminist and critical ethnography has problematized traditional ethnographic methods, suggesting that ethnography requires reflexivity and sensitivity as it takes into account the ways in which power, privilege, and voice are established and maintained in relationships between researcher and informants. Ethnographic fieldwork with children demands this reflexive commitment as well. Children's voices are notoriously difficult to access ethnographically. Not only are they often overlooked, but they remain obscured and often inaccessible even when these voices are intended to be the focus of the research. Children are sometimes hesitant to answer direct questions about their spiritual practices and beliefs, whether out of concerns about giving the "wrong" answer or out of uncertainty about what is expected of them. In some cases, parents of minority religions who may face real or imagined social repercussions for their unusual beliefs warn their children against discussing these beliefs with strangers. Fortunately, this reticence is not a quality all children share, and some children were more than happy to regale me with endless amounts of information—most of it fascinating, if unrelated to the topics at hand. Some of my younger informants became enthralled with the accoutrements of the study, constantly interrupting themselves and other children and asking to listen to the odd sound of their own voices on the recorder. Naturally reserved children were sometimes overshadowed by their more extroverted siblings or friends, as well. As four-year-old Rhia explained a ritual in which she had participated, her older sister Raven grew impatient with her version of the events:

RHIA: Yeah, the labyrinth was so cool. We saved some bugs. And I even caught two bugs. Yeah, in the same hand! A grasshopper and . . .

RAVEN: A grasshopper.

RHIA: A grasshopper and another grasshopper. And we did incense. And Raven and Cricket went with us, and I kept up with them. And we maked these [marks in the dirt with her fingertips]: It's someone's fingerprint, so that they know you're here. Okay? We did that. And we did incense. . . . We went all the way around the circle, and then we did that, and when we were going around in the circle or something—

RAVEN [interrupting]: She's a weirdo. Can we listen to the tape now?[6]

Raven's interruption and dismissal of her sister's ritual narration illustrate some of the difficulties involved in fieldwork with very young children. Allowed to proceed in her own pace in the telling of her story, Rhia might have eventually found the words to describe her experience, or she might have eventually become frustrated by the difficulty of this endeavor, choosing instead to tell me what she believed I wanted to hear (or to tell me nothing at all). Fieldwork with children demands a continuous awareness of the power dynamics at play in the researcher/informant—and adult/child—relationship. The perceived social status of the adult researcher, the intentional or accidental influence of parents and other children, and a host of other factors can potentially affect the fieldwork environment and the accessibility of children's voices within it.

In addition to a mandatory reflexivity, ethnographic work with children can benefit from a level of methodological flexibility beyond the ordinary uncertainties of the field. Flexibility regarding potential research outcomes is essential; as children struggle to gain control over their emotions and their environment, their willingness and ability to participate in a long-term fieldwork situation can seem capricious. Fatigue, hunger, or parental discipline can render a normally garrulous informant taciturn and aloof. Expanding fieldwork methods beyond the scope of ethnographic interviews and structured participant-observation can increase the kinds of information researchers can glean from interactions with children. Observing children's interactions with parents, siblings, and peers can offer significant information unavailable from ordinary methods.

2. Into the Labyrinth: Children's Religious Expressions

At the Council of Magickal Arts (CMA) festival in Texas, a permanent labyrinth has been built by the festival community into a section of the land. The children sharing my campsite were fascinated by this area, and visited it often over the course the weekend. Children at the CMA festival are generally respectful of this space and of others within it (although they seem to find running the labyrinth path preferable to quiet, meditative walking). Signs at the entrance to this part of Spirit Haven land, where the CMA festivals are held, inform visitors that they are "Entering Sacred Space," and another sign near the outer gate of the labyrinth sets the tone for activities there, asking visitors to "Declare your intention to travel to the heart." The "heart" to which the path leads is represented by the "Heart Rock," a huge piece of rose quartz in the center of the clearing.

I walked the labyrinth path one afternoon with eight-year-olds Raven and Cricket, five-year-old Rhia, and Cricket's mother, Freya. Once inside the gate, the girls ran the labyrinth path as Freya and I followed. The circular path of the labyrinth winds back and forth on itself, so the girls and I passed each other at every turn and Cricket high-fived me each time her path met mine. In the center, Freya helped the children carefully light sticks of incense, and the girls sat quietly near the heart rock for several minutes, meditating (or watching the bugs crawl in the grass). Another adult entered the second gate of the labyrinth behind us, and he sat on a bench a short distance away, waiting to walk the path. As the girls lit incense and candles, Freya approached them and quietly said, "I think this man is waiting because he needs to walk the labyrinth alone today," gently encouraging them to begin walking the path out. Her comment reminded the girls of a number of different concepts at once: the need to be empathetic and aware of the "energy" of their environment, to trust their intuition, and to remember that spirituality can be practiced alone or in community.

The older girls followed Freya out of the circle, but Rhia was not ready to leave yet. She walked to the center of the circle, knelt down, and put both hands on the pink heart rock. With more gravitas than one would expect from a five-year-old in a foam wizard's hat, she said, "It makes it hard to breathe." Somewhat alarmed at suddenly being the only adult present—did she have heat exhaustion? a bee sting?—I asked her, "What makes it hard to breathe?" She answered, "When I touch the rock, because it's so powerful. It makes my tummy hurt." I reminded her that we could leave the circle, but she kept both hands on the rock and insisted she wanted to stay. She stood up, put her hands together with index fingers pointing up, and said, "I'm costing [casting] spells here. I'm magic. I have to close my eyes and do this to cost spells." Rhia had watched her parents cast circles both with their coven and in smaller family rituals, and her actions mirrored many of those she had witnessed from adults—although her physical response to the heart rock was entirely her own. She looked around the center of the labyrinth and exclaimed, "This place is magic. This whole campground is magic!" Kneeling by the heart rock again, she closed her eyes, pointed her joined index fingers at the rock, and began mumbling an incantation of her own invention. She finished by informing the rock, "We need opportunity. We need help. Okay? Now you have to leave the spell in your head." She looked up from the rock and suddenly announced, "This is a scary place. It's creepy. There might be a snake in the grass." I asked her again if she was ready to leave, and she shook her head no.

The adult who had been sitting on the benches started slowly walking the path into the center. As the only other adult present, I had felt responsible for encouraging Rhia to leave the center so that the adult who was waiting could enter. Watching her "cost spells" here and witnessing her reluctance to leave this area—a place that clearly had a powerful effect on her body, mind, and spirit—it eventually dawned on me that she had as much right to this space as the adult visitor. I slowed down to walk at her pace, and as the man in the tie-dyed sarong passed us on the labyrinth pass he smiled, nodded at Rhia, and commended her on her "good energy."

Winding our way out of the labyrinth, I realized that my perception of the other adult—that he was impatiently waiting his turn, and that Rhia's presence would be disruptive to his meditation—was a reflection of my own normative understandings of child and adult spirituality. The spiritual world of the other adult visitor included Rhia's presence, however marginal to his own experience. For her part, Rhia's spiritual experience of the labyrinth was remarkably reflective of—but distinctly separate from—that of the adults around her. The range of emotions and responses to the labyrinth, the heart rock, and her own "spells" that Rhia experienced during our visit to the center draws a complex and multilayered picture of children's participation in ritual and other spiritual practices. The combination of Rhia's focus on her own improvised ritual and her sensory experiences of the labyrinth, my anxiety as her ad hoc adult liaison to the labyrinth and the other visitors, and our tie-dyed companion's perceptions of children's spirituality, Rhia's "energy," and the shared religious space of adults and children together illustrate many of the ambivalences, tensions, and idiosyncrasies of the religious worlds of Pagan adults and children.

3. "Abundant Events" and the Religious Imagination of Children

Contemporary Paganism's reliance on the realms of the magical, fantastic, and enchanted both refutes and rejects modern understandings of religion. For contemporary Pagans—and even more so for Pagan children, raised in these magical worlds—the "real" world *is* the enchanted world, and vice versa. Pagan children—children raised in households in which one or both parents practice some form of contemporary Paganism, often Wicca—exhibit an extraordinary fluency with the religious idioms of their parents' traditions. Pagan parents frequently go to great lengths to avoid "indoctrinating" or "inculcating" their beliefs into their children, instead espousing an ethic of radical intellectual freedom and religious choice for these children. What parents strive to instill in their children is not religious tradition, theological belief, or inflexible "dogma." Rather, their spiritual legacy to their children is an intimate familiarity with the enchanted, magical, and supernatural. Pagan adults—most of them adolescent or adult converts to the religion—construct a spiritual and ritual rhetoric of enchantment and magical presence.

The magical and sacred presences that permeate the Pagan world—goddesses, gods, tape-recorder fairies, nature sprites, dream animals, cosmic energies—comprise a body of phenomena akin to what religious studies scholar Robert Orsi has called "abundant events." These events are those characterized by "aspects of the human imagination that cannot be completely accounted for by social and cultural codes, that go beyond authorized limits. . . . Abundant events are saturated by memory, desire, need, fear, terror, hope or denial, or some inchoate combination of these."[7] The Catholicism Orsi observes is one infused with a supernatural presence, a world that rejects post-Enlightenment assessments of religion, rationality, and "denial of presence."[8] Despite the obvious theological differences, the world of supernatural presence and abundance inhabited by American Catholics is one that might be oddly familiar to contemporary American Pagans as well.

Pagan children, more than most, inhabit a thoroughly magical world that takes for granted these abundant events and provides children with the tools to understand these extraordinary events as ordinary occurrences. Pagan children's fluency with the religious activities and idioms of this new religion illustrates both the ritual creativity that arises from children's immersion in this magical world and the necessity of constructing, as Orsi suggests, a "radical empiricism of the visible *and* invisible real"[9] that allows scholars to study the significance of this magical presence in daily religious life. The spontaneous rituals created by Pagan children make it clear that these children understand at least the spirit (if not always the theological messages) of the rituals in which they participate. It is also apparent that Pagan children integrate messages from their parents and other adults regarding the magical, spiritual, and ritual aspects of daily life. Beyond this, however, these improvisations can be empowering for Pagan children, helping them to develop confidence in their ritual improvisational skills and in their place within their religious worlds. These improvisations illustrate the ritual fluency and religious imagination of Pagan children, as they take the foundations of ritual from adults and add imaginative, fantastic, child-centered elements.

The labyrinth holds a powerful appeal for the children at CMA festivals, and over the course of a festival weekend Rhia, Raven, and Cricket spend hours in its dusty paths. One afternoon, the girls huddle together over water that pools in a shallow indentation of a large rock. Dressed in long black cloaks and tennis shoes—their standard festival attire—each girl concentrates intently on a black rock held in her hand. Raven has cast a makeshift circle for the group by walking around the circle and drawing a pentagram in the air with a tree branch, and she proudly informs the other girls that this is the third circle she has cast since her father first showed her how, a skill that seems to earn her the role of de facto ritual leader. She instructs the others to think about a person or animal that has died, explaining that they can wish that their loved one were still alive, or just think about them quietly. All three girls place their rocks in the pool of water, and then each child lights three incense sticks from a box left in the labyrinth by other festival goers. Raven takes up her circle-casting branch and walks counterclockwise around the other girls, to "pop" the magical circle she previously created, and then—in a ritual closing that seems mutually, if tacitly, agreed upon—the three girls spend several minutes carefully scooping insects from the pool of water and placing them on the grass. "Poor bugs," sighs Rhia, the youngest of the trio. "Poor bugs. We'll save them." An adult observer—whether Pagan or not—of the activities in the labyrinth could be forgiven for assuming that the girls' spontaneous ritual concluded with Raven's "popping" of the sacred circle and that the "saving" of the insects marked an abrupt shift from ritual imitation and creation to another kind of play. When asked later to explain the ritual, though, all three girls were careful to include the "bug saving" in their accounts as the ritual's dénouement. Ritual improvisations such as these illustrate the religious fluency and imagination of Pagan children, as they take the foundations of ritual behavior from adults and add elements that crystallize adult attempts to codify a Pagan moral and religious world. It is difficult to imagine an adult coven—no matter how explicit their emphasis on compassion, karma, or the ecological interconnectedness of all life—closing a ritual meditation on death by scooping flies from the elemental water bowl. For the second-generation children of this new religion, though, this connection is intuitive and integral.

4. "I'm not a Pagan, I'm a snake."

Adolescents and adults bring certain expectations to their conversion to contemporary Paganism. Most converts to the religion have become familiar with it through an assortment of literary sources, including the works of seminal figures such as Aleister Crowley, Gerald Gardner, Raymond Buckland, or Starhawk, and popular works aimed at a younger or general audience, such as those by Silver RavenWolf, Scott Cunningham, and the offerings of

Llewellyn Publications. First-generation converts manipulate this medley of fictional and nonfictional literature, informational and community-centered online sources, personal contacts, and previous religious experience to construct a functional Pagan identity. In many cases, the journey toward this Pagan identity becomes a central part of the adult Pagan's autobiographical mythos, functioning as a rejection of his or her childhood religious experience and a tale of personal spiritual evolution.[10] The religious identities of second-generation Pagan children, however, are the product of a radically different process—family tradition rather than spiritual journey. Understandably, Pagan children's uses of religious idioms can differ dramatically from those of adults. Rather than embracing Paganism as an oppositional identity that differentiates them from mainstream religious cultures, Pagan children take a Pagan identity for granted, using it instead as a departure point for their own spiritual explorations. Overhearing the adults discussing the formation of a new coven, five-year-old Rhia asked, "What's a Pagan?" Her father, Atashih, the high priest of the new coven, responded, "*You're* a Pagan, Rhia." "No, I'm not. I'm a snake," Rhia countered, then pointed at her sister: "And Raven is a tiger."

In his classic discussion of "primitive mentality," intelligibility, and religious belief, historian of religions J. Z. Smith considered alternatives for ethnographers and historians of religion encountering seemingly nonsensical statements, such as the Bororo tribe's assertion that they "are" parrots. The relative "truth" of this statement, Smith suggests, may be beyond the scholar's purview; the statement "functions as expressive in certain situations. The principles of rationality are upheld and the problem becomes one of finding the situation in which the statement will function in a noncontradictory way."[11] Similarly, the magical, enchanted worlds in which Pagan children are immersed raise questions for the ethnographer about levels of commitment to and belief in the metaphysical aspects of the religion. When a Pagan parent tells a child "all rocks are magical,"[12] asks her if she is "channeling pixies" when she seems hyperactive, or informs her that dandelions gone to seed are fairies that need to be "helped on their way," they construct a world for their children (and for themselves) in which the magical and supernatural are an accepted part of daily life. The extent to which Pagan adult converts "believe" in these events and presences is difficult to gauge. For Pagan children, however, these events and presences are presented by adults as ontological facts, and children's interpretations and manipulations of these kinds of events accompany an understanding of the world as "really" imbued with this presence.

Rhia's response reflected a conversation she had overheard earlier in the day, when her older sister Raven and several of the adults discussed their Chinese astrological signs; she was correct, in fact, in remembering that she was born in the Year of the Snake, her sister in the Year of the Tiger. Her father, however, had not participated in the earlier conversation, and Rhia's announcement that she and her sister were animals rather than Pagans seemed apropos of nothing. His response, however, was to accept this statement as an indication of his daughter's belief in totem animals, magical properties, and transmutation. These are, after all, the building blocks of his daughter's childhood religious vocabulary. Rhia's comment may have had a more mundane origin in this case, but Atashih was correct in assuming that his daughter was intimately familiar with these concepts and fluent in their applications for daily usage—whether in explicitly "religious" practice or for more quotidian uses. Through religious instruction, everyday conversation and jokes, and modeling behavior, Pagan parents like Atashih make the magical and supernatural real for their children by incorporating these idioms into their family religious practice. Drawing on contemporary Paganism's ideological roots in Romanticism, Victorian ideals of childhood innocence and purity, and nineteenth-century magical and occult movements, Pagan parents construct a world in which "abundant events" become everyday companions.

Children's responses to these types of supernatural, sacred, or extraordinary events may vary radically; contemporary Paganism is nothing if not a religion of individual response and improvisation. The world may be rife with magical events, but not all inspire reverence and awe. At a festival campfire Robin, an eleven-year-old boy, drops a marshmallow that has been toasting on a stick into the fire, and informs his mother that he can divine the future from the marshmallow drippings, using the obscure—and newly invented—art of "mallowmancy."[13] Robin's clever response to the marshmallow spatters (and his mother's indulgent attempts to "read" the marshmallow omens with him) is typical of the fluency with which Pagan children manipulate their religion's repertoire of symbols and idioms. Children raised among these practices—even if the religious "traditions" themselves only date back to their parents' generation—find ways to include these themes in their daily lives and their play. Second-generation Pagan children in the United States hold funerals for pet fish (complete with pentacles carved into popsicle sticks), "manifest" parking spaces for their parents in crowded parking lots, and draw pentacles, moons, and affirmations of love for the Goddess on craft projects. Pagan family life is infused with an attention to the supernatural meant to awaken and instill in children a kind of everyday imaginative spiritual practice. Pagan children live their lives in these enchanted worlds, so it is little wonder that they are adept at manipulating the elements of structured Pagan practice and worship to construct and perform rituals that reflect their orientation toward and immersion in the imaginative and magical.

The invisible world made visible to Pagan children is a world of magic, enchantment, and fantasy, a world that both shapes and authenticates children's (and adults') fascination with the magical. Pagan children inhabit a world—and experience a religion—where spirits, fairies, nature sprites, and magical powers are present, tangible, and fully validated by adults. Pagan adults construct and maintain these magical religious and moral worlds, drawing on Victorian and Romantic ideals of childhood, spiritual texts established by other converts to the religion, fantasy literature, and a multitude of other sources. Pagan children, in turn, manifest this moral and religious imagination in their daily lives, in ways that organically integrate a synthetic Pagan ethos with larger society.

The relationship between adult expectations of children's religious participation and children's own spiritual experiences is complex, dynamic, and often fraught with ambivalence. Adults consciously shape the boundaries of children's religious worlds, unconsciously encourage or discourage religious activities and experiences, and interpret children's actions and experiences in ways that reinforce Pagan values and adult ideals of childhood. For their part, Pagan children navigate the religious worlds offered to them by adults at the same time that they construct their own ritual experiences—experiences that may have little or no need for adult presence at all. Pagan adults begin from a mainstream religious perspective to consciously architect a contemporary Pagan ethos. Children take for granted a world imbued with spiritual presence as they manipulate the elements of these constructed religious idioms—both literally and figuratively—to create a coherent religious imaginary.

NOTES

1. Lawrence A. Hirschfeld, "Why Don't Anthropologists Like Children?" *American Anthropologist* 104, no. 2 (2002): 611.

2. Additional fieldwork during 2006-2007 was conducted among families affiliated with SpiralScouts International, a Pagan-oriented scouting organization for children of minority religions.

3. R.B. and J.B., personal interview, May 23, 2006.

4. Pia Haudrup Christensen, "Children's Participation in Ethnographic Research: Issues of Power and Representation," *Children & Society* 18, no. 2 (2004): 166.

5. At my second visit to a Covenant of Unitarian Universalist Pagans circle during an early phase of fieldwork, I was asked to assist in "calling Quarters" by reading the invocation to the powers of the West. A large number of those present were attending the circle for the first time, and my previous visit apparently granted me some measure of seniority. I was handed a paper with the text of the invocation, and pointed toward the correct candle to light. At another CUUPS ritual a member explained to me that this inclusivity and improvisation was part of the group's attraction, remarking, "If you come back here twice, they're already asking you to call Quarters, so you get Quarters being called all these different ways, by whoever was asked to do it" (North Shore CUUPS, October 27, 2002, Salem, MA).

6. Council of Magickal Arts Samhain Festival, October 20, 2006.

7. Robert A. Orsi, "When 2 + 2 = 5: Can We Begin to Think about Unexplained Religious Experiences in Ways That Acknowledge Their Existence?" *American Scholar* 76, no. 2 (2007).

8. Ibid.

9. Ibid.

10. For an excellent analysis of this phenomenon see Sarah M. Pike, *Earthly Bodies, Magical Selves: Contemporary Pagans and the Search for Community* (Berkeley: University of California Press, 2001), chapter 5, "Children of the Devil or Gifted in Magic? The Work of Memory in Neopagan Narrative."

11. Jonathan Z. Smith, *Map Is Not Territory: Studies in the History of Religions* (Leiden: Brill, 1978), 286.

12. Atashih, Council of Magickal Arts Beltane Festival, May 2005.

13. Council of Magickal Arts Beltane Festival, 2007.

8

"*La Virgen*, She Watches over Us"

What Cholos and Cholas Can Teach Us about Researching and Writing about Religion

KRISTY NABHAN-WARREN

We sat under some mesquite trees as he caressed the black and white tattoo of the Virgin of Guadalupe etched on his right forearm. A crochet rosary in green and red hung around his neck, next to the gold medallion of the Virgin of Guadalupe that his *abuelita*, his grandmother, gave him when he was a little boy. Mark, a member of the South Phoenix gang Wetback Power (WBP), narrated his life story; he spoke passionately about his love for "*la Virgen de Guadalupe*," his "*familia*," and his "*nueva familia*," his gang peers. He talked about his faith, shooting rival gang members to protect himself and his "homies," and his belief that *la Virgen* protected him at all times. In good times and bad, Mark emphasized that it was *la Virgen* who was "there for me" when others failed him. He was a devout Catholic whose faith was strong.

This essay focuses on what scholars of religion can learn about the religious lives of young adults and about religion, more broadly speaking, from the perspectives of Mexican American male and female gang members. In the 1990s, while working with *cholos* and *cholas,* I reconsidered the categories I had taken for granted in the study of religion. Pervasive notions of "good" and "bad" religion dominate academic discourse, no matter how much we hope to move beyond such dichotomizations.[1] These gang members with whom I worked challenged my assumptions about what "religion" is and what constitutes a "religious" person. The gang members I interviewed constructed modes of conduct and comportment that reflected their geographic, socio-economic, and ethnic realities. Once I shelved preconceived notions I had of religion (good/bad, real/unreal) and similar dichotomizations of youth (good/bad, normal/deviant), I was drawn into the urban religious phenomena I was studying. Religion walked in the streets, talked, yelled, shot bullets, and was worn on bodies and the cars that carried those bodies.[2]

Gang members' lives were the focus of my research in the early 1990s and my entryway into Catholicism in the barrios of South Phoenix. *Cholas* with teardrop tattoos and *cholos* with tattoos of the Virgin of Guadalupe walked the streets as newspaper articles on gang violence proliferated and outreach programs struggled to reach them. Gang members in South Phoenix invented religious rituals and symbols that were born out of dispossession and an intense yearning for love and acceptance. Ritualization of violence and desire was a "strategic *way* of acting."[3] Religious symbols took on new meaning in the barrio across generations—Christ and Mary were alive and walked with the men, women, and children who lived there.[4]

Cholos and *cholas* were not the "deviant" or unredeemable youth they were often portrayed as in the media.[5] I found these young adults to be searching for answers to their very real problems and turning to their Catholic faith, to their religious icons, and to each other for guidance and support. In some ways they were unconventional in their beliefs yet in other ways they were conventional. They attended mass frequently, alone or with family members, looked forward to receiving Eucharist, and always carried their rosaries with them. But they also created forms of religiosity that spoke to and addressed their needs—much like other American Christian teens who move beyond their parents by adding their own creative touches to their faith. While evangelical Christian teens participated in the 1990s "What Would Jesus Do?" wristband craze, Mexican American Catholic *cholos* and *cholas* internalized the cultural religiosity of their grandparents and parents. Anglo American Christian youth often chose to wear Jesus on their bodies in various forms. In contrast, gang members tended to wear and carry images of the Virgin of Guadalupe, signifying her importance in their lives. Street processions of the *Virgen de Guadalupe*, murals that depicted Christ's and Mary's suffering and agony, and tattoos on the bodies of barrio residents reflect a "visual piety" that stands as a "collective representation of personal relationships or community."[6]

For Mexican American Catholics in Phoenix's south side, Christ and the Virgin of Guadalupe live alongside them. They have grown up hearing stories about the "Mexican National Virgin," and they relate to her in ways that are culturally consistent with their religious genealogy.[7] Their faith in the salvific power of Christ and Mary is so secure that they can be seen as radical devotees. Their belief is unshakable. Much as Mexican armies have held aloft the image of the Virgin of Guadalupe, rival gang members display their affection and devotion to their divine *madre* and believe that she champions their particular cause.[8]

All fifteen young men and women, nine male and six female, between the ages fifteen and twenty whom I interviewed spoke of the violence in which they lived, the Catholicism of their homes, and their own personal religiosity, which neither completely rejected nor completely conformed to the religion of their *familia* or culture. These young men and women created spaces for themselves that allowed them to confront the realities of their barrios. The religion that they made was raw and searching—a reflection of the tenuousness of their daily lives. Christ and the Virgin of Guadalupe showed love and concern for them when everyone else failed them. Any brokenness they experienced in their familias was eased by their fervent belief that *la Virgen* and Christ loved them and would not, unlike human family members, hurt them in any way.

Like mainstream American youth, these *cholas* and *cholos* wanted to feel love and acceptance, and they sought out others who might support them. Yet these youth came from homes and families that experienced various forms of dispossession and violence, and their yearning for love and acceptance took on new levels of significance.

"It's Your Family"

For eighteen-year-old Isabel, member of Southside Thirty-Fifth and its female offshoot the Squirrels, her gang and her homegirls and homeboys are her *puro familia*—her real family. She had been let down by her nuclear and extended family far too many times for her to remember, and as a result of an anxiety-ridden childhood, she didn't consider them to be true family. "Just because you're born into a family doesn't mean that it is right for you," she told me. Isabel, like the other *cholos* and *cholas* with whom I spoke, talked at length about the "craziness" of her home life, the lack of love and affection she felt from parents and siblings, and the constant feeling of being unwanted. Recounting her childhood, Isabel cried at several points, wiping her eyes to declare, "I don't believe in getting married. I think marriage is just a piece of paper that's gonna tell you you're going to get a divorce. My parents are always fighting and there's no love."[9]

According to Isabel, she was ignored at best, physically abused at worst. The only daughter in a family of six children, she was treated "like I was stupid." She eventually found a group of individuals who welcomed her and who made her feel special. Isabel's experience was mirrored by the other *cholos* and *cholas* I interviewed; they all experienced neglect and abuse by their nuclear family and sought out a new community where members pledged themselves to each other. While much has been written about Mexican American family life, affectionately referred to as *la familia*, much less has been written about religion in *familias* that experience failures.[10]

Fifteen-year-old "Jesse," a member of Wetback Power (WBP), acknowledged that many families in the barrio are "messed up real bad." For Jesse, joining WBP was a way to find homies who really cared about him and who "have my back at all times." He experienced abuse and neglect in his *familia* and knew that WBP had a reputation of being "like a family but better than most because a lot of families in the barrio are like, God, . . . so fucked up." When I asked Jesse how he dealt with the acts of violence committed by members of his gang and his own involvement, he shrugged and said that "you just do things for your family. Sometimes you have to do what might not seem right but it is . . . because you're protecting your turf and what's right." Jesse admitted that he was "sometimes scared" and didn't want to die but that he was willing to do drive-bys when they were deemed necessary by his gang because "hey, you have to do what is right for your homies and your family." *Cholos* and *cholas* who come from abusive, violent families and situations often legitimate gang violence. Violence for the common good of the gang *familia* takes on a sacred meaning. Pain and suffering become the paths toward a new identity. A gang member is transformed into someone who is better, stronger, even sanctified.

Sacred Violence and Sacrifice: "La Virgen, She Has Our Backs"

While there has been much written about the violent, deviant, and illegal aspects of gang membership, nothing, as far as I can discern, has been written about the sanctifying, religious aspects of violence for these young men and women. Each of the fifteen gang members I interviewed described the process of initiation into their gang, and how the rite of passage gave them a profound sense of accomplishment and meaning. The physical violence that these young women and men endure gives them a sense of transcending their everyday realities and empowers them. For them, "the act of hurting is not the extension of the ego's domain over the body, properly speaking. Instead, the self as a phenomenal organization of perceptions, motivations, commands, and actions emerges out of the violence and out of the hurtful feedback it generates."[11] Violence can lead to a kind of redemption from *la vida loca*, this crazy life. Several of the young men and women I spoke with talked about how "good it felt" to feel pain and to see and feel the blood running down their faces (and other parts of their bodies) after being jumped in to their respective gangs—violently initiated into the gang by peer gang members. Rites of passage into gang life, including being jumped in, having sex with one or more members, or engaging in activities such as stealing alcohol or money, involve liberating the use of the body in support of a greater cause.

To gain membership into WBP Jesse had been "jumped in," beaten by "about ten other guys" to prove his loyalty and devotion to the gang. Jesse's initiation was physically painful; "I hurt real bad for weeks," he said, but the bodily pain was outweighed by the power he felt at enduring such agony. Jesse told me that even though he "had the crap kicked out of me," he had never felt better about himself before and felt that he was part of something important. He was given a purpose and a sense of self-worth in his gang that he had never had in his nuclear family, where he "felt like a piece of garbage, just shit, you know?" Soon after his successful initiation, Jesse had a tattoo of a cross emblazoned on the left side of his neck and of the Virgin of Guadalupe on his back. The latter tattoo application took several visits to the tattoo parlor as it was so elaborate and involved. Jesse compared the pain of his initiation to the pain of being tattooed and said they were both "worth it because I am part of a family that cares about me and I am showing respect for my mother, *la Virgen*, who watches over me and my homies and who loves us so much."[12]

Jesse, like the other *cholos* and *cholas* I encountered, underscored the importance of legitimating suffering on his terms and how *cholos* and *cholas* seek out and embrace bodily pain to prove their loyalty to the gang and to their way of life. Gang members drew deep connections between their suffering and Christ's and *la Virgen's* when she saw her dead son on the cross. These associations with pain, suffering, and the divine were gendered: the *cholos* I interviewed tended to talk more about Christ's sacrifice, emphasizing how they related to Jesus Christ because he "hurt so bad and like so many people, like, hated him" whereas *cholas* I talked with stressed their connection with *la Virgen* "because, I mean, she saw her son *die!* Can you imagine that?!"[13] Both Christ and Mary resonate powerfully as symbols and as real people because they endured pain, ridicule, and ostracization—like them.

While *cholos* talked about their admiration of Christ, they signified their devotion to his mother, *la Virgen*, by wearing beautiful, professionally done tattoos of her. This is a life commitment and is taken seriously as a rite of passage, a ritual initiation into gang life where she is seen as watching over them at all times. While *cholos* wear large tattoos of the Virgin of Guadalupe on their backs and forearms, as well as crosses on necks and forearms, *cholas* tend to have understated, small teardrop tattoos to represent Mary's crying for her son as well as for their own sadness for incarcerated and dead gang members. During my fieldwork in South Phoenix I never met a *chola* who wore a large tattoo of the Virgin of Guadalupe but did meet several who wore smaller, black-etched tattoos of *la Virgen*, delicate, like intricate lacework, on their shoulderblades. These tattoos, small or large, are testimonies of devotion and are a form of prayer. For Mark, his sacred body art helps protect him from the ever-present dangers of gang life: "Every time I go out I know that I am being watched by someone from another gang and that I could be killed. But I know that *la Virgen* is watching over me and I pray to her constantly when I'm out there."[14] Mark, as with all eight of the other *cholos* I interviewed, went out of his way to tell me that he stopped in front of his church, St. Catherine of Siena, regularly, to genuflect and to bend down and kiss his rosary, which was in his gang colors. Gang-colored rosaries were another form of protection that, in addition to their tattoos, is meant to keep them safe on the streets of South Phoenix. Tattoos, rosaries, and even their decked-out cars are gang members' sacramentals, a form of material culture that can "nourish, strengthen, and express belief."[15]

The *cholo/a* Christ and Mary are alive and they walk with them each and every day. They are living symbols who help them navigate the urban terrain in which they live. Christ and *la Virgen* are living, breathing, bleeding beings who protect their urban street children and die for and with them. In the *cholo/a* cosmology of South Phoenix, religion is rarely nice; it is wary of the world and it condones and prescribes violence. For *cholos* and *cholas*, living in community means that you pledge to commit acts of violence to protect your family and violence is seen as sacred. *Cholo* religion—a blend of Catholicism, ethnic pride, family-centeredness, and urban wherewithal—does not fit neatly into academic understandings of religion largely because it can be frightening and violent as much as it can be beautiful. Scholars of religion have the moral imperative to study and think about phenomena such as gang violence and the construction of cosmology—those "practices that make us uncomfortable, unhappy, frightened."[16]

Christ and the Virgin are ever-present realities in the barrios of South Phoenix. It is they, unlike parents, brothers, and sisters, who do not abandon their children. For the *cholos* and *cholas* of South Phoenix, religion is never romanticized. Their Jesus does not have long, flowing hair and a beatific smile. He is not their close friend or buddy; he is a man they respect from afar for his bloody and agonizingly painful self-sacrifice. They respect and embrace his suffering in the deepest way possible and see themselves as kindred martyrs for their *causa*: protecting their turf and their gang *familias*. The *cholo* Christ of South Phoenix reflects their cultural surroundings and deepest desires. The *cholo* Christ is both an "iconoclast as well as an icon," as he is for other Americans.[17] Much like other Americans, who, as Stephen Prothero has shown, make Jesus into their own image, these young people in Arizona "have hailed Jesus as a personality who stood out from the maddening crowd" and have "applauded him the loudest when he has walked and talked like them."[18] Embracing what they interpret to be a sacrifice for the gang and their freedom as gang members to make their rules and live by them, *cholos* and *cholas* draw connections to Christ's sacrifice for "his people."

Likewise, the *cholo/chola* Virgin of Guadalupe is a warrior woman, and is imagined and lived much like the Aztec goddesses Tonantzín and Coatilecue were in fifteenth- and sixteenth-century Mexico. The *cholo/a* Guadalupe is unafraid of street violence and gang warfare. She is not relegated to the inside of the church—she *wants* to be with her children.[19] *La Virgen de Guadalupe* is emblazoned on cholos' backs, shoulders, and arms in colorful tattoos—she is no shrinking violet, relegated to the inside of the church. She is out there with her children, walking with them, emblazoned on their bodies. She is a reflection of their gritty lives and stares down violence on a daily basis. Her image on gang members' bodies is an act of religious and cultural devotion. Their devotion is no less powerful than is their *abuela's* Catholic-church-related societies in honor of the Virgin of Guadalupe or her home shrine, *altarcito*, which reserves a special place for *la Virgen*.[20] In this way, respect for her cuts across generations. And while devotion to Guadalupe and Christ is unwavering, belief in God, at least for the *cholos* and *cholas* I encountered, wavers because he cannot be seen or heard or represented in a physical way as Christ and Guadalupe can be shown. Isabel's declaration during one of our interviews was supported in other conversations I had with South Phoenix gang members: "I'm a churchgoer and when I am in church I believe in God but when I'm outside in the real world, I don't believe in God."[21] To Isabel and other *cholos* and *cholas*, God seems distant, removed, and even uncaring. Isabel, as well as fellow and rival gang members in South Phoenix, wrestled with the role of "religion" in their lives, which they equate with organized religion. Religion is distant and unrecognizable to them because it stems from church involvement and Catholic theology, all of which seem painfully irrelevant in their lives.

To me, my philosophy is, if there is a God, there would be no killings, there would be no shootings, there would be no Devil, just peace, you know? So that is one of the reasons I don't turn to religion because why should I turn to religion when it's like . . . God gives us faith sometimes but most of the time we need him.[22]

As Isabel's remark highlights, *cholo* and *chola* theodicy—an attempt to explain the ever-present violence in their lives using theological language— views God as distant, even uncaring. He has abandoned them. It is Christ and the Virgin of Guadalupe who come to their aid and who show that they care. Importantly to *cholos* and *cholas*, these part-human, part-divine beings have proven their loyalty to them because they themselves endured bodily pain and suffering. By contrast, God is an ethereal, almost make-believe being whose distance from their lives is obvious. He cannot be seen or experienced in ways that his son, and the mother of his son, can for these *cholos* and *cholas*.

Guadalupe, the warrior woman of the streets, is appreciated by her *cholo* children because she is "down" with them and comes to their aid. For *cholas*, *la Virgen* is the only one who understands what they go through and what lengths they will go to for their gang. Sexual acts sometimes take on a ritual dimension as forms of sacrifice and a sign that you are "down" with your gang. Among *cholas*, having sex with male gang members is a rite of passage, initiation into the gang. Isabel's gang family, like Mark's, required an initiation and most *cholas*, like Isabel, were told to have sex with one or more *cholos* to prove their loyalty to the gang. "Sometimes, you know, you are asked to go all the way for the gang and to prove your loyalty. After I had hung with them for awhile and had shown them I wanted to be down with them, the *cholos* in Thirty-Fifth looked at me and over to this guy Art and told me 'to fuck him for Thirty-Fifth,' so I did."[23] Isabel looked down at the ground for a moment when she was recounting this story to me, but she quickly looked up and said it made her feel "important, like I was doing some good for somebody, you know?"[24] Isabel chalked up her actions as a "personal sacrifice" and stressed that her sexuality was a small price to pay for inclusion in a largely supportive group; "if you want something you gotta give something."

In contrast to the gang members' experiences in the barrio of South Phoenix, middle-class American sexual ethics have encouraged "safe sex."[25] Dovetailing with the widespread "Just Say No" antidrug campaign that was spearheaded by former first lady Nancy Reagan, the safe sex campaign was popularized in public schools before and during Isabel's school days.[26]

According to youth advocate and educator Apple-White, "just saying no" to drugs for poor Black and Hispanic kids in the barrio is difficult at best, nearly impossible: "Until you really know what it is like to wake up every morning and not have alternatives, and to go to school hungry and to see your big brother coming in with some McDonalds or Kentucky Fried Chicken because he went out and sold some drugs. . . . You have to put yourself in that circumstance to understand it, you know?"

Cholos who surrounded themselves with guns, cool cars, and drugs were guaranteed success with girls. Having sex with girls affiliated with your gang as well as outside your gang was to prove that you were "down" with your homeboys and girls. The idea of wearing a condom or "saving yourself for marriage" was unheard of among the young women and men I interviewed. Safe sex and chastity were impractical at best, dangerous at worst, especially for *cholas* because of the expectation to share yourself and to offer your body as a sacrifice to the gang. To them, it is a small price to pay for admission into a family that will stand by you, unlike your biological one. The *cholos* I talked with all spoke about having sex at a young age, fourteen and fifteen, and said that it "was no big deal to have sex," as one *cholo* put it. "You just do it and then it's like over," another *cholo* said. Like the other young men I interviewed, this young man saw sex and sexuality as detached from morality. Acting on physical desire was normal and abstaining was seen as aberrant and risky because of what others would think of you ("faggot," "gay," or "a lesbo"). Arturo, a *veterano* and cofounder of one of the oldest South Phoenix gangs, stressed how it was *muy importante* to show that you were a real *hombre* by having sex with numerous women. Arturo stressed that in his experience, *cholos* and *cholas* try not to get too attached to each other and that sex should not be taken too seriously.

The idea that these men and women have a "choice" is further complicated, as they believe that they individually make the decision; as Isabel has emphasized, a *chola* must sometimes prove her loyalty to the gang family and way of life by offering herself sexually to a young man or men. Young women like Isabel and "Roni," a member of Phoenix's Dupa Villa Projects gang, challenge feminist consciousness and notions of women's right to determine their bodies' actions. Isabel claims that it was ultimately "up to me" to have sex with Art and to thus prove she was "down for" Thirty-Fifth Street—she was adamant that she wasn't forced and that she chose to do it. Like Isabel, Roni made a bold statement of self-determination and declared at age seventeen that she wanted to become pregnant; "I want a kid. . . . I hope I'm pregnant now. I want to have a kid and it can be part of me before I die."[27]

Their proximity to the U.S.-Mexico border, combined with their hybrid blend of popular and official Catholic piety, fueled gang members' desire to establish an identity for themselves. As religious beings who must live between worlds and construct their own realities, *cholos* and *cholas* create symbols and rituals that work for them in their given time and place.[28] What worked for their *abuelos* and *abuelas*—being involved in religious societies dedicated to Christ and Mary—does not work for them and their life situation, especially when they feel as though the church has, as most of the *cholos* and *cholas* told me, "let me down."[29] Those who go to church "feel good" when they are there, but once they are out on the street, they no longer feel the warmth or protection of God, the church, or the church community. Nevertheless, some religious figures reached out to these youth. The late Father Doug Nohava was highly respected among South Phoenix *cholos* and *cholas* because "he showed that he cares for us and it isn't just talk, you know?" as one *cholo* explained.[30] "Father Doug" gained respect in the barrio among these youth for his insistence on not judging but rather mentoring these young adults. During his tenure with St. Catherine of Siena parish church, Father Doug worked closely with gang members and helped them attain their GEDs, secure jobs, and renounce a life of crime. He asked them to take responsibility for their lives, but he understood the depths of poverty, oppression, and violence in which they were immersed. He especially understood *cholos'* and *cholas'* devotions to the Virgin of Guadalupe because "initially she came to a poor Indian peasant, spoke his language and showed her love for him. These young people need love and *la Virgen* has a pretty good track record of showing her love for her Mexican children!"[31]

Working with Cholos, Cholas, and Their Adult Mentors

As an outsider, a non-Latina, nonbarrio resident, and an academic, I would never have had the kind of access I had to these young people if it had not been for the support and encouragement of certain individuals who encouraged my research and who helped me set up interviews and appointments with these young adults. As religious studies ethnographer Susan B. Ridgely has noted in *When I Was a Child*, scholars of religion who work with children and young adults rely heavily on support networks, adult figures, and others who trust us and who relay this trust to the young people in their care.[32] The vulnerability of children and young adults must be safeguarded by their adult caregivers, and we as scholars must be mindful of our reliance on others when we engage in ethnography with children and youth. In my case, I had to meet with Father Doug Nohava, Arturo Weis, Danita Apple-White, and Estela and Reyes Ruiz before I could gain access to gang members in South Phoenix. I had to spend lots of time in the church rectory and social hall as well as other visible, public places where I could be observed and where I could prove myself as trustworthy to these adult figures.[33] Susan B. Ridgely writes in her introduction to this volume that scholars who turn their attention to children and religion "might need to attend to new social environments and the effects of those environments on the religious realm, including environments such as schools—public and private—and the playground."[34]

The words we type at our computers in the safety of our homes can indeed hurt those we study, and I was ever mindful of the power I had over these young adults when I was a guest in their world. I was aware of the moral obligations I had to them, to help safeguard their identities and to not divulge their information to law enforcement officials. I learned to tread lightly and carefully and above all else, be a quiet and careful listener.

I was cognizant of my identity as a double outsider in their lives. I strove to gain their trust by showing my interest in their lives and their experiences. These young men and women have experienced so many disappointments, and I certainly did not want to be yet another one for them. Gangs are attractive to young women and men who have been let down by their families. Like Isabel, Mark left his family home. He shared living space with several other *cholos* and worked odd jobs to help pay the apartment's rent. Mark and his "homie" Jessie spent a lot of time at Estela and Reyes Ruiz's backyard Marian shrine, where they felt "at home." They experienced the warmth of the Ruiz family and in the safe haven of the backyard shrine they prayed to the Virgin of Guadalupe and the Virgin of the Americas, who was appearing to Estela Ruiz throughout the 1990s. Sitting on a bench in the backyard, Mark said softly, "I feel like I can really breathe here, you know, and I know that *la Virgen* is listening to me because this is where she lives." My own ethnographic experiences with young adults confirm that we must meet them on their turf, where they are most comfortable. In the course of my research with *cholas* and *cholos* I met them in restaurants, at youth groups, at community centers, and in a backyard Marian shrine—places they frequented and where they felt comfortable meeting me to talk.

Conclusion

As scholars of religion who want to understand the experiences and voices of youth, what can we learn from *cholos* and *cholas* from Phoenix's south side? What I learned from these young men and women was to suspend any and all white middle-class conceptions of what religion is and what it should be. I gained a deeper appreciation for the intense challenges facing these young people, and I realized my own economic and class privilege. In almost every way, the *cholos* and *cholas* I encountered had had radically different childhoods, and their relative lack of options directly informed the paths they took, whether it was engaging in acts of violence, becoming pregnant at a young age, or selling drugs. As scholars of religion we need to pay closer attention to children's and youth's narratives and the unique contexts of their lives. We must attend to ethnic, cultural, and class peculiarities in the practice of religion. As American youth, *cholos* and *cholas* share in some of the hopes and dreams of mainstream, middle-class youth but are limited by their economic and ethnic status. Neither "mainstream" nor "deviant," these young men and women desire love and acceptance, much as do other youth—even more because they have been so unloved. They have formed a Catholic faith and family, and they want love, acceptance, and guidance. In the end, despite what might be vast differences in class, ethnicity, and family structure and support, *cholos'* and *cholas'* dreams and desires are really not so different from those of mainstream American youth.

By paying close attention to bodily and verbal cues, as well as hanging out with gang members in more casual venues, I learned that rather than being deviant and irreligious, these young women and men harbored a creative and pragmatic spirituality that they carried with them, quite literally, each day. These young women and men craved a connection with the divine. Some looked to the Virgin of Guadalupe for protection and codified their belief by tattooing their bodies, others wore rosaries the color of their gang, and still others saw their gang leader as their "priest." These young women and men, even while they were engaged in a culture that included and even encouraged violence, continued to see themselves as God's children and as Catholics. These youth challenge us as scholars of religion to rethink our methods as well as our definition of religion. *Cholos* and *cholas* blur the "sacred" and "the profane" and create their own category of what religion is and how it can apply to their oftentimes tenuous existence. As scholars, we must engage in and understand the gritty urban realities in which they live.

1. Jonathan Z. Smith explores this pervasive dichotomization of religion as good or bad by religious studies scholars in his essay "The Devil in Mr. Jones," *Imagining Religion: From Babylon to Jonestown* (Chicago: University of Chicago Press, 1988).

2. In Robert Orsi's *Gods of the City*, Orsi as well as the contributing authors write about the peculiarities of urban religion and how the space of cities deeply impacts the faith of their inhabitants. See Robert Orsi, ed., *Gods of the City* (Bloomington: Indiana University Press, 1999).

3. Catherine Bell, *Ritual Theory, Ritual Practice* (Oxford: Oxford University Press, 1992), 5.

4. While I want to empathize with and understand this religious world, and the poverty, violence, and dispossession that go along with it, I do not want to romanticize this world, either. At this time a few of the *cholos* expressed interest in me being their girlfriend, and I had to negotiate those requests and interests as well. I cut my hair short, dressed androgynously, and wore no makeup so as to appear like a boy—or at the very least a nonsexual being. I thank NYU Press editor's Jennifer Hammer, who edited my first book, *The Virgin of El Barrio*, for asking me to write this essay, which prompted me to go back to the richly detailed fieldnotes I had written as a master's student in religious studies.

5. During the time of my fieldwork, newspaper articles on gang violence appeared in the newspapers and on television each day. Socioeconomic factors were rarely discussed and the religious lives of gang members were never mentioned.

6. David Morgan, *Visual Piety: A History and Theory of Popular Religious Ideas* (Berkeley: Unversity of California Press), 206.

7. The folklorist Eric Wolf referred to the Virgin of Guadalupe as the "Mexican National Virgin" in his influential essay "The Virgin of Guadalupe: A Mexican National Symbol," *Journal of American Folklore* 71 (1958): 35-39.

8. D. A. Brading chronicles the competing images of the virgins during Father Miguel Hidalgo's rebellion against Spanish domination. He writes about the "spectacle of Catholic priests using religious symbols for violent, political ends" and notes that this was "not confined to Spain" (230). "In effect, throughout the hispanic world, provincial patriotism still found expression in the invocation of traditional, religious symbols" (230). *Mexican Phoenix: Our Lady of Guadalupe, Image and Tradition across Five Centuries* (New York: Cambridge University Press, 2001).

9. Interview with Isabel, 11/19/92.

10. See Griswold De Castillo, *La Familia: Chicano Families in the Urban Southwest, 1848 to the Present* (Notre Dame, IN: University of Notre Dame Press), 1984, for a good example of this kind of hagiographic history of Mexican American families.

11. Ariel Glucklich, *Sacred Pain: Hurting the Body for the Sake of the Soul* (New York: Oxford University Press, 2001), 101.

12. Interview with Jesse, 2/10/93.

13. Interview with Jesse, 2/10/93; interview with Luisa, 11/5/92.

14. Interview with Mark, 9/20/92.

15. Colleen McDannell, *Material Christianity: Religion and Popular Culture in America* (New Haven, CT: Yale University Press, 1995), 19.

16. Robert Orsi, *Between Heaven and Earth: The Religious Worlds People Make and the Scholars Who Study Them* (Princeton, NJ: Princeton University Press, 2005), 5.

17. Stephen Prothero, *American Jesus: How the Son of God Became a National Icon* (New York: Farrar, Strauss, and Giroux, 2003), 300.

18. Prothero, *American Jesus*, 294.

19. *Cholos'* and *cholas'* experiences with and interpretations of Guadalupe mirror the contributors to *Goddess of the Americas: Writings of the Virgin of Guadalupe*, ed. Ana Castillo (New York: Riverhead Trade Books, 1997). The thirty contributors to this volume emphasize the empowering aspects of Guadalupe, her overlap with the Aztec goddesses Tonantzin and Coatilecue, and her pivotal role in their lives as U.S. Latinos and Latinas. Many of these authors have constructed inventive devotions to Guadalupe, and they interpret her as watching over them and protecting them, much as *cholos* and *cholas* do.

20. See Timothy Matovina, *Guadalupe and Her Faithful: Latino Catholics in San Antonio, from Colonial Origins to the Present* (Baltimore: Johns Hopkins University Press, 2005) and Roberto Treviño, *The Church in the Barrio: Mexican American Ethno-Religion in Houston* (Chapel Hill: University of North Carolina Press, 2006) for two recent studies of Mexican American devotion to the Virgin of Guadalupe.

21. Interview with Isabel, 11/19/92.

22. Ibid.

23. Ibid.

24. Ibid.

25. The fear of HIV- and AIDS-related deaths resulted in a widespread government campaign in and outside of the United States to promote the use of condoms. The safe sex campaign occurred well before the largely evangelical Christian abstinence-only campaigns that began in the late 1990s. See Sara Moslener, "By God's Design? Sexual Abstinence and Evangelicalism in the United States, 1979-Present," Ph.D. dissertation, Claremont Graduate University, 2009.

26. Nancy Reagan's "Just Say No" to drugs campaign was influenced by psychologist Richard Evans's "social innoculation" model, which focused on effective strategies to combat peer pressure. See R. I. Evans, "An Historical Perspective on Effective Prevention," in *Cost-Benefit/Cost-Effectiveness Research on Drug Abuse Prevention: Implications for Programming and Policy,* eds. W. J. Bukoski and R. I. Evans (National Institute on Drug Abuse Research Monograph Series No. 176, NIH Publication no. 98–4021) (Washington, DC: U.S. Government Printing Office, 1998).

27. Michelle Campbell, "Girls in Gangs," *State Press: Arizona State University's Summer Weekly*, August 6, 1992, 7.When we spoke last, Isabel was neither in nor out of the gang; she had decided to try to get a "normal" life but realized that this was difficult because once you are in a gang, you can never truly leave. Neither wanting to return to Thirty-Fifth as a hardcore member nor wanting to live a life without her *cholos* and *cholas*, Isabel struggled to find a place for herself where she felt that she had a purpose and meaning.

28. For an extended look at borderlands theory, particularly as it applies to the fields of history and religious studies, see my forthcoming essay "Borderlands" in *Companion to Religion in America*, ed. Phil Goff (Malden, MA: Blackwell, forthcoming 2011).

29. Interview with Angel, 4/9/93.

30. Interview with Jésus, 2/5/94.

31. Interview with Father Doug Nohava, 11/14/92.

32. Susan Ridgely Bales, *When I Was a Child: Children's Interpretations of First Communion* (Chapel Hill: University of North Carolina Press, 2005), 14.

33. Places where I frequented included St. Catherine of Siena's church rectory, Estela and Reyes Ruiz's backyard Marian shrine, and AppleWhite community center. I attended fundraisers for the church and various community meetings held at the church hall. I also had lunch with *cholos* and *cholas* at Ponchos, a local restaurant.

34. Bales, *When I Was a Child,* 3.

Studying Children in Schools

Going through the Motions of Ritual

Exploring the "as if" Quality of Religious Sociality in Faith-Based Schools

SALLY ANDERSON

It was lunchtime in the teachers' room of a Danish Jewish day school on the last day before Passover recess. At the door, two fourth-grade girls asked politely for their Judaics teacher. "Is it all right if we go home too? The other class has finished and gone home." The students looked hopefully at their teacher, who answered, "No, we're going to stay. We still have the *afikoman*, the blessing, and the songs" (April 2008).

This excerpt comes from field notes taken on the day of the Model Seder. Just two weeks into fieldwork at a Danish Jewish school, I was excited at being allowed to witness this important Jewish observance. My knowledge of Seder proceedings was unfortunately meager, and I had struggled all morning, aided by the teacher, the students, and the Danish translation of the Haggadah, the ritual text, to make sense of this ritual meal performed by two friendship classes, in which children in a younger grade are paired with children in an older grade for various activities. Like the two girls in the hall, I was not sure why we were staying when other classes had chosen to finish the Seder before lunch and go home. Did the students I was observing have to perform the *whole* thing, so I might get a sense of the *real* thing, or did their Judaics teacher want them to experience the entire Seder for their own sakes? What was this about?

This chapter explores the relationship between children and ritual observance in a school setting. Based on ethnographic fieldwork carried out in Danish faith-based private schools, it probes the question of why religious inculcation is important to adults, what adults want children to learn about religion, and how they go about teaching religion to children. It also seeks to understand how children experience and relate to religious practices in school and to each other as "religious" peers. It draws on observations of classes, religious rituals, and holiday observances, as well as interviews with administrators, teachers, and students in a Jewish day school.

A central question is the nature of the relation among children, religion, and society, and how this relation is forged in school settings. I explore this question through an account of a Model Seder jointly celebrated by a fourth-grade and an eighth-grade class on the last day of school before Passover. Based on observation rather than interview, the account positions both children and adults as performative informants (Fabian 1990). Although much recent research privileges verbal articulation as children's authentic perspectives on the worlds in which they live, the analysis here focuses on modalities of engagement with ritual observance to probe the ways in which "children," and more specifically "classmates," are socially and culturally situated performative categories. This approach hones our understanding that children are never "just" children and allows us to explore the relationship between social categories and performative genres. While children are inherently social actors, they are differently positioned and framed as "children" in different settings and situations. When studying children as a social category, then, we must attend to the ways in which the relationality of a setting inflects "children" as a performative category. Even as we carefully construct children as human *beings* rather than human *becomings* (Qvortrup 1994: 4) and as social actors in their own right (James and Prout 1997), it is important to remember that children often live in environments that classify them as somehow different, and distance them from the *real* society of adults. A performative approach allows us to investigate the multilayered liminal framing of school, children, and religious ritual, all of which index "other worlds"—beyond school, beyond the present, and beyond this world.

Incorporation through Ritual and Rehearsal

In a paper on the invisibility of children in anthropological research, anthropologist Jean La Fontaine (1997) asks whether children are really "people." In this vein, we might also ask whether children are really "in society." Adults employ a variety of means to embed children in meaningful cosmologies and form them as full-fledged members of collectivities (Gottlieb 2004). Yet despite ascription at birth, there remains a sense that children must be further drawn, through ritual and rehearsal, into the collectivities into which they were born. In many societies—though not all—childhood practices, experiences, and performances are perceived as preparatory rehearsals for and previews of what children will become when they "step forth . . . from the venues of childhood" (Dyck 2010: 150).

My research into the ways in which religion is taught and articulated in school settings points to questions of how this shapes children's future affiliations, and engages a host of concerned interlocutors: researchers, teachers, school boards, religious heads, and faith-based communities, not to mention concerned governments peering over their shoulders. All are grappling with questions of how faith-based schooling impacts children's identities and affiliations, how religion sets faith-based schools and schoolchildren apart, and how religion is (and should be) articulated in school settings (cf. Glenn 1988, 2003; Judge 2002).

One way to begin to address this last question is to sort out which school activities are framed as "religion" and which as "just school." Yet the answer is never straightforward. Among those who believe God is everywhere, determining where "religion" stops and starts in a school setting may prove a futile exercise. Others have misgivings about whether religious practices in school settings really count as "religion" per se (Stambach 2009). Such misgivings lead us to consider how conceptual frames of "religion" and "school," despite their entwinement, pull in different directions, often held apart by conscious efforts to distinguish pedagogy from preaching (*forkyndelse*) (Petersen 2002, 2007). Such misgivings also lead us to consider what, if anything, counts as *real* in schools. How is religion made *real* in schools, which themselves set children apart from *real life* (*virkeligheden*)? In my work, I have found that schools are often spoken of as once removed from *real life,* as sites of rehearsal for a future life *out in the real world.* I suggest that such cultural assumptions about where the *real* is located and what is *really real* in relation to religion, children, and school impact the way religious observance plays out in school settings. I will return to this after a brief excursion into the history, demography, and educational mission of the Danish Jewish school.

Danish Free Schools

The Danish constitution has from the start (1849) guaranteed freedom of education (*skolefrihed*). By law, all children must receive an education, but they are not required to attend school. This freedom has not led to home schooling, but to a free school movement,[1] championing parents' rights to establish not-for-profit schools. "Free" schools receive (on average) 75 percent of public school subsidies. The state relinquishes its right to specify teacher qualifications and teaching methods as long as free schools teach subjects and produce educational results comparable to those of public schools. These policies allow parent groups with relatively small means to start schools premised on their own educational preferences.

Whereas the earliest free schools (1850s) were established to ensure the religious and pedagogical freedom of an emerging rural middle-class, many free schools established in the twentieth century grew out of alternative philosophical, pedagogical, or political movements. Schools established by religious and ethnic minorities are among the eldest (Jewish) and the most recent (Christian, Muslim) additions to the free school arena. Today's faith-based free schools strive to affiliate children with both Danish society and particular religious communities. Teaching religious cosmologies, core cultural practices, and the socio-spatiality of being Jewish, Christian, or Muslim, faith-based schools aim to produce particular kinds of "educated persons" (Levinson and Holland 1996) and incorporate children into particular local, national, and transnational spheres of faith-based belonging.

The Danish Jewish School

Dating back to the 1600s, the Jewish enclave in Denmark was long a parallel society that took care of its own religious and economic affairs (Buckser 1999: 193). Upon receiving rights of citizenship and access to trade guilds in the early 1800s, Jewish leaders established two schools, one for boys (1805) and one for girls (1810). Governed now by the free school law, the present Jewish school is a private, coeducational day school (grades K-9) enrolling approximately two hundred students. Located in an unassuming renovated factory on the outskirts of Copenhagen, it is one of the top schools in Denmark.

During my fieldwork, teachers often related the ironic story of the school's past and present mission. Founded to educate poor Jewish children and integrate children of Jewish immigrants into Danish society, the school's present mission is to integrate the children of well-assimilated and often out-married Jews into Jewish society. The school aspires to facilitate a Jewish identity by conveying knowledge and understanding of Jewish religion, culture, and tradition, the history of the Jewish people and modern Israel, and Hebrew as a living language, as well as the basis of original texts and religious services. Together with families and the Jewish Community, the school aims to generate a desire for an active Jewish life. In keeping with this mission, the school teaches Hebrew and Judaics, provides kosher meals, teaches the ritual, prayers, and songs of Shabbat, observes all Jewish holidays, celebrates Israel's birthday, and invites elder members of the community to speak of their experiences during World War II. Through such activities, the school endeavors to forge strong links to Jewish society, while teaching—and striving to practice—tolerance for the myriad ways in which local families choose to affiliate themselves with the Jewish societies of Denmark, the diaspora, and Israel.

Diversity and Distinction

The Jewish population in Denmark is small, numbering about seven thousand, yet "in their understandings of what Jewishness is, and its place in everyday behavior, the Danish Jews encompass virtually every point in the Jewish ideological spectrum" (Buckser 2003: 8-9, n. 239). Approximately twenty-four hundred are members of the organized Jewish Community of Denmark, and about 150 of these send their children to the community's school, the only Jewish school in Denmark. The school is obligated to accept all children whose parents are paying members of the community.

While founded on orthodox principles, the organized Jewish Community describes itself as pluralistic. Over the last decades, it has become more inclusive, open to Jews who, regardless of background or nationality, wish to be part of the community.[2] Struggles over access to membership in the organized Jewish Community impact the school. Striving to accommodate children from all corners of the community, the school presently accepts children from Orthodox, Lubavitch, mainstream, cultural, and secular Jewish families, as well as children of mixed-faith parentage. Administrators, school board members, and teachers have met regularly in recent years to develop the school's Jewish vision. Their goal has been to iron out and deflect conflicts over the intent, content, and scheduling of Judaics and Hebrew, and to forge a school acceptable to all Jews who wish to enroll their children. The school's tolerant stance in the face of diverse claims is not just ideological. With its existence hinging on student enrollment, these new pluralistic policies are necessary survival tactics.

Children attending the Jewish school represent the entire spectrum of local Jewish distinctions. When asked about family background and religious practice, children commonly described their families in relation to these distinctions. One boy noted that the main synagogue was not orthodox enough for his family: "We go to the little synagogue, because the big one isn't religious enough; they don't do things right." Another told how his family shied away from the main synagogue: "We never go to the synagogue—the people there are all snobs." Another told of how his immigrant mother used the family's connection to the school to gain social access to Jewish society: "My parents put me in this school to try to get closer to the Jewish community." A girl whose mother chose the school to access a "good education" explained at Rosh Hashanah: "We don't do any of this holiday stuff at home."

Children were aware of how their families positioned themselves, and were positioned by others, within the local set of available distinctions. Children were also aware of family members' varying degrees of religiosity, candidly noting, "My father is very religious, but my mother isn't"; "I'm trying to keep kosher, but my parents don't"; or "My grandmother is religious, so we hold Shabbat at her house." My young informants were also conscious of religious differences based on countries of origin—Yemen, Poland, Russia, India, or Argentina—and where their relatives resided. Statements such as "Grandma lives in Florida" and "Dad's brother's in England—that's London, not Manchester" indicated affiliation with particular kinds of Jewish communities in other countries.

All of this suggests that to know any particular individual in this environment requires insider knowledge of family background, religious practice and affiliation, place of origin and residence, internal family differences, and, on the whole, which distinctions are relevant in which contexts. Yet it is important to note that religious differences were not the only relevant differences. As in most schools, differentiation based on age, gender, socioeconomic status, grade level, academic and athletic ability, behavior, appearance, popularity, and choices of clothing, music, and media was also relevant. The Jewish students knew who had the best grades, the latest electronic gadgets, the greatest number of tunes, the most text messages, and the coolest vacations. In sum, this small school with its fragmented Jewish identity field was held together by a common set of measures and assumptions about children, students, and the many ways of being Jewish made relevant there.

Enclave, Refuge, and Incubator

The anecdote of the Jewish school's inverted educational mission sheds light on the conceptual whereabouts of "society" in relation to schoolchildren. Teaching immigrants enough Danish, reading, and writing to integrate them into "Danish society," and teaching assimilated Jews enough Judaism and Jewish heritage to integrate them into "Jewish society" both index the assumption that "society" and "school" are somehow separate, and that for children, "society" is accessible only through years of schooling. I suggest that this semantic logic reflects assumptions about social order that impact the relational orders and performative modalities of school settings.

With reference to "Danish society," the Jewish school was often likened to an *enclave*. Teachers spoke deprecatingly of the school as villagelike with its interrelatedness, gossip, and conflicts. They characterized it as a somewhat claustrophobic place, from which, after nine years, pupils could not wait to escape. Older students spoke excitedly about "getting out" and going to other schools where they would be with "all kinds of people." First graders knew about "those kinds of schools where *all* children go," and one fourth-grade girl assured me that she often went "out among Danes." Although obviously not blind to the fact that they lived in Denmark, adults and children alike spoke as if "Danish society" were beyond the fence that enclosed school grounds. Everyone else, "all children" and "all kinds of people," were "out among Danes." Children attending the Jewish school were, semantically speaking, not in that open space of universal "Danish" sociation except perhaps after school, on weekends, and upon graduation.

The vice-principal characterized the school enclave positively, as a small, sheltered (*tryg*) setting where no one was anonymous, where everyone knew each other. Invoking the image of a *refuge*, she argued that this sheltered quality allowed children to "test themselves," to "dare to try things," and to "take stock of their own origins and foundations as human beings and as Jews." The vice-principal felt it was important for the children to develop their own standpoint because everyone knew that "when they get out of here, they risk meeting all those who are not fond of Jews." Teachers and students also spoke of the school as a refuge in the sense of a place where it was safe and normal to be Jewish, where Jewish children did not feel different or feel they had to constantly defend themselves as Jews. Older students saw this in contrast to secondary schools with many Muslims, or school where "teachers have negative attitudes towards Jews." They also saw this in contrast to public transportation, where some had experienced verbal or physical abuse, and to the street, where not all (boys) felt safe wearing *kippahs* or football jerseys sporting the Star of David.

Teachers also likened the school to an *incubator*, a protected space for developing a sense of oneself as a Jew. As one teacher explained, "these kids are Jews. They'll need to be able to hold their own out in society. It's not become any easier to be a Jew in Denmark, and they'll run into discussions out in society. They need to know a lot about themselves, and to have the courage to join in the debate." As both refuge and incubator, then, the school provided a sheltered space for developing a Jewish identity that might withstand the weight of difference and opposition, and allow children to add their voices to society "out there." The school's new mission statement revealed that a Jewish education is about religious and cultural knowledge, history, self-knowledge, identity, loyalty, and community participation. In striving to accommodate the differences threatening to dismantle local Jewish institutions, this particular minority school struggled to maintain a strong focus on Jewish life without closing the circle to newcomers or turning away from Danish society at large.

Teaching Religion in a Plural Fashion

Faith-based schools are not necessarily the one-eyed sectarian enclaves critics expect, even though students, as here, have the same religious and cultural background. Even when students to some extent share a religious background, schools find themselves embracing a wide range and degree of observance. This inevitably shapes the way teachers teach religion as well as the way children engage in religious events and rituals in school settings. A brief excerpt from a first-grade Judaics lesson serves to illustrate how a teacher attempts to make room for believers and nonbelievers alike.

> TEACHER: We're going to talk about Shabbat today. We do something like Shabbat in class on Fridays, but there's more to Shabbat than that. Some of you know something about this, others don't know as much. Some of you do this at home. But who can tell me why we hold Shabbat?
>
> BENJAMIN: HaShem was finished creating the earth.
>
> TEACHER: Then what happened?
>
> JAKOB: He had to rest.
>
> TEACHER: The people should also rest. He wanted to give the people a present. That's if you believe in God. Not all believe in God. It's something you know in your heart. But do we believe in a God that gets tired? Don't worry, there's no right or wrong answer here.
>
> NATHAN: Yes, it was hard work.
>
> ADAM: No, God's not tired because he has to help if you need him.
>
> TEACHER: That's right, if we believe in such a one. God doesn't just shut the door to his office and tell you to come back on Monday.
>
> EMMA: It's morning in other countries when it's night here. If God has to be there all the time, he can't be resting.
>
> TEACHER: Does God need food, rest, and sleep?
>
> SOME: Yes.
>
> OTHERS: No, God doesn't eat.
>
> BENJAMIN: But, we sacrificed animals to God.

TEACHER: Yes, but does God rest on the seventh day? Everybody needs a break. But is the break for God or for us?

CHILDREN (*shouting*): For us!

TEACHER: That's right, for God is never tired. We need a break, and Shabbat is God's gift to us. (May 2008)

Throughout this dialogue, the teacher invokes a collective we—"*we* believe," "gift for *us*," "*we* need a break." At the same time, she makes it clear that not everyone believes in God; believing is a personal choice, a choice of the heart. Which children in this class might "believe" and which might not remains implicit until the teacher asks them to "draw what you do on your day of rest." When Nathan asks, "But what if we don't hold Shabbat?" the teacher answers, "Draw what you do on your own Shabbat—your own day of rest."[3]

Walking around the room, I noted drawings of watching TV, riding horses, going to the synagogue, lighting Shabbat candles, skipping rope, playing with Lego blocks, playing computer games, playing football, and making scrambled eggs. At the bulletin board, taking down drawings of Moses in the desert to make room for the new drawings of Shabbat, the teacher quietly informed me,

> The children at this school come from all kinds of families. It's important to tell the children about Jewish traditions, but also to make room for everybody. There's a whole book of rules about how to hold Shabbat in the proper way. A whole book with lots of rules! And I can tell you that the really religious wouldn't be happy with the pictures these children have drawn. Synagogue, family dinners, walks in the woods with family are OK on Shabbat, but not TV, football, and computer games!

The excerpts show how the teacher firms up a collective Jewish affiliation— the *we* who have been given Shabbat—while concurrently highlighting the possibility of observing this day of rest in different ways and acknowledging (in a quiet aside) that not all would approve. The teacher's focus on making room for everyone by making sure that none of the children feels that what he or she does at home is wrong here trumps "the book of rules."

The teacher's approach is most likely tempered by respect for the families whose children she is teaching. Yet not all dilemmas of connecting children to religion in school settings are explicable in terms of respect for disparate religious observance. This teacher's approach may also be attributed to pedagogical ideals of respecting children as individuals and stimulating their feelings of self-worth, as well as to the importance Danish teachers attach to establishing an inclusive atmosphere in classes that remain together for all nine years of schooling (Anderson 2000, 2003). Thus it appears that when religious orthodoxy meets pedagogical orthodoxy, the latter prevails. The drawing exercise leads the teacher to focus on *personal* ways of observing Shabbat, in order to maintain an inclusive class atmosphere. While clearly compromising and challenging any semblance of religious orthodoxy, this inclusivity allows children to develop the insight that there are many ways of being Jewish and perhaps even of being religious. Although it is important to understand how the age-grade organization of schools and pedagogical truths might order and influence religious observance, it is still difficult ethnographically to isolate "religion" from "school" in a school setting. I hope to make this difficulty clear in the following account of a Model Seder.

The Model Seder

The Model Seder I observed was a joint affair between a fourth- and an eighth-grade class. It also included several sixth graders, who on the previous day had thoroughly cleaned the classroom to rid it of *chametz* (crumbs of leavened bread), and then set the tables with white tablecloths, floral napkins, and spring flowers. The same sixth graders arrived early on the day to prepare place settings with *matzoh*, salt water and Seder plates of egg, lettuce, a radish, a sprig of parsley, a pinch of fresh horseradish, and a spoonful of *charoset*, a mixture of chopped fruits, nuts, and red wine, "that brown stuff" meant to recall the mortar used by the Israelites to bond bricks when they were slaves in Egypt. There was also juice and a plastic shot glass for wine. Each child had a bound copy of the Haggadah, with ritual texts in both Hebrew and Danish.

We were seated in the fourth-grade classroom, approximately 30-35 students at two long tables, the large fourth grade along one table and the smaller eighth grade at the other. The Seder mother and father, chosen among fourth graders, said the proper blessings, heavily prompted by the teacher. Then students came to the front, one after the other, to read their assigned portions of the Haggadah. After each reading, the teacher explained the text and asked questions. At the proper times, the attending sixth graders poured the Seder wine. Students sang the more rhythmic songs, like "Dayenu," with gusto, and mumbled their way through others. Although this was an abridged version of the Seder, things moved slowly, and we had to reassemble after lunch for the final parts of the story.

There is no space here for the many details of this school version of the Passover Seder. What I want to convey, however, is the modality of the students' participation. As Susan B. Ridgely (2005) observed in Catholic faith formation classes, there were many involuntary and reluctant participants here. A group of first-grade boys saw the playground bonfire to ritually rid the school of leavened bread as an excellent opportunity to continue their recess role play. Teachers had just barely run down the last of these escapees when the rabbi launched a short prayer. Those standing around the fire talked so loudly it was difficult to hear his words. Later, upon leaving the teachers' room to act as Seder moderators, teachers joked that their *real* role here was that of police ("Nu skal vi ned og lege politi."). A number of students—including some who had been selected to read parts of the Haggadah—had simply chosen to stay home.

Once the ritual started, it was apparent that few children had practiced reading their parts. As they stumbled over words, the ritual plodded along to a constant undertone of student chatter and teacher "shhhs". Many eighth graders distanced themselves from the ritual proceedings, smirking, fooling around, and singing off-key and against rhythm. Most fourth graders appeared bored unless it was their turn to read. The constant undercurrent of chatter, laughter, and scuffling made it difficult to hear students reading their assigned parts, or the teacher reading parts assigned to absent students. Most sang selectively—some songs, certain verses and lines—while others refused to sing at all. The result was a disjointed, half-mumbled drone beneath the teacher's solo, except for toward the end, when some of the rhythmic choruses were enthusiastically rendered in mocking falsetto by eighth graders who were working on finishing off the Seder wine. At one point, a girl sitting near me, who was entertaining herself by dripping patterns on her napkin with salt-water "tears," sighed deeply, "Thank God we don't have to do this at home! Thank God!" Had I recorded this Seder, a listener would hear a constant undertone, or perhaps overtone, of chatter and shushing, a subtextual soundscape that lent the ritual much distance, irony, and an ambivalent sense of mattering and not mattering. The students' ambivalent displays of disorder and self-restraint were incessant, yet well-orchestrated, never too much, right on the edge, but never over.

Coming to this fieldwork with childhood recollections of religious sociality in New England Protestant churches, I was ill prepared to interpret this Model Seder, my first Seder. Expecting a certain measure of solemnity, I found spoofing. Expecting some measure of unison, I found dissonance. Expecting some semblance of familiarity and identification, I found selective and furtive engagement as well as disinterest and resignation. Watching the Model Seder unfold in shifting modalities of fun, boredom, reluctance, obligation, and ironic engagement, I was not sure which framing might help me understand my performative informants. Was this ambivalent and mocking modality the students' response to Judaism, to religion in general, or to religion in school? Did this ritual modality index a generic student or age-grade sociality, or perhaps the many years of anti-authoritarian reform pedagogy in this progressive urban free school?

My effort to understand the multilayered framing of this event on the basis of ethnographic observation points to general problems of interpretation—for researchers and laypersons alike. While it is often quite easy to discern a dominant frame, such as "lesson" or "ritual," it is more difficult to grasp the myriad of concurrent subframes that impinge on and inflect a dominant frame. Such subframes do not necessarily fall into the simple dualisms of "adults'" and "children's," or "teachers'" and "students'" perspectives. Understanding ritual modalities requires more fine-grained analyses of the multitude of perspectives made relevant to the ritual performance.

As argued above, depending on the setting, children are not just children, nor are adults just adults. They are variously positioned in relation to each other as siblings, parents, second cousins, aunts, classmates, teachers, antagonists, friends, neighbors, and fellow parishioners, to name just a few relationships. Jean la Fontaine (1997) urges us to include both children and adults in our analyses, warning that studying children as a distinct category of individual risks just confirming Western perceptions of children. From an anthropological perspective, it is important to investigate rather than unwittingly reiterate cultural assumptions about children's separateness and about intergenerational relations as discontinuous (Olwig 2000). Thus, in analyzing "children's perspectives," it is important to look beyond crude dualities of adults and children to the plurality of performative categories made relevant in settings under study.

Placing the Real

We have seen how colloquial ways of speaking about the location of "the real" set children and school semantically apart from the *real* life taking place "out in society." Cultural understandings of both children and school as once removed from society (*samfund*) and reality (*virkelighed*) lend a liminal, "as if" quality to much school practice. School becomes a place for *modeling* the real world in rehearsal of future participation and affiliation, and children's lives are cast in a present-as-future tense, where what they do previews things to come. I suggest that this normative nonreal quality of both children and school rubs off on religion. Based on cultural assumption that *real* rituals are performed elsewhere with other sets of practitioners, religious practice become less than real in school settings.

Unlike me, the students I observed had experienced other Seders, either in school or at home. Although I have since learned that any singular, standard version of the Seder exists only as an ideal (cf. Cernea 1995), students were aware that, like the Shabbat performed in the lower grades on Fridays, this Seder was not a *real* version. *Real* Seders do not take place in school, among classmates from different grades, with eleven-year-olds presiding as Seder mother and father and class teachers struggling to keep order. As with other school versions of rituals belonging to venues and hospitalities beyond the school, the "as if" quality of the Model Seder—with no real host or hostess, or invited gathering of family and friends—may have rendered it relationally and performatively less imperative.

The once-removed framing of school, children, and (school) religion affords one explanation of the students' going-through-the-motions approach to the Model Seder, for to whom did the Model Seder *really* matter on the last day of school before spring recess? Observation suggests that sixth graders took their duties as table setters and wine pourers quite seriously. The Model Seder also appeared to matter to the Judaics teacher who made a conscientious effort to explain the Seder to those she knew did not celebrate Passover. Having a small ritual part seemed to matter to some students, though not to all. Moreover, participation mattered to students, such as the rabbi's grandson, whose self-conscious engagement distanced him from his more playful classmates.

Despite cultural assumptions and semantic conventions of placing the *real* somewhere beyond children, school, and religion, all are, of course, aware that daily school life is exceedingly *real*. Indeed, the very reality of school-based sociality may play a strong hand in the way children and teachers engage ritual. For example, any event, including religious ritual, held just before a school holiday has to contend with the more relaxed and anticipatory atmosphere of such days, perhaps particularly in Denmark, where everyone knows that the last day of work or school before a holiday need not be taken seriously. With regard to pedagogy, we have seen how the pedagogical orthodoxy of social inclusion coopts the religious orthodoxy of Shabbat. Moreover, the resistive license with which most eighth graders approached the Model Seder may be explained by their being forced to hold Seder with fourth graders, a lower grade of student in the school's age-based hierarchy. Finally, as I discovered in interviews, students were often shy about revealing their own religious inclination among classmates whose inclination and affiliation might vary from their own. In this pluralistic setting, then, students might prefer the ironic distance provided by fooling with classmates in order to avoid sticking out as the only ones seriously engaged in the unfolding ritual.

Despite the liminal, "as if" aspects of both school and children, the excruciating reality of school social life—its temporality, generationality, inclusive pedagogy, age hierarchy, and social grouping—may strongly influence the way students and teachers engage with ritual. Although schools may be understood as once removed from *real life*, the *real life* of schools compellingly coopts any models of society rehearsed in school settings.

Ritual Levity and Ritual Appropriation

Positing that school organization and relationality trumps ritual performativity in school settings may explain the students' and teachers' going-through-the-motions approach to the Model Seder, but it provides a less adequate explanation for the fooling, mocking, and embellishing that I observed. Nor do I find satisfactory the intuitive inclination to refer students' penchant for fun making to children's natural affinity for play, to boredom, or to inevitable prevacation rambunctiousness. We conclude therefore with a brief discussion of ritual levity.

Religious studies scholars Selva Raj and Corinne Dempsey (2010) call attention to the way scholars of religion have traditionally overlooked playfulness as an integral aspect of ritual.

> While the Western academy's focus on Christianity might have contributed in some measure to the current lack of interest in the study of religious levity, it is also due—at least in part—to the general tendency among scholars and nonspecialists alike to view ludic expressions and behaviors as no more than superficial and marginal aspects of human life, incongruent with the seriousness and solemnity normally associated with religion. (Raj and Dempsey 2010: 2)

Given cultural assumptions about the natural affinity of children and play, it is no surprise that Ridgely finds that ritual scholars also tend to overlook children in their focus on "the actions and interpretations of well-practiced ritual participants" (2005: 174).[4] The scholarly penchant for studying prototypical actors in their authentic sites[5] seems to marginalize both ludic expression and childlike actors in serious ritual analysis, despite anthropological claims that ritual liminality is "particularly conducive to play" (Turner 1982: 85) and insistence that it makes no sense to dismiss children, as "their ideas are grounded in their experience and thus are equally valid" (Toren 1993: 463).

Raj and Dempsey define ritual levity as both lighthearted and serious, including an array of moods, attitudes, and expressions such as "mocking, clowning, play, parody, imitation, jest, laughter, fun, role reversal and competition" (Raj and Dempsey 2010: 3). This describes well the attitudes and expressions students displayed at the Model Seder. Contrary to my interpretation of such ludic expression as resistive license or embellishment, Raj and Dempsey argue that it is an integral part of any ritual. Building on anthropologist Victor Turner's concept of liminality (1967), and theologian Tom Driver's assertion that no matter how playful or foolish ritual liminality may be, "there is substance to it" (1998), Raj and Dempsey conclude that levity is "neither an anomaly nor aberration but an essential, intrinsic part of ritual that serves multiple—both tangible and intangible—functions" (2010: 5). Ritual levity provides relief, however brief, from social conventions, casts doubt on hierarchic order, and challenges established orders both earthly and cosmic (ibid., 5-6). Yet by playing *in opposition to* and, thus, *up to* these conventions and orders, ritual levity also serves to reinforce and restore them.

Anthropologist Eric Gable makes this point in his analysis of religious skepticism among Manjaco youth, who despite their pervasive derisive, mocking mimicry of the elders' religious practices and beliefs, continue to participate in community ceremony and ritual (2002: 41-42). Doubtless informed by intergenerational antagonism, a modality common in many societies, the self-consciously playful skepticism of youthful mimicry serves, as Gable argues, both to parody and to appropriate ritual and belief (ibid.: 51, 54). Even when mocking and mimicking a ritual, the young are appropriating it, because in order to produce a play on genre, young people must have a basic knowledge and understanding of the ritual they are parodying. Thus, when interpreting children's engagement with ritual in school and other settings, we must not jump too readily to intuitive, normative conclusions about the relationship between displays of reluctance, fun making, parody, and resignation and children's appropriation of and commitment to the ritual at hand.

Whether students chose to join in the Seder fun or resign themselves to boredom, I am convinced they were appropriating some basic tenets of Judaism. Certainly even a boisterous and mocking rendition of all fifteen verses of "Dayenu" conveys a basic appreciation of HaShem's overwhelming gifts to the Jewish people. Most students also appropriated the laid-back posture associated in the Haggadah with being free men. Moreover, in having to return after lunch "to do the *afikomen* and the blessing," students surely gained some sense of the importance of the Seder's narrative chronology.

Yet as anthropologists David Berliner and Ramon Sarro (2007) argue, there is more to learning religion than acquiring content. It also entails appropriating the contexts, relations, emotions, and attitudes associated with ritual. With regard to context, the students' going-through-the-motions approach to the Model Seder may be inflected by their firm grasp of the relational and social conventions of the school setting. It may also indicate a clear grasp of ritual context, of the where, when, and with whom a Seder should be held, if at all. Finally, it may point to a firm understanding that "what is interesting about religion" (Stafford 2007) does not take place in school, where classmates avoid displaying earnest engagement with blessings, songs, and ritual texts in the copresence of diversely Jewish and equally self-conscious age mates. In brief, school may be seen as the wrong context and classmates as the wrong relations for *real* Seders. This raises a question of how "wrong" or nonprototypical and unconventional contexts and relations might impact ritual attitudes and modalities. Might the students' multiple postures of guarded interest, semicompliance, genre exaggeration, cool distance, and forthright mockery that constantly threatened to turn the Model Seder into a Mocked Seder be an example of the way ambiguous relations and ambivalent contexts lead to ritual levity?

According to Raj and Dempsey, the very "plurality of significations and inherent elasticity" of ritual levity make it difficult to pin down (2010: 3). In ritual played out in school settings, this protean quality of ritual levity is greatly augmented by the multilayered liminality of schools. Driver notes that "what distinguishes performance in the ritual mode from other kinds of events is that the *performer assumes roles and relates to what is going on in an 'as if' way not appropriate to the workaday world* (1998: 98, cited in Raj and Dempsey 2010: 5, italics mine). Yet, as I have attempted to show, in any school setting, there are many "*as if*" *ways* and multiple *workaday worlds*. First, children often find themselves in "as if" modes, particularly in educational settings where they are expected to rehearse and model the real world. Second, although schools have their own workaday worlds, what goes on in schools is often referred to as a once-removed, "as if" version of the *real* workaday world. Bringing otherworldly religion into the double-up liminality of children and school adds another coating of "*as if*"*-ness*, including the "as if" mode of ritual performance. Ritual levity, with its own "as if" take on the "as if" performativity of ritual, adds yet another reflexive layer. If, as Turner posits, "liminality is conducive to play," we can begin to glimpse, in this multi-inflected liminal setting, the vast contours of a veritable playground of intersecting symbols and significations, appropriate and inappropriate contexts, roles and relations on which students (and teachers) may draw in the artful work of ritual play.

Concluding Remarks

This chapter has explored the multifaceted relationship between children and model ritual observance in a Danish Jewish school. The analysis of the Model Seder illuminates the shortcomings of interpretations that uncritically refer to certain performative modalities—going through the motions and ritual levity—to the natural proclivity of children to play or students to resist teacher authority. It underscores the need to attend to the culturally constructed liminality of children, school, religion, and ritual—and perhaps even being Jewish—at play and at stake in this school setting. Ritual levity may indeed be a way of forging a semblance of commonality across the multiple liminal modes and diverse Jewish distinctions intrinsic to this setting. And, lest we forget, children *do* take cues from adult performativity. Engaging in the Passover Seder with a good portion of irony and fun making may very well be a culturally transmitted, acquired convention of being and doing "as if" Jewish.

To conclude, it is important not to assume from the outset that we know the nature of "children," "religion," and "school" or the relationship among them. We must pay close attention to the conceptual, organizational, and historical frameworks in which they are embedded, to modalities of expression and overlapping relational frameworks. In this chapter, we have seen how the performative categories of "children," "religion," and "school" bend to the context of a small Jewish free school complying with norms of Danish school organization and pedagogy and serving the reproductive needs of a small yet diverse Jewish community. We have also seen how conceptualizing children and school as once removed from the *real* world, coupled with educational aims to teach religion through model ritual, acutely complicate the "as if"-ness of performance in the ritual mode (Raj and Dempsey 2010). With Gable (2002), we may argue that even when improvising reluctant and mocking modalities of engagement, children appropriate both ritual content and context. Further study should investigate what children appropriate about the *workaday worlds* of school, religion, and society when engaging with religious ritual in school settings. In performing model rituals in school, children are expected to take on roles and relate to what is going on in "as if" ways appropriate to the *real "as if" way* of ritual marked by its own inappropriateness to the workaday world. Surely learning to navigate this complex world of mirrors teaches children something about appropriate contexts, roles, and ways of relating intrinsic to the workaday worlds of school, religion, and even society.

NOTES

1. The free school movement of the 1850s was inspired by the popular teachings of the Danish priest N. F. S. Grundtvig (1783-1872) and further developed by Christen Kold (1816-1870).

2. From the website of Det Mosaike Troessamfund (The Jewish Community), http://www.mosaiske.dk/index.php?option=com_content&view=article&id=46&Itemid=34, retrieved April 5, 2010.

3. Here, the teacher recasts the collective ritual, Shabbat, not held by all, as a collective day of rest that all hold.

4. An exception is Christina Toren's excellent work on children and ritual in Fiji (Toren 2004, 2006).

5. I have argued elsewhere that, in studying social categories designated by peoplehood (the Nuer), age (children), gender (women), or profession (doctors), we often focus on prototypical informants in categorically authentic sites. In Denmark, this inevitably leads to studying children in schools and institutions and ministers and priests in churches (Anderson 2003).

10

Catholic Children's Experiences of Scripture and the Sacrament of Reconciliation through Catechesis of the Good Shepherd

JENNIFER BESTE

Joining a growing number of childhood studies scholars who advocate child-centered research, I was interested in exploring how Catholic children encounter and respond to scripture and its impact on their relationship with God. I decided to focus on a particular faith formation program called Catechesis of the Good Shepherd (CGS) because it views its programs and its theological content as completely child centered. From February to May 2007, I observed six-to-nine-year-olds at a Catholic Montessori school during their weekly two-hour class. I must admit that my own interest in conducting child-centered research with CGS children stemmed in part from a sense of incredulity as I read the works of Sofia Cavalletti, the founder of CGS. I skeptically wondered whether Cavalletti's and other catechists' reflections on children were based broadly on their experiences of all children in their atrium or represented the select few who were spiritually precocious for their age. I felt that the only way to truly access children's perspectives in CGS atria was to engage in child-centered research and choose a variety of ethnographic methods. For four months, I observed children in the six-to-nine-year-old atrium, and took notes on the children's class discussions and individualized choices of work. Then, I interviewed those second graders who volunteered to talk to me and signed an assent form about their first Reconciliation. After asking them what the Sacrament of Reconciliation was like, I asked followup questions about second graders' understanding of the sacrament, its effects on them, and reasons why they received the sacrament.

In this chapter, we first explore assumptions about the religious potential of children that underlie CGS. Next, we examine how children from age three to age nine encounter and respond to scripture through this method. I also find it helpful to contrast the CGS method of relating to scripture with the traditional Catholic religious (TCR) educational method that relies on a textbook with scripture stories. For this, I will draw on my field research observing four TCR classes from December 2006 to March 2007 as they prepared for Reconciliation. Third, I will attempt to gauge the impact of this catechesis on children's spiritual and moral development. I will focus especially on comparing CGS and TCR students' interviews of their experiences of Reconciliation. Finally, I will reflect on what I have learned from conducting this child-centered research and how such insights may assist other religious scholars as they design their child-centered projects.

History and Method of Catechesis of the Good Shepherd

In 1954, when Hebrew scripture scholar Sofia Cavalletti agreed to teach a friend's son and other children about scripture, she was immediately struck by her young students' keen interest. Inspired by their joy and curiosity about scripture, Cavalletti combined her biblical expertise with leading Montessori educator Gianna Gobbi's grounding in Montessori education to create a faith formation program. Eventually named "Catechesis of the Good Shepherd," the program's aim is to provide children with the opportunity to engage scriptural passages on their own terms and learn to participate meaningfully in the liturgical life of the Catholic Church. Begun in Catholic parishes in Italy, CGS has spread around the world and is used in many Christian denominations.

In her work *The Religious Potential of the Child*, Cavalletti argues that young children from the ages of three to five possess a deep spiritual hunger to know and relate to God, but need guidance from adults and the Holy Spirit to nurture their relationship with God: "Anecdotal evidence from children . . . reveal[s] to catechists that God and the child have a unique relationship, particularly before the age of six."[1] Her years of experience reading scripture and praying with children have convinced her that faith formation should begin at age three because it fulfills a deep spiritual need that facilitates children's holistic development as healthy, well-integrated persons.[2] This also represents a crucial age, argues Cavaletti, because young children have a unique capacity to enjoy and trust in God's loving presence with their whole being, an ability that becomes more complicated as children grow more aware of moral issues and perceptions about God's judgment. CGS focuses on providing children the sacred space to "fall in love with God" and "enjoy God's presence in their lives with deep awareness and great wonder."[3] The basic idea underlying CGS philosophy is to "foster the child's natural inclination to live in relationship to God, rather than creating a mold in which to force the child's soul."[4] To enact this philosophy, faith formation takes place in a specially prepared room called an atrium filled with child-sized, hands-on Montessori materials intended to encourage children to enter into a meditative and prayerful space in which they learn how to deepen their relationship with God.

The task of the catechist is not to teach but rather to serve children by reading scriptural passages and wondering with the children about the meaning of texts.[5] The underlying belief is that children possess an "Inner Teacher"—the Holy Spirit—who guides them in their work as they deepen their relationship with the divine. Consequently, catechists self-consciously attempt to refrain from imposing their own views about the meaning of the text when discussing scriptural passages with children; with few exceptions, they limit themselves to asking questions and guiding group discussion.

Cavalletti's commitment to nonintervention is also manifest in her insistence that the integrity of the scriptural text be respected and that it is essential for children to encounter texts precisely as they are in the Bible rather than be given simplified versions of texts found in children's Bibles: "God's Word has many aspects and resounds in each person in a unique way: if we limit ourselves to giving the child one or two verses of our choice, . . . we intervene unduly between the text and the child, imposing on the child *our* experience with the text, *our* way of listening to it."[6] When constructing and modifying the curriculum, Cavalletti and Gobbi selected those passages to which children consistently responded with enthusiasm, wonder, and joy.

In a postmodern context, where the very term "the child" and "childhood" is being deconstructed and the significance of social location is emphasized, GCS's claim that children cross-culturally share similar religious needs and respond to the same core themes of scripture will be met with skepticism by many childhood studies scholars. To attain a more accurate understanding of children's religious needs, it would be helpful for CGS catechists to document in greater detail their process of trial and error when introducing themes and materials to children throughout the world. Are children's religious needs static throughout history or do they vary, given an individual child's historical and social location? Are there not *any* relevant differences in children's experiences of God in atria throughout the world? How do racism, sexism, classism, and social location affect children's spiritual experiences in atria globally?

Comparing CGS's and "Traditional" Religion Classes' Method of Encountering Scripture

When comparing my ethnographic field notes of CGS classes held in the atria with my observations of four TCR religion classes that followed a more common method of relying on a textbook, it was clear that the CGS and TCR classes were drawing on very different models of childhood development and approaches to how children should encounter scripture. Rejecting the idea of textbook because it dilutes and simplifies scripture and reflects adult views of the Christian message, CGS aims to "try to put the child in touch with those 'sources' through which God reveals and communicates Himself in living form; namely, the Bible and Liturgy, in balanced proportion."[7] Putting children in touch with the direct source enables them to appropriate the meaning of God's word on their own terms. When I pressed Mr. Butler, the CGS catechist, about this issue, he elaborated: "If you reduce a sacramental mystery to a series of questions/answers on a workbook page, you have bled the soul out of it. The method most suitable to the mystery it seeks to convey is the method of Jesus himself—the parable method."[8]

The model of childhood development undergirding CGS curriculum, then, emphasizes children's own agency; children are the ones to demonstrate when they are developmentally ready to learn certain materials and concepts through their interest in the work stations. It is the task of educators to be aware of children's sensitive periods in which they can learn concepts most easily and to expose children to these materials at developmentally appropriate times.

In contrast, the TCR teachers I observed focused their lessons directly on textbook chapters and actively sought to educate children about religious concepts and doctrine. Many of these textbooks were developed on the basis of the developmental theories of Piaget, Erickson, and others whom directors of religious education had read as part of their own training. When I asked several catechetical directors what view of the child underlies Catholic religious education, some mentioned (not uncritically) a common assumption of children being blank slates: many adults assume it is the responsibility of the Catholic Church and religious educators to fill children with knowledge about Catholic teachings and form them in their faith by participating in the church's liturgical and sacramental life.[9] Emphasizing the teacher's role in disseminating knowledge does not imply, however, that TCR catechesis has not moved beyond rote memorization of the catechism: according to catechetical leaders and religion textbook editors and representatives I spoke with, their overarching goal is to help children understand the Catholic faith and appropriate the lessons of it for their daily lives.[10] Most likely influenced by religious educator Thomas Groome, some of the textbooks often follow a variation of his method that offers teachers a structured way to get students to connect Catholic doctrine to their everyday lives.[11]

In order to compare and contrast CGS and TRC methods of teaching, we will contrast class conversations of two TCR classrooms that relied on the textbook with the CGS class discussions. In the TCR classes, students read every chapter in the *The Gift of Reconciliation* aloud and discussed it. During TRC class observations, I frequently found that to ensure comprehension teachers asked students if they had any questions about the topics they were reflecting on. I never heard anyone ask children about their thoughts and feelings concerning reception of this sacrament, except once in Mrs. McManus's[12] class. When asked how they were feeling about receiving Reconciliation, students eagerly raised their hands and responded, "joyful but a little nervous," "happy," "excited," and "nervous." Mrs. McManus enthusiastically responded, "You can't believe how happy you will feel." She then sought to address possible concerns that might contribute to nervousness. "Will Father ever scold you?" "No!" the class shouted. "You're right. Father will be there standing in Jesus' place," she assured them. In contrast, some second graders in a different religion class actually interrupted the flow of the lesson by raising their concerns and feelings. In the midst of a lesson, Justin raised his hand: "Do we need to tell all of our sins of our whole life?" "No, you can just confess several sins. If you forget some, you'll still be absolved," Mrs. Adams answered. Hunter enthusiastically raised his hand: "When you tell Father sins, should you tell him the most serious ones or does it not matter?" "The most serious," Mrs. Adams said. "Is it okay to be afraid?" Lily asked. "It's normal to be a little afraid," Mrs. Adams answered. Jack was the next to be called on: "Do we *have* to go?" Mrs. Adams responded, "Yes, if you are Catholic." Stephanie raised her hand: "What if you are very nervous and you start to cry during Reconciliation?" Mrs. Adams responded, "Very good question, but you won't cry." She then looked at me, and said, "Emotions can run high." She then addressed the children: "We're not going to get all worked up about this, we're just not." She then redirected the class back to the chapter for that day.

Two Approaches to Scripture

Besides these different educational methods and assumptions of child development, I noticed clear differences between CGS and traditional religious educators with respect to the way students encounter scripture. The TCR teachers who rely on a textbook present scripture stories as part of a larger religious or moral lesson. The scriptural passages in these textbooks are also reworded in language that is easier to understand, and children can readily grasp and explain the correct answer about the meaning or moral of the story. For instance, one textbook introduces children to the parable of the vine, and teachers are advised to say the following:

> Point out that the vines and branches intertwine and the grapes depend on the branches, which in turn depend on the vine. . . . A branch cannot be healthy on its own. It needs the vine or the stem to bring it nourishment and to give it life. Point out we, too, are like branches. We must remain close to Jesus who is our vine, so we can grow in his love and life. This is what we mean when we speak of "bearing much fruit" and becoming Jesus' disciples.

In contrast to this rather bland prescription in the textbook, the CGS class had a long and vibrant discussion about the parable of the vine. Most of the kids interpreted the parable to mean that Jesus was the vine and they were the branches. They believed that Jesus is telling them to remain in him, abide in him, keep loving him, do not leave Jesus, and be like Jesus. Mr. Butler affirmed their comments and added, "Yes, Jesus is saying, 'Remain within me; we are very close and connected.' Jesus needs us because you can't really have a vine without branches." He then changed the direction of the conversation: "Now, during Jesus' time, grapevines needed special care. What does a plant need for life?" After several answers like "water," "food," and "sun," Mr. Butler told them about the sap that runs through plants to bring the water and nutrients. "What does the sap represent in this parable?" "Jesus, God," several students called out. "Well, we know from prior classes that God is the vine grower and Jesus is the vine," Mr. Butler answered. After much discussion, Nathan suggested that the sap might represent rubber. Several kids disagreed, suggesting that the sap in the parable represents the Holy Spirit. Although Mr. Butler said Jesus is the vine and God is the vine grower, some kids continued to press the idea that Jesus or God could also be the sap. "I think the sap is Jesus, coming to visit us when we pray," Ryan asserted. Aubrey answered, "Since we're the branches, the sap is probably God's love streaming through, giving love to the branches." Tara reflected, "I think the sap is God in your heart creating you." Thomas continued, "God *is* everywhere so He could be in the sap." Samantha asked, "Who really made God?" Justin further questioned, "How *did* God get created? If he has always been. . . ." Jared concurred: "Yeah. If there's no beginning or end to God—well, how does this work?" John added, "I can't really think 'forever' in my head."

After the children sat for a few moments in silence trying to wrap their minds around God's infinity, Mr. Butler responded: "These are all great questions. It is all a great mystery—God is greater than anything we can understand." He then directed the conversation back to the issue of sap, asking the students to examine a small plant. "Do you notice how some leaves are not healthy and dried up? What would keep the leaves from being healthy?" "They don't get enough of sap—of God," Joseph answered. "Do you think God wants to give sap to all people?" "Yes!" many students answered. "But if that is true, what is blocking the sap?" Mr. Butler asked: "How do you think sap gets clogged up in people?" Nathan found that question quite easy and quickly responded, "In bad guys, the sap gets clogged up." When Mr. Butler asked why the sap gets clogged or blocked, Amelia answered, "Sin blocks the sap: it's like I'm saying 'I don't want all of that love.'" When saying this, Amelia put her hands to her chest, palms outward, as if demonstrating how we as humans have the capability to block God's love. "What happens to the branch if the sap is clogged?" Mr. Butler asked. "It doesn't bear fruit," Jamison answered. Mr. Teller then returned to God: "What do you think the father thinks when the sap gets clogged?" Melanie promptly raised her hand: "The branches don't love him." Adam added, "I think it makes him sad." As the class continued to talk about sin and the sap getting clogged, Mr. Butler encouraged them to think about how the Catholic Church offers a special way to keep the sap flowing through them: receiving the Sacrament of Reconciliation is a way in which Catholics can experience God's forgiveness and be freed from the blockages of sin. Maria expanded on this idea: "In Reconciliation, some of the blockages go away so that I can get sap. Jesus removes the blocks so that sap can run through us." Mr. Butler then asked the children to listen carefully again to the parable. After he was finished reading, he asked, "What did you hear this time? What are the words you love the most?" The kids who spoke now focused on the theme of the branches bearing fruit. Aubrey spoke: "The sap gets to be so much that it has to bear fruit." Claire explained, "The fruit is all of the good things we do. God needs us to bear fruit." "Bearing fruit means we will abide with Jesus and remain in him," Sarah reflected. Mr. Butler asked, "How do you feel about being a branch?" Anna raised her hand and simply shared, "I feel really happy to be born in this world and be part of the branch." After Mr. Butler remarked that Anna had just said a beautiful prayer of thanksgiving, he invited the class to go and do their own work, and consider thinking about what Jesus said in the parable that they liked the most: "You may wish to express what you think through artwork, or write a prayer card saying something back to Jesus."

In the next class, after having the children summarize what they had learned about the parable the preceding week, they discussed how all the parables reveal God's reconciling love and desire to be incredibly close and connected to all people. Mr. Butler then sought to help them examine their consciences and identify blockages of sin in their own lives by asking the following questions: (1) Has there been a time when I have not stayed close to Jesus, the good shepherd, when I have strayed away from God and Jesus like the sheep? (2) Has there been a time when I have not taken the sap of God's love fully into me? (3) Has there been a time when I've said something hurtful, didn't listen to someone, didn't do what I know I should have done? (4) Have there been times when I haven't loved others the way God loves me? He also suggested that they spend time reviewing the scriptural maxims when examining their consciences: "For example, how well have I done being good to those who hate me?"

Along with guiding lessons through summaries of what the children said and encouraging questions, Mr. Butler occasionally stepped in when students were venturing into theologically incorrect territory. In another parable-of-the vine discussion, the children were again reflecting on the problem of sin and what happens when a vine branch falls off the vine. Affirming the class's consensus that the branches represent humans and the sap represents God's love, several children started theorizing that maybe the branches got too much sap, broke off, and died. Marcus suggested, "When a branch falls off, maybe it gets too much of God—maybe the branch is saying, 'This is too much.'" "Maybe we *can* get too much of God and want to die," Tara considered. After asking other children what they thought, Mr. Butler directly objected to this idea that receiving too much of God could result in death: "Remember—scripture reveals that Jesus is life, not death. So you don't have to worry about getting too much of God and then dying." When this class discussion ended and children dispersed to choose their own work, Tara quickly walked around in the atrium picking up various scriptural quotations and objects. She promptly returned to Mr. Butler and started debating with him that there are other scriptural passages that suggest we might die or be fearful if we are confronted directly by God. He took time explaining the meaning behind the scriptural passages she had brought to him and said that some words should not be taken literally. Tara appeared satisfied with his explanations and went off to choose her work. I was deeply impressed by how this seven-year-old could remember and synthesize scriptural quotations, gather them quickly, and select pictures and other objects to support her idea. I also was struck by how comfortable Tara was challenging and arguing with her teacher over her interpretation. When I later asked Mr. Butler whether his decision to refute students' ideas that too much of God's love could result in death was consistent with Cavalletti's emphasis that adults cannot impose their scriptural interpretations onto children, he affirmed this emphasis. However, he argued that there are exceptional times when he feels a need to correct an interpretation of God that directly contradicts the core tenets of Catholic faith. If he were to remain quiet, many children might get disturbed or leave class with religious ideas that are directly opposed to Catholicism's basic convictions. There are certain basic limits, then, to which interpretations of scripture and religious ideas are considered valid during class discussions.

These group conversations are great examples of how wide the parameters are for children to pursue the questions they are interested in and to ponder challenging questions from their teacher; the discussion is so open they are free to explore whatever questions arise for them and even bring up topics that are not obviously related to the parable, such as God's infinity. This is quite different from the parameters in a traditional classroom where the religious content is presented and children are asked to answer questions based on the content. Throughout these discussions preparing for Reconciliation, I was struck by CGS children's insightful questions as they sought to make sense of sin, our relationship with God and others, and Reconciliation. For instance, a student asked, "If we are able to say these things [recognize sins and confess them] to the priest, why can't we do the right thing in the first place?" The children sought to figure this out, suggesting that people often avoid doing hard things, can be lazy, and are not perfect.

In contrast, after encountering scriptural stories and parables in their textbooks, TRC children were encouraged to participate in adult-designed activities during religion classes and at home with family in order to better comprehend religious concepts contained in scripture. For instance, one textbook recommends that children might only understand the parable of the lost sheep if they act out the story; the suggested class activity is to choose one child to be a shepherd and send him or her out of the room. Another child hides a toy symbolizing a sheep. When the shepherd enters the room and looks for the sheep, the other children are to say "baa" if the shepherd is getting closer and should say "moo" when the shepherd gets farther away. When the shepherd finds the toy, children are supposed to cheer.[13]

Overall, throughout my ethnographic observations of the four traditional religion classes and the CGS atrium, I was struck by how different the quality and depth of discussions were in each classroom. My ethnographic notes of CGS classes, as well as submissions of children's drawings and conversations from CGS catechists, strongly indicate that children are capable of theological reflection and rich insights when teachers and parents convey this expectation of children's capacities and give them opportunity to appropriate scripture on their own terms. In the brief moments when the children in the TRC classes were asked for their interpretations, they too showed an eagerness to be heard, although they had fewer opportunities to hone their analytical skills. During our interviews about the Sacrament of Reconciliation, I asked them some questions about certain issues that were never addressed in the textbooks or the classes I observed. For instance, I asked them what they would say to a friend who decided not to receive this sacrament because she decided instead to pray and confess her sins directly to God that night. What would they say to their friend? The vast majority of second graders in the TRC classes disagree that this would be just as good. When I asked why, some could not articulate why they thought confessing their sins in the sacrament was better. Others, however, thought for a moment or two, and then offered a diverse set of creative responses, including the following:

> I'd disagree because if you just say, "Oh sorry, God, I sinned," it's not really doing anything. In Reconciliation, the priest is acting as God so you tell God. At the last part of reconciliation, there's absolution so you know you're forgiven. (Robbie)
>
> You should still go because the priest will understand and forgive because you might have done more sins than you think, and if you tell him, that'd be much better because he can make them gone forever. (Aaron)
>
> It's important to talk to the priest because when you talk to him you feel more confident that God's going to hear me. If you do it talking to God you don't feel as confident. (Claire)

Spiritual and Moral Impact of the Catechesis of the Good Shepherd

It is obviously difficult to assess or measure in any definitive way the impact of CGS on children's moral and spiritual development. There are writings of a community of catechists throughout the world who testify to the powerful spiritual and moral impact this method has on many children.[14] Such testimonials, however, are all adult-centered accounts, revealing only adult perceptions about CGS's effects on children's spiritual and moral development. My research offered the children's interpretations of these events. Interviewing sixteen CGS second graders and fifty-nine second graders in "traditional" classes individually seemed to be the most reliable way to access their interpretations of their experiences.

While the vast majority of the seventy-five second graders expressed feelings of nervousness and anxiety prior to receiving the sacrament, their experiences during and after the sacrament diverged. Three overall responses emerged that I categorized as "lukewarm to negative," "positive," and "very positive." While the majority of second graders (80 percent) expressed either positive or very positive emotions and attitudes after they received the sacrament, a minority of second graders (20 percent) were mostly indifferent or focused on negative aspects of their experience. They emphasized feeling nervous or scared prior to the sacrament and did not volunteer how they felt during the sacrament.[15] Taking into consideration nonverbal cues such as facial expressions and gestures as well as their verbal responses to subsequent questions, I categorized these second graders' experiences as "lukewarm to negative." Jack, for instance, said he didn't remember feeling anything during the sacrament or remember much at all except the party afterwards. He thought kids should be older because they would understand the sacrament better and have more courage. When asked how they would explain this sacrament to their peers, some of these students said they would tell second graders to "just do it and get it over with" or that they just have to "do this" if they wanted First Communion. It is also characteristic of this "lukewarm" group that they did not notice any change in themselves or their relationship with God or others after the sacrament.

In contrast to the "lukewarm to negative" group, 58 percent of second graders reported a positive experience and 22 percent reported a very positive experience of the sacrament. When analyzing the data, I found the "very positive" group's enthusiasm to be qualitatively different. During the interviews, I was often caught off guard by the degree of joy and enthusiasm these second graders expressed when reflecting on what it was like to receive the sacrament. These second graders also differed from their "positive" peers in the rich, often moving, way in which they described encountering God in the sacrament. Rachel, for instance, stated, "I felt a lot holier. I felt I was more in God's family. I felt it after and when he put his hands on my head. I did my penance and I kneeled and started praying and thanking God for my life." This "very positive" group of second graders also offered the most detail about how the sacrament positively affected their relationship with

God, their view of themselves, and the way they treat others. For example, when asked if the sacrament affected her relationship with God, Catherine reflected, "I want to make my relationship with God better than it is now. I think and feel it in my heart. I felt that way after the sacrament. I felt happy and joyful and knew I was filled with God's grace because I was forgiven."

When asked if the sacrament has changed them in other ways, including how they act toward others, most second graders in the "positive" and "very positive" groups answered affirmatively. They reported being kinder and nicer to siblings and friends, not fighting, acting "less difficult" and more obedient. A significant percentage of second graders in these groups also believed that the sacrament would help them avoid committing the same sins in the future. Catherine stated, "It [the sacrament] shows me what I'm doing wrong to make me do better." Michael, along with other children, connected being happier and committing fewer sins: "[The sacrament] makes me more happy and makes me not do sins again so I'm closer and closer to God. You're talking to the priest and telling him your sins and after that you try not to do the same sins again."

When comparing the percentages of lukewarm, positive, and very positive responses among the second graders in TCR classes (fifty-nine second graders) versus CGS (sixteen second graders), 20.3 percent of TCR second graders had a lukewarm to negative response, 61 percent had a positive response, and 18.6 percent had a very positive response to the sacrament. As for the CGS second graders, 18.7 percent had a lukewarm to negative response, 37.5 percent had a positive response, and 43.8 percent had a very positive response to the sacrament. While I cannot justifiably draw definitive conclusions about these percentages due to the small smaple, studying and comparing all of the second graders' positive and very positive responses indicated that CGS students typically offered the most depth in their answers about the sacrament's meaning and its spiritual impact. For instance, when asked how she felt after the sacrament, Claire confided, "It's feels like I get to start over and try to be closer to God and it doesn't feel like you've done anything wrong and like you've just been born. Like you're a baby."

When asked if the sacrament had changed her relationship to God, Robbie stated, "I feel that I have more God in me. I feel closer after my sins are forgiven." Tara responded, "I feel like I've come deeper into him and more close to him. I know what he wants of me. He wants me to believe in him and go straight and do what he wants me to do." Tara's description of coming "deeper into him and more close to him" evokes mystical language, challenging the adequacy of many adult perceptions of children's spirituality that minimize or trivialize children's ability to form a relationship with God. The CGS students also expanded in the greatest depth about how the sacrament motivated them to avoid past sins and act "better" or "nicer." For instance, Claire stated, "It feels like 'Oh my gosh I just received the sacrament' and 'I want to start all over and try to be better at this. . . . I want to be better at this and confess less and try to do better and I think about it and I don't want as many sins.'"

Lessons Learned: Reflections on Ethnographic Child-Centered Research in Schools

What can religious scholars learn from child-centered research that they would not learn otherwise? This ethnographic research project has convinced me that the only way to truly access children's perspectives is to observe children and interview them individually. While children, like adults, are deeply influenced by their families, religious communities, schools, and American secular culture, my experiences interviewing children strongly persuade me that children are not blank slates that passively absorb religious knowledge and the constant messages they receive from secular culture, but are actively coconstructing meaning and their reality. They are also capable of deepening their relationship with God in distinctive ways when given a supportive environment, as demonstrated by the CGS children's interviews. When I told Catholic second graders in all classes that no religion scholar had ever interviewed children about their religious experiences of Reconciliation and that I would truly like to know what they experienced and thought about this sacrament, many of children's eyes lit up with interest; I sensed that they appreciated being asked and listened to about their religious experiences and perspectives. And yet, having said this, my experiences throughout this study gave me a deeper appreciation of how complicated it truly is to access and write accurately about children's experiences and perspectives. Just as catechists' own perspectives of children influence their observations and accounts of children, child-centered researchers also bring their own theoretical lenses about children to their research. As I engaged in this project, I continually sought to remain open to what I observed and heard from children, attempting to be constantly self-critical about how my own assumptions of children might be narrowing my vision of what I observed in these classes.

Furthermore, the power differential that exists between teachers and children can also serve as an obstacle to accessing what children *really* think and feel. While my individualized interviews were the activity during which I felt most satisfied in terms of accessing children's views, I still wondered to what extent unspoken norms about good behavior coupled with norms about being a good Catholic discouraged children from expressing ideas or feelings that were more negative. I sensed my approach of consistently conveying to children that they were the experts on their experiences and thoughts and that I was the student who wanted to learn from them was key in fostering an environment in which children could communicate what they really experienced and thought about Reconciliation and their relationship with God.

Overall, my experiences during this research project left me with many more questions than answers. My hope is that childhood religion scholars will initiate a dialogue with leaders and religious educators from all religious traditions about what the ideal "child-centered" religious faith formation program would look like. In my ethnographic observations of Catholic religious education, the CGS faith formation program is the most child-centered Catholic pedagogy; I am still left wondering, however, how catechists worldwide negotiate the tension between empowering children to interpret God's word on their own terms and guiding children through discussion questions toward some interpretations of a parable (consistent with Christian tradition) and away from others. I suspect that CGS catechists would respond that being child-centered does not mean embracing a theological relativism that entails affirming all theological claims or scriptural interpretations offered by children; "faith formation" implies a commitment to form children in one way rather than another. This research project has made me more aware of how complicated the commitment to engage in a child-centered pedagogy and practice in religious formation truly is.

As a Christian ethicist who is concerned about what it means to treat children justly in religious communities and our broader secular culture, I sense that there is a great need for creative and frank dialogue among child-centered scholars and religious leaders and educators about how religious traditions can form children in their faith traditions in a way that respects and honors children's own desires, needs, and agency. I strongly suspect that further research interviewing children about what *they* think about their religious experiences, participation in religious rituals, religious communities, and relationship with God may very well alter or even shatter our dominant assumptions about children's intellectual, religious, moral, and spiritual capacities, allowing us greater understanding and appreciation of the actual children in our midst.

NOTES

1. David Kahn, "Modern Montessori in Search of a Soul," in *Catechesis of the Good Shepherd: Essential Realities*, ed. Tina Lillig (Chicago: Liturgy Training Publications, 2004), 83.

2. Sofia Cavalletti, *The Religious Potential of the Child* (Chicago: Liturgy Training Publications, 1992), 22, 40-45.

3. Ann Garrido, *Mustard Seed Preaching* (Chicago: Liturgy Training Publications, 2004), 45-46; Cavalletti, 13-14, 43.

4. Luigi Capogrossi, "An Opening into the Way of Love," in *Catechesis of the Good Shepherd: Essential Realities*, ed.Tina Lillig (Chicago: Liturgy Training Publications, 2004), 17.

5. "Characteristics of the Catechesis of the Good Shepherd," *Journal of the Catechesis of the Good Shepherd* 13 (1998-2002): 5.

6. Ibid., 53.

7. Cavalletti, 28.

8. Email correspondence with Mr. Butler, 3-10-2010.

9. Interviews with catechetical directors, March–April 2010.

10. Interviews with catechetical directors and representatives from all major U.S. Catholic religion textbooks (March–April 2010).

11. See, for example, Sister Catherine Dooley and Monsignor Thomas McDade, eds., *Reconciliation: Pardon and Peace* (Allen, TX: RCL Benziger, 2006); Sister Catherine Dooley and Monsignor Thomas McDade, eds., *Reconciliation: Pardon and Peace; Catechist Edition* (Allen, TX: RCL Benziger, 2006); Rev. Richard N. Fragomeni and Jean Marie Hiesdberger, *The Gift of Reconciliation* (Glenview, IL: Silver Burdett Ginn, 2000); *We Believe Jesus Shares God's Life: Parish Edition Catechist Guide Grade Two* (New York: William H. Sadlier, 2011); *We Believe and Celebrate First Penance* (New York: William H. Sadlier, 2006); *Reconciliation: We Are Your People, the Sheep of Your Flock* (Allen, TX: Resources for Christian Living, 2003); Christiane Brusselmans and Brian A. Haggerty with the assistance of Jacquelyn Mallory, *We Celebrate Reconciliation: The Good Shepherd* (Morristown, NJ: Silver Burdett and Ginn, 1990); Christiane Brusselmans and Brian A. Haggerty with the assistance of Jacquelyn Mallory, *We Celebrate Reconciliation: The Lord Forgives* (Morristown, NJ: Silver Burdett and Ginn, 1990).

12. All names in this chapter are pseudonyms to protect the confidentiality of teachers and children.

13. Dooley and McDade, *Reconciliation: Pardon and Peace; Catechist Edition*, 16.

14. See Victoria M. Tufano, *Journals of the Catechesis of the Good Shepherd* (Chicago: Catechesis of the Good Shepherd Publications, 2003); Victoria M. Tufano, *Journals of the Catechesis of the Good Shepherd, 1984-1997* (Chicago: Catechesis of the Good Shepherd Publications, 1998).

15. Seventeen second graders expressed a lukewarm to negative response to the sacrament, thirty-nine expressed positive views of the sacrament, and sixteen expressed very positive views of the sacrament.

11

Religion and Youth Identity in Postwar Bosnia Herzegovina

RUQAYYA YASMINE KHAN

Mosques, churches and temples once lined
Your beautiful landscape
Sometime ago your bridges connected
Generations of lives, of Muslim, Croat and Serb
Sometime ago, you were more than just a news story
More than just a city, more than just a name
Sometime ago, you were the heart
The heart of a nation

Hajat Avdović, high school student

Vice-president Joseph Biden quoted the poem above on May 19, 2009, as he stood before the Bosnian Parliament and delivered a speech that was generally a well received by the Bosnian press. The words of Hajat Avdović, who left Sarajevo when he was a child and moved to America with his family,[1] profoundly convey his feelings about religion and conflict in his birthplace.

A need to access precisely such words and worldviews of Bosnian youth and children prompted me to conduct research as a Fulbright fellow at the Faculty of Islamic Studies, University of Sarajevo (Fakultet Islamskih Nauka, Sarajevski Univerzitet) in Bosnia Herzegovina (hereafter BiH) during spring 2009.[2] With the assistance of my Bosnian colleague, Mujesira Zimić-Gljiva, I designed a survey assessing Muslim youth attitudes toward religion.[3] We then applied this instrument at a selection of public schools in BiH's capital city, Sarajevo, employing a two-stage process, which generated raw data contained in over one thousand student surveys.[4] No doubt, the topic of Muslim youth identity in a uniquely European country currently commands global attention in both popular and academic circles.[5] BiH offers a glimpse into the attitudes and experiences of Muslim youth in a Southeastern European country where Islam has been an indigenous, majority presence for over five centuries.

This chapter aims to share some of these insights as it offers suggestions for researchers working with surveys as a method for accessing the words and worldviews of children and youth.[6] We unintentionally prepared this research instrument using both child-centered and adult-centered methodologies where they seemed appropriate. Reflecting on the survey and its results reveals the strengths and weaknesses of both approaches in ways that may be illuminating to future researchers. Specifically, our work with these Bosnian teenagers emphasized the importance of tapping into child/youth input with regard to the design of the survey.

Brief Background on Religion in the Western Balkans

Sarajevo is a small, cosmopolitan city centered in a valley ringed by the mountains of BiH. Biden, in his May 2009 speech, also quoted English writer Rebecca West, who observed that arriving in Sarajevo was like "'walking [into] an opening flower.'"[7] Biden noted new construction in Sarajevo and spoke about a cautious air of optimism in the country. The flower that is Sarajevo is the capital of the only truly multireligious country in the Western Balkans, namely, Bosnia Herzegovina.[8] Nearly 50 percent of its population is Muslim, and the remainder consists of both Orthodox Christians and Roman Catholics. In the Western Balkans, three religious traditions prevail: Orthodox Christianity, Roman Catholicism, and Islam.[9] Three Western Balkan nations are predominantly Orthodox Christian: Serbia, Montenegro, and Macedonia.[10] Two are mainly Roman Catholic, namely, Slovenia and Croatia.[11] Albania possesses a Muslim majority.[12] Only BiH, as noted already, is multireligious.

For centuries, up until the late 1300s, the Western Balkans region (located at a midpoint between Rome and Byzantium) was the arena for conflict between two rival forms of Christianity: Orthodox Christianity and Roman Catholicism.[13] Between the fourteenth and nineteenth centuries, the Western Balkans became part of the Ottoman Empire, and as such, this region formed the borderland between Islam and Christian Europe for nearly five hundred years.[14] Religion and nationalism are more often than not intimately linked in the Western Balkans, so that, for example, in Bosnia, "Serbian" is synonymous with Orthodox, "Croat" is synonymous with Catholic, and "Bosniak" is synonymous with Muslim.[15]

Getting into Their Heads: Bosnian Youth and
BiH Confessional Religious Education

In the late 1980s, "religion" made a big comeback in BiH society and has continued to have an important presence for the past two decades.[16] Consequently, the issue of religious education in the public schools has risen to the fore in BiH society and as Ahmet Alibašić (scholar of Islamic thought and history, University of Sarajevo), the author of an important policy paper on the subject, points out, "Speaking broadly, BH citizens and politicians are obviously still searching for the effective solutions to the challenges of common living in a pluralist BH. The position of religion in public schools is just an aspect of that wider context."[17] Over the last twenty-five years BiH has embraced in its public shool system theologically oriented (think "Sunday school") education, which is termed "confessional religious education" (henceforth, CRE). Currently, there exist heated controversies over the implementation of CRE in the BiH public school system.

The formation of Bosnian youth identity is an issue that taps into charged popular and intellectual debates regarding national unity and socialist Yugoslav legacies, as well as postwar politics and grievances. Questions such as the following surface in these discussions: Is the implementation of CRE helping or hindering social cohesion in the country? Should the CRE model be revised or banned? Should academic or comparative religious studies courses (*cultura religia*) replace or supplement the CRE model (the latter advocated by Catholic and Islamic leaders)?

Despite all the adult concern over the implementation of these courses, few studies, if any, have been done of just what the youth or students themselves think and feel about the system. Indeed, Alibašić personally communicated to me that it was surprising that no or so little data was available conveying what those most affected by the implementation of CRE thought about the whole matter. BiH educators, policy makers, clergy, and parents continue to face the task of "centering children and youth" in the CRE system, i.e., of obtaining *their* perspectives and views. While the objective of our scholarly research was to examine the experiences of Islamic CRE for Bosnian youth during the postwar period, the data yielded from our survey project hopefully contributes toward addressing the lacuna for Bosnian educators and policy makers in this area.

CRE, in Sarajevo, embraces the teaching of all three religions (Islam, Roman Catholicism, and Orthodox Christianity) on a weekly or biweekly basis in the primary and secondary public schools. Students, with parental approval, can voluntarily sign up for or opt out of taking these classes focused on any one of these three religions. At the beginning of the school year, parents and students together decide about the matter of whether or not to enroll in CRE. Children are deemed "minors," so schools have to obtain parental permission. These religion courses are electives, and each course elective is equal in credit to other courses in the school curriculum. Students can drop the course if they desire.

"Children as Consultants": The Two-Stage Process

Our case study demonstrates the utility, in Ridgely's words, "of engag[ing] children as consultants in a . . . project."[18] This happened inadvertently through the use of a small-sample pilot survey (120 respondents, open-ended questions) before we conducted the large-sample survey. Such a two-stage process of surveying (e.g., pilot followed by a large-sample survey) is nothing unusual as regards survey methods.[19] What is important here is that because it gave us direct access to the prevailing words, idioms, themes, ideas, and expressions of the youths being surveyed, it proved to be invaluable when we began to code responses into forced-choice options for the large-sample survey.

The target group was grades seven, eight, nine, and ten, in which students were born either during or slightly after the era of the recent Bosnian war, ca. 1992-1995. As regards both the pilot and large-sample versions of the survey, my colleague and I first devised them in English and then subsequently translated them into Bosnian/Croatian/Serbian, or BCS[20] (the Bosnian insider term is "Bosanski"). From January to March 2009, we worked on designing the survey and we then applied this instrument primarily during the months of March and April 2009, in a two-stage process that generated raw data contained in over one thousand student surveys from public schools in BiH's capital city, Sarajevo. The survey instrument allowed controlled access to the experiences and interpretations of Bosnian Muslim youth and the sizable sample renders it "generalizable" to the larger population.

The pilot survey consisted mainly of open-ended questions and the fulsome responses to these open-ended questions presented us with a treasure-trove of themes and expressions with which to code the forced-choice options for the large-sample quantitative survey (April 2009, 888-890 respondents). Admittedly, the analysis of the pilot data was tricky given the shuttling back and forth between the Bosnian language and English in which my Bosnian colleague and I engaged. In the coding, we were very careful with the choice of words (in Bosnian/Croatian/Serbian, or BCS) and we sought to use as much as possible the language (i.e., vocabulary, phrases, dominant themes and insights) of the students/youths themselves as accessed from the earlier pilot survey. The large-sample survey was designed such that it could be ultimately analyzed without knowledge of the language BCS.

The overall pool of students consisted of about 890 students. Of this total, 465 were from grades seven and eight (i.e., middle school), and 425 were enrolled in grades nine and ten (i.e., high school). Pilot data demonstrated that middle-school students, perhaps because they were less guarded, were inclined to write more abundantly and hence respond more fully to survey questions than their older peers. In the pool of about 890 students, the number of females was somewhat larger: 477 females and 365 males (N/A or "No Answer": 48). The survey instrument consisted of two sections. The first section elicited basic information and consisted of mostly coded prompts with the exception of two to three "fill in the blank" questions.[21] The coded prompts concerned the following items: grade level, gender, and *mektab* attendance (i.e., Islamic equivalent of weekend religious schooling).[22] The survey demonstrated that the majority of students did not attend *mektab*: 542 students coded "no" with 228 coding "yes" (118 N/A). As for the second section, it consisted of twelve numbered questions, of which approximately eight were coded. The questions/issues framed in this portion were essentially for both the pilot instrument and the large-sample survey.

The five coded questions from the second section all yielded different results on the basis, in part, of who helped to craft them: two (#2 and #6) where we successfully engaged, albeit accidentally, in a child-centered methodology; another two (#3 and #4) where we cobbled together adult-centered and child-centered methods; and lastly, one question (#9), where our approach was mainly adult centered to the detriment of data results. Question #2 dealt with *identity*, specifically Muslim identity, whereas question #6 addressed the issue of *choice*, i.e., youth agency in choosing the Islam religion course. As for #3 and #4, they both concerned performance of *Islamic religious practices*. Question #3 dealt with Islamic daily prayer, whereas #4 addressed the observance of Ramadan (i.e., the month of fasting). Finally, question #9 attempted to engage students on the issue of *interfaith relations*, i.e., relations with members of the Orthodox, Catholic, and Jewish faiths.

The Proof Is in the Pilot: Child-Centered Methodology

Question #2, on "Being Muslim": Overwhelmingly the students indicated that they view themselves as "Muslim." In response to question #2, "Do you consider yourself a Muslim?" ("Smatraš li sebe muslimanom/kom?"), the count was as follows: 837 students "yes," 44 "no," with 7 abstaining from any answer. To some degree, prior assumptions were made that our target audience was mainly Muslim (after all, the capital city of Sarajevo is majority Muslim); however, we desired explicit information on this issue. The data results elicited by #2 demonstrate that the survey was indeed undertaken by an almost full majority of Muslim students.[23]

Although a majority of the students deemed themselves "Muslim," this uniformity breaks down in the followup question to #2: "If so, describe what being Muslim means to you." It is in this followup to #2 that we see the benefits of the pilot survey, the benefits of engaging the youth/children as consultants. Both the range of *five* forced-choice options and the language employed in wording these options were taken from the initial pilot survey results:

A. "Honesty, good, moral conduct" ("Poštenje, dobrota, ponašanje u skaldu sa moralnim principima");
B. "Means a lot to me, I am proud to be a Muslim" ("Meni znači jako puno, ponosan/sna sam što sam musliman/ka");
C. "Belief in and worship of one God;" ("Vjerovati i obožavati samo jednog Boga")
D. "Prayer, fasting, and following other Islamic prescriptions and practices" ("Klanjati, postiti i izvršavati ostale islamske propise")
E. "Respect everyone, including people of other religions" ("Poštovati svakoga uključujući i pripadnike drugih vjera").

Importantly, the followup question to #2 asked the youth to select only *two* out of these five forced-choice options.

We are able to obtain some compelling information from the analysis of the followup data. The results of the survey shed light on how Bosniak Muslim youth view and construct their religious identities given the recent war and Bosnia's unique traditional Islamic status within Europe. The first tenet of belief in Islam (i.e., unity of God, belief in one God), not surprisingly, is a determinative factor in "what being Muslim means" for these Bosnian students.[24] Creed or profession of faith in the oneness of God, enshrined also in the first of the five pillars ("I bear witness that there is no god but God. . . .") is formative. In sum, the data results assign emphasis to three patterns:[25]

- The belief in and worship of one God is constituent to Bosniak youth religious identity and its expression (options: AC, CD, CE).[26]
- Valuation of ethical, moral conduct ranks almost as high as belief in one God, particularly valuation of conduct reflecting honesty and integrity (AC and CE).[27]
- Both belief and religious practices are deemed very important (CD).[28]

We were intrigued by a number of elements yielded by the pilot data. For example, it was interesting that a number of the youth responses to "being Muslim" in the pilot data were not particular to Islam, but rather reflected general ethical and moral principles. Importantly, we transferred these insights into coded options that resonated with the youth taking the large-sample survey. Also, from our adult-centered perspective, we probably would not have thought of, much less devised the wording of, the option reflecting youth pride in religious identity is (e.g., "Means a lot to me, I am proud to be a Muslim."). In sum, through a close consultation of the data (open-ended responses) to question #2 and its followup in the pilot survey, we gleaned enough information to devise a spectrum in the coded responses ranging from creedal elements to interfaith relations. Accessing the words and world-views of Bosnian youth directly through the pilot survey data permitted us to implement a child-centered methodology that rendered the survey more inclusive and meaningful.

Question #6, "Choosing" the Class: This survey was geared toward those schools that offered an Islam elective class, and survey question #6, queried students on whether or not they were "currently enrolled in an Islam elective subject or class." Once it was ascertained that a youth was enrolled in such an elective, we wanted to investigate whether students were subject to external pressures in signing up for this class. The schools' official line was that *students make the decision* in consultation with their parents. Reflective perhaps of our adult-centered views, we were keen on exploring whether these Bosniak teenagers were subject to parental pressures in particular. That, to one degree or another, parents influence children and/or youth on their views of religion is a commonplace. Indeed, the initial pilot survey contained a question that asked students to rank (in order of importance) a series of categories that "shaped their view of religion." The categories consisted of parents, friends, *mektab*, religious school subject, and "other" (i.e., as a "write-in"). Consistently, the pilot data revealed that these Bosnian youth ranked "parents" ("*roditelji*") as #1 in terms of factors "shaping" their view of religion.[29]

On the pilot, the followup to question #6 asked the enrolled students, "If so, how did you choose this particular class?" Here again, both the range of forced-choice options and the language employed in wording these options were taken from the initial pilot survey results. The followup to #6 in the large-sample survey asked the students to "select *one* phrase that best describes how you chose this class": (1) "My friends are taking it" ("Pohađaju je i moji prijatelji"); (2) "My parents wanted me to" ("Roditelji su me natjerali"); (3) "To better understand my faith" ("Da više naučim o svojoj vjeri").

Of the total sample, 703 affirmed that they were signed up for the course while 168 stated "no" (i.e., they were not taking the elective; 13 N/A). Data from the followup yielded 673 total responses and the breakdown was thus: 576 ("To better understand my faith"); 73 ("My friends are taking it"); 24 ("My parents wanted me to") with 190 N/A.[30] Clearly, an overwhelming majority indicated that they enrolled in this course for their own edification and benefit. Indeed, the smallest number indicated that they signed up for the course because their parents desired this. It is instructive to note the disparity between our adult-centered assumptions (i.e., majority may have been thrust into the course by parents) and the youth-centered data (i.e., they chose to enroll for their own benefit).

Combo Approach: Adult-Centered and Child-Centered Methods

Questions #3 and #4, Religious Practice: Several reasons contributed toward mainly an adult-centered methodology when it came to the questions concerning religious practice on the survey. I and my colleague, Mujesira Zimić-Gljiva, as researchers and scholars of religion in general, were interested in learning about religious practice and observance among Bosniak youth. Moreover, my colleague was also interested in this from a pedagogical perspective; after all, she was a lecturer at the Faculty of Islamic Studies, which licensed the teachers that staffed the Islam elective courses in the canton of Sarajevo. And as a practicing Muslim active in the Bosnian Islamic community and the mother of a teenager, she keenly desired to assess the degree of Islamic practice among Bosniak teens.

Ultimately, however, *both* child-centered and adult-centered methodologies drove our handling of the two questions regarding religious practice on the large-sample survey. For instance, consider the decision regarding *which* religious practices to query Bosnian youth about on the survey. The choice of Islamic daily prayer (*namaze*) and the annual fast (Ramadan, or *ramazan*) was chiefly adult driven. My Bosnian colleague maintained that these two were among the religious practices most adhered to by Bosniaks in general,[31] including possibly their youth. Hence, these two were represented on the pilot, and the data corroborated her assumptions. Actually, on both the pilot and large-sample versions, two questions (with followup forced-choice options) are found concerning Islamic daily prayer (*namaze*) and the annual fast (Ramadan, or *ramazan*), respectively. The child-centered approach surfaces in the narrowing of forced-choice options from three to two (based on the pilot data) for these two questions on the large-sample instrument. For example, the followup to #3 (Islamic prayer) on the pilot contained the following three options regarding frequency of prayer observance: "All five regularly"; "At least once a day"; "From time to time." On the large-sample survey, we eliminated the middle option from those itemized above due to minimal response rate.[32] Again, the pilot data further assisted us in fine-tuning the questions and their followup.

Let us look at the data concerning question #3 (on performance of daily prayer): As regards *namaze*, over two-thirds responded "yes" to the question, "Do you perform prayers?" ("Da li klanjaš?"). From among the count, 615 responded "yes" and 263 responded "no." When students were asked the followup question, "If so, how often?" the result was skewed: the two choices were "All five daily" ("*sve propisane namaze*") and "From time to time" ("*povremeno*"). Only 85 respondents checked the box concerning "All five daily" whereas 546 checked the box "From time to time," along with 255 providing N/A or no answers. Clearly, the "bell curve" here falls in the gray area of "From time to time," whether that may imply one prayer or so daily, or two or so weekly, or one to three monthly.

When we turn to question #4, it was phrased, "Do you fast during Ramadan?" ("Da li postiš uz ramzan?"). The followup question was, "If so, how often?" and the two choices consisted of "The whole month" ("*Cijeli mjesec*") versus "Several days" ("*Nekoliko dana*"). Structurally, this question is identical to #3 except that here the religious practice in question is fasting. Intriguingly, the yield to this question reflected a trend that was the reverse of the prior one. Overwhelmingly, the students responded with "yes" (779), with only 98 indicating a "no"(11 N/A). Moreover, in response to the followup question, the data suggested an approximate half-half division: 324 students chose "The whole month" while 450 opted for "Several days," with 113 N/A.

The data yielded from these two queries reflects what we desired to know *as adult researchers*. While I am not sure we really obtained much in the way of insights into the Bosnian youth experience of and relation to these two religious practices, the data was not unproductive. Perhaps, it was less revealing than that yielded by, for example, questions #2 and #6. Yet, a significant result derived from the relevant data is that fasting during Ramadan is by far the more observed of these two religious practices. Arguably, among Bosnian youth, fasting during Ramadan may be the most observed pillar from among the Five Pillars.[33] In discussions with my Bosnian colleague, it became clear that Ramadan fasting is a "more societally observed" ritual, and given its public, festive, and visible dimensions compared to, for example, daily prayer, this particular practice is perhaps more subject to peer and family pressure(s).

Falling Short: Queries concerning the "Other"

Question #9, Relations with Members of Other Religions: In this area, we were less than successful in eliciting meaningful results in either the pilot or the large-sample survey. Our problems began in the pilot survey, which contained two questions, the first one querying youth about "learning about different religions or people of other religions" and the second one asking them about class influence on their "relations with people who are Bosnian Orthodox or Bosnian Catholics." Moreover, the wording of the followup to the latter question on the pilot was especially problematic: "How and why not?" Not surprisingly, the student responses to both questions were confusing and scattered.

For the large-sample survey, we reworded the question concerning "relations with people who are Bosnian Catholic or Bosnian Orthodox" to read, "Does this class have an influence on your relations with Bosnian Orthodox, Catholics, or Jews?" ("Da li vjeronauka utječe na tvoj odnos prema bosanskim pravoslavcima, katolicicma ili Jevrejima?"). The large-sample tabulation was as follows: 546 students coded "yes" with 346 responding with "no" (N/A 35). For the followup to #9 on the large-sample survey, we designed two coded responses reflecting either the presence or absence of "social distance" vis-à-vis a member of another faith. For those who coded "yes" to #9, we asked them to select *one* of the following two:

A. "I respect their faiths, but do not socialize with them because they are different from me." ("Uči me da postujem njihovu vjeru ali da se ne družim s njima jer su oni drugačiji od mene.")
B. "I behave the same with everyone regardless of their religion." ("Uči me da se ponasam isto prema bez obzira na njihovu religiju.")

The results were skewed: 550 checked "B" whereas 42 chose "A" (N/A 293). With 293 students not responding at all to the followup and the imbalance of those who did respond, I deemed the results unproductive.

In retrospect, it would have been far more effective to instead have a series of *concrete* questions indexing "social distance" vis-à-vis members of these other religions. For example, we could have devised a series of yes/no questions querying them about specific social interactions with peers of other faiths: e.g., whether or not they engaged in sports activities with them, whether or not they visited their homes, and/or whether or not they had attended a religious service associated with them. This also would have reflected a more child-centered methodology, as it would have queried them about interactions within their own age group. Indeed, the lack of success is partially attributable to the prevalence of an adult-centered lens in approaching this issue: given the recent history of war and genocide in the region, I, as an adult scholar of religion, deemed it salient and significant to poll Bosniak students on their relations with members of other faiths, but maybe Bosniak *youth* do *not* perceive their Catholic or Orthodox or Jewish peers in terms of the "other." I also think those doing survey work with youth should be wary of devising questions that ask teenagers to be analytically reflective and/or introspective about influences of any kind, especially in the context of a timed survey. Such questions yield weak data. Lastly, it's instructive to reflect on how my colleague and I (both of us possessing a Muslim heritage, with our own preconceived adult notions and biases) struggled with the exact wording of the aforementioned followup to #9.[34]

Conclusions

The survey instrument permitted us to fairly reliably access the words and interpretations of the youth/students themselves. The two-stage process provided us with direct access to the prevailing idioms, themes, ideas, and expressions of the youths being surveyed—access that enriched our ability to meaningfully code responses into forced-choice options for the large-sample survey. Reliance upon the initial pilot survey as a research tool facilitated our capacity for "getting into the heads" of my youthful subjects, of accessing and obtaining "their own words" as regards the issues about which they were polled.

Of course, the survey, as a research tool, also had many limitations. I will comment on only two that loomed large in our project. The analysis of the data based upon forced-choice options (devised in the large-sample survey) presented several challenges.[35] While this permitted both quantitatively based assessments and, to a degree, qualitative interpretations, the data did not allow much in the way of insights into youth emotions and affects; in other words, we could measure or evaluate the way students framed a particular issue, where they stood on a particular question, aspects of their social interactions and activities, and even what something meant to them, but we could not access the *quality of their feelings* (e.g., the affects or feelings behind their responses). For instance, regarding religious practice, we were able to assess something of the degree and/or nature of their religious observance, but not the feelings and sentiments associated with the performance and/or the lack thereof. Again, regarding the issue of "Muslim identity," we were able to assess the complex aspects of identity language and self-ascription, but not so much the feelings behind these identity markers.

Moreover, the survey tool presented hurdles in polling youth in a recently war-stricken society and culture where religion remains a heavily charged issue. We faced challenges in the limits imposed by the survey tool to adequately allow for youth to express and articulate trauma experienced by them and their kin. A survey is far from a narrative. The common English phrase "loaded words" is especially relevant to querying and assessing trauma in any context, and as regards the survey instrument, we struggled with how to phrase words touching on, for example, interfaith relations and the recent war in Bosnia. This may shed further light on why we were less than successful in eliciting meaningful data from the question pertaining to relations with other religions.

What the survey tool imposed in terms of limitations was offset by the choice of the "school" as research site. In the case of BiH, we were especially fortunate in having fruitful ground for research as the BiH state sanctions the teaching of religion (i.e., CRE) in the public schools. Logistically, we had a captive child/youth audience at the school sites, and generally, Bosnian teachers and other staff were eager to facilitate the research project. However, even in contexts where religion is not taught in public schools, there are myriad ways to approach the study of religion and childhood using the institution of the school as a site. Space does not permit me to outline these ways, but two that are certainly relevant to the United States' milieu concern the increasingly multireligious nature of the student bodies in American schools and the charged debates swirling around religion and science in school curricula.

1. To read Hajat's poem as part of Biden's address see http://www.pims.org/news/2009/05/20/vice-president-joe-biden-address-to-the-parliament-of-bosnia-and-herzegovina.

2. The Faculty of Islamic Studies in Sarajevo is the oldest and most prestigious institution of Islamic learning in the Balkans and Southeastern Europe as a whole. It offers both undergraduate and postgraduate programs in two areas: theology (*usuluddin*) and religious education (*et-terbijjetu-d-dinijje*). Both programs are committed to integrating insights from "the most important disciplines in the Humanities and Social Sciences" (undergraduate study bulletin, 2005-2006).

3. I am greatly indebted to Mrs. Mujesira Zimić-Gljiva (teaching assistant, Faculty of Islamic Studies, University of Sarajevo) for her assistance in this research project. Without her interest in and diligence as regards this project, I could not have undertaken the work.

4. Religion is taught in the Bosnian public school system, and the fact that my institutional affiliation was responsible for licensing the teachers that staffed the Islamic religion classes facilitated our contacts with the public schools in Sarajevo.

5. Indeed, the topic of Islam in Europe is of compelling interest to many audiences in the twenty-first century.

6. I am indebted to the Fulbright Scholar Program, Council for International Exchange of Scholars, Washington DC, for their generous support. In particular, I thank Jean McPeek, deputy assistant director–Europe, Council for International Exchange of Scholars.

7. Author's notes, 20 May 2009.

8. Anne Stensvold, "Introduction to the West Balkans' Religious Scene," in *Western Balkans: The Religious Dimension*, ed. A. Stensvold (Norway: Sypress Forlag, 2009), 10.

9. Ibid.

10. Ibid.

11. Ibid.

12. Ibid.

13. Ibid., 12.

14. Ibid., 13.

15. Ibid., 9.

16. Ahmet Alibašić. The fall of communism and the death of Marshal Tito both helped usher in the end of Yugoslav socialist rule in the Western Balkans. Ahmet Alibašić, "Religious Education in Public Schools in Bosnia Herzegovina: Towards a Model Supporting Coexistence and Mutual Understanding," Open Society Fund Bosnia & Herzegovina, OSF BH: http://www.soros.org.ba/images_vijesti/stipendisti_2009/eng_ahmet_alibasic_full.pdf (accessed July 2010).

17. Ibid.

18. Volume introduction, p. 000.

19. I am very grateful to Gene Roehlkepartain for first suggesting the two-stage process to me: "I would suggest piloting the instrument in, say, one or two schools to be sure it's working well (before doing a large survey). This is particularly true since you have a lot of open-ended items. I would tend to use a survey like this one on a small sample (under 100 to 200), then code their responses into forced-choice options for a larger-sample quantitative survey." Personal communication, March 2009, Gene Roehlkepartain, vice-president, Search Institute, Minneapolis, MN, gener@search-institute.org.

20. "Serbo-Croatian," http://en.wikipedia.org/wiki/Serbo-Croatian_language.

21. These questions asked students to list "Father´s occupation," "Mother´s occupation," and/or "Suburb or city or village where you live."

22. Another coded element was the response to the question, "Which relative(s) are bringing you up?" with coded responses including "mother and father," "only mother," "only father," "grandparents," and "other." Overwhelmingly, the students indicated that they were being brought up by two parents: mother and father, with "only mother" being the second most often coded choice.

23. A factor that may have influenced the data results to #2 is discerned in the analysis of question #6 (see relevant portion in this chapter); this analysis demonstrates that those youth who were enrolled in an Islam elective may have had a higher degree of interest in Islam—personally and academically—than the larger populations of their schools.

24. The three most often coded "slices of the pie" were combos of AC, CD, and CE, in which "C" consistently represents "Belief in and worship of one God."

25. Hereafter, the computation of all data results is based upon those results in which the student(s) responded correctly by filling out the appropriate answer(s).

26. Again, the three most often coded "slices of the pie" were combos of AC, CD, and CE:
> AC: "Honesty, good moral conduct" *and* "Belief in and worship of one God";
> CD: "Belief in and worship of one God" *and* "Prayer, fasting and following other Islamic prescriptions and practices";
> CE: "Belief in and worship of one God" *and* "Respect everyone, including people of other faiths."

27. The combo response with the most quantitative weight is AC. The two combo responses AC and CE I would describe as responses that combine "doxy" (e.g., belief system) with ethical, moral factors:
> AC: "Honesty, good moral conduct" *and* "Belief in and worship of one God";
> CE: "Belief in and worship of one God" *and* "Respect everyone, including people of other faiths."

28. Of the three most popular combos (AC, CD, and CE), only the middle, CD, incorporates religious practice: "Belief in and worship of one God" *and* "Prayer, fasting, and following other Islamic prescriptions and practices." Two other responses that brought in close numbers to these three are
> BC: "Means a lot to me, I am proud to be a Muslim" *and* "Belief in and worship of one God";
> AE: "Honesty, good moral conduct" *and* "Respect everyone, including people of other religions."

Out of these five possible combinations, again, only the last one, AE, absents the theological centrality of belief in one God. I would place CD at one end of the spectrum and AE at the other end of the spectrum, CD representing perhaps the "orthodox, exclusive" stance and AE representing the "liberal, inclusive" position.

29. We eliminated this question from the large-sample survey for several reasons, including the need for brevity and the perception that it would be too onerous to tabulate the rankings for a large sample of one thousand surveys. Perhaps, this serves as an example of where we missed an opportunity to productively use data from the pilot survey.

30. Based upon those results in which the student responded correctly by filling out one answer.

31. Other Islamic practices included Qur'an-related activities (reciting, memorizing the holy book), attending *Juma* congregational prayer, and/or attending *mektab*. Indeed, the pilot survey contained the following question concerning these other practices: "From *namaz* [Islamic daily prayer], *sawm* [fasting], *qir´a al-Qur´an* [Qur'an recitation] and others, which Islamic ritual or practice shapes you the *most*? Why?" Again, we dropped this question from the large-sample survey. We thought it unnecessary for the large sample, and more importantly, we discovered that questions that ask teenagers to reflect on and/ or be introspective about impact, shaping, or influences of any kind yielded poor data. For example, 27 out of a total of 120 students (on the pilot survey) failed to respond to the aforementioned question.

32. Likewise, due to the pilot data on the followup for #4 (regarding fasting), the large-sample survey eliminated the middle option from those itemized below:

The whole month _____
About half the month _____
Several days _____

33. The Five Pillars consist of profession of the following: faith, daily prayer, fasting during Ramadan, alms-giving, and performing the pilgrimage (*Hajj*).

34. Before settling on this version for the large-sample survey, my colleague, an observant Muslim, offered to draft it in the following manner (a manner that I found objectionable because of the specificity and tone of the first choice):

"I respect their religions, but keep away from them because they eat pork and drink alcohol." _____
"I behave with them exactly like I behave with anyone else." _____

35. Space does not permit me to discuss some technical glitches we encountered. For instance, problems arose regarding students correctly coding responses in the large-sample survey, even when we made the directions very clear; some students did not follow instructions properly (e.g., a student coding "no" in a yes/no query, and yet still coding response(s) in the followup to the "yes" option in spite of this).

Using Adult-Generated
Material about Children

Sources and Methods for Accessing

Children's Voices from the Past and Today

The Battle for the Toy Box

*Marketing and Play in the Development
of Children's Religious Identities*

REBECCA SACHS NORRIS

"Will you join 'The Battle for the Toy Box'?" asks the poster in large letters across the top. The seriousness of this battle is shown through the image of muscular Samson and Goliath action figures locked in combat and the accompanying text: "one2believe, a faith based toy company, has been given an opportunity to spread the word of God to children throughout America. . . . one2believe is in a Battle for the Toy Box. Which side are you on?" ("Battle for the Toybox" 2007: 190).

What's going on here? Aren't toys supposed to be fun?

Playthings are indeed fun, but they are not *merely* fun, especially today, when marketing research and media promotion are so thoroughly embedded in the materials—television, movies, and computers as well as toys— that children are exposed to on a daily basis. For those doing research with children, it is important to consider the cultural contexts and multiple subtexts of ordinary items found in children's daily lives. Seemingly innocent or harmless items such as toys are potentially formative influences, their influence being shaped by diverse motivations such as parental needs and wishes, socioeconomic factors, neuroscientific research, profitability, and the intentional or unintentional impact of graphic images. In light of these types of factors, children's needs or wishes may seem to have become distant, dim, and distorted, or even to have disappeared.

The Battle Is Joined

While toys may not commonly be regarded as battle weapons, as in the scenario above, they are implements in parental struggles to prepare their children for what parents want and expect them to become. Playthings are supposed to do this by instilling values and developing social, mental, and physical skills. Buying toys with these anticipated results also reassures parents about their parenting abilities and helps them feel better about themselves. Although material about toys, especially educational toys, seems to be child-oriented, it is largely the parents' hopes and fears that are being addressed. Moreover, marketing plays a strong part in creating these items, bringing into question who really benefits from them. Religious games and toys, which are directed toward parental moral and religious concerns, are a growing segment of the educational toy industry.

Contemporary religious games and toys are fascinating, perplexing, and often contradictory. Although they abound online, many people are unaware that they exist. As well, on first sight many adults are not sure what to make of the games. Are they serious or satire? Are they for children or adults? While there are satirical games, most current religious games are not satirical. Games such as Missionary Conquest, Episcopopoly, BuddhaWheel, The Hajj Fun Game, or Kosherland, and toys that include a variety of talking Bible dolls (Christian) as well as Razanne and Fulla (Muslim), and Gali Girls (Jewish) bring together religion, commerce, play, and politics. Just as play is used in kindergartens, elementary schools, and religious schools as a fun way to attract children to the learning tasks at hand, these games call on the intrinsic appeal games have for children. Most are colorful; many include humor (not always successfully) or attempt to be contemporary and relevant. They are intended as educational tools, meant to instill morals as well as implant knowledge, to be one more element in a child's spiritual formation.

As religious studies scholar Susan B. Ridgely notes (2005), most studies of children's religiosity and spirituality are from the adult perspective. Books on children's spiritual formation present what *adults* need to do to develop and form children's religious identities. As adults, can we ever know children's inner spiritual lives? We are limited by having to comprehend children's worlds through the lens of our adult experience and understanding. Knowing children's *play* lives is much more difficult, because one of the difficulties of researching children's play is that when it is supervised, it changes.

Chaya Kulkarni, the director of Infant Mental Health Promotion (IMP) at the Hospital for Sick Children in Toronto, asserts that children get much more out of toys and that it is "far more meaningful" when a parent participates in the play as well ("Do 'Educational Toys' Really Teach?" 2009), but these interactions are not that simple, since children don't like adult interference in play,[1] to the extent that they may even change their activities when observed (Kline 1993: 190). Children's play cannot be completely isolated from parents; for one thing, it is inevitable that younger children play in the presence of parents.

Adult influence on children's play is not limited to personal interaction during the play event either, since even when children are older, parents still buy toys for them. However, even though parents buy them, there may a gap between the intended use and the way children actually use a toy. For example, subversion is a natural accompaniment to children's play; notable are the ways in which Barbie is often treated—drowned, decapitated, or mutilated. There is some "play" in the way educational toys are used as well: "children in effect refuse to use the smart toys provided with their implied conceptual enrichments, and instead use them in terms of their own preexisting more simplified play predilections" (Sutton-Smith 2004: ix). It is reasonable to assume that religious toys are just as likely to fall prey to children's own interpretations and usages as other toys, regardless of the motivations behind parents' efforts. There are a number of essential factors to keep in mind when researching children's play or toys; one is the impossibility of separating the worlds of children and adults. It is difficult, or perhaps even impossible, to isolate children from adults or adult influence when doing research. One can never see how children play when separate from adults, as the act of observation changes the observed. This is not to say that there is some platonic ideal, a "pure" play that we can strive to observe, however. It is simply that these relationships must be taken into consideration.

Another aspect is motivational complexity, whether within an individual parent, between parents, or among parents and educators, and perhaps even including the researcher. Competing formative influences—education, marketing, science, and mass culture, for example—are also evident and advance their own agendas. While my focus on the religious category may provide a more direct avenue to analyzing competing motives, these forces exist in the larger world of toys and play as well, and need to be made visible by the researcher. This may be difficult, since our own cultural beliefs and perspectives can correspond so fundamentally with those of the people we are studying that they are difficult to discern. For example, who would question that we should teach children morals or that educational toys are useful? But deeper investigation shows us that we need to question who is shaping those moral lessons, and how the concept of educational toys developed.

Educational Toys and Play

The impulse to use toys as moral regulators is not new. The kindergarten movement, for example, led to "a consumer market for children's products" through pressure from manufacturers to have educational toys in schools to ensure "normal child development" (Dehli 1994: 209). It became imperative as well for middle-class parents, especially mothers, to have the proper toys and books available at home, creating a market for educational toys. Current parental concerns about children's play include social development as well as athletic skills, education, and brain training.

But Americans are confused. We bemoan the loss of unstructured and outdoor play time for children, but we spend vast amounts of money buying educational toys to make sure our children's play is productive. Educational toys help resolve our American ambivalence—the contradiction between negative Puritan views of play and the belief that play is a healthy pastime (Elkind 2007: 34). Our ambivalence is evident also in the complementary yet contradictory emphasis in articles on toys and play—one side emphasizes the importance of educational play and toys (make that play time useful!) and the other insists we should be having as much fun as possible (Bado-Fralick and Norris 2010: 119-21). Play is seen as a crucial element in social development, a therapeutic tool, a pedagogical method, and a necessary part of childhood.[2]

These perspectives, inevitably, are adult views—what grownups think play and toys *should* be. Discussions of the importance of choosing the right toys took place throughout the last century, for example, in *The Wise Choice of Toys*, originally published in 1934 (Kawin 1938). In the article "Toys as Learning Materials for Preschool Children," education is foremost; the word "fun" is used only once in the whole article, and this viewpoint is evident in its focus on play as "the children's workshop" (the title of one of the sections).

> Whether the child's place of business is a classroom, a remodeled home, an architecturally planned preschool educational facility, or a church basement, there is agreement that it should be not only attractive and inviting but should encourage exploration. The arrangement should be made with the child's point of view in mind and should be responsive to him. (Zimmerman and Calovini 1971: 642)

While this attitude claims to keep the child's perspective foremost, the adult's view of what the child needs is still central. "A good toy is attractive and inviting, well constructed and durable, safe, nontoxic, challenging, and fun. It also stimulates a child's curiosity and imagination, and lets him discover that which it was *expected* he would learn" (Zimmerman and Calovini 1971: 644; emphasis mine).[3]

The idea that children *need* to have the correct toys in order to develop properly is now well embedded in American and British cultures. Assumptions about the value and uses of educational playthings abound, assumptions that appear to be so natural that it can be difficult for the researcher to identify them as culturally specific and historically distinct ideas, for example, that educational toys are valuable assets to parents and educators. But according to education professor Linda Cameron, all toys can teach something; an educational toy is simply one that is defined by the manufacturers that way ("Do 'Educational Toys' Really Teach?" 2009). As researchers, we need to be aware of and question our own cultural beliefs—a difficult task. Essentially we are doing fieldwork on ourselves.

Game-Playing Modes

As I have noted, the focus of educational toys is on adult expectations for children. Similarly, religious toys aim at shaping children's religious identity according to adult views of religiosity. Games try to do this through a number of devices, including emphasizing knowledge, moral conduct cards, and spiritual game rewards. For example, most of the Muslim games, as well as some Christian and Jewish ones, are Trivial Pursuit–type games, which require knowledge of ritual, religious history, and so on, for a player to move forward in the game. The Hajj Fun Game asks questions of varying levels of difficulty, e.g., "Where is the birthplace of the prophet Mohammad located?" or "What is Rukn Aswad?" Moral conduct cards are common in many games, the level of the ethical issue being based to some extent on the recommended age for the game. For example a card in the Armor of God game (Christian, ages five to nine) states, "You are tempted to lie about the lamp you broke, but you tell the truth instead." In some games, moral conduct cards will move you forward or back; in this game, having told the truth, the player gets a spiritual reward: the Belt of Truth, one of the Armor of God playing pieces needed to win. Event cards may also have moral implications; picking up the wrong Career Event card in the Vatican game will land you in the Cesspool of Sin. Another approach altogether is that used in more evangelical games like Salvation Challenge, "which imparts clear judgments about proper Christian behavior. This game bestows greater rewards to those who jump up, put their hands in the air, and loudly proclaim 'Jesus, Save Me!' when they land on the cross than to those players who merely say it" (Bado-Fralick and Norris 2010: 4). While there are similar motives to these games, the methodologies are different.

Religious games employ imagery as well, in order to appeal to children; the style of imagery also varies. Karma Chakra, a Buddhist game, is almost completely abstract, with intensive thought put into each color and element (Ghartsang 2007), while the BuddhaWheel board is the Buddhist Wheel of Life. Muslim game boards may have images of mosques, but for the most part they are simple and abstract, probably because of Islamic restrictions on sacred images. Judaism has similar restrictions, but many of the Jewish games, such as Kosherland, Let My People Go, or Exodus, are freer in their expression—with bright colors, nasty pharaohs, and even a "wheel of plagues" in the Exodus game.

Christian boards display the most variety, in part because there are more Christian games in general, a natural result of the history of Christianity and commerce in the United States, as well as the Christian call to spread the gospel in any way possible (Bado-Fralick and Norris 2010: 70-78). The design of Vatican: The Board Game is largely symbolic, with different sections of the board representing through color and geometry steps on the way to becoming pope. The Journeys of Paul game board is a map of the Mediterranean around the time of Paul, with cartoon-style realism used on the event cards. Bibleland uses children's cartoon images to represent Adam, Eve, the serpent, and even the crucified and resurrected Christ. In these images it is hard to imagine Christ suffering very much on the cross, since he is so cute and chubby-cheeked.

Shaping Religious Identity

While these games are intended to teach particular religious concepts through their playing cards or game strategies, children also learn from the images themselves. Stephen Kline, a professor of communications, notes that children are not able to work with abstract concepts as well as adults, that they are not as self-reflective, and thus that market researchers should use techniques that "rely on pictures" since children are responsive to visual impressions (Kline 1993: 187). Indeed, one of the most interesting things about these religious games is their role as sensory objects and the way that they utilize imagery. In some ways they are no different than any other children's games; in other ways their religiosity creates a unique set of conditions.

What effects will religious cartoon images have on children's developing religious identity? Will later studies of the efforts of the Apostle Paul evoke cartoon images of Roman soldiers? Will reflection on Christ's suffering bring chubby-cheeked Bibleland images to mind? Will sneering pharaohs be a part of one's inner Seder for decades to come? Graphic images are powerful. They communicate polysemically, and more directly than words. Images are the language of the subconscious. Television and computers make use of this fact, as does advertising. The power of imagery can be seen in religious efforts to control it: the Taliban destroying Buddhist statues, Jewish and Islamic restrictions on images of God or Muhammad, or the Reformation, for example.

Images are powerful from another perspective as well. It may seem an exaggeration to be questioning religious cartoon images—these are just games, so how can we take these images seriously? Yet if we consider how religious enculturation takes place, it is clear that these images will become part of a person's religious associations—associations that are the underpinnings of religious experience and understanding. Images communicate directly to the emotions, which are a vital and essential part of religious life. Emotions, unlike other aspects of our experiential lives, have an interesting quality: when emotional memories are evoked, they are reexperienced. This quality is part of the internal structure through which we are enculturated into specific religious worldviews and experiences (Norris 2005: 194).

Images and other sensory input construct an ever-changing interconnected web of associations that inform our religious identities and experience. Thus these games, meant to inculcate religious ideals and values, do so not only through information conveyed through game cards or board structure but also through their graphic style. Another unintended factor is the limitation of the game structure itself; the knowledge conveyed is necessarily restricted and incomplete. Although these toys may not be the primary factors in a child's religious upbringing, they will have some effect. And just as the banning of religious images reveals their power, the fact that religious games and dolls are being marketed as players in the "Battle for the Toy Box" reveals that some adults view toys as significant sources of transmission of cultural and religious information. The psychological impact of toys is evident in other domains as well. Psychologist Brian Sutton-Smith notes that "a toy or tool can sometimes become an *identity* around which the child organizes his or her actions and concepts of the world" (1986: 207; emphasis in original). Toys are also used in play therapy—another indication of their potential and influence.

If the game imagery and materials, or the shape and clothing (such as a *hijab*) of religious dolls are formative of religious identity, then we also need to ask ourselves what is influencing their forms and content. Unlike most toys, these are meant to instill religious ideas and values, but like other toys they are objects in the marketplace, competing for parents' money and children's attention.

The Toy Market

Toy manufacturers depend on children's visual orientation to the world, and religious toys must compete with toys that are advertised widely and readily available. The forms and imagery used in religious games are necessarily influenced by those of popular games. They must be visually appealing and fun to play. Some games are simply religious reflections of secular ones, with religious terms replacing secular ones, as with Catholicopoly; dolls (or "action figures") exhibit much of the same mirroring. Farah, a Muslim doll as popular in the Middle East as Barbie is in the United States, has almost as many accessories as Barbie, and Jewish Gali Girls are similar to American Girl dolls. For these dolls to successfully serve as examples, they have to compete with their rivals.

Religious dolls are of two basic types. The religious action figures and most talking dolls are overtly religious, while Muslim dolls like Razanne and Farah, or Jewish dolls like the Gali Girls, are presented as modest role models, to counteract the effects of immodestly dressed and consumer-oriented dolls like Barbie. In contrast to that female modesty, Samson and Goliath are muscular action figures, a form that corresponds to their biblical characters and their roles as major players in the battle for the toy box. Their design reflects the militaristic attitude behind their creation as well as the competition with other action figures for a market share.

In order to attract children or even teenagers to religion, marketing and models from popular culture are put into play. For example, in the following promotional recommendation for a child-oriented Bible, if one were to remove the words "Bible" and "biblical," there would be nothing to set it apart from advertising for a secular book:

> Parents and kids alike are instantly drawn to the Read With Me Bible for its outstanding, action-filled artwork. . . . [K]ids respond to the bold, humorous depictions of Bible characters, and easy-to-understand stories. And now this beloved Bible storybook for 4-to-8-year-olds is updated, with even more artwork, a new typeface, and a fresh, eye-catching cover. . . . Christian parents are always in the market for creatively designed, value-priced Bible storybooks for young children. They want a sound biblical message, but they want it packaged in a novel, state-of-the-art way. The Read With Me Bible has a proven track record of strong popularity with consumers. ("Read with Me Bible" 2009)

The quantity and variety of religious merchandise available reflect the marketplace as well. Board games and dolls are not the only examples of child-oriented religious commodities. Other examples include party favors, baseball caps, and children's Bibles—one website alone (tbnwebstore.org) offers 136 children's Bibles, including the "Children of Color Bible" and the "Precious Princess Bible." The apostles might be quite surprised to see the "252 Backpack Bible-NIV,"[4] which "also contains twelve color tip-in pages that show boys how they can grow smarter, stronger, deeper, and cooler to be like Jesus" ("252 Backpack Bible-NIV" 2009).

The effort to serve many masters is evident in the conflicting qualities exhibited by religious games and dolls. For example, as games, they are marketed as "fun," even though the relation of fun to some religious practices, such as *salat* (prayer, one of the five pillars of Islam) in the Madinah Salat Fun Game, seems an uneasy one at best. Moreover, apparently to be fun, a game must also be easy; a number of the Christian games note that no Bible knowledge is required. These games are marketed as Christian alternatives that will help instill values, yet the need to promote and sell them leads to contradictory claims.

Another example is the talking Bible dolls. One is the Holy Huggables talking Esther doll that one site claims speaks "actual scripture verses to introduce children of all ages to the wisdom of the Bible" ("Talking Esther Doll" 2009). While Esther's sound bites may be derived from scripture, "My natural beauty won the king's heart" is a far cry from most versions of Esther 2:12-17. If these phrases are meant to "introduce children of all ages to the wisdom of the Bible" what wisdom are the doll's creators aiming for? Their talking Jesus doll does not fare much better. While his scripture quotations may be more accurate, few of his phrases are from the Bible; "'I love you and I have an exciting plan for your life'" is not in any version of the New Testament that I am aware of.

The creators of some of these toys are not aiming for textual accuracy; they are more interested in the relationship between the child and the doll, a "faith-based and wholesome alternative to teddy bears and stuffed animals" that can "give kids a special source of comfort" ("New 'Holy Huggables' Plush Dolls Pack Fun and Faith into One Lovable Kid-Sized Package" 2007). This warm and fuzzy approach relates primarily to contemporary concepts of a "sweet and sentimental Jesus" (Bado-Fralick and Norris 2010: 179) but also to the use of play in religious schools—based on the idea that children can be attracted through games and play. This approach to education calls deeply on current understandings of play as necessary to development.

Play and Religious Education

The role of play in learning has been understood at least since Plato's time, and is the subject of much scholarship. But the relationship of play to religious education is not as clear, and evidence of scholarly interest in this topic is scant.

Religion and spirituality are set apart from fun, even though festivals and other games and enjoyable activities are an integral part of children's experience of religious life. This integration is acknowledged in some traditions—Hinduism, for example, in which festivals are so widespread that they can hardly be ignored. Although the enjoyable aspects of these activities are recognized, overall they are regarded by scholars more as occasions to "involve children in the spiritual and religious life of their elders" (Agarwal 2005: 26), and the fun or playful aspects of festivals or other beliefs, texts (such as myths), or practices may even be ignored altogether in a serious discussion of their aims. Academics apparently do not see these practices as the "religious" part of religion, and with rare exceptions (e.g., Bado-Fralick and Norris 2010; Raj and Dempsey 2010) do not consider them worthy as a focus of academic investigation.

Despite the fact that play is rarely acknowledged by scholars in their discussions of religious and spiritual development, it is nonetheless a common element in Sunday schools as well as religious nursery schools and kindergartens, not only in the United States but in other countries as well. In the Baby School (ages two to four) associated with the Choongshin Presbyterian Church in Seoul, Korea, for example, "educational activities consist of free play, singing and dancing, gym, worship, Bible stories, as well as family play, field trips, doll play, concerts, presentations, Mothers' class, and other special activities" (Dawson and Park 2005, 242).

To a certain extent the dichotomization of religion and play is understandable, since religion is serious business. Religious traditions inform our deepest identities and relationships with the cosmos. They address our most serious inner concerns—who we are, what it means to be human, what happens after we die, what the universe is. When it comes to religious education, children's souls are considered to be at stake.

> Parents who neglect to give this necessary Christian training and instruction to their children, or who permit them to go to schools in which the ruin of their souls is inevitable . . . that such parents, if obstinate, cannot be absolved [in confession] is evident from the moral teaching of the Church. ("Instruction of the Propaganda Fide concerning Catholic Children in American Public Schools" 2008: 57)

There appears to be a marked contradiction between adult understanding of the seriousness of children's spiritual development, on one hand, and the use of play in religious education or even the existence of religious games and dolls, on the other. For many people, the risk of trivializing religious concerns puts play and religion in opposing camps.

Religious toys are meant to inculcate religious ideals and values and to do so through play, by their very existence dissolving the apparent boundaries between play and religion. Religion can include play; the open and reciprocal relationship between religious and ordinary life, which has always been there, is acknowledged and evident in the place of religious toys in home and school, and in the influence of marketing and popular culture on religious toys.

Conclusion

Most toys are marketed to parents but also directly to children, a development driven by television (Kline 1993: 163-72). In the case of religious toys it is largely the parents' wishes and concerns that drive the market. Most religious games and dolls are simply religious alternatives to secular ones, aimed at instilling ethical values and religious concepts. Although they rely on children's attraction to play, the impulses behind religious playthings have more to do with adults than children; they aim for results that *adults* desire *for* children. This is true of toys in general; adults, whether parents, designers, or marketers, direct children's play toward their own ends. In research done by children's toy manufacturers and marketers, children appear to be the "experts" (Ridgely, chapter 5 this volume), but their voices are sought primarily in order to increase profits.

Religious toys both exploit and resist children's culture, a culture created in large part by toy manufacturers and television. As a subset of educational toys, they take advantage of contemporary marketing techniques as well as current attitudes towards play and educational toys, yet at the same time they resist contemporary toy culture by aiming to encourage ethical thinking and behavior and by serving as alternatives to games and dolls understood to be violent or immoral.

The impulse behind religious games and dolls is understandable. Religious and spiritual beliefs are part of our deepest identity; instilling those beliefs in their children or students assures parents and educators that their identity has value. But there is another side. America's cultural imperative of fun and the manufacturer's needs for profits shape the toys that inform children's developing religious identities. Marketing takes precedence over accuracy in many cases, and even when this is not the case, the medium shapes and limits what can be transmitted.

Marketing of religious games and toys affects religious identities in another way as well. In an interesting twist, there is a strong similarity between marketing toy lines through shows like Masters of the Universe, and marketing religions through religious toys. Catholicopoly, Mormonopoly, and Episcopopoly are a form of religious branding, aiming to ensure the continuity of distinct religious factions, each one in competition with the others.

At the extreme, religious toys become weapons in the battle for the toy box, a battle that separates and divides people from each other. It dichotomizes "us" and "them," proper religion from practices of "others." These interesting and evocative games and dolls, which by their very nature cross boundaries, can paradoxically be used to build them.

Most of these observations are relevant not just to religious games and toys but to all toys. Focusing on religious toys, a subset of educational toys (which are themselves a subcategory, albeit a vaguely defined one), brings issues to light that are relevant to those doing research with children, especially on games, play, or fun. The main points for researchers are that we can take toys seriously as sources, but we need to keep in mind how to approach them, what they are likely to tell us about the adults who created and use them, the historical and cultural contexts in which the children meant to play with them are living, market influences, and other factors that shape toys, play, and even conceptualizations of childhood. The uses (by adults or children) and influence of toys and games are not limited to their stated or intended aims, which are not necessarily the same thing, and may even be contradictory, as with intensive marketing of educational toys. The sensory and material dimensions of these items can also have a deeper influence than parents or educators may understand, as seen with graphic images, for example.

Another aspect to keep in mind is one's own cultural assumption about toys and children's play. What is considered "natural" in one time and place is anything but that in another. Our culturally embedded understandings are hidden from view, but we carry them with us and they color our observations and conclusions. It may be that questioning our assumptions about children is made more difficult *because* of contemporary attitudes toward children and childhood, and we need to be aware of how these and other beliefs shape our perceptions and thinking.

Finally, it is evident from my work in this area that there is a substantial area of study that is currently not being addressed by scholars: religious education and play. Considering that play makes up a significant part of religious education, in terms of time, attention, and resources, it is clear that this is an area ripe for research. There is ample opportunity for participant observation and a wealth of resources, including internet research and primary materials. I hope that others will hear this call to investigate the complex intersection of play, religion, education, and marketing.

NOTES

1. This is not a new phenomenon by any means. See, for example, Nasaw 1985: 20, 37.

2. For a more comprehensive discussion of play see Bado-Fralick and Norris 2010)

3. It is also interesting to note that among the photos at the end of this article is one of a mother playing with her child, with the caption, "Show your child the tenderness and love you feel for him" (Zimmerman and Calvolini 1971: 646). It is the mother's work to show her child love, and she apparently needs instructions to do this, just as the child needs the right learning tools to develop properly.

4. 252 Basics, which produces the backpack Bible, offers "a unique approach to curriculum for churches and Christian schools. It is built around three Basic Truths every child should embrace according to what Jesus modeled in Luke 2:52" ("252 Basics" 2009).

13

"God made this fire for our comfort"

Puritan Children's Literature in Context

PHILIPPA KOCH

The seventeenth-century English world witnessed a proliferation of literature designed for children. Puritans and other dissenters from the Church of England after the 1662 Act of Uniformity wrote much of this literature, from which emerged a new genre—a child's martyrology—that collected accounts of children dying with admirable piety. Historians have used these books to scrutinize adult intentions and psychology and to argue that Puritan childhood was fear filled and repressed. A focus on children and religion in the study of this literature, however, challenges historians to reexamine the sources, to reevaluate historical method, and to consider how literary narrative can reflect and shape life experiences.

This chapter focuses on two of the earliest and most successful books in this genre, James Janeway's *A Token for Children* and Thomas White's *A Little Book for Little Children*, to demonstrate both the perils and possibilities the study of this literature presents to modern scholarship. Puritans wrote this literature both about and for children. Historians cannot know with what accuracy this literature depicted children's actual experiences. Historians can demonstrate, however, that the Puritan community's narrative of faith and perseverance played a vital role in children's education and daily lives. The new literature merged catechism and martyrology into works that both instructed and entertained, that emphasized both theological correctness and appeal to children, and that encouraged children's interaction and creative engagement in their religious worlds.

Historiography and Methodology

Scholarship on children's literature often makes Puritans the low starting point in a narrative of progress, illustrated by the title of a recent anthology: *From Instruction to Delight: An Anthology of Children's Literature to 1850.*

Puritans are located on the "instruction" end of this continuum, reserved for works characterized as "uniformly repressive." The other end, "delight," consists of works "more sympathetically expressive." The editor, Patricia Demers, describes books like *A Token for Children* as "grim" but acknowledges the chasm between modern readers and Puritans, for whom "everything was charged with spiritual meaning."[1] Despite this concession, her narrative emplotment implies a progressive triumph of modern children's literature over past endeavors.[2]

This narrative of progress enables historians to measure past attitudes toward children against their own. Such an approach takes a selective view of the sources, disregarding what their construction and context might suggest about Puritan childhood and focusing instead on parental intentions and possible psychological repercussions in adults. Further, the approach lacks appreciation for different historical and religious contexts in which systems of belief foreign to the modern scholar infused life with spiritual import.

Francelia Butler, a foundational figure in the study of children's literature, offers one example of this approach. Appalled by the treatment of death in early children's literature, Butler described a "commercial and psychological exploitation of children through a special literature aimed at them alone."[3] While recent scholars of Puritan childhood usually acknowledge historical contexts and beliefs, many remain, like Butler, fixated on psychological implications and troubled by a perceived cultivation of fear.

Philip Greven's classic study, *The Protestant Temperament*, does not address children's literature but has nonetheless influenced scholarship on it.[4] Greven analyzes how early Americans' "psyches were shaped by formative experiences of childhood." Greven's sources for these childhood experiences come from adults, because, as he claims elsewhere, "one can deduce childhood experiences without any evidence whatsoever being available by knowing about the theoretical origins of adult psychological disorders."[5] Greven argues that children raised by parents of an "evangelical" temperament, including most Puritans, faced "a policy of unrelenting repression" and grew into adults who lacked a sense of self. He later describes them as "victims of violence and abuse."[6]

Greven judges "evangelical" childhood fearful and repressive, but had he focused on these children as children, and not as future adults, and had he considered theology, he might have read and interpreted the sources differently.[7] Greven does not offer a chronological narrative of progress; he proposes three different temperaments that exist concurrently. These temperaments inhabit a continuum of progress, with the "traumatized," self-assaulting evangelicals and the self-assured "genteels" forming the two extremes and the self-controlled, reasonable moderates occupying the middle.[8]

Historian David Stannard also explores the role of fear in Puritan childrearing. Part of his study of death in Puritan New England, the discussion appears in a helpful context; Stannard explains that a young married couple in the late seventeenth century probably understood that "in all probability *two or three* of [their] children . . . would die before the age of ten." He points to similarly high mortality rates in England. Stannard argues that Puritans loved their children but also saw them as "polluted with sin and natural depravity." Books like *A Token for Children* were used "to remind children of the ever-nearness of death and its possible consequences." He notes that "what we would consider a painfully early awareness of sin and death" was, for Puritans, necessary for "the well-being of the child and the community." Despite his attention to context, however, Stannard betrays a modern concern for the psychological toll of Puritan education, which, together with "the disquieting complexities of Puritan theology," produced "a culture permeated by fear and confusion in the face of death."[9] This modern concern limits the role of Puritan theology to fear and denies children any individual or creative role in its interpretation.

Literary historian Gillian Avery reaches similar conclusions. Citing the large amount of "juvenile death literature," including "sensational accounts of martyrdom," Avery argues that Puritans "sought to cause fear and used very considerable eloquence to depict the appalling prospects in store for children who were not savingly converted." Avery's evidence includes New England Puritan Samuel Sewall's journal entries describing conversations with his children about anxiety over death. Avery uses an adult source without considering why Sewall recorded these conversations—which perhaps he saw as moments of spiritual progress. Further limiting discussion of the theological context in which this literature emerged, Avery's only examples of the way children understood the literature are negative reflections from two nineteenth-century adults. The central focus on fear and sensationalism prevents a thorough examination of context. Avery suggests that children's literature began "with seventeenth-century Protestant concern to rescue children from hell," implying that these books represent a necessary, if unpleasant, starting point in the narrative of children's literature, which became "gentler" by the 1860s.[10]

Scholarship on Puritan children and their literature suffers from an implicit narrative of progress. This bias leads to a reading of the sources based on modern concerns and prevents historians from seeing constructive possibilities for the role of religion in children's lives. The first step in changing this approach involves asking what these texts say about children themselves.[11] The answer is not straightforward. Historians must examine the texts' contents and assess their popularity within Puritan communities and then look to clues such as the author's sources, editorial decisions, narrative construction, and possible motivations. Finally, historians should consider the books as a whole, within their literary and religious context, and attempt to understand the world the books reflected and promoted. This world was significant for both author and reader, and we can approach it through a critical examination of the texts.

Modern historical method only brings us so far in the study of Puritan children, because the sources we have are by adults and are deeply religious. Historian Dipesh Chakrabarty argues that a "certain kind of historicism, the metanarrative of progress, is . . . deeply embedded in our institutional lives." This secular understanding of progress, which has shaped narratives of Puritan childhood, is also ingrained in the discipline of history itself, with its standards of evidence and proof.[12] What should historians do when much of the evidence about Puritan children lies outside a desirable source base, infused with religious meaning and transmitted by adults?

To use this evidence when writing about Puritan children, we must move from our secular understanding of history and interpret a community in which a concept such as individual agency was, if anything, extremely limited—a community that saw God as the supreme actor. This movement, what Chakrabarty calls "translation," is difficult: we cannot make the Puritans' God an actor in the history we write, but we can make room for the importance of God in Puritan belief. The work of "translation" helps us to recognize and question modern assumptions about religion and repression. Translation, however, is limited, reminding the historian that her subjects inhabited a very different world, one that she can never completely know or narrate. Incorporating Puritan children into the historical narrative entails the significant work of both broadening the story and recognizing history's limits.[13]

How then do we get from highly structured, adult-written Puritan children's literature to the child's experience? Childhood studies scholars Pia Christensen and Alan Prout suggest the possibilities of the "new social studies" of childhood. Scholarship now sees children as "active in the construction and determination of their social lives," but Christensen and Prout emphasize the need "to recognize children as *both* restricted or encapsulated by social structures and as persons acting within or towards the structure."[14] Puritan children's literature illustrates the way social circumstances—like the literary and theological worlds that both codified and informed Puritan self-understanding and identity—shaped children's lives, as well as the way children might have made meaning within these circumstances. In reading this literature critically and exploring its context, we can reconsider previous accounts of Puritans and their children.

The Sources: Content, Publication, and Reception

In addition to two central sources, James Janeway's *A Token for Children* (hereafter *Token*) and Thomas White's *A Little Book for Little Children* (hereafter *A Little Book*), this chapter makes use of several other works of Puritan or dissenting literature, all published in (or near) the seventeenth century, and selected on the basis of popularity among Puritans, prominence in secondary literature, and usefulness as supplementary evidence to make a historical, theological, or literary point about the other texts. The methodology outlined above presents several questions: How were the sources constructed? What popularity did they achieve? Did they reflect the religious concerns of the authors and Puritan community? How did earlier literature influence them? And, finally, what can these books tell us about children and how they understood their world? The following sections will address each of these questions in turn. It is important to note that Puritan childhood and youth encompassed the years from age seven to the midteens, and, because of the centrality of reading in the religious communities of the English-speaking transatlantic world, childhood literacy flourished.[15] The texts considered here comprised two of the earliest and most widely available children's books of this time period.

Both *Token* and *A Little Book* were written in England in the 1670s by dissenting ministers. *Token* contained prefaces to adults and children and stories of thirteen children who demonstrated exemplary piety at their deaths. Originally published in two parts, some editions of *Token* published after 1673 also contained the second preface halfway through the volume.[16] *A Little Book* contained four sections: advice for children, historical examples of youthful martyrs, contemporary examples of pious, dying children, and a conclusion.[17]

The popularity of these texts can only be estimated from their publication record and references in other textual evidence. *Token*, first published in England in 1671, was followed by a second part in 1673. Both parts were reprinted in 1676 as a single edition, which made its way to the American colonies by 1677, when Increase Mather discussed it in a sermon as "a Book which many of you have in your houses, that giveth an account of thirteen Children."[18] Colonial booksellers began advertising *Token* in almanacs by 1692. It was first published in the colonies by 1700, with an addition by Cotton Mather titled "A Token for the Children of New-England," and remained in print through the eighteenth century.[19]

The publication record is less complete for *A Little Book*. Its first year of publication is unknown. In his preface to children in *Token*, Janeway wrote, *"get your Father to buy you* Mr. White's *Book for little Children,"* which suggests *A Little Book* predated *Token*'s 1671 publication date. One scholar notes that *A Little Book* was in its twelfth edition by 1703. It appeared in New England by 1702, and an advertisement provides evidence that it was published as late as 1726 in the colonies.[20] The record provides enough information to show that these books achieved a high level of popularity in the late seventeenth century.

These records pertain to an adult world of publishing, sermonizing, and bookselling and buying; they do not provide evidence for how the books might have been shared within a community and family,[21] nor how seventeenth-century children read and reacted to them. The only evidence for the latter is often from the books themselves. White encouraged children to actively engage in reading: "as you read (if the Books be your own) mark in the margin, or by underlining the places you find most relish in, and take most special notice of, and that doth most concern thee, that you may easily, and more quickly find them again."[22]

Both White and Janeway included accounts of children who developed strong connections to certain books. Janeway wrote of one child, John Sudlow, who "was hugely taken with the reading of the Book of *Martyrs*, and would be ready to leave his Dinner to go to his Book."[23] White told of John Langham, who loved his catechism so much that he "would often have it to bed with him."[24] These examples suggest that Puritan children were encouraged to have an active reading life and to enjoy texts like John Foxe's *Book of Martyrs* and the catechism, books with themes similar to those written by Janeway and White. These texts, however, were generated by adults; we need to assess whether these sources provide accurate depictions of children's experiences by evaluating how authors gathered evidence and shaped accounts.

Assessing the Sources: Standards of Evidence and Editorial Influence

Both Janeway and White claimed that their narratives were true representations of actual events. Their methods for collecting evidence seem similar to the demands of modern history: accounting for sources, including eye-witnesses, using verbatim accounts or transcriptions, and reporting character witnesses. Investigating the accounts closely, however, reveals significant differences between their methods and assumptions and our own standards—as seen in their heavy and not always forthright editorial hand, their use of hearsay, and their ultimate reliance on God as arbiter of truth.

In the first account of a child's death in *A Little Book*, White called himself "an Ear witness" to many of the events he recorded and, as to the "other things which I shall speak of him, I am fully satisfied." White's sources for the other accounts differed. He mentioned no source for the second, the source for the third was a minister who was also the father of the child, the fourth was transcribed from a funeral sermon, and the fifth was transcribed from the child's letters.[25] Two of White's accounts can be checked against the historical record: the funeral sermon still exists—and White faithfully transcribed his account from it[26]—and parts of the first account appear in another book.

The first account described the life of a child who died at age eight. The child "was frequent in reading, he would read two or three hours at once," and he marked his books, just as White suggested children should.[27] White reported that he had "several books of [the child's] marking, [such] as *Mr. Baxter's Call to the Unconverted*, wherein he hath marked many precious things, as you shall hear hereafter." In the following pages, White transcribed the child's eighty-four marked passages. At first glance these passages appear to offer a wealth of information about the child's reading habits and experiences. One passage reads, "These are not inventions of men to terrifie, but truths to reform you," suggesting that the child recognized the constructive role books like *A Call to the Unconverted*—with difficult themes like conversion and death—should play in his faith. Looking into the origins of these passages, however, complicates matters. The first thirty-one passages came from Baxter's *Call to the Unconverted*, which White earlier mentioned the child reading, among "several" other books.[28] Yet the last fifty-three passages came from only one source, *A Method and Instruction for the Art of Divine Meditation*, written by White himself.[29]

White failed to claim those later passages as his own work, perhaps fearing to discredit his objectivity. His unknown process of selection also raises issues. Did he transcribe every passage the child marked? If not, how did he choose the passages he used? Finally, there is the question of whether an actual child existed or an imagined child was created as a literary foil. While there are no certain answers, we can surmise that if the child existed, and if White knew him well enough to be an "Ear witness," it is likely that the child had access to White's book. We cannot ignore, however, White's editorial involvement in shaping the text's religious meaning.

Janeway also sought to explain his evidence-gathering methods. In his preface to parents and teachers, he wrote,

> *What is presented, is faithfully taken from experienced solid Christians, some of them no way related to the Children, who themselves were Eye and Ear witnesses of God's works of Wonder, or from my own knowledge, or from Reverend Godly Ministers, and from persons that are of unspotted reputation, for Holiness, Integrity and Wisdom; and several passages are taken verbatim in writing from their dying Lips.*[30]

Janeway emphasized first-hand accounts from unbiased sources—often non-relatives—of excellent reputation. Accounts also came from himself, ministers, reputable laypersons, or transcriptions of the child's words.

Despite Janeway's explanation, *Token* met with skepticism. His preface to the second part, published in 1673, addressed critical responses to the first part. Readers objected principally to the second example: the story of the child who "*began to be serious* [about religion] *between two and three years old.*" Readers feared that the incredibility of this account "*might somewhat prejudice the authority of the rest.*"[31] Janeway responded to this criticism in two ways. If his critics were "*bad*" people, "*it is no wonder at all to me, that the Subjects of Satan should not be very well pleased with that, whose design is to undermine the interest of their great Master: nothing will satisfie some, except Christ and holiness may be degraded and vilified.*" No evidence could satisfy these critics, Janeway contended, because they objected to the accounts in their entirety, including the faith the stories both relied upon and propounded.[32]

If Janeway's critics were "*godly,*" however, he was willing to "*give them reasonable satisfaction.*" He wrote that his witness, "*Mrs.* Jeofries," was known "*for her exemplary Piety, Wisdom, Experience, and singular watchfulness over every punctilio that she speaks.*" Her name was "*precious to most of the Ministers of* London," and her authority "*almost*" equaled that of those ministers. Responding to the criticism, she called on "*God to witness, that she hath spo-*

ken nothing but the Truth; only in this she failed, in that she spake not by far so much as she might have done concerning that sweet Babe." Janeway also pointed to corresponding cases of children equally young, described by "*a godly gentleman*" and in the books of "*Reverend Mr. Clark.*"[33]

As in his first preface, Janeway called on multiple sources of evidence, but here he implied that truth and authenticity relied on the proximity to the church of both the witness *and* the reader. He criticized those who questioned his accounts: "*I think most of Gods [sic] works in the business of Conversion call for Admiration: And I believe that Silence or rather Praise would better become Saints than questioning the truth of such things.*" For Janeway, these "*wonders*" were the work of God. While Janeway's standards of evidence seem familiar—with eye-witnesses, verbatim records, and character references—his ultimate claim to truth was God: "*Hath God said he will work no more wonders?*" Children's experiences still mattered to Janeway; indeed, they were of the utmost importance because they demonstrated God's wonders in everyday life.[34] This did not, however, place their stories beyond the editorial hand.

An account in *A Little Book* illustrates how authors could slightly alter stories for religious and political ends. White included a narrative based on II Maccabees, in which seven young Jewish brothers suffered persecution and death because they refused to "Contemn the . . . superstitious belief of [their] Countrey-men, and embrace [the ruler Antiochus's] Religion." White prefaced his account by drawing parallels to his young readers' lives: "My dear little Children, do not you find *your* hearts willing if ever Persecution should arise, to *Dy* rather than to *Deny* Christ and turn Papists? Would *you* not rather sing at the stake to be burnt, then [sic] worship Images?"[35]

White's version of II Maccabees came from the works of Josephus, translated by Thomas Lodge in 1602.[36] White followed Lodge's translation but made some telling changes. Historian Erin Kelly recently demonstrated that Lodge's translation of Josephus revealed his Catholic sympathies, particularly in the story of the seven brothers, although Kelly remained uncertain that Lodge's contemporaries recognized the problematic aspects of the translation.[37] A close comparison of Lodge's and White's versions of the Maccabees story shows that White edited Lodge's account, deleting many of the references to "tyranny" as well as to intercessory prayers.[38] White took care in framing the martyrological message for his audience of Puritan and dissenting children. He edited out Lodge's underlying Catholic political and religious statements and emphasized themes important to his historical and religious context: the steadfast faith of the brothers against demands for religious conformity.[39]

White's alterations to this story, along with Janeway's ultimate reliance on God for truth, demonstrate why we must carefully examine these sources. Understanding how White and Janeway presented the evidence and fashioned their stories allows us to see these texts as historical documents permeated with religious sentiment. These depictions of children were undoubtedly formed by religious motivations, yet the books' popularity suggests that these depictions appealed to children and their parents—either as reflecting childhood experiences or as ideal examples.

Literary Influences: Catechism and Martyrology

Finally, it is important to consider *Token* and *A Little Book* within their literary and religious context. Janeway and White relied on existing genres of religious literature, including catechisms and martyrologies, in order to develop instructional and entertaining books for children. Both catechisms and martyrologies encouraged interaction. The question-and-answer format of catechisms was employed to instill confidence in the theological system that shaped Puritan lives and communities, and martyrologies provided Puritans with examples of suffering, resistance, and perseverance in faith. By adapting these interactive texts into a single literature about and for children, Puritans gave children an opportunity to individually and creatively engage in and react to their social world.

A crucial part of children's literature, the catechism permeated both *Token* and *A Little Book*. Catechizing involved set questions and answers and further examinations into the answers to test understanding. Older children learned accompanying proof texts in order to gain a deeper, biblical knowledge of the catechism.[40] White's account of John Langham described an exemplary attention to catechetical instruction:

> He learned his Catechism throughout (*the Assemblies shorter Catechism*)[41] and began to learn it over again with the Proofs of the Scripture at large, wherein he had made some Progress, yet did he not learn these things as a Parrot, by rote without understanding what he said, but could give a good account (*much beyond what might be expected in one of his Years*) of the sense & meaning of what he learned.[42]

Catechizing encouraged a high degree of inward knowledge and appropriation of the catechism. Rote memorization was not enough.[43]

The order and theology of the catechism shaped the very structures of *Token* and *A Little Book*. The prefaces encouraged children to use these books to think about God and their utter sinfulness, to despair of their ability to fulfill the moral law, to give themselves up to Christ, and to "resolve in well doing all your days"—that is, the process of sanctification—by praying secretly, obeying parents, reading good books, avoiding bad company, and not lying.[44] This catechetical order also influenced the narratives of children's deaths. Janeway's fifth example was a child who had not grown up in the church but "was by the Providence of God, brought to the sight of a godly Friend of mine" and "brought to a liking of the things of God." The passive tense emphasized the child's inability to fulfill the moral law and come to God without God's providence and effectual calling.[45]

Recognizing sinfulness and inability to fulfill the moral law, many of the children in these accounts went through a period of weeping, praying alone, and reading. Janeway described one child who "is still more and more broken under a sense of his undone state by Nature: He is oft in Tears, and bemoaning his lost & miserable Condition."[46] Puritans considered weeping a normal part of spiritual turmoil; one of the passages White recorded in *A Little Book* read, "Mine Eyes are dry, as mine Heart is hard."[47] A hardened heart—like dry eyes—implied an inability to witness the works and word of God;[48] weeping and tears, though, could be a sign of election.

After repentance, the accounts, following the catechism, moved to justification and sanctification. Janeway offered a detailed description in his eleventh example. Susannah Bicks, who died in 1664 at age fourteen, prayed for comfort in Christ's arms, and later exclaimed, "I lye here as a Child, O Lord I am thy Child, receive me into thy gracious Arms. O Lord, Grace! Grace! and not Justice! for if thou shouldest enter into Judgment with me, I cannot stand, yea, none living should be just in thy sight." Bicks described the comforting presence of the Spirit, sent by God as promised in the Bible.[49] She acknowledged that God redeemed her from sin and meditated on receiving the "*Spirit of Adoption*." Following the catechism, she spoke of her soul leaving her body at death, to be reunited at the resurrection, "albeit the Worms eat up my Flesh, yet with these Eyes shall I behold God."[50]

Allusions to the catechism also occurred at key dialogue moments in both *Token* and *A Little Book*. Adults quizzed dying children with questions about death in a manner similar to the question/answer structure of a catechism. White described one such scene: "When he fell last sick, of which he died, his

Father asked him, whether he would die or live? he answered, he had rather die: his Father asked him, why he would rather die? he said, that he might go to God; but how dost thou know thou shalt go to God when thou diest, said his Father? he said, I love GOD."[51] Janeway described similar scenes, including one in which a minister tested the child:

> John, Art thou not afraid to Die? He answered, No, If the Lord will but comfort me in that Hour. But said the Minister, How canst thou expect comfort, seeing we deserve none? He answered, No, if I had my deserts I had been in Hell long ago. But replied the Minister, Which way dost thou expect Comfort and Salvation, seeing thou art a Sinner? He answered In Christ alone.[52]

We cannot know that Puritans questioned their dying children so resolutely, but the theme recurs throughout the literature. While some scholars may find such quizzing fear inducing, the catechetical nature of these books illustrates how Puritan parents prepared their children for both life and death within a comprehensive theological system. The books gave children examples of how to enact the catechism. Catechisms had set answers, and answering its questions correctly could give children confidence—especially those who suffered or faced death.

A public declaration of faith at the time of death also appeared in martyrologies. Some martyrs recited their faith in triumph immediately before their deaths, others responded faithfully in the examinations that convicted them.[53] Like the catechism, martyrologies played a significant role in shaping the accounts that appeared in Token and A Little Book. White urged children to read and take notes "in the Book of Martyrs," and Janeway approvingly noted one child's fascination with the "Book of Martyrs."[54] First published in 1563, John Foxe's Acts and Monuments, more commonly known as the Book of Martyrs, was a key text of the Protestant martyrological tradition in seventeenth-century England and the colonies. Foxe recorded the "Acts and Monuments" of the recent Marian martyrs because he recognized, historian Brad Gregory noted, "that a long Elizabethan reign was far from guaranteed." Foxe wrote to keep these examples of faith in the minds of his fellow believers.[55]

Foxe's martyrs followed the tradition of the Ars moriendi, which told of the last five temptations a Christian encountered on his deathbed—a moment of struggle between God and the devil. The Christians described in this work suffered but persevered in faith, reassuring their loved ones of their hope for salvation.[56] Foxe's attention to the hour of death resembled this tradition; patient suffering and community witness formed central aspects of his martyrs' deaths, yet his martyrs were ultimately sure of their salvation.[57]

Foxe drew his martyrs vividly, historian John Knott has argued, as ordinary people within a community. Focused on the drama of the scene, Foxe included humanizing details, incorporated documents such as letters, and described events like trials. He depicted the martyr as a real person whose actual words survived within a "larger narrative chronicling the resistance of individuals and the ultimate triumph in England of the true church."[58] Foxe hoped that readers might "imitate [the martyr's] death (as much as we may) with like constancy."[59] The *Book of Martyrs* conferred a powerful religious self-understanding to Puritans, who, even in the absence of the intense religious persecution of the Marian age, maintained this tradition.[60]

Writers extended this martyrological legacy to children. The popular *New England Primer*, first published between 1686 and 1690,[61] reprinted the story of the first Marian martyr, John Rogers. Among the *Primer*'s lessons appeared a poetic version of Roger's dying exhortation to his children: "Abhor that arrant Whore of Rome, / and all her Blasphemies; / And drink not of her cursed Cup, / obey not her decrees." Just as Foxe described his martyrs' transcendence over pain and their certain salvation, so did the *Primer*'s account of Rogers' death: "Though here my Body be adjudg'd / in flaming Fire to fry, / My Soul I trust will straight ascend; / to live with GOD on high."[62]

Janeway and White developed their books within this martyrological tradition but chose to focus on child martyrs. Publication records suggest both the success of this choice and that parents found these works engaging and suitable for children. The books featured exemplars of children's own age—pious youths who lived and died heroically and contributed to their community's narrative of faith and perseverance.

Sarah Howley, Janeway's first example, demonstrated how to suffer and die in imitation of the martyrs. Converted between the ages of eight and nine, Howley devoted time to the spiritual welfare of her siblings. At age fourteen, Howley "brake a Vein in her Lungs (as is supposed) and oft did spit Blood, yet did a little recover again, but had several dangerous relapses." As Howley neared death, she—like Foxe's martyrs—assumed the role of spiritual advisor. When her mother movingly asked, *"How shall I bear parting with thee, when I have scarce dryed my eyes for thy Brother?* She answered, the God of love, support & comfort you: It is but a little while, and we shall meet in Glory, I hope." Howley bequeathed her Bible to her brother, exhorting him to make his "Calling & Election sure, while you are in Health." Later, surrounded by her father's servants, she prayed to God to *"finish thy work upon their Souls.* It will be my Comfort to see you in Glory, but it will be your everlasting Happiness." When her grandmother chided her for expending so much energy, Howley declared, "I care not for that, if I could do any Soul good."[63]

Janeway's account of Howley's life and death bore similarities to themes in Foxe's *Book of Martyrs.* Howley persevered in suffering as she awaited God's grace, and she comforted others and stressed the work of conversion in her dying moments. These efforts echo Foxe's martyrs, such as Thomas Bilney, who distributed alms en route to execution and comforted his fellow minister, encouraging him to "[f]eed your flock, feed your flock, that when the Lord cometh, he may find you so doing." Further, like all of the children in Janeway's volume—and like Foxe's martyrs—Howley died surrounded by an audience. This audience prayed and rejoiced with her, but did not equal her spiritually. As death approached, her faith surpassed that of her parents and grandmother, who worried about earthly things such as comfort in sorrow and physical ease in death. Howley, a child, achieved a heroic death worthy of emulation.[64]

Charles Bridgman's account offers an explicit connection between Janeway's volume and the *Book of Martyrs.* Janeway describes Bridgman as a thoughtful child who rebuked "his Brethren" for poor Christian behavior and whose "Sentences were wise and weighty, and well might become some ancient Christian." Falling ill, Bridgman reflected on the "Nature of his Soul" and became sure of his "Hope" in salvation. After his pains increased, the catechism-like quizzing began. Asked "*[w]hether he would rather still endure those Pains, or forsake Christ?*" Bridgman answered,

> Alas . . . *I know not what to say, being but a Child; for these Pains may stagger a strong Man; but I will strive to endure the best that I can.* Upon this he called to mind that Martyr *Thomas Bilney*; who being in Prison, the Night before his burning, put his Finger into the Candle, to know how he could endure the Fire. O (said the Child) *had I Lived then, I would have run through the Fire to have gone to Christ.*[65]

Although it did not occur at the stake, Bridgman's death represented suffering within a martyrological context. The reference to Bilney's actions on the eve of his execution allowed Bridgman to act as a youthful intermediary between the *Book of Martyrs* and Janeway's young audience.[66]

Both Janeway and White emphasized the importance of testing and its constructive possibilities. Near his conclusion, White wrote of the fires that awaited wicked children in hell and paused to play with the idea of fire. Referencing Bilney's account, White reminded children, "Alas, our fire is but as painted fire to that of Hell, and if this burn so fiercely, what will that do? God made this fire for our comfort, but that only for torment."[67] Historian Michael McGiffert has demonstrated that anxiety and assurance often occurred simultaneously or cyclically in Puritan piety, one of its central paradoxes.[68] Like Foxe's martyrs, Puritans understood this life as a life of testing—or "proving"—that prepared them for death and could offer a sign of election.[69] For Puritans, tests could be painful and challenge belief, but successful perseverance brought faith, sanctification, and the hope of heaven.

Puritan children's literature incorporated the martyrological tradition and made its themes accessible to youth. Accounts like those in *Token* and *A Little Book* showed that ordinary children could suffer and die extraordinary deaths—just like Foxe's martyrs. Martyrological influences made the literature entertaining in its dramatic biographical accounts of children overcoming suffering within a community of faith. By merging catechism and martyrology, Janeway and White vivified the catechism and demonstrated how to enact the martyrology's call to an active faith. They produced a literature that tested children individually and included them within the community's narrative of perseverance. Like the genres from which it derived, Puritan children's literature encouraged interaction; elements of fear and control emerged in these texts, yet the literature treated children as participants through grace in their own salvation and sanctification.

Conclusion

Scholarship on Puritan children's literature has suffered from a focus on adults and from an implicit progress narrative that privileges the present. In researching this remarkable body of literature, which achieved high popularity in its time, historians should cast a critical eye at existing scholarship, which often neglects the crucial question: what can these sources tell us about children and religion?

Asking this question transforms our approach to these sources and suggests a method for analyzing children's religious literature from other eras and communities. Scholars should evaluate texts for authorial intentions as well as for literary and religious influences. In the Puritans' case, we learn how theologically charged these texts were, how they reflected Puritans' understandings of themselves and their communities, and how the authors adapted complicated theological ideas for a child's understanding.

The careful reading pursued in this chapter also cautions against making modern psychological assessments of children of the past, particularly when these assessments can only be based upon religious and devotional literature written by adults. Thus this essay warns against the simple assumption that Puritan children were repressed or abused. Without the children's own writings we cannot know how they responded to these books, yet it is clear that the books were written to teach children how to participate in their community and how to live the essential elements of faith in their daily lives. The texts encouraged children to engage their religious world in constructive and meaningful ways and proffered the possibilities of hope and heroism in the face of death.

NOTES

1. Patricia Demers, *From Instruction to Delight: An Anthology of Children's Literature to 1850*, 2d ed. (Ontario: Oxford University Press, 2004), xvi, 46, 56.

2. On emplotment, see Hayden White, *Metahistory: The Historical Imagination in Nineteenth-Century Europe* (Baltimore: Johns Hopkins University Press, 1973), 7-11. On the progress narrative in scholarship on Puritan children, see Catherine Brekus, "Children of Wrath, Children of Grace: Jonathan Edwards and the Puritan Culture of Child Rearing," *The Child in Christian Thought*, ed. Marcia Bunge (New York: Eerdmans, 2000), 328.

3. Francelia Butler, "Death in Children's Literature," *Children's Literature* 1 (1972): 104.

4. See, for example, Diana Pasulka, "A Somber Pedagogy: A History of the Child Death Bed Scene in Early American Children's Literature, 1674-1840," *Journal of the History of Childhood and Youth* 2 (2009): 176-77, 194 nn. 18, 22.

5. Philip Greven, *The Protestant Temperament: Patterns of Child-Rearing, Religious Experience, and the Self in Early America* (Chicago: University of Chicago Press, 1977), 14-15; Philip Greven, "The Protestant Temperament Reconsidered," *Through a Glass Darkly: Reflections on Personal Identity in Early America*, eds. Ronald Hoffman, Mechal Sobel, and Fredrika J. Teute (Chapel Hill: University of North Carolina Press, 1997), 367-68.

6. Greven (1977), 35, 61; Greven (1997), 366.

7. Greven (1977), 17.

8. Ibid., 12-14; Greven (1997), 368-69.

9. David E. Stannard, *The Puritan Way of Death: A Study of Religion, Culture, and Social Change* (Oxford: Oxford University Press, 1997), 55-60, 65, 69.

10. Gillian Avery, "Intimations of Mortality: The Puritan and Evangelical Message to Children," *Representations of Childhood Death*, eds. Gillian Avery and Kimberley Reynolds (New York: Macmillan, 2000), 87-89, 98-103.

11. See Pia Christensen and Alan Prout, "Anthropological and Sociological Perspectives on the Study of Children," *Researching Children's Experience: Approaches and Methods*, eds. Sheila Greene and Diane Hogan (London: Sage, 2005), 47.

12. Dipesh Chakrabarty, *Provincializing Europe: Postcolonial Thought and Historical Difference* (Princeton, NJ: Princeton University Press, 2000), 88-89, 99, 106.

13. Ibid., 95, 107, cf. 106, 112.

14. Christensen and Prout, 50, 42. Their emphasis.

15. Brekus, 302; David Hall, *Worlds of Wonder, Days of Judgment: Popular Religious Belief in Early New England* (Cambridge, MA: Harvard University Press, 1989), 32, 6. See discussion of literacy and distinction between reading and writing abilities: 32, 262-63.

16. James Janeway, *A Token for Children the Second Part* (London: D. Newman, 1673); James Janeway, *A Token for Children* (London: D. Newman, 1676); James Janeway, *A Token for Children* (Boston: Nicholas Boone, 1700). Unable to locate the 1671 edition, I use the 1676 edition unless otherwise noted.

17. Thomas White, *A Little Book for Little Children* (Boston: T. Green for B. Eliot, 1702); Thomas White, *A Little Book for Little Children* (Boston: T. Green for N. Buttolph, 1702). The former, hereafter "White (Eliot)," is the most accessible edition but lacks the last page. The latter has a partially readable final page.

18. Avery, "Intimations," 95; Increase Mather, *A Call from Heaven* (Boston: J. Foster, 1679), 106-7; see Hall, *Worlds*, 50.

19. *Boston Almanack* (Boston: B. Harris and J. Allen, 1692), appendix; Cotton Mather, *A Token for the Children of New England* (Boston: T. Green, 1700).

20. Janeway, xviii; cf. Hall, *Worlds*, 36; F. J. Harvey Darton, *Children's Books in England: Five Centuries of Social Life* (Cambridge: Cambridge University Press, 1932), 59; White (Eliot); White (Buttolph); William Cooper, *The Service of God Recommended to the Choice of Young People* (Boston: T. Fleet, 1726), appendix. The Toronto Public Library has a version of *A Little Book* attached to a 1660 book by White. Thomas White, *A Manual for Parents* (London: J. Cranford, 1660). I am unsure if *A Little Book* was added later or if this suggests an earlier publication date.

21. See discussion of book lending in New England in Hall, *Worlds*, 44-45.

22. White (Eliot), 19.

23. Janeway, 2: 4.

24. White (Eliot), 74; cf. use of catechism in Janeway, 1:24, 51, 2:3, 19, 23, 71-72.

25. White (Eliot), 54, 72, 73, 78.

26. See Thomas Burroughs, *A Soverain Remedy for All Kinds of Grief*, 2d ed. (London: T. R., 1662).

27. White (Eliot), 54, 59, 19.

28. Ibid., 60-71; Richard Baxter, *A Call to the Unconverted* (London: R. W., 1658).

29. Thomas White, *A Method and Instruction for the Art of Divine Meditation* (London: Thomas Parkhurst, 1672).

30. Janeway, v, 1:55; italics in original. Janeway attributed Bridgman's narrative to "*Mr. Ambrose's Life's Lease*," a text I could not locate. Janeway, 1:49.

31. Janeway (1673), ii.

32. Ibid., ii-iii.

33. Ibid., iv. "Rev. Clark" was probably Samuel Clark, whose writings included *The Lives of Sundry Eminent Persons in this Later Age* (London: T. Simmons, 1683).

34. Janeway (1673), iii-v.

35. White (Eliot), 38-39.

36. Ibid., 39; cf. Avery, "Intimations," 95; Thomas Lodge, *The Famous and Memorable Works of Josephus* (London: J.L. for Luke Faune, 1655), 802-13. According to Early English Books Online, Lodge's text appeared in at least sixteen editions by 1670.

37. Erin E. Kelley, "Jewish History, Catholic Argument: Thomas Lodge's 'Workes of Josephus' as a Catholic Text," *Sixteenth-Century Journal* 34 (2003): 997, 1003.

38. Lodge, 802-13; White (Eliot), 39-54; cf. Kelley, 1003.

39. White (Eliot), 51-53. On the Maccabees in Catholic and Protestant traditions, see Brad Gregory, *Salvation at Stake* (Cambridge, MA: Harvard University Press, 1999), 123.

40. Cf. Cotton Mather, *Bonifacius: An Essay upon the Good* (Boston: B. Green, 1710), 56-57.

41. Westminster Assembly, *The Shorter Catechism* (London: Company of the Stationers, 1657).

42. White (Eliot), 73-78.

43. Cf. Janeway, 1:24, 51, 2:4, 19, 23, 72.

44. Ibid., vii-xviii; White (Eliot), 3-25; cf. Westminster.

45. Janeway, 1:50-51; cf. Westminster, 10-12, 17.

46. Janeway, 1:60; cf. 1:2-4, 21-23, 27-30, 34-35, 39-40, 53, 2: 29, 69.

47. White (Eliot), 67.

48. Cf. Exodus 4:21.

49. Janeway, 2:23-46; see John 14:16.

50. Janeway, 2:46-53, 60; see Job 19:26; cf. Westminster, 17-22.

51. White (Eliot), 58.

52. Janeway, 2:13.

53. See, for example, John Foxe, *Acts and Monuments* (London: Company of Stationers, 1641), 278, 578-80.

54. White (Eliot), 19; Janeway, 2:4.

55. Foxe, title page, 15-16; Gregory, 173.

56. Gregory, 52-53.

57. See John N. King, *Foxe's Book of Martyrs and Early Modern Print Culture* (Cambridge: Cambridge University Press, 2006), 201; Gregory, 109, 177.

58. John R. Knott, "John Foxe and the Joy of Suffering," *Sixteenth-Century Journal* 27 (1996): 721, 725, 728-29, 733.

59. Foxe, 15-16.

60. See Susan Juster, "What's 'Sacred' about Violence in Early America? Killing, and Dying, in the Name of God in the New World," *Common-place* 6 (2005) [online]; cf. Gregory, 7, 137-38.

61. Gillian Avery, *Behold the Child* (Baltimore: Johns Hopkins University Press, 1994), 29.

62. *The New-England Primer, Enlarged* (Boston: S. Kneeland & T. Green, 1727), 29-36. Rogers's story first appeared in Benjamin Harris, *A Protestant Tutor for Children* (Boston: S. Green, [1685]). See also Juster.

63. Janeway, 1:1-18.

64. Foxe, 278; Janeway, 1:10-18.

65. Janeway, 1:46-49.

66. The *Book of Martyrs* includes a woodcut of Bilney. Foxe, 277.

67. White (Eliot), 89.

68. Michael McGiffert, ed., *God's Plot: The Paradoxes of Puritan Piety; Being the Autobiography and Journal of Thomas Shepard* (Amherst: University of Massachusetts Press, 1972), 20, 24-26.

69. See Psalm 66:10-12.

14

Childhood in the Land of Hope

Black Children and Religion in Chicago, 1920-1945

MOIRA HINDERER

Bronzeville's devouter church people are almost unanimous in
their belief that "our young people are on the road to hell."[1]
Black Metropolis, 1945

The fears about the religious and moral lives of children expressed
in the quotation above were not exclusive to Black Chicago; rather, these
concerns were common among adults of many races, religions, and regions
in the twentieth-century United States. In the case of Black Chicago, adult
fears reflected a gap between adult and child experiences of urban life. The
generation of children growing up in Black Chicago between 1920 and 1945
could be called "the gospel generation." While not all of them listened to
or performed gospel music, they were a generation of migrants growing
up in a city that was home to a vastly expanding urban, Black vernacular
culture, of which gospel was a central expression. Many adults described
this diverse, commercial, loud, and fast-moving environment as one filled
with dangers, including the loss of adult religious authority. Adults often
sought to regain this lost authority by stressing formal religious participation, including church and Sunday school attendance, and adherence
to denominational behavior standards. For young people, the simple rules
prescribed by adults often proved to be a framework insufficient to help
them make sense of their complicated lived experience of religion. Adults,
for example, often described religion as a set of formal experiences and
encouraged a strict divide between sacred piety and secular pleasure, while
children in Chicago experienced both a commercial world of religion and
a spiritual world of commerce and entertainment. While children sometimes used the same formal terms as their elders, they also discussed religion in terms of sensory awareness, personal relationships, and everyday
experiences. Uncovering these wide-ranging religious experiences requires

scholars to look beyond texts that focus on the formal religious practices of children and instead seek evidence of the holistic world of religion described by young people.

Like other groups, Black children in Chicago had historically and culturally specific experiences of religion. In the decades after World War I, the Great Migration of Black southerners to the urban North produced vibrant and rapidly expanding communities. Churches were widely recognized as important organizations in Black Chicago and other African American communities in northern cities. A study conducted in Chicago found five hundred predominantly Black churches from more than thirty denominations with two hundred thousand members in a general African American population of 278,000 in 1940.[2] Despite the recognized importance of churches, and the popular belief that religion was a solution to the perceived "youth problem," there remains much that scholars do not know about the religious beliefs of Black children and youth in migration-era Chicago.

A majority of churched Black children in the city were Protestants, but smaller numbers of Catholics, Muslims, Bahais, and other groups also shaped the religious landscape. For many of Chicago's Catholic children of European heritage, life was dominated by the parish model, which infused geography, education, and social relations within the spiritual life of the Catholic Church.[3] By contrast, most Black children went to public schools alongside children of many denominations, and also lived and played in this racially segregated but religiously mixed environment. Most African American children in the city were children of migration—either migrants themselves, or children of migrant parents. Particularly for rural migrants, Chicago presented a new and amazing array of commercial and religious options.[4]

Most churches offered activities specifically for young people, ranging from church-sponsored parties and events to Bible-study and prayer groups. Youth services were also popular events at churches. These services allowed young people to practice all of the church positions normally occupied by adults, including preacher, choir director, and usher. Denominations that valued spirit-led public expression encouraged children to begin offering simple prayers and testimonies while they were young and to continue building their skills over time. Thus, the religious participation of young people could constitute a broad range of activities, from attending a dance to studying and praying with other young people to preaching before an entire congregation.

The basic historical information above provides evidence of the world of formal religious practices of Black children in the mid-twentieth century, yet it leaves many questions about the religious experiences and beliefs of young people unanswered. Scholars of religion who wish to know what children thought and believed set themselves a difficult task. The question of how people receive texts that they read, view, or hear is always complicated, and it is made more so when those individuals are children. Because adults were once children, the terrain of childhood feels familiar, and that can make us think we know more than we actually do about the experiences of young people. Adults occupy positions of power and author most texts, making it very difficult to reconstruct the voices of historical children. There are, however, specific techniques that scholars can employ to address these challenges. Using historically sensitive interpretation, consulting a variety of sources, and seeking patterns within those sources can bring historians closer to an interpretation of children's religious experiences.

One of the most challenging tasks facing scholars is trying simultaneously to understand and take seriously our informants from the informants' points of view, while also placing that point of view within a broader historical analysis. This type of reading asks scholars to look beyond direct statements made by sources and seek unexpressed ideas and multiple explanations. For example, if we took the statement that opened this essay as fact, we would assume that Black children in Chicago were indeed "on the road to hell," or at least that the young people of the migrant generation were growing less religious than their parents and grandparents, perhaps distracted by a modern city that offered many forms of entertainment. While there is no quantitative historical evidence of growing irreligion among young African Americans, this statement is still useful because it exposes a cultural tension around issues of age and religion.

This chapter locates those adult concerns as a starting point for exploring a cultural conversation between adults and children. Religious leaders, like the one quoted above, expressed adult fears of loss of control over young people in a new environment, as well as concerns about a broader cultural shift in religious practices. Meanwhile, children seemed to feel comfortable in a diverse and changing religious environment. Young people continued to feel strong ties to religious beliefs and practices, although those beliefs and practices sometimes differed from those of their parents. Reading from a child-centered perspective reminds scholars to be attentive to tensions within historical documents and to explore not only the point of view of the creator of the text but also the point of view of the subject of the text.[5]

Children and the Religious Landscape of the Great Migration

The years between 1920 and 1945 discussed in this chapter were a period of religious transition and conflict, both in Black Chicago specifically and in the United States as a whole. This was the period of the birth of both Christian modernism and Christian fundamentalism.[6] Contemporary scholars, as well as scholars and everyday people during the migration era, all agreed that the religious practices and beliefs of individuals were closely tied to social class. Before the Great Migration, Black churches in Chicago were dominated by mainline Protestant churches with fairly well-off congregations who were wary of emotional styles that they associated with poor, rural people. As large numbers of poor and working-class African Americans came to Chicago, they brought distinctive religious practices that often clashed with the restrained style of many established African American churches. Some new migrants responded by establishing their own churches more attuned to the emotional and miraculous, while others joined established churches, which they then pressured for change.[7]

By the 1930s, the new form of worship music known as gospel exploded, first from Holiness-Pentecostal churches, and then more broadly from churches like Chicago's Pilgrim Baptist. Adult participants in these churches and outside observers agreed that the opportunity to participate in gospel quartets and choirs drew young people to these churches. Gospel provoked controversy in many Chicago churches while also achieving popular success in the marketplace.[8] Gospel's blend of religious sentiment and popular musical styles provoked the ire of many adults in the city who questioned the religious and moral legitimacy of the form; conversely, for many young people in Chicago, gospel's blend of pleasure and spirituality, religion and commerce both shaped and reflected their own experiences of the religious landscapes of the city.

Historical sources generally agree that there was widespread participation by African American children and youth in Chicago in formal religious services. The authors of the extensive sociological study *Black Metropolis*, published in 1945, suggested that even unchurched parents tended to send their children to "Sunday School as a part of their 'right raising.'"[9] The scholars also noted that for many young people, religious instruction on Sunday was one part of a larger social scene that involved dressing up in one's best clothes, meeting friends out on the street, and after services going out to the movies or hanging out in a local park.[10] For many adults this mix of sacred and secular amusements was highly disturbing, a slippery slope toward immorality. Young people themselves, however, offered a more complicated analysis.

In 1925, an observer sat in on a Sunday School lesson for a group of junior high school–aged girls. After the girls studied their lesson on the Ten Commandments, they moved on to the topic of keeping the Sabbath holy. According to the observer, who was researching the content of Sunday school education in Chicago,

> Some of the members decided that if attending the theatre was not done at the expense of Sunday School and was attended as a substitute for some less constructive activity, then to attend the "movie" on Sunday was not failing to keep the day holy. They talked on the types of pictures which stimulate thought about life's meaning and agreed that pictures of this kind were decidedly not conductive to the abuse of Sunday, the day set apart in our social order as a day for repose and worship. Others questioned the baseball game and similar sports in relation to Sunday and discussed the factors that make ball playing and engaging in other sports sinful.[11]

These girls appeared comfortable with the idea that there was not one correct answer to the question of how to spend Sunday. They also seemed to feel that they could speak fairly freely, and even offer opinions that might contradict those of another girl. The conclusions reached by the girls were in line with the teachings of many liberal Protestant churches at the time that focused on ethical training rather than rigid codes of conduct, while also encouraging young people to be engaged with the wider world.

Other children came to similar conclusions about the relationships between religious participation and secular amusements despite, seemingly, spending less time analyzing the issue. One girl growing up in an African American neighborhood on Chicago's West Side told an interviewer casually that "[s]ometimes we go to church, and sometimes we go to the show."[12] She expressed no fear that going to the movies instead of attending church was bad or sinful. Rather, this—admittedly fragmentary—response suggests that church services and movies were simply two ways to spend time in the city. While many adults expressed concern about the blurring of lines between secular entertainment and religious participation, young people, like those discussed above, appeared untroubled by these intersecting worlds.

Some young people expressed concerns about secular culture that were similar to those of their parents, but such concerns did not necessarily influence their behavior. Eighteen-year-old Moselle, growing up in a poor family on Chicago's West Side, played a variety of religious and popular songs, moving from "Just a Little Talk with Jesus" to the popular tunes her brothers and sisters jitterbugged to. A researcher conducting an ethnographic study of the family noted wryly that "despite Moselle's own active social life, or perhaps because of it, she judged others, believing many Christians violated their own rules of behavior, and believing that dancing and Blues music has a negative effect on morality."[13] Moselle's performance of popular music, even though she found it problematic, offers the valuable lesson that we cannot expect that beliefs and actions will necessarily correspond.

A smaller group of youths completely rejected the views of their parents and religious leaders. Sixteen-year-old Ruby scoffed that the minister at her parents' church "tells our parents that we are being lost."[14] Ruby complained that the minister was a hypocrite who "doesn't know that we know he does lots of things that ain't so hot. . . . Then he can preach a whole sermon on the sins of the younger generation." Ruby also objected to his strategy of trying to control the behaviors of young people by warning them of the terrible fate that would await them if they sinned. In response, Ruby said simply that the "older people do as they please anyway, so can we."[15] Ruby's rejection of her parents' church was tied to her general frustration with the poor community in which she lived—one that seemed to offer her few options for the future. Ruby had befriended girls in other parts of the city who had more recreational, educational, and religious options. Ruby appeared to believe that rejecting the local minister was one step toward a better life outside the community in which she had grown up.

Despite adult fears that many young people would adopt the views held by Ruby, the available historical evidence suggests that a large percentage of young people growing up in mid-twentieth-century Chicago attended church—at least occasionally—and participated in religiously affiliated activities. In a survey conducted in 1930 about the lives of Black children, the small sample of respondents nearly all celebrated Christmas and Easter, and most attended church at least weekly.[16] Many children also reported saying grace and prayers with their families, and a significant minority reported family Bible reading. It is clear that a large percentage of children participated in at least some religious activities, which occupied a spectrum from devout participation in religious ritual to occasional participation in church-sponsored social events. Children also encountered religious imagery and concepts embedded in popular culture, during interactions with friends, and in the built environment of their neighborhoods. Given this widespread exposure, what can we say about the religious experiences of young people? The following sections will consider several types of historical sources as well as the problems and opportunities they present to scholars.

Autobiography

In his book, *An Autobiography of Black Chicago*, Chicago businessman Dempsey Travis reported that as a young man he encountered a new regime of home religion when his Seventh Day Adventist grandmother came for an extended stay during the 1933 world's fair. She quickly instituted a Friday evening service to welcome the Sabbath. During this time Travis began his "106 week engagement as the family musical director for opening and closing the Sabbath."[17] Despite the new rules about food and behavior that Travis was required to observe in his grandmother's presence, he appeared to enjoy his religious status under her tutelage. He was proud to lead his family in song, and he chose to memorize 180 Bible verses, despite only being required to learn thirty. None of Travis's memories, recorded more than fifty years later, focused on theology. Rather, he remembered the practices of religion, and his own religious participation was linked to a sense of personal pride, as well as to the bonds of love and affection that he shared with his grandmother. It is likely that the particular narrative Travis created regarding religion was influenced by the fact that, among other factors, he did not consider himself particularly religious as an adult. If Travis had grown up to be a committed Adventist, he might have attached more spiritual importance to his childhood religious experience. This religious introduction might have been described as part of a serious story of religious salvation, rather than as a light-hearted family tale.

While Travis was drafted into one particular religion, children from unchurched families found that Chicago could be a religious marketplace where they could choose between many religions. In her autobiography, *Another Way Home: The Tangled Roots of Race in One American Family*, Ronne Hartfield remembered that while her parents rarely attended church, "their position was that our involvement wasn't likely to hurt us."[18] Despite the fact that they did not participate in formal religious services, Ronne remembered Christmas and Easter as a special time—one for new shoes and dresses—and Sunday as a day when everyone dressed up.[19] The Hartfield children followed their older sister, who admired her Catholic friends, into the Catholic Church. Hartfield eventually went on to explore a wide variety of churches: Catholic, Episcopalian, AME, Baptist, and Holiness. Quickly rejected was the "hellfire church" she attended once with a friend, which made both her and her parents uncomfortable. Ultimately Hartfield chose to become an Episcopalian because she was attracted to the liturgy and music of the church. Her impressions of each religion were not limited strictly to theology as she remembered a variety of sights and sounds, including the heavy lace mantillas worn by Catholic women and the "soul filled human voice" that poured from gospel records.

Like Travis, Hartfield created this narrative of religious experience as an adult remembering childhood. As an adult Hartfield went on to study and teach at several elite universities. In 1982 she earned a master's degree in theology and literature at the University of Chicago. The influence of this liberal academic religious environment, with its emphasis on free inquiry, intellectual analysis, and multiple religious traditions, can be seen in Hartfield's autobiography. If Hartfield had joined a church that discouraged participation in other religious denominations, or if she had attended a more conservative religious college, she might have considered her youthful church-hopping a foolish or even dangerous experiment, rather than a useful religious education.

Both Travis and Hartfield offer evocative memories of their childhood religion that share similar themes of the personal power and love that they associated with religious participation. Such memories can provide scholars with information about youthful experiences of religion that would otherwise be inaccessible. However, while there is no reason to believe that writers who reflect on their childhoods are untruthful in their reporting of the past, it is also important to consider how adult experiences can shape an individual's narrative of childhood.[20] Scholars must closely examine the source, asking why the informant might remember the event in this particular way, and what multiple interpretations can be applied to this life narrative. While it is not an exact mirror of the past, memory is an extremely useful source of historical information, one that must be interrogated with respectful scrutiny.

Diary

Born in 1909, Willard Motley grew up in a relatively well-off African American Catholic family in a predominantly white neighborhood. . As a teenager Motley was editor of the "Defender Jr.," the children's newspaper column in the popular African American–owned newspaper the *Chicago Defender*, and as an adult he had a successful career as a novelist. Motley's diaries, which begin when he was sixteen, reveal little interest or comfort in religion. In one of the few entries to mention religious activities, Motley describes a Sunday in January: "Blue Sunday. Church. Movies. To-day is the end of holiday, vacation."[21] This entry suggests that church was just another event that brought Motley little happiness. Christmas was the only religious holiday referenced by Motley, and his 1928 entry was representative: "Dull—dull—endless day was Christmas—much as many of my other Christmas'. Life is really miserable when you have no inseparable pal nor a girl or sweetheart to be with, to talk with, to laugh with on such days of wholesome joy and when dreams seem empty."[22] Instead of seeking joy in religion, Motley found joy in school, football, books, and writing. He worried about not being a "regular fellow" and often described deep loneliness, but Motley never described turning to religious faith in times of uncertainty and sorrow. Yet the first time he fell in love, Motley relied on religious imagery to describe the depth of his feeling, and he expressed his concerns about the sexual morality of others in religious terms, suggesting that he had internalized some of the lessons of his religious training even if he did not discuss them in his diary.

As Motley grew older, he wrote more frequently about religion and religious themes, but even then, religion was simply one element in his moral, ethical, and philosophical landscape, and one that seemed to bring him little comfort or certainty. For Motley, religion seemed to exist primarily in the background, only becoming important as he sought to make sense of challenging situations as a young man.

In contrast to memoirs, diaries, like the one kept by Motley, recorded events as they occurred. Diarists generally do not undertake the work of reshaping their experiences into a polished narrative designed to appeal to an audience. This difference could lead scholars to view diaries as a less mediated historical source than memoirs, and thus, as a truer account of Black childhood in Chicago. While the diary is a valuable text, it is important not to expect too much of it. Unlike a memoir, a diary of this sort is not a developed narrative of a person's youth. Instead, it is a fragmentary account that leaves out many issues and events in which scholars may have interest. In addition, while the diary was written as a private document, in this case it was written by a young man who was a published author and intended to pursue writing as a profession. It is quite possible that Motley hoped the diary would one day be published. Even if he did not, there is a certain performative aspect to the diary, as Motley used the diary both to record the world around him and to shape the person the world would perceive him to be. Diaries are valuable sources for information about childhood and youth; however, they must be analyzed with the same critical approach used to evaluate other, seemingly less intimate sources. Diaries are most valuable when they can be placed in context with additional information about the historical and social context of the author's life.

Popular Culture Sources

These tensions within Motley's writing between his inner thoughts and the way he hoped to be seen by others are further revealed through a comparison of his diary and the "Defender Jr." newspaper columns he wrote as a teenager. Begun in 1921 and published in the *Chicago Defender* newspaper, the "Defender Jr." was a weekly column for children. The column was one of many media forums for youth, part of a world of vastly expanding media and consumer goods marketed specifically to children during the late nineteenth and early twentieth centuries.[23] The "Defender Jr." was distinctive because its intended audience was African American children, a group ignored or maligned by many publishers and toy makers. The anxiety many adults in Chicago expressed about the influence of popular culture on children makes the "Defender Jr." a particularly interesting source for examining the relationship between secular entertainment and religious life. Like other children's media, the "Defender Jr." provides insights into the ways in which children negotiated religion in their everyday lives.

The *Defender* was one of the most widely read Black-owned newspapers in the nation. The "Defender Jr." was a forum for young people containing both columns written by an editor—the pseudonymous "Bud Billiken"—and letters, photographs, drawings, poems, stories, and recipes sent in by young readers. Readers were also encouraged to join one of the many Bud Billiken clubs sponsored by the "Defender Jr." and to write to other club members. The club was officially open to children of all faiths and races with the stated objective of "making better boys and girls, which will, in turn, create better men and women of the Race."[24]

Religion was one of many topics discussed in the children's page of the *Defender*, and those discussions often pointed to the diversity of children's religious experience and the frequently blurred lines dividing the sacred and secular in Chicago.[25] While Motley seldom discussed religious themes in his diary, he referenced them more frequently in the "Defender Jr." during his two-year stint as editor. In one particular column, Motley reminded his young readers, "Billikens, don't forget that tomorrow is Easter Sunday. We have over 30,000 Billikens in the club and each of them should be in church Sunday. Billikens, Easter is not only a day of joy, a day to strut around in new clothes, etc., it is a day that we should all get serious and think of Christ and what he has done for us."[26] While such explicitly religious sentiment was not reflected in his diary entries, those diary entries did often reference a desire to be a young person who did the right thing, so Motley may have felt internal pressure to be a positive religious role model in his columns. It is also possible that his adult editor suggested that he include these religious sentiments.

As part of its participatory format, the "Defender Jr." published letters from children, sometimes as many as one hundred a week. These letters appear to have been minimally edited. Most children described family, friends, school, and play in their letters, but a significant minority of children did discuss religious beliefs, church-related activities, and religiously oriented poetry and art. A letter from a girl named Tillie, for example, described a tragic recent event in her life. She wrote, "I am feeling very sad and lonely today so I thought I would write. Last month my little three and a half year old sister left us but I shall see her again when the gates of Eternity swing wide, I hope. I would like very much if some of the members would write me."[27] This short letter suggests some of the ways in which children may have used their spiritual training to make sense of the complicated world around them. In a time of sorrow, Tillie seemed to draw comfort from religious teachings about a spiritual life that continued after the death of physical bodies and about a heaven where believers would reunite after death. By writing this letter Tillie was not only expressing her own beliefs but also teaching other child readers of the "Defender Jr.," and in the process reaffirming or challenging their own beliefs.

The "Defender Jr." column and clubs served different purposes for different children. For some children the "Defender Jr." was pure entertainment, while for others, like Tillie, it was a forum in which to share life's challenges with others. Clubs could be spontaneous groups of friends or neighbors, while others were more organized affairs with adult chaperones. The inclusion of formal religious elements like prayers and hymns appears to have been highly correlated with the presence of an adult chaperone. For example, one club reported that "the Bud Billiken club met at the home of Mrs. M. L. Danforth. The meeting was opened with a song, 'What a Friend we have in Jesus,' and the Lord's Prayer in unit [sic]."[28] An observer noted that another club, held in a Chicago church, was "as nearly like [a] church service as possible."[29] This type of club produced tension between the adult leaders and child members. The children pressed to sing popular songs and play games, but these suggestions were rejected by the adults in favor of hymn singing and crafts. While the younger children pushed against the limitations of the club, older youths rejected it completely. One young man who had previously been a Billiken member complained,

The Bud Billiken [club] would be all right, only they never do anything but sing hymns and piece quilts, that's all right for little kids, but can you imagine me or some of the other kids here getting a kick out of piecing quilts or singing hymns and all that stuff.[30]

Like this young man, some members saw Bud Billiken clubs as a form of entertainment, and they resented the imposition of adult rules and religious content on a recreational activity. In contrast, when child-led clubs included religious elements, their presence appeared more spontaneous, such as a hymn or mock religious ceremony that was integrated into other games and play.

In 1932, the "Defender Jr." also began sponsoring an Easter music festival featuring performances by young people. The festival was largely organized by David Kellum, the "Defender Jr." editor who succeeded Willard Motley. Kellum was a Bahai, who brought an emphasis on peaceful international relations to the festival, which was celebrated in Christian churches outside his own religious tradition. The nondenominational Metropolitan Community Church was the first site of the festival, but the event quickly expanded to include additional Baptist and Methodist churches. While the festival was described explicitly as a celebration of the "resurrection of Jesus Christ," religion was integrated with political and artistic goals.[31] Many of the festival programs opened with the song "Lift Every Voice and Sing," a song also referred to as the "Negro National anthem." This song choice pointed to one of the larger goals of the festival, which was to showcase the talents and potential of Black youth. While the participants and audience for the festival were primarily African American, advance publicity for the event stated that "no color line will be drawn on the participants in next year's festival. Children of all races will be extended an invitation to display their talents."[32]

The festival highlighted political themes uncommon in many Easter celebrations, and it also embraced a wide range of musical styles not limited to church music. Selections performed at the festival, many by children, included opera, spirituals, and the French national anthem. One advertisement noted that "Chicago's favorite dance band will lay aside Jazz on Easter Sunday afternoon, April 16, and play classics and college songs at Bud Billiken's Second Annual Music Festival."[33] While jazz was apparently considered inappropriate for an Easter performance, most other types of music were deemed acceptable. For organizers of the Easter festival, the event was designed to be a celebration of the future possibilities of Chicago's Black community, represented through the talents of its youths. In this event and in the "Defender Jr." columns, the editors often sought to avoid doctrinal disputes by hosting religiously themed events with broad political and entertainment appeal. The *Defender* staff saw religion as one integrated part of a full life, an approach that seemed similar to the religious beliefs expressed by many of the children discussed in this article. This similarity suggests that even as children were shaped by the ideas presented in the "Defender Jr.," so the column was also shaped by its child participants.

Like other forms of interactive children's media, the "Defender Jr." provided a forum where young people could discuss their religious faith if they so chose. "Defender Jr." clubs could also incorporate significant religious elements into their operation. Children who spoke about religion often described the comfort and protection they found in their faith, but more common were discussions of increasingly commercialized religious holidays. Despite the admonishments of Motley, talk of Easter eggs and Christmas presents dwarfed discussions of religious beliefs. Nevertheless, these topics reveal the religious landscape that many children were experiencing and recreating, one in which there were no clear lines between the sacred and the secular.

These types of participatory forums were common in newspapers and magazines in the twentieth century, and they provide a wealth of sources for scholars interested in reconstructing children's historical voices. As a source, children's media does not give scholars a full picture of the religious lives of children; however, it does offer revealing information about the everyday religious experiences of children, as well as information about the religious ideas and practices children were exposed to through media and popular culture. These sources should be approached carefully, with the understanding that they may have been influenced by an adult editorial hand, or by a young writer's desire to maintain community standards of thought and expression in a public forum. Despite these limitations, children's public writings can tell us a good deal about their everyday religious lives, as well as their perceptions of appropriate public expressions of religiosity.

The Sacred and the Secular

The young people discussed above constitute a group with diverse religious beliefs and practices, and this diversity creates challenges for the historian's job of developing a coherent historical narrative. Creating a narrative is also complicated by the fact that the materials left by children describing their own religious or spiritual lives are often fragmentary. Despite these issues, when we allow young people to tell their stories, they present themselves as thoughtful observers of their own lives. In the case of migration-era Black children in Chicago, one common theme described by young people is the diverse, complicated, and sometimes contradictory nature of religious experience, which often transcended adult-sanctioned boundaries of formal religious practice. Their having had multilayered religious experiences did not mean that Chicago's children had a shallow faith. On the contrary, many began a lifelong journey of deeply felt religious belief as children. Instead, the multiplicity of religious beliefs and practices among young people suggests that many of them learned as children that there were multiple ways to be a religious person, and that nurturing an authentic spiritual self required careful consideration of the world.

The example of Willard Motley and other Chicago youth suggests that young people can simultaneously absorb religious lessons even as they resist the adult imposition of religion. Like other groups of children, migrant African American children were a new generation creating themselves from the materials they had at hand—popular movies, comic books, school lessons, and Bible stories all mingled with the sights, sounds, and smells of city streets, creating something new. Like the growing number of gospel performers in the city, these children were fusing diverse materials as they created new forms of expression that would reflect their own spiritual lives. It is clear that children were not simple empty vessels to be filled with religious lessons; instead, children interacted, pondered, and remade the religious materials they were given. Some adults feared these actions, seeing them as a move toward irreligiosity; however, children seemed to embrace their religiously diverse environment, understanding their experiences as part of a generational shift in belief and practice and not a rejection of religion. In this process, young people were actors changing their religious landscape.

None of the texts analyzed in this chapter offers a comprehensive perspective on the religious lives of children. Memoirs reveal narrative memories of childhood, often created and reworked over the course of decades. Diaries provide a snapshot of childhood beliefs and experiences as they are happening, but are often fragmentary and impressionistic. Children's writings in magazines and newspapers tell us a good deal about what children believed was socially acceptable, but they do not necessarily explore the inner lives of child writers. In addition, many of the sources used in this chapter are not specifically focused on religion, which can make it more difficult to fully reconstruct religious lives, while also making it easier to locate aspects of informal everyday religious experience. Despite the limitations of individual sources, however, taken together they describe shared themes. They point to a generational change in process, as young people did not actively reject the religious practices and beliefs of their parents, and may have embraced them, but nevertheless brought a distinctive set of cultural experiences to their practice of religion. Understanding the process of change over time is central to the discipline of history, and texts created by children can provide clues about how children become agents in larger patterns of historical change.

NOTES

1. St. Clair Drake and Horace Cayton, *Black Metropolis: A Study of Negro Life in a Northern City* (New York: Harcourt, Brace and World, 1970), 684.

2. Drake and Cayton, *Black Metropolis*, 412.

3. Eileen McMahon, *What Parish Are You From? A Chicago Irish Community and Race Relations* (Lexington: University Press of Kentucky, 1995); John McGreevy, *Parish Boundaries: The Catholic Encounter with Race in the Twentieth-Century Urban North* (Chicago: University of Chicago Press, 1996).

4. James Grossman, *Land of Hope: Chicago, Black Southerners, and the Great Migration* (Chicago: University of Chicago Press, 1989), 159.

5. Marina Warner, *Managing Monsters: Six Myths of Our Time* (London: Vintage, 1994); Emily Cahan et al., "The Elusive Historical Child: Ways of Knowing the Child of History and Psychology," *Children in Time and Place: Developmental and Historical Insights*, eds. Glen Elder, John Modell, Ross Parke (New York: Cambridge University Press, 1993); Anna Davin, "What Is a Child?" *Childhood in Question: Children, Parents, and the State* (New York: Manchester University Press, 1999), 15-36.

6. William Hutchinson, *The Modernist Impulse in American Protestantism* (Cambridge, MA: Harvard University Press, 1976); George Marsden, *Fundamentalism and American Culture: The Shaping of Twentieth-Century Evangelicalism, 1870-1925* (New York: Oxford University Press, 1980).

7. Wallace Best, *Passionately Human, No Less Divine: Religion and Culture in Black Chicago, 1915-1952* (Princeton, NJ: Princeton University Press, 2005), 8-9.

8. Best, *Passionately Human*, 104-96.

9. Drake and Cayton, *Black Metropolis*, 416.

10. Ibid.

11. William Andrew Daniel, "Negro Theological Seminary Survey" (Ph.D. diss., University of Chicago, 1925), 78-79.

12. Jones Notes, March 21, 1944, Allison Davis Papers (ADP), Box 40, Folder 1, Special Collections Research Center (SCRC), University of Chicago Library, Chicago.

13. T. S. Downs, Research Notes, March 27, 1943, ADP, Box 39, Folder 2, SCRC.

14. Ruby Manse Notes, 1934, Ernest Burgess Papers, Box 89, Folder 5, SCRC.

15. Ibid.

16. My Friends and Family Survey, Ernest Burgess Papers, Box 80, Folder 8, SCRC.

17. Dempsey Travis, *An Autobiography of Black Chicago* (Chicago: Urban Research Institute, 1981), 53.

18. Ronne Hartfield, *Another Way Home: The Tangled Roots of Race in One American Family* (Chicago: University of Chicago Press, 2004), 133.

19. Hartfield, *Another Way Home*, 119.

20. Mary Jo Maynes, Jennifer L. Pierce, and Barbara Laslett, *Telling Stories: The Use of Personal Narratives in the Social Sciences and History* (Ithaca, NY: Cornell University Press, 2008), 76-82.

21. *The Diaries of Willard Motley*, ed. Jerome Klinkowitz (Ames: Iowa State University Press, 1979), 3; Maynes, Pierce, and Laslett, *Telling Stories*, 82-92.

22. *The Diaries of Willard Motley*, 17.

23. Gary Gross, *The Cute and the Cool: Wondrous Innocence and Modern American Children's Culture* (New York: Oxford University Press, 2004); Lisa Jacobson, *Raising Consumers: Children and the American Mass Market in the Early Twentieth Century* (New York: Columbia University Press, 2005).

24. *Chicago Defender*, April 27, 1935, 15.

25. Colleen McDannell, *Material Christianity: Religion and Popular Culture in America* (New Haven, CT: Yale University Press, 1995).

26. *Chicago Defender*, March 31, 1923, 14.

27. *Chicago Defender*, May 3, 1924, A2.

28. *Chicago Defender*, August 6, 1932, 16.

29. Bud Billiken Notes, 1934, Ernest Burgess Papers, Box 89, Folder 5, SCRC.

30. Ibid.

31. *Chicago Defender*, March 11, 1933, 16.

32. *Chicago Defender*, April 29, 1933, 16.

33. *Chicago Defender*, March 18, 1933, 16.

15

The Baptism of a Cheyenne Girl

ANN BRAUDE

This chapter approaches the rite of Christian baptism through the eyes of a Cheyenne child.[1] The eight-year-old girl was baptized into the Episcopal Church in a gold mining town in Colorado in 1866. Baptism is intended as a signal event in the life of an individual, as well as for his or her family and church community. This baptism was all those things, but its meaning also extended beyond its immediate environs. Delicate treaty negotiations between the United States and the Cheyenne nation felt the effect of this baptism during a particularly violent period of the military conquest of the West. This child's religious outlook concerned the federal government, influencing its response to the Cheyennes' demand that she be returned before they would be willing to sign a treaty with the United States.

This particular child had enormous symbolic importance for all the parties involved in Indian-U.S. relations during the Civil War period because she had been taken captive by Union forces in the notorious Sand Creek Massacre. One of the few massacres of Native people officially condemned by Congress, the event still resonates today. It is a particularly sensitive issue for the many Cheyenne and Arapaho people descended from survivors, who keep the memory of Sand Creek alive through tribal scholarship, oral knowledge, and family traditions.

From the moment of her capture, this little girl's fate had as much to do with the symbolic status of the massacre in which she was orphaned as it had to do with her as an individual. Yet an exploration of her religious choices suggests that the seemingly intractable political forces shaping her experience framed, but did not subsume, her individuality. The question of where her perspective leaves off and those of the adults around her begins is both complicated and intensified by constraints placed on all religious expressions entangled with the contest for land during the westward expansion of the United States.

Because not one word exists in her own hand, the effort to reconstruct her experience is speculative. This chapter explores what fruit such speculation may bear. It proceeds by attempting to stand in her shoes wherever the documents tell us her location. The resulting fragments of experience suggest a somewhat obvious conclusion that nevertheless bears repeating because it pulls against adult pieties about the young: childhood provides no exemption from the political contexts of religiosity. While this child's story intersects with one of the major political developments of American history, the conquest of Native America, all children who engage religion do so in some political context. Though they may be presented as props in adult political negotiations, elements of children's religiosity come into focus as we look across the historical record. In this case, exploring the political context of a ritual helps to distinguish the perspective of one child from that of others who participated.

Perhaps the most important lesson of this story for students of children's religiosity is a reminder that context is only one piece of the puzzle. Faith sits at the intersection of internal and external experience, of self and other. The ritual of baptism illustrates the joining of internal transformation to membership in a community. At this intersection children, like adults, are capable of making the same religious motions either as concessions to conformity or as heroic personal commitments, or, most likely, at some indefinable point in between. This story suggests that historians are poorly served by assuming they know exactly where a child's piety sits on this continuum.

To begin, we retrace the steps that led to the baptismal font.

On the chilly morning of November 29, 1864, the Third Regiment of Colorado Volunteers under the command of Colonel John Chivington attacked a peaceful Cheyenne and Arapaho village camped under government protection on land assigned them as a reservation on a dry wash called Sand Creek. Following instructions to take no prisoners, soldiers killed over one hundred women and children, and fifty or so warriors and old men. After the massacre they turned over the bodies searching for survivors, shooting or stabbing any who were not already dead. They mutilated the bodies, cutting off scalps, fingers and toes, and sometimes genitals as trophies to take home, along with buffalo robes and buckskin dresses.[2] A few children they chose not to kill—instead they took them captive. One of these children soon died, another was later returned, and another—the subject of this chapter—was never returned.

The girl and her sister were pulled from a sand pit full of corpses and icy water late on the afternoon of the attack. George Bent, son of a Cheyenne mother and a prominent trader, was in the pit and described the scene:

Her and her sister and her father and Mother, were all in the same hole with me and others about 19 or 20 persons all together. I was sitting next to their father and mother when their father was killed. . . . Balance of them were all killed, and the two girls taken away.[3]

The girl saw her father die before her mother, too, was killed. Later in the day the troops fired howitzers into the sand pits to kill any who still sought shelter there. The girl and her sister survived this as well.

According to George Bent, "the girl[']s father[']s name was . . . Who-ho-mie. . . . one of the Medicine M[e]n. My brother Robert," he recalled, "had great faith in him as Medicine Man. [H]e cured him of sickness that white Doctor had given up." One eyewitness recalled, "One or two medicine men must have been shot in the pits, as the contents of medicine bags were scattered about very freely."[4] The surviving daughter probably saw her father's medicines dispersed and desecrated with the rest of the booty collected by the Third Regiment.

Fifty years later an old-timer recalled that late on the afternoon of November 29 the two sisters were found "huddled among the dead in a sort of cavity under the bank of the stream." Billy Weiss, the soldier who found them, planned to kill them in accordance with orders from Col. Chivington. But George R. Shrock, a 29-year-old miner from Central City, leaned over the bank and insisted that Weiss pass the children up to him.[5]

Together with other trophies of the fight, the children were loaded onto the tired horses of the Third Regiment. They spent three weeks in the army camp, constantly on the move, before the Third made its triumphant return to Denver. One of the captives, a boy, was taken by a soldier who displayed him in a circus. Another, probably the younger daughter of Who-ho-mie, soon died. When the regiment was mustered out, it was decided that the oldest child, the subject of our story, should be kept by the men who saved her as a "living mascot" of their unit, Company B of the Third Colorado Cavalry. They called her Minnehaha.[6]

Minnehaha. The fictive Indian maiden, heroine of Longfellow's "Song of Hiawatha." Longfellow (mis)translated the name as "Laughing Water." Even if the little girl could not respond when asked her name in English, this query could easily be expressed in sign language. Maybe she was reluctant to give her name to the men who murdered her family, or perhaps the soldiers could not understand when she said her name in Cheyenne, and Minnehaha was as close as they could come. In any case, she was now called by the name of a tragic maiden, beloved of Hiawatha, who perished of fever before her husband disappeared into the sunset with the arrival of the white man.

What did the name signify to the soldiers who applied it to their eight-year-old captive? What did the orphan share with Laughing Water, "Loveliest of Dakotah women," who, in Longfellow's poem, walked naked through the cornfield at midnight to ensure its fertility?[7] Did the soldiers think that like Minnehaha and Hiawatha, this child was doomed to perish with the coming of the whites? Or by associating her with the Indians of Longfellow's poem, were they distinguishing her from the people they had killed and mutilated, and associating her with the good Indians who existed in the realm of romantic poetry, the realm of childhood games and of the imagination? Perhaps they were ignorant of literary allusions, and simply thought of "Minnehaha" as a generic name for a female Indian, just as the miners gave the name "Pocahontas" to a Cheyenne woman living in Denver with her trader husband.[8]

The girl called Minnehaha traveled with the Third Regiment of Colorado Volunteers to Central City, their home in the heart of Colorado's gold mining district, high in the Rocky Mountains. There she remained for the next three years.

Meanwhile, Tsis tsis tas, as Cheyenne tribal members called themselves, persistently demanded her return. The Sand Creek Massacre united the indigenous inhabitants of the Plains in a war of vengeance against the United States. As violence disrupted communication with Colorado, the government sent a series of treaty officers and agents to make restitution to the survivors of Sand Creek, and to try to restore peace on the Plains. At every meeting with federal officials over the next two years, Cheyenne chiefs demanded the return of the captive children. Government officials required the return of white captives before treating with any Indian nation; the chiefs now proposed to hold the United States to the same standard.

It is in this context that the child taken captive at the Sand Creek Massacre prepared for baptism. While government officials promised her return to her family, the rite of baptism formally incorporated her into a new community, and gave her a new identity. Finally—two years after the massacre—a new Colorado territorial governor, Alexander Cummings, responded to the request of the commissioner of Indian Affairs that he locate the children. His longest report concerned the older girl:

The third child is at Central City in this Territory, kindly cared for by the family of Mrs. Ford. She is a regular attendant at the school and church of Revd Mr. Jennings; speaks English only; is attentive at school, and will acquire a good education. The family with whom she lives are tenderly attached to her, and she to them. They both feel sorrow and aversion at the prospect of having the child taken from the home and Christian influences with which she is surrounded and returned to the savage life of the Indians of the Plains.

She would not go willingly; and her forcible return to the Cheyennes would—in the opinion of the entire community among whom she now lives happily—be so grievous an injury to her whole future life, that I have taken no further steps in the matter, but have informed her friends that a statement to the Department of the facts would, no doubt, restrain further proceedings.[9]

The commissioner of Indian Affairs did indeed concur.

How much of the child's perspective can be gleaned from this letter's report? The governor described the unnamed Cheyenne orphan as a valued member of a loving family, welcomed by the entire community. This description contrasts sharply with other accounts of public sentiment toward Native Americans in Central City. Here is the view of David Collier, editor of the daily paper, who, as superintendent of public instruction, was the town's leading advocate for children's education. "As long as the business is to kill Indians, we cannot see what difference there is in the mode adopted," he wrote. "We are glad the 3d regiment killed as many as they did, and wish not one had escaped to tell the tale." The soldier's mutilation of their victims' bodies was actually a humanitarian measure because it struck terror into the survivors, "the killing of a less number accomplishing the same purposes."[10]

Editor Collier was not alone in his enthusiasm for killing Indians. Congregationalist reverend W. Crawford found this to be the universal demand of the district. "'Let them be exterminated,' people say, 'men, women and children together,'" he reported. He assured the Home Mission Board that he did not join in such un-Christian sentiments, but explained that his views had changed since moving to Colorado. Unlike the "ideal Indians" in the works of Cooper, he found live Indians "a filthy, lazy, treacherous, revengeful race of vagabonds." These were strong words indeed for a Christian clergyman.[11] What sort of welcome did this town offer the Cheyenne orphan brought to Central City as a living trophy of the event that was now the rallying point for anti-Indian hysteria? Why would she be so eager to remain in this environment?

Contrary to Rev. Crawford's claim, the Indian-hating editor did not represent all the citizens of Central City. Central City divided over the morality of the fight in which its new resident had been orphaned. Shortly after the troops returned from Sand Creek, the Montana Literary Society debated whether "the indiscriminate massacre of all Indians without reference to age or sex, is contrary to humanity, religion, and common sense, and involves on our part a return to the spirit and practice of barbarism."[12] Readers of the *Sunday School Casket* might have found the tone of this resolution more familiar than the *Register's* call to kill women and children. Although a few scalps were displayed in public, Central City did not respond to the massacre with the celebratory orgy witnessed in Denver.

One person in Central City clearly took an interest in the girl: the Reverend Mr. Jennings. Albin Barlow Jennings arrived in Central City during the summer of 1865, six months after the Cheyenne girl. Before that there is no evidence that anyone expressed concern about her spiritual state. By far the largest church community in Central City, the Methodists, whose presiding elder, Col. Chivington, led the Sand Creek Massacre, would hardly have welcomed her. Nor would the Congregational Church, whose minister's skepticism about bringing Native people "under the blessings of the gospel" is quoted above.

A. B. Jennings seems to have brought a new perspective to Central City when he answered a plea from the Episcopal missionary bishop of the West for men and money to build western churches. The energetic young priest found seven communicants when he arrived at St. Paul's Church, but soon attracted many more, and placed the mission church on a self-supporting basis. Jennings's most ambitious undertaking was the establishment of a school in the church basement. Within a year he also held classes for African Americans, who were excluded from the public school by Superintendent David Collier. On Sundays, Jennings conducted a second service in the afternoon for African American communicants. One contemporary described Jennings as "the zealous young rector of Saint Paul's, who believes first of all in good works, and is himself a noble and vigorous exponent of his creed."[13] As part of this creed, he took on the elevation of the Indian orphan.

The Cheyenne girl was one of the first students at Jennings's school. An orphan, whose guardian, Mrs. Ford, was probably a widow, could not have paid the tuition of eleven dollars per term. More likely the Rev. Mr. Jennings, with his belief in good works, admitted her without fee. Here was a tractable heathen at close hand—an attractive opportunity for an eager missionary.

When Governor Cummings assured the commissioner of Indian Affairs that the child attended church regularly, she had not yet been baptized. That rite waited until December 24, 1866, at Saint Paul's festive Christmas celebration. Let us now walk through that baptismal ceremony, adhering as closely as possible to the perspective of the child brought to Central City as a living mascot by the Third Regiment of Colorado Volunteers.

The church, festooned with evergreens, began to fill early in the evening. Miners had denuded Central City of trees, so the decorations provided a welcome change from drab piles of scree and slag. The Christmas tree, lately introduced to America by *Godey's Lady's Book*, connected the mountain church to the most civilized Victorian parlors. The children "came in by classes, in company with their teachers, and took their places in a body." Next, the rector administered the rite of baptism. Eleven children came forward, ten joined by their parents at the baptismal font. One child was without her parents—the child taken captive at Sand Creek. Instead, two loyal churchwomen, Mrs. Arnold and Mrs. Bissell, stood up with her, and Rev. Jennings himself joined in sponsoring her.

When Jennings recorded the child's baptism in the parish register, he wrote the word "Indian" in the column for the parents' names. This was all he included of her origins, recording neither the name of her parents nor the date of her birth. The parish record noted adoptions, when members brought adopted children to the church to be baptized, and in this case they, rather than the birth parents, appeared in the register. But Mrs. Ford was not a member of Saint Paul's, and did not appear as an adoptive or foster parent, or as a sponsor for the little girl who lived with her. This suggests that the child's attendance at church and school were initiated not by Mrs. Ford but rather by Mr. Jennings.

The eleven children presented for baptism on Christmas Eve ranged in age from four to eleven, most, like the Cheyenne orphan, between seven and ten. They had been preparing for this day in Sunday School, and must have been familiar with the baptismal service.

Jennings asked the children or their sponsors on their behalf, "Dost thou renounce the devil and all his works, the vain pomp and glory of the world, with all covetous desires of the same, and the sinful desires of the flesh, so that thou wilt not follow, nor be led by them?" And they replied in unison, "I renounce them all; and, by God's help, will endeavor not to follow, nor be led by them." The rest of the baptismal service followed.

At the conclusion of the rite, Jennings baptized each child. When he came to the child for whom he himself acted as a religious sponsor, he said to Mrs. Arnold and Mrs. Bissell, "Name this child."

"Minnie Haha," they responded.

Repeating the name of Longfellow's fictive Indian maiden, Jennings dripped water on the girl's head, baptizing her as a Christian, saying,

We receive this Child into the congregation of Christ's flock and do sign her with the sign of the cross, in token that hereafter she shall not be ashamed to confess the faith of Christ crucified, and manfully to fight under his banner, against sin, the world, and the devil, and to continue Christ's faithful soldier unto her life's end.[14]

What did these words mean to the child orphaned in the Sand Creek Massacre? When she renounced the devil and all his works, what did she renounce? Did she think of the Cheyenne ceremonies she had seen most years until this one, ceremonies that her baptismal sponsors certainly considered to be among the devil's works? Did the daughter of the medicine man Who-ho-mie renounce the medicines that had saved the life of Charles Bent's brother before they scattered amidst the carnage of Sand Creek? Or, when she renounced the devil, did she hope that her new faith might guard her from the living hell she had survived two years ago? Or did she simply mean that she renounced evil, and promised to be good, doing as Mrs. Ford said and not taking sweets from the pantry? When she confessed her faith in Christ crucified, did she think of the Cheyenne men who pierced their bodies in the Sun Dance, sacrificing their flesh, as Christ did, for the welfare of the people? Or did she believe, with her sponsors, that Christ had come to save humanity from such barbarous practices? When she promised to be Christ's faithful soldier, and to fight under his banner against sin and the devil until her death, did she see herself marching behind the soldiers of the Third Regiment when they fought to protect the white settlers of the territory, or did she think of the Cheyenne warrior societies, who promised to fight unto death in defense of their people? Did the Reverend Albin Barlow Jennings explain who Christ's soldiers were in Colorado? Perhaps she joined an army of the righteous that included both her Cheyenne family and her new friends at St. Paul's. No documents answer these questions, yet asking them may open us to the internal tensions and contradictions of a child's-eye perspective.

In baptism participants enact a symbolic death and rebirth: a death to sin and a second birth as a soul cleansed by Christ's redemptive suffering. "None can enter into the kingdom of God," Rev. Jennings read from the Book of Common Prayer, "except he be born anew of Water and of the Holy Ghost."[15] The conferral of a name fuses the identity of the individual with his or her new status as one who has received remission of sins by spiritual regeneration, one who may "enjoy the everlasting benediction of thy heavenly washing" (274). Minnehaha was hardly a name to evoke rebirth and regeneration as a Christian. Indeed, it suggested the primacy of the child's Indianness for those among whom she lived. Yet it did bespeak a transformation—it was not a Cheyenne name. Rather, it was a name evoking the imaginary Indians of American popular culture.[16]

The girl repeated Rev. Jennings words as he led the people in addressing "almighty and immortal God, the aid of all who need, the helper of all who flee to thee for succour." There was no aid at Sand Creek, no succor for those who fled. As the soldiers attacked the camp, Moketavahta (Black Kettle) raised the American flag, given to him by the commissioner of Indian Affairs, to identify himself as a friend of the U.S. government and an advocate of peace.[17] White Antelope displayed the Peace Medal he had received on a visit to Washington, equally convinced that the village was under protection rather than threat from the army.[18] Was this God mighty enough and loving enough to help a little girl when powerful chiefs could not help themselves?

"Spare thou those, O God, who confess their faults," the girl repeated after Mr. Jennings in the Confession of Faith. God had not spared the other nineteen people in the sand pit at Sand Creek. Yet he had spared her. Did she escape death by accident, or did God spare her to bring her to St. Paul's Central City to hear his word and learn his ways? Did her decision to embrace Christ continue the successful strategies that had kept her alive in a mining camp full of people who wished all Indians dead? The baptismal rite may have brought her as close as she had come since Sand Creek to the moral world of her childhood, with its encouragement to sacrifice for others, and to attend carefully to spiritual truths. Were the values of the Episcopal Church more consonant with Cheyenne traditions than the gross immorality she witnessed during six weeks with Colorado's Third Regiment.? Did she expect, in keeping with some Plains Indian traditions, that captivity could lead to adoption into a family and a new identity among one's captors?[19]

Whatever the significance of this event to the child now called Minnehaha, it marked an important watershed to the adults around her. It signified her redemption from savagery, her entry into civilization. From their perspective, she was now one of Christ's flock, to whom God had given this great land, not one of those who stood in the way of God's plan to spread his United States across the continent, from sea to shining sea. She had been plucked from the living death of heathenism to enjoy the blessing of eternal life.

After the fact, baptism would be included among the primary reasons why the child was never returned to her family. By declining to return her, the territorial governor of Colorado and the commissioner of Indian Affairs concurred in a measure that they had been repeatedly informed would threaten national security and jeopardize the lives of white settlers. Did they really believe the welfare of one Cheyenne child justified such risks? Perhaps, with extraordinary hubris, they believed her relatives would agree that the child was better off where she was, and that once they learned of her situation they would stop demanding her return. This view is supported by the fact that the government did take steps to locate, and did eventually return, the boy taken captive with her. Instead of being sent to church and school, he was being displayed in a circus—a situation deemed less advantageous to him than return to his family.[20]

One other line of reasoning suggests itself for the government's willingness to exacerbate the Indian Wars by refusing to return the girl taken captive at Sand Creek. Perhaps the symbolic significance of a child, and of this child in particular, being successfully rescued from savagery and incorporated into a Christian community was so great that it *was* worth taking some risks. Perhaps everyone involved, from Mrs. Ford to the commissioner of Indian Affairs to the Central City men who had by now reenlisted as Indian fighters, needed tangible proof of the superiority of civilization over savagery, and could see it in the bright girl who was "a regular attendant at the school and church of Revd Mr. Jennings."

According to the territorial governor, Minnehaha shared with her guardian "sorrow and aversion" at the prospect of being "taken from the home and Christian influences with which she is surrounded and returned to the savage life of the Indians of the Plains." If she understood the words of the baptismal rite in the same way as her sponsors, this may indeed have been her view. Having come so close to losing her life at Sand Creek, she knew that her survival in a community that publicly condoned anti-Indian violence depended on the approval of those concerned about her welfare. If they expressed "sorrow and aversion" at the prospect of her removal, perhaps she echoed their sentiments.

The baptism of Minnehaha joined the transformation of her personal beliefs and identity to the nation's need for expiation following the attacks on indigenous inhabitants necessary to its territorial expansion. For the government and the church, baptism into the Christian community also meant baptism out of her tribal community. It justified withholding from Tsis tsis tas the reparation they wanted most following the Sand Creek Massacre— their own child.

But the baptism of the child now known familiarly as Minnie was not the end of her Cheyenne identity. A resilient child by any measure, her survival of the massacre and its violent aftermath, and her embrace by a community rife with anti-Indian sentiment, required intelligence and tact as well as good fortune. Psychologists report that the children who succeed in recovering from extraordinary trauma are those who are able to establish reliable bonds with supportive adults.[21] In the Episcopal Church she found the community's chief advocates of racial tolerance, and a faith that promised protection for her soul.

Cheyenne peace chiefs' demands for her return did not abate when they were informed of her new circumstances. "Where are the little children the whites hold as prisoners that belong to me?" Black Kettle asked U.S. Indian agent Jesse Leavenworth. "If our father would have known how our hearts would have danced at seeing them he would have had them here." Leavenworth informed his Senate supervisor, "Black Kettle said they wanted the children more than anything else."[22]

The summer after Minnie's baptism, Congress appointed a new Peace Commission to treat with the Cheyennes and other tribes. The commissioners sent an agent to Central City to bring Minnie to Medicine Lodge Creek to rejoin her extended family as part of the government's fulfillment of its previous treaty obligations. He found that "she declined to go and that he could only get her away by kidnapping her." Peace Commissioner Samuel F. Tappan, who had chaired the military investigation of Sand Creek and heard countless eyewitness accounts of atrocities perpetrated by the Third Regiment, then traveled to Central City himself. "I saw the child," he wrote, "and found that she was unwilling to go."

Minnie must have been exceedingly effective in asserting her preferences. The adults around her might have been forceful in objecting to her return to Tsis tsis tas. But Tappan was a strong advocate for reparations for Sand Creek, and should have been convincing in explaining the security interests at stake in her return. That is, he should have been unless he too believed her baptism changed her in some essential way. Instead of pressing for her return, he made a suggestion contradicting the Peace Commission's charge. "I then asked if she would go to Boston and attend school. She replied that she would."[23] She would? Tappan's first assertion, that she was unwilling to return to her extended Cheyenne family, is consistent with Governor Cummings's letter of the previous year. But the second statement, that she agreed to go east to attend school, seems to contradict the claim that "the family with whom she lives are tenderly attached to her, and she to them."

This disjuncture may be an opening through which we can glimpse the child's perspective, a moment when her voice is faintly audible through the political posturing, the adult agendas, and the passage of time. If so, then less than a year after her baptism, Minnie made an extraordinary decision; she would leave the familiar surroundings of Central City, bid farewell to Mrs. Ford and Mr. Jennings, and travel east with a man she barely knew to take advantage of the opportunity to continue her education. Was the decision Minnie's, or was she acquiescing in the preference of proximate adults? She had no legal guardian to consent or object. It is not clear who was paying for her food and clothing, or her education. Perhaps once the Third Regiment was mustered out and Sand Creek became a source of national disgrace rather than glory, the living mascot outlived her appeal. A Colorado mining town held dim prospects for a Cheyenne schoolgirl.

Minnie might have met Col. Tappan before, but probably did not know him well. An occasional Episcopalian with ties to Central City, he never appeared on St. Paul's membership rolls. Raised a Congregationalist, he became a faithful participant in spiritualism, the religious movement professing that contact with the spirits of the dead provides empirical proof of the immortality of the soul. In addition to collecting testimonies of the Sand Creek Massacre for the army, he regularly visited spirit mediums with whom he communed with the spirits of dead Indians at the séance table.[24]

Tappan brought Minnie to Boston after completing his work with the Peace Commission. Here she became a valued member of a new religious community, this one espousing doctrines quite different from those she affirmed at her baptism. Minnie attended public school, and spent Sundays at the Children's Progressive Lyceum, the spiritualist answer to the Sunday School. Sunday Schools, they complained, taught "unhappy lessons" that led children "to believe in unhappy thoughts." There "young minds are being constantly *mis*educated by the supporters of the popular dismal theologies." At the Progressive Lyceum Minnie learned more optimistic doctrines, that children were born good, not bad, and needed no cleansing in the symbolic waters of baptism. "From this point we start—affirming the interior purity of the child's spirit, and denying that the infant nature inclines to everything that is evil and wicked."[25]

Spiritualists' embrace of Minnie reflected their claim that Indian spirits were among their most valuable and helpful friends in the world beyond. Through their enthusiasm for Indian spirits, spiritualists participated in a distinctive way in "the cant of conquest." Espousing love and admiration for dead Indians who frequented their séances, they contributed to a view of Indians as part of America's past, as a vanquished people who lived on as a spiritual resource for those who now occupied their land.[26]

Inclusion among the dead Indians with whom mediums held daily conversation was at best a problematic environment for an adolescent girl establishing a new identity in Boston. Yet it encouraged her to bring to the fore memories apparently buried at Sand Creek and abandoned at her baptism. She told her new friends about her father the medicine man, and about his encounters with spirits that she witnessed as a child. These were stories that interested spiritualists more than they interested a missionary priest in Colorado.

And she told them her name—or perhaps she did. Col. Tappan reported that Minnie's Cheyenne name was Em-mu-ne-eska, a name that does not mean anything in Cheyenne.[27] Most likely it is a corruption of whatever her Cheyenne name was, a name she had not spoken since the massacre. This explanation is suggested by the transformation of her father's name by Col. Tappan and the Boston spiritualists. The man whose Cheyenne name was Who-ho-mie became Omwah, a shortened rearrangement of the same sounds. Or perhaps she chose not to share the names exactly, to shield them and their power from non-Cheyennes eager to use them for their own purposes. In any case, the fact that she revealed at this juncture aspects of her Cheyenne identity that she had retained but concealed until this point complicates the interpretation of her baptism as acquiescence in the values of her captors. Her embrace of Christian baptism must be seen in the context of other choices at other moments. As a child's life unfolds, one year or one ritual may not tell the whole story.

Minnie's decisions radically changed the course of her life. On the East Coast Minnie met Indian rights reformers who advocated "civilizing" rather than exterminating the Indians. She sat on the platform when the great antislavery orator Wendell Phillips gave a riveting account of the massacre in which her family perished.[28] Like spiritualism, reform rhetoric provided a language that allowed Minnie to combine commitments of her baptism with those that predated it. According to Colonel Tappan, Minnie wanted to pursue her education because she hoped "to return to her people as a teacher." This ambition and her academic credentials gained her a scholarship to the preparatory department of newly founded Howard University.[29]

Before she could complete her education and realize her ambition to return to Tsis tsis tas, Minnie died of tuberculosis, the scourge of civilization. She was sixteen years old. She spent her last days in the nation's capital, in a dormitory at Howard University, cared for by the daughters of freedmen who hoped to contribute to the uplift of their people.

Conclusion

The story of Minnie's baptism begins with the United States' assault on the lives, cultures, and lands of indigenous nations. After the Sand Creek Massacre she had little access to the religious way of life in which her family surely expected her to be raised. Yet her story loses much if focused exclusively on the losses she endured, or if approached in a way that obliterates her individuality. The historical record does not reveal why Minnie made the religious choices she did. But it does reveal that she made choices. Her ability to embrace first the Book of Common Prayer and then the very different doctrines of the Children's Progressive Lyceum suggests that her conversion to Christianity should not be seen as a rejection of her past, but rather as engagement of the best opportunity at hand for her spiritual and personal development. Minnie's adaptability and emotional accessibility were among her most important survival tools, allowing her to bond with new sets of adults on whom her future depended. Her religious choices were deeply embedded in these contexts, but they remained hers.

In dramatic fashion, Minnie's story suggests the enmeshed constraints and possibilities of the religious lives of children in relation to politics, both local and national. While her case could be dismissed as anomalous because of the extraordinary collision of her childhood with national events, this extreme case exposes a set of questions that may be usefully applied to other children. To go beyond the obvious impact of violence on religiosity, one might ask about how other political contexts frame children's religious lives: the Cold War and the arms race, immigration law, the civil rights movement, trade unionism, or Zionism, for example. What kept children up at night? When children learned in school to "duck and cover" in case of nuclear attack and to contemplate a nuclear apocalypse, did they bring these lessons with them to church? On what issues did adults communicate their anxieties?

While political interventions framed the disparate worlds in which Minnie engaged various faiths, they hardly determined her religious outlook. In ethnographic studies, concerns of confidentiality may discourage in-depth biographies of religious children. Historical studies present opportunities to emphasize the individuality and religious creativity of children like Minnie, who defy odds and expectations, flexibly navigating religious worlds adults might find daunting.

1. Dozens of people have commented on and assisted with the research on which this paper draws. Most immediately I am indebted to C. P. (Kitty) Weaver, David Halaas, the Reverend Canon Cyril F. Coverley, Laird and Colleen Cometsevah, Molly Ladd-Taylor, Leigh Schmidt, and Gary Roberts.

2. Senate Executive Document No. 26, 39th Cong., 2nd Session, *Report of the Secretary of War, Communicating . . . Sand Creek Massacre* (Washington, DC: Government Printing Office, 1867), p. 110. Hereafter cited as *Sand Creek Massacre.*

3. Als George Bent to Samuel F. Tappan, Feb. 23, 1889. Samuel Forster Tappan Papers, Denver; State Historical Society of Colorado.

4. Morse H. Coffin, *The Battle of Sand Creek* (Waco, TX: W.M. Morrison, 1965), p. 34.

5. *Field and Stream*, Nov. 30, 1918, p. 8.

6. Ibid.

7. Henry Wadsworth Longfellow, *The Song of Hiawatha* (New York: Hurst, 1898), pp. 165-67.

8. Stan Hoig, *The Western Odyssey of John Simpson Smith* (Glendale, CA: Arthur H. Clark, 1974), p. 114.

9. Gov. Alexander Cummings to Commissioner of Indian Affairs Lewis Bogy, Nov. 12, 1866. Office of Indian Affairs, Letters Recieved, Upper Arkansas Agency, National Archives, Washington, DC.

10. *Central City Miner's Register*, Jan. 5, 1865.

11. "Public Estimate of Indians," Rev. W. Crawford, *The Home Missionary* 37 (January 1865), pp. 214-15.

12. *Central City Miner's Register*, Jan. 25, 1865.

13. *Echoes from Acadia* (Denver: privately printed, 1903), p. 53.

14. Protestant Episcopal Church, *The Book of Common Prayer, and Administration of the Sacraments* (New York: Nelson, 1864) , p. 273.

15. Ibid., p. 264.

16. Phillip J. Deloria, *Playing Indian* (New Haven, CT: Yale University Press, 1998).

17. *Senate Report No. 142*, 38th Congress, 2nd session, *Massacre of Cheyenne Indians* (Washington, DC: Government Printing Office, 1865), p. 5.

18. George Bent, *A Life of George Bent* (Norman: University of Oklahoma Press, 1968), p. 157. *Sand Creek Massacre*, p. 70.

19. Her father's name, Who-ho-mie, which George Bent translated as "Sioux," suggests that adoption could have been part of her family history.

20. Cummings to Bogey, Nov. 12, 1866.

21. Roberta J. Apfel and Bennett Simon, eds., *Minefields in Their Hearts: The Mental Health of Children in War and Communal Violence* (New Haven, CT: Yale University Press, 1996), p. 46.

22. Als S. F. Tappan to Gen. F. A. Walker, Commissioner of Indian Affairs, Aug. 6, 1872.

23. Ibid.

24. Samuel F. Tappan Diaries, collection of C. P. Weaver.

25. Andrew Jackson Davis, *The Children's Progressive Lyceum* (Boston: Bela Marsh, 1867, 6th edition), pp. 13, 7.

26. Francis Jennings, *The Invasion of America: Indians, Colonialism, and the Cant of Conquest* (New York: Norton, 1976).

27. Tappan Diary. I am indebted to Colleen Cometsevah for the discussion of the relation of this name to the Cheyenne language.

28. *Banner of Light*, Nov. 14, 1868, p. 4.

29. Tappan to Walker, Aug. 6, 1872.

16

Examining Agency, Discourses of Destiny, and Creative Power in the Biography of a Tibetan Child Tertön

AMY HOLMES-TAGCHUNGDARPA

Introduction

Ascertaining a child's perspective and experience of religious tradition and practice can be a difficult feat, made all the more complex by the tendency for adults and scholars to reinterpret, overlook, or even omit children's explanations of their experiences in depictions of religion. While recent scholarship (particularly by the scholars included in this volume) has introduced the child's voice into studies of religious ritual and experience in a number of cultural contexts, in studies of Tibetan religion, children remain largely absent as agents and participants. Establishing the perception of historical children and their experience is made all the more difficult by the lack of source material available, since most of what can be found has been written by adults *about* children. What can these sources reveal about a child's perspective on religion? This essay will explore a culturally Tibetan case, but will address the challenges faced by those wishing to do child-centered research across many (if not most) religious traditions in the absence of an archive created by actual children.

One way to develop a child's perspective is to examine general scholarship within a religious tradition that features children. An important genre of such scholarship is religious biography that features children or, in some cases, has children as their subject.

In traditional Tibetan scholarship, there are several sources that not only indicate the role of children in religious life but also suggest that in certain traditions particular children played important roles of authority beyond that of lay ritual participation. The obvious example of this is the Tibetan tradition of recognizing children as emanations or incarnations (*Tibetan Sprul sku*) of deceased religious masters. Granted authority through complex cultural matrices of destiny and spiritual virtuosity, these children receive specialized training and education after they are recognized as incarnations of former masters. Following confirmation of their new identity, they are placed on a trajectory of activity, or a career, that they are expected to enact as they grow into adults. The most famous example of these emanations is the institution of the Dalai Lama, who acts as a religious, cultural, and political authority within Tibetan culture. Although not all children are emanations, many are often recruited into monastic life at a young age, or are born into a family that transmits its own set of teachings and ritual practices on a heredity basis.

There are also children in Tibetan history who exemplify several of these strands at once but who were unique in that, from a young age, their activities contributed to the formation of Tibetan religious and intellectual systems. One prominent example is that of Tertön Namchö Mingyur Dorje (Gter ston Gnam chos Mi 'gyur rdo rje, 1645-1667; hereafter Namchö Mingyur Dorje),[1] a prominent teacher in the Nyingmapa (Rnying ma pa) tradition of Tibetan Buddhism who in his short life is held to have transmitted the influential collection of Sky Treasure (Gnam chos) teachings. Namchö Mingyur Dorje is a significant case study for the examination of children and their experience of religion for a number of reasons: first, Namchö Mingyur Dorje was regarded as a prominent religious teacher and practitioner from his childhood. However, unlike with other incarnations, his authority was gained through his participation in different, almost apocryphal discourses of destiny. He was believed to have been a Treasure discoverer (*gter ston*) who was predestined to "discover" religious relics and teachings that had been concealed in the eighth century CE by the important religious master Guru Rinpoche, a figure who had played a crucial role in the dissemination of Buddhism in Tibet. Therefore, Namchö Mingyur Dorje's precociousness and virtuosity were not remarkable due to his age: instead, it was his place within broader systems of knowledge associated with Treasure revelation that brought him recognition from Buddhist communities within Tibet.

Namchö Mingyur Dorje appears, then, to be a pertinent example for this volume of a child who gained significance within a religious culture despite (not necessarily because of) his age, and in this culture, his own experience and understandings of rituals and visions were believed to be extremely important and therefore were meticulously recorded. Does this case study suggest a traditional example of what we are trying to uncover: of a child's religious agency and voice being restored to the academic archive? While in some ways it might, herein lies the rub: it was not always Namchö Mingyur Dorje who recorded his experiences but instead his teacher and student

Karma Chagme (Kar ma chags med, 1613-1678), who was an adult and over thirty years older than his youthful teacher.

In this chapter, after providing more context for Namchö Mingyur Dorje's life and legacy, I will examine depictions of his childhood in his biography, *The All-Pervading Sound of Thunder: The Outer Liberation Story of Tertön Mingyur Dorje.*[2] In these depictions, I will be specifically looking for instances where his age is important, so as to consider the influence and potential power of age in a Tibetan context. It is also interesting to see where his age is not mentioned or glossed over. This often occurred for complex reasons that in turn assert and deny agency to Namchö Mingyur Dorje himself. I will then expand on these depictions by drawing out several theoretical considerations that this case raises—especially the necessity to examine the ambiguity of agency in assessing biographical sources regarding children. To what extent do such sources, written by adults, actually capture a child's voice? Where are the moments when a child's agency or voice is particularly heard? If such sources are ultimately contrived by adults and therefore serve to reduce a child's agency in articulating his or her religious experience, where else can we look for information regarding historically significant children in a written archive? The obvious answer is in autobiographical material, or, in Namchö Mingyur Dorje's case, his ritual and meditation cycles of teaching instructions. Agency, here, however, can also be difficult to discern. In this case the issue becomes even more complex, due to the discourses of destiny surrounding him in his role as a Treasure discoverer and representative of Guru Rinpoche. Discourses of destiny render the task of identifying a child's agency more ambiguous within the Tibetan context, and raise important methodological questions for negotiating historical sources about children and by children in religious settings. Outside of the Treasure tradition in Tibet, other religions also interpret religious behavior according to their own belief system. Thus, the child's words and actions can never be fully separated from communal perceptions and definitions of them. However, ultimately biographies of children and textual records regarding their religious experiences are still important to consider in drawing attention to children's voices. To discover some of the glimpses of actual children that can be found in these adult-authored texts, scholars need to be aware that these writings simultaneously tell the child's story and serve to create a legacy for the religious tradition that the child helped to promote. Thus this chapter demonstrates ways in which researchers can both be mindful of what the authors have at stake in the portrayal of the young person and work diligently to seek out places in that adult agenda where the perceptions of the child seem to have survived the editorial process.

An Overview of the Life of Namchö Mingyur Dorje

Namchö Mingyur Dorje was born in 1645 in an area named Ngom in Eastern Tibet to parents who had links to the ancient Tibetan kings and the aristocracy.[3] As a child, he often made religiously significant hand gestures (*mudra*), performed yogic exercises, and claimed to have been a lama in his past lives.[4] His biography records that nobody believed him and he was sent to live with his grandfather, and that within ten years of his birth, his family's condition and wealth decreased. After much effort on his part, at the age of ten Namchö Mingyur Dorje finally managed to trace the man who was to become his main teacher and at the same time his initial student, Karma Chagme. After initially being tested for authenticity, Namchö Mingyur Dorje was determined to be an incarnation of a previously significant teacher, and so he was enthroned and began a formal education.

Namchö Mingyur Dorje showed great natural talent in meditation and ritual practice. After several spells of illness, he began to receive visions in which he "discovered" the Namchö (Nam chos; Sky Treasury) cycle of teachings. These were new teachings that he was held to have been destined to reveal, and that spanned thirteen volumes, including meditation instructions, texts for ritual offerings, instructions for preliminary and more advanced Tantric practices, and philosophical commentaries. The most famous characteristic of these teachings was their incorporation of Pure Land meditation practice and iconography, particularly practices and iconography that incorporated Sukhāvatī, an extremely popular pan-Asian Buddhist practice.[5] These teachings are found throughout Tibetan cultural areas of China and the Himalayas up to the present day and form an important part of the Palyul (Dpal yul) lineage of the Nyingmapa tradition of Tibetan Buddhism, though they are also transmitted in other traditions as well.

After he completed revealing the Namchö teachings in his early teens, Namchö Mingyur Dorje went to Chamdo for a period of time. During his later teens, he developed a reputation for opening new sacred places for pilgrimage. He was also known for serving his community with rituals that started and stopped rain and cured illness, as well as for sponsoring religious rites that were intended to bring benefits to the wider community.

At twenty-three[6] years of age, Namchö Mingyur Dorje became ill, suffering from a "brown phlegm,"[7] and soon after passed away.[8] While there was some controversy immediately after his death over how he died (which will be outlined below), it was generally held to have been caused by a tragic illness. However, Namchö Mingyur Dorje's death was not the end of his preco-cious career—instead, it reconfirmed his reputation as a Treasure discoverer, destined to remain for as long as needed in this life in order to pass on to the next to benefit more beings.

Childhood and Treasure Discovery

Treasure cycles (*Gter ma*) are teachings, meditation practices, prophecies, and ritual texts that are organized into "cycles" that form important and controversial parts of the Tibetan Buddhist canon. While they are cultur-ally distinct to Tibet, an overview of their traditional system is helpful in raising broader questions regarding agency in sources about children. This is the case because the most distinctive part of Treasures that gives rise to controversy is their origin. Unlike other practices within Tibetan Buddhism, they do not derive from Tibetan translations of Indian texts traced back to the Buddha. Instead, they are held to have been "discovered" at predes-tined times by preordained individuals, and are apocryphal in nature. These individuals are believed in their previous lives to have been linked to Guru Rinpoche (Sanskrit Padmasambhava) in the eighth century CE. In their pre-vious incarnations, they received teachings that were then reconcealed to be "discovered" at times of need in the unspecified future.

While Namchö Mingyur Dorje followed in the footsteps of a well-estab-lished tradition of Treasure discoverers, the way in which he did so was slightly different due to his young age. Many Treasure discoverers exhibit unique signs of intense religiosity from a young age; however, few are recog-nized immediately, or actually begin to reveal comprehensive cycles of teach-ings at a young age. The process of Treasure revelation is often a drawn-out one, and a single cycle may take years.[9] This aspect of his biography draws attention to issues of agency and authorship in children's biographies, and will be developed in this section. In particular, I will explore the literary devices used to emphasize Namchö Mingyur Dorje's uniqueness and outline tools for unpacking these, in order to offer a broader perspective on how to negotiate adult depictions of children.

The biography of Namchö Mingyur Dorje often emphasizes his young age as having been important in establishing his credibility as a unique person, and is a good example of the biography of a significant child fig-ure within a religious tradition. Important parts of his biography also raise useful questions for biographies from other traditions, as many details regarding his life can also be found elsewhere in descriptions of talented children from other religions. Identifying these literary devices is useful in demarcating where an adult's interpretations end and the behavior of an actual historical child begins.

To begin with, gaining recognition and thus the opportunity for a religious education was not automatic or immediate within the Tibetan tradition for all Treasure discoverers. People within communities of Treasure discoverers are also careful to authenticate a new Treasure discoverer. Namchö Mingyur Dorje's biography records that when he began to talk, he claimed that he was a lama from Kathog (elsewhere in eastern Tibet) and discussed in great detail the landscape of the area and his experiences of Buddhist practice from his previous life. However, nobody around him took any notice of his stories, regarding them as a child's imagination, and "nothing more happened then."[10] This is an interesting point, for it demonstrates that the subject of the biography was not automatically powerful. This raises the question, at what point is a child recognized for his or her religious virtuosity in a biographical text? In our case study, only Karma Chagme, Namchö Mingyur Dorje's biographer, took him seriously, and warned his grandfather to take care of him after it was revealed that the child had spontaneously learned the alphabet without any study.[11] This kind of remarkable precociousness is found in many religious biographies about children, and appears to be more a literary device than evidence of miraculous intelligence, as it reinforces the idea that the child was set apart from others at a young age and therefore has a special and unique fate within the religious tradition.

More miracles appeared elsewhere in Namchö Mingyur Dorje's biography. When he was five, Namchö Mingyur Dorje went to live with his grandfather, named Adrup Gyal (A 'grub rgyal, dates unknown). During this period of living with his grandfather, at the age of seven Namchö Mingyur Dorje had his first vision, in which he met a religious master in an unknown city surrounded by retinues of singing women. He was inspired by this vision to go into the mountains, where he saw Karma Chagme from afar. He repeatedly attempted to go and join Karma Chagme, but his grandparents would not allow the small child to leave.[12] After Namchö Mingyur Dorje received several more visions, Karma Chagme decided to meet with the boy's parents to explore the possibility of Namchö Mingyur Dorje coming to live and study with him, as he decided the boy was certainly a reincarnation of a well-known teacher, and if he did not begin to study Buddhism he would certainly fall ill.[13] This discourse of urgency, with the threat of illness, can also be found in biographies from other religious traditions, and acts to reinforce and legitimate the child's special identity.

After receiving recognition and enthronement from Karma Chagme, Namchö Mingyur Dorje embarked on an intensive career of study and retreat. Karma Chagme rarely acknowledges his age, though, other than to express concern over a small child living in such austere living conditions with rats. For this reason, he allowed Namchö Mingyur Dorje to sleep alongside him.[14] Namchö Mingyur Dorje himself also does not appear in the text to behave in a childlike manner, and instead exhibits remarkable meditative feats and intelligence. This aspect of religious biographies about children is particularly challenging, as the actual child's experience is excluded. This may be due to the editing of the text, which could have intentionally excluded references to play or tantrums. Despite acknowledging the creative power of children and their imagination, other manifestations of that creativity, such as play, are not often apparent in biographical depictions, which sanctify their subjects. Only on one occasion in the case study at hand does Namchö Mingyur Dorje ever express a lack of confidence. After giving an empowerment to a small group of students, the boy appears preoccupied. Afterwards, he recounts an experience he had during the empowerment:

> When I was giving the empowerment, wisdom and mundane dharma protectors assembled like a gathering of clouds filling all of space. The entire land was crowded with innumerable gods and demons, as well as local deities major and minor, all of them laughing out loud. I thought they might be making fun of me since I know little about empowerments. I asked them, "Are you laughing at me?" Rather than insulting me they said they were laughing from joy, happy with the flourishing of Lord Buddha's teachings. They pledged to protect the Namchö teaching and offered their life force mantra.[15]

In this instance, Namchö Mingyur Dorje appears as a small boy—unsure and self-conscious about his ability to perform the ceremony appropriately, and also concerned with the appearance of laughing deities in the visions (what is noteworthy, though, is that he does not note the visions as unusual themselves). Rather than believe that Namchö Mingyur Dorje did not play, though, for the reader to remain aware of the editing of this behavior is helpful for understanding more about social norms within different religious traditions and cultures. This editing also makes sections such as the excerpt above all the more noteworthy.

Throughout the remainder of the biography, however, such concerns are not present, and it is therefore difficult to unpack the actual child from his textual representation. For example, at one point, a confident ten-year-old Namchö Mingyur Dorje exclaims that he merely "pretends" to receive empowerments and oral transmissions and to study, as he has already received all the teachings he needs in a past life.[16] Indeed, this confidence is reaffirmed through the boy's apparent virtuosity. Within a short amount of time after joining Karma Chagme, he receives brilliant visions in retreat, confirming his talent, the reemergence of knowledge of previous lives, and his unique destiny.[17] In order for the reader to receive a glimpse of any child-like behavior in biographies such as Namchö Mingyur Dorje's, very close and critical reading of the text is necessary, and even then, as in the excerpt above, the actual precocious nature of the experience is not commented upon.

The most famous aspect of Namchö Mingyur Dorje's childhood was his revelation of the Namchö cycle, which most firmly attaches him to the Treasure tradition and its cultural discourses of destiny. A couple of years after he joins Karma Chagme and begins his training, a series of obstacles befall him and his family: he is criticized by the local king, his family accrues debt, and his father dies at thirty-seven years of age. He also experienced frequent bouts of ill health:

> Tertön Migyur Dorje himself sometimes became paralyzed for two or three days, unable to even sit or stand, and then suddenly, without medicine or treatment, he recovered and walked, ran and jumped. This happened again and again. . . .
>
> Until the time he revealed the Namchö treasures the Tertön sometimes acted as though he were mentally ill, running, jumping and even throwing the shrine objects far away.[18]

Though he apparently could not remember these incidents later, it is interesting that "running and jumping" are childlike activities, and it may be that Karma Chagme was attempting to explain some of his pupil's childlike behavior.

For several years Namchö Mingyur Dorje had intense and frequent visionary episodes in which he revealed systematically the Namchö cycle. Karma Chagme assisted him in recording the visions and texts that emerged from them, and was surprised when the Tertön wrote down thirteen unfamiliar Sanskrit words as quickly as he wrote Tibetan. He also recorded a few Sanskrit words at the top and the bottom of the treasure texts along with various coded sign letters of protection and some drawings that I did not understand. Most of these letters appeared to him directly; some came from his meditative experience and some from his dreams.[19]

The entire process took over three years, up until Namchö Mingyur Dorje was approximately fourteen to fifteen years old. When the revelations ended, his visions ceased as well,[20] though he did continue to reveal other teachings.[21] He did not teach all of them, though, at one point telling Karma Chagme that not all of his mind treasures were "clear in his mind, and he didn't feel comfortable enough to write them down."[22] This comment suggests some self-consciousness and is another revelatory part of the text depicting a hesitation befitting the subject's age.

Namchö Mingyur Dorje remained actively engaged in meditation practice for the remainder of his short life but also began to teach publicly after completing a three-year retreat. During this time, Karma Chagme records that he had great power over others.

> Being quite young, he looked like a child. But, those who came to see him—leaders, great lamas, learned geshes and so on—regardless of their own pride and prestige, were outshone by his charisma when they entered his presence. They could not speak well and became cautious, indicating the auspicious coincidence of the Tertön being able to overpower the perceptions of others.[23]

These comments should be approached critically as part of the author's broader attempts to create a particular and powerful image of his subject. However, comments from other people about biographical subjects are always interesting to note for what they suggest about the reaction of broader society to children.

Despite this charisma, though, Namchö Mingyur Dorje always had his detractors. In his later teens he began to undertake a series of expeditions to open up new pilgrimage sites for lay devotees, and fell ill at twenty-three with a mysterious and eventually fatal phlegmatic illness.[24] After he passed away, very suddenly, Karma Chagme was left with a variety of strange rumors to negotiate: "Lama Nyima had written to me of doubts about the Tertön's mysterious illness. The doctors who were present had different opinions. Most diagnosed that the Tertön had consumed poison."[25]

After further investigation, Karma Chagme decided that Namchö Mingyur Dorje's death was "no one's fault."[26] He did this based on his belief that the religious people who had surrounded Namchö Mingyur Dorje before his death were all too devoted to him to have poisoned him. He also argued that lay people would be incapable of poisoning such a powerful being. Therefore, Karma Chagme sadly accepted his teacher's death, as well his lack of immediate incarnation.[27]

Karma Chagme does attempt to provide some explanation for the loss of the young man. He explains toward the end of the biography that Treasure discoverers do not always live long, only living to fulfill their predestined responsibilities.[28] Karma Chagme provides this explanation partly to refute rumors about Namchö Mingyur Dorje being inauthentic, as some critics have claimed that, having been so young when he died, he could not possibly have completed all of his revelations and so must have been a fake. However, maybe it was also a way for him to reconcile with what is always a difficult experience—the death of a loved colleague who must have become like his own son and who passed away at a tragically young age. In this sense, at the end of the biography, Namchö Mingyur Dorje's age does become ultimately significant, as his early loss cannot be easily explained considering his remarkably prolific short life.

The early death of Namchö Mingyur Dorje is significant in other ways, however, as it means that as an adult, he did not have the opportunity to write an autobiography in which he retrospectively defines and explains his childhood and experiences. This adult retrospection is another challenge to overcome in reading children's autobiography, as, due to cultural conditioning and the passage of time, the memory conveyed within an autobiographical text also portrays an adult explanation of childhood events.

Theoretical Considerations

This look at Namchö Mingyur Dorje's biography and the influence that his young age had on his activities raises a few issues that remain problematic in exploring this depiction of the life of a child in a position of religious authority. These issues also point to broader questions about dealing with children's religious biographies, including questions of authorship, agency, and interpretations.

First, the remaining archive about Namchö Mingyur Dorje was largely written or recorded by an adult, Karma Chagme, which raises the question of how to negotiate the authorship of biographical sources about children. In this case, though Namchö Mingyur Dorje did have autobiographical notes at the end of his teachings and the Namchö cycles are attributed to him, Karma Chagme was the scribe in most cases, and he was the person who had the last word in his role as the biographer of his teacher. Adults have a variety of different influences and motivations that may lead them to record biographies of children in certain ways. In this instance, as an adult, Karma Chagme had a variety of complex motivations in his composition of the text. Though the boy was originally his student, in time he became the teacher in the relationship and therefore occupied a position of respect, which may have tempered Karma Chagme's perspectives of Namchö Mingyur Dorje. It is important when dealing with a child's biography to acknowledge the age of the scribe, and the scribe's relationship with the subject, as well as other contextual information, in order to understand the full repercussions of the adult status of the biographer, which include power differentials and particular interpretive frameworks.

Also important is that, as the main holder of the Namchö cycle after Namchö Mingyur Dorje himself, Karma Chagme had a personal interest in seeing the lineage continue, which draws into question the sociopolitical context of a biography. Biographies have historically been a crucial tool for the propagation and survival of religious lineage in Tibet and elsewhere, and therefore depicting a biographical subject in as efficacious and uncontroversial a way as possible is of great importance. In this instance, where we know that there was controversy and criticism of the boy and his authenticity, the biography of Namchö Mingyur Dorje becomes even more important as a means to confirm legitimacy and efficacy. The depiction of Namchö Mingyur Dorje's miracles and visions in the biography are not just present for posterity but are essential in consolidating an image of him as a powerful and authentic Treasure discoverer—in spite of, not because of, his young age. Precociousness is not emphasized in Karma Chagme's text. Precociousness, however, is very much present, and does need to be addressed in this case and in the discussion of other children's biographies. What about a child's circumstances may have contributed to this precociousness? What does it tell us about the educational and social systems of the society in which he or she lived? And also, as in the case of Namchö Mingyur Dorje, when is a child's intelligence played down or emphasized? These questions can lead to new directions for understanding the religious society and community that the child subject lived in. In this instance, we find that Karma Chagme does not emphasize Namchö Mingyur Dorje's age or precociousness. This is the case because it does not fit within his intention of creating a biographical relic of his teacher as a powerful religious practitioner and teacher. The appearance or absence of age as a factor in a child's religious experience is not arbitrary, but is of immense relevance to understanding more broadly the literary devices at work in the text, as well as its broader intention, and how the child subject's own agency can be located within it.

Excavating the child's voice in such a biography and the remainder of Namchö Mingyur Dorje's corpus is extremely difficult and points to broader problematics for religious biographies with child subjects. Although, as seen above, there are moments of childlike hesitation and self-consciousness, in this case Namchö Mingyur Dorje appears overwhelmingly adult, and at the age of eleven he is already composing teachings and prayers using traditional literary forms. His participation in the discovery of the Namchö cycle of Treasure teachings complicates his agency even further, as he appears within traditional accounts as a conduit for Guru Rinpoche's teachings, and an adult, Karma Chagme, writes them down. However, he also surely conveys his own perspective in some measure in his writing, though to what extent is hard to confirm.

This point ties into wider issue of exploring Namchö Mingyur Dorje's religious experiences from the perspective of a child. The strong discourses of destiny that tie him into the broader cosmodramas of Guru Rinpoche and Tibetan history are mentioned throughout the biography and his other works. They are essential to his self-identity, and to others' perceptions of him. They also render extremely difficult attempts to truly understand his own agency as a child, as they create yet another layer of adult voices and expectations molding his experiences and, crucially, the way he describes those experiences. These discourses are common across religious traditions, however, as while the actual terminology used is different, the concept of destiny is a powerful one that is used to explicate and define a child's behavior in certain ideological contexts. Attempting to demarcate the boundaries of these discourses is a crucial task for understanding more of the historical child's motivations and understanding of his or her experiences.

In Namchö Mingyur Dorje's biography, it could be argued that we only really see his own childlike, nondestined nature in one instance: when he hesitates during a vision due to concern that the deities he sees are laughing at him and his immaturity and lack of knowledge. However, even this excerpt suggests what is most interesting about this case study: his involvement in the creative process of seeing visions and *interacting with them*. For, even if we do see the adultness of the archive in which Namchö Mingyur Dorje's life has been written, we cannot deny the potential to also see the lineage and life of Namchö Mingyur Dorje as a wonderful example of the way a child's creative and imaginary potential can shape the religious world around him. The Namchö cycle of teachings is distinctive: vibrant, potent, and yet accessible. If we interpret his involvement with the process of revealing them as it has been set out in Karma Chagme's biography, we see an eleven-year-old's version of how a meditation should be visualized; how a ritual should be performed; and how imagination can be used as a powerful means for reconceptualizing the world—something children do naturally and that Tibetan Buddhism attempts to institutionalize as a path to freedom.

Conclusion

The biography of Namchö Mingyur Dorje remains as an excellent example of a child's life story in the Tibetan context, and provides fascinating information about a religiously powerful child. Unlike other sources that describe the childhood of religiously powerful figures, in this biography, the main figure passed away at a tragically young age, which means that he has not had the opportunity to reinscribe his own life story from an adult perspective.

As well as providing a wealth of information about Treasure discovery and Tibetan culture, this biography raises important questions for negotiating other biographical texts about children. Most prominently, many biographies have been written by adults about children that introduce to their depictions of a child's life complex issues of power and agency, and this phenomenon is in some ways a drawback of using this form of literature, as it is not actually conveying the voice of the actual child. In this case, the main teacher and student of Namchö Mingyur Dorje, Karma Chagme, has conveyed his life story from an adult perspective in the biography he composed in the late seventeenth century. It is a biography of an adult-child—a child who is wise beyond his years, and who does not act like a child except in brief moments in which we can see emerge the hesitation, nervousness, playfulness, and imagination of a child's view of the Tibetan religious cosmos.

This potentiality is the greatest advantage of using biographical literature to study children. It is these moments, which can be unpacked from the broader literary devices created through the sociopolitical context of the author, that make biographies of children rich sources of information. While in some ways this biography is merely another example of an adult interpreting a child's perspective of the religious world through the adult's own perspective, it can also be interpreted as an example of a culture that takes the imaginative potency of children seriously. The Namchö cycle of teaching attributed to Namchö Mingyur Dorje remain an accessible and widely popular series.

The biography of Namchö Mingyur Dorje raises pertinent and important questions regarding the complexity of determining the agency of children within a Tibetan Buddhist context. It can also be seen as an affirmation of a child's creative power, and encourages nuanced readings of children in religious, historical, and cultural texts across cultures. Within a culturally specific context, Namchö Mingyur Dorje was not perceived as religiously powerful because of his age, or even in spite of his age—instead, he is a significant figure in Tibetan history because of what is considered his miraculous connection to a broader spiritual destiny. Perhaps this perception of him suggests ultimately the new way in which we may read children's relationships with and perceptions of religion: as the site of imagination and creativity, but also with the potential to redefine previous paradigms. If we can unpack and identify the literary devices and broader contexts and motivations of the authors of biographies, as well as their institutional affiliations, we may gain a glimpse of this creativity, which can allow us new perspectives on religious traditions and childhood within them.

NOTES

1. In their first instance, Tibetan words are given phonetically, followed by their full spelling in the Wylie transliteration system.

2. The original Tibetan text has been published as Kar ma chags med, "Sprul sku mi 'gyur rdo rje'i phyi'i rnam thar kun khyab snyan pa'i 'brug sgra (phyi'i rnam thar)," in Mi 'gyur rdo rje, et al., *Gnam chos thugs kyi gter kha snyan brgyud zab mo'i skor* (*Collection des Tresors par gNam-chös Mi-'gyur rDo-rje*) [The Profound Essence of the Aural Lineage of the Sky Treasury Teachings] (Paro: Dilgo Khyentsey Rinpoche, 1983), vol. 10, 6-533. An accessible and fluent translation of this biography has recently been published in English as Karma Chagme, *The All-Pervading Sound of Thunder: The Outer Liberation Story of Tertön Migyur Dorje*, translated by Lopon Sonam Tsewang and Judith Amtzis (Taiwan: Palri Parkhang, 2008). In order to facilitate further research into and access to this source, in citations below I will include the pages of the English translation, with their original spelling and punctuation retained.

3. Sonam and Amtzis 14-22. This lengthy section discusses in great detail the family connections that explain how the family was connected with the aristocracy. This information is often included in Tibetan biographies as a form of increased legitimacy for the family's authority and, most importantly, spiritual potency.

4. Ibid., 26.

5. See Georgios Halkias, "Pure-Lands and Other Visions in Seventeenth-Century Tibet: A Gnam-chos sādhana for the Pure-Land Sukhāvatī Revealed in 1658 by Gnam-chos Mi-'gyur-rdo-rje (1645-1667)," in *Power, Politics, and the Reinvention of Tradition: Tibet in the Seventeenth and Eighteenth Century*, B. Cuevas et al., eds. (Leiden: Brill Publishers, 2006), 121-51. This article outlines the development of the Pure Land tradition in Tibet.

6. This is according to the Tibetan method of counting age—according to the Western system, he was twenty-two.

7. Sonam and Amtzis 204.

8. Ibid., 210-11.

9. For more on this process, see Holmes-Tagchungdarpa, Gardner, and Janet Gyatso., *Apparitions of the Self* (Princeton, NJ: Princeton University Press, 1998) and Amy Holmes-Tagchungdarpa, *The Social Life of Tibetan Biography: Textuality, Community, and Authority in the Lineage of Tokden Shakya Shri* (New York: Lexington Press, forthcoming).

10. Sonam and Amtzis 26-27.

11. Ibid., 27.

12. Ibid., 30-31.

13. Ibid., 33.

14. Ibid., 60.

15. Ibid., 84-85.

16. Ibid., 50.

17. Ibid. For examples, see 53, 60-61.

18. Ibid., 73.

19. Ibid., 82.

20. Ibid., 91-93.

21. Ibid., 112.

22. Ibid., 114.

23. Ibid., 130.

24. Ibid., 217-18.

25. Ibid., 217.

26. Ibid., 219.

27. Ibid., 208-10; his eventual actual reincarnation is again mentioned on 232-33.

28. Ibid., 222-24.

Memory Work and Trauma
in Research on Children

DIANE WOLF

Sometime in 1942, Max's grandfather took him by train to Friesland. At the train station at Leeuwarden, he gave Max to a stranger who was waiting for them.

> My grandfather said to me, "You have to go with that gentleman, and he'll take care of you." My grandfather popped in the train, and he was gone. And . . . then you can feel your heart pounding. "What's going to happen to me?" And . . . well, the man, he took me by the hand and, well, he was talking to me, but I couldn't understand him because he spoke Frisian, not Dutch. When I came into his house, my foster mother, she came towards me and she hugged me and she said things like, "Oh my poor child! You must be cold, because you don't have woolen stockings! Well, I will see to it that you get everything you need and . . ." Well, she was very kind.

Max was welcomed into the man's family, which consisted of his very maternal wife and two other foster children as the couple could not have children of their own. As Max adapted to village life in Friesland, he learned the language, excelled in school, and loved his foster parents as they did him. He knew he was different—a dark-haired boy among blondes—and he knew his name was not Friesian, as people often commented that Max is a dog's name, not a person's name. But he did not know he was Jewish. He played constantly with his friends and, like most village boys, accompanied his family to church on Sundays.

After the war, in 1945, someone Max described as *"der dikke vette man"* (the fat man; *"dikke"* and *"vette"* both mean "fat") whom they called his "father" came to visit occasionally. Max found *"Vader"* (father) a strange and distant term, since he used Frisian terms—*"Mem"* and *"Heit"*—to address his foster parents, whom he believed were his real parents. He had no idea who this man was or what the term "*Vader*" was. He did not interact with this man, nor did the man talk with him.

Max was the first of seventy people I interviewed in Holland, Israel, and the United States for a project on hidden Jewish children in the Netherlands during World War II in which I analyzed their experiences before, during, and after the war in terms of family dynamics in both their hiding family (or families) and their family of origin (Wolf 2007). In order to contribute to future research on children and religion, this chapter draws from these cases to illuminate some of the challenges of working with a group that has a strong memory of trauma in childhood. I will focus on methodological issues, quandaries, failures, and successes, including the ethics and sensitivities involved in studying traumatized children

Although my research is historically based, this particular case is relevant for dealing with the memory of trauma in a range of contemporary situations such as (1) a people being pursued and driven out or murdered due to religion, race, or ethnicity; (2) groups having to hide their identity and disguise it, or having their identity forcibly transformed; (3) children placed in foster care in the United States being bounced in and out of multiple families, where they must adapt their identities, including their religious affiliation and practices; and, finally, (4) those who were sexually abused by clergy in their youth. All of these categories potentially link religion with the memory of trauma during childhood and require special attention to the sensitivities of those being interviewed. This chapter focuses on three main areas concerning the memory of childhood trauma: the formation of distinct memories during childhood; memories of childhood that are difficult to access; and making sense of these memories once they are accessed. This chapter underscores two important points relevant for research on childhood and religion. First, religious identification should be seen as fluid across the life span rather than something fixed and static. Second, it is important to consider the context of the state and its various tentacles, which affect both childhood and religion in specific contexts.

Before delving into the memories of childhood trauma, it is important to understand the context from which they emanated. I more or less fell into this research topic after learning about an unsavory aspect of Dutch history (Verhey 1991). After World War II's end, the Netherlands was the only European nation to create a committee that would decide the futures of those Jewish children in Holland who had been orphaned by the war. Typically, these children had been in hiding with a Dutch gentile family and had lost their parents. Often, surviving Jewish kin wanted their children returned to them. However, some hiding families were attached to the child and wanted to keep him or her. The decimated Jewish community wanted all of the children reared in Jewish families. A professor of international law, Gesina van der Moelen, was appointed chair of the committee. That she was a member of a faith—reformed Calvinism—that did not view Judaism as a legitimate religion was significant in the way she picked the committee members, a majority of whom were not Jewish, as well as in the decisions made by the committee. Many of the decisions about orphans were made with anti-Semitic under- and overtones. Needless to say, this was not the Holland of Anne Frank with which I was familiar.

This startling discovery led to a full-blown research project on those Jewish orphans over whom there had been fights about guardianship. However, after I met and talked with Dutch scholars, Jewish leaders, and some former hidden children, my topic shifted to a focus on family dynamics among hidden children whose parent(s) may or may not have survived the war. My main research findings were surprising in that those interviewed largely focused on the trauma they experienced *after* rather during the war. When surviving parents found their children, the majority of whom in my sample had been hidden between their first day of life and five years of age, the child did not recognize his or her parents and ran away from them. This resulted in Jewish children feeling dragged away from the people they thought were their family by strangers whom they did not particularly like and with whom they had no connection. Because children tend not to have consistent memories before the age of five, they did not remember their biological parents. Their world as they knew it completely came apart as they learned that their hiding family was not their "real" family and, to top it off, that they were Jewish. Although these same children would have also suffered when they were first separated from their parents at a young age, they did not remember that, or perhaps it came up again and was expressed through this subsequent trauma.

The first publicity I received about the project was in a newsletter for HOK (Het Ondergedoeke Kind), the Hidden Child association in Holland. Shortly after it came out, I received a phone call from a man in New Jersey; at that time, my family and I lived in The Hague. "I have been waiting for over fifty years to talk about this," he said in his deep voice and heavily Dutch-accented English. He began sobbing as he spoke about his postwar life as an orphan. I knew at that moment that the topic I was pursuing was the right one.

Children and Memory

In the 1930s and 1940s, parents did not seek out the feelings, desires, and opinions of children in Western Europe—children were to be seen but not heard. In the case of hidden children, this attitude and practice was intensified in the extreme. Parents felt forced to give up their child(ren) to complete strangers in the hope that by being separated and hidden elsewhere, the child(ren) and perhaps the entire family had a better chance at survival. Parents made these excruciating decisions and arrangements but usually explained nothing to the child when giving him or her to a complete stranger. Children from the ages of a few hours old up to age eighteen were hidden with non-Jewish families and were either integrated into the family's life or hidden clandestinely. The majority spent most of their hiding period integrated into a family's life, playing with other children, going to church and perhaps to school. Their entire identities were usually changed, including their name, place, family of origin, and religion. Hidden children had to memorize this new information and were forbidden to talk about their previous lives; any slip was potentially dangerous. And for those in clandestine hiding, they could neither be seen nor be heard for fear of being found out and betrayed.

Although the sociology of childhood emphasizes a focus on children as social actors, this particular history casts a different light on overly sanguine notions of children's agency. Powerless European Jewish children (and adults) in hiding were completely dependent upon the help of strangers. In such circumstances or others mentioned earlier—e.g., children in settings where they must change their identities to be safe—we must recognize that agency is highly limited and constrained.

Because children cannot usually estimate time accurately, researchers cannot focus their research questions on the veracity of dates or, in this case, the exact lengths of time spent in different families. I sought instead the emotional reaction to these relationships from the perspective of the hidden child, who had filtered his or her memories through a good fifty-five years of experience. My main interest centered on how these former hidden children viewed family dynamics in their family of origin before the war and after the war, if parents survived, as well as in their hiding family.

Of course it is very possible that former hidden children had forgotten some important events or dynamics while embellishing others. And they also were able to reflect on these relationships as adults, most of whom had become parents and grandparents in the meantime. Oftentimes, repressed memories resurfaced when their own children or, more frequently, their grandchildren reached the age at which they went into hiding. I am quite sure that if I had interviewed any surviving biological parents or hiding parents, I would have heard a very different perspective about the same people. However, my interest was located in the child's experience and views of these relationships and their texture.

It always struck me how these survivors, now in their seventies and eighties, still refer to themselves as "children" in terms of having been "hidden children." They are part of a global network of Child Survivors of the Shoah who gather every year in a different city to meet, hear lectures, and have workshops. Those who went from Germany and Austria to England on the KinderTransport (child transport) still refer to themselves and are referred to as "the Kinder," or "the children." This labeling only began in the 1990s when the first conference of hidden children occurred and former hidden children "came out of the closet" (their terminology) and claimed their memories and identity. This collective endeavor empowered many who then appropriated the terminology of "hidden child" as part of their identity. This group of surviving Jewish adults feels very connected to their childhood and the ways in which it defined their entire lives. Whether this improves their memory of that period is unclear, but it is obvious that those who belong to such organizations or attend meetings and congresses base part if not all of their identity on having been Jewish children in Nazi Europe.

After the war, if their biological parents survived and returned to claim them, hidden children found that parents did not want to hear about their wartime experiences. Parents shut them down by stating that "children don't have a memory," perhaps to assuage their own guilt about separating from their children. Parents brushed off their children's experience, telling them how much they, the parents, had suffered. Thus, not only during the war but after the war as well, hidden children experienced a highly intensified version of "being seen but not heard." Neither did anyone else want to hear from them—their classmates, friends, teachers—and broader Dutch society felt just as victimized, was not interested in Jewish suffering, and in some instances expressed anti-Semitism. Although most hidden children had memories, they were forced to spend the next decades with their memories in hiding. This simply continued their wartime practice; however, this hiding changed in the early 1990s when global conventions began for former hidden children.

By centering on children's memories, my research challenges any popular notion that children do not have a memory or cannot remember. Indeed, they do and they can, from about age five on, although some can recall certain experiences before age five. Almost everyone I interviewed can still easily recall their feelings, living with a family or families, and the radical changes they confronted after the war—with the exception of a few people whose entire hiding experience occurred under the age of two or three.

Early childhood memories were usually in the form of fragmented emotional memories. Mary was four when there was a raid of her family home by the Nazis. She remembered "a lot of noise . . . and my mother screamed and screamed" (Wolf 1997: 127). Peter was five when the police raided his apartment and dragged his grandmother away. He wept as he recounted "the shouting, the yelling, the crying and my mother's helplessness" (1997: 128). When he was sent into hiding, he recalls, "I remember the first night. When they took me to bed and I started to cry, 'I want to go home!' But I couldn't go home. I cried the whole night." Naomi was three when her parents sent her into hiding: "That's such a trauma, you always remember that." She recalled crying herself to sleep at night. She was moved to four different hiding places and recalled, "All I did was cry" (1997: 137). Peter's and Naomi's memories of their fear and desperation clearly remained with them. However, at such a young age, memories do not remain consistent and cohesive.

Accessing Memories of Trauma

Seeking out those who were hunted and experienced trauma earlier in their lives—religious or otherwise—creates particular challenges for researchers, necessitating a high degree of awareness, sensitivity, perhaps creativity, and understanding to obtain volunteers to interview. It took over fifty years for many of these former hidden children to be able to talk about their experiences; had I begun this research some years earlier, several of the most fascinating individuals would not have volunteered for an interview. A few interviewees explained to me that it felt like a major accomplishment to them to participate in the interview since they had been unable previously to discuss their past. After making contact and a date with those who volunteered to be interviewed, I went to their houses to conduct the interviews. I was always treated hospitably.

Each person was first given a sheet of paper concerning informed consent and asked to sign it. It followed a format most relevant for experiments in medical science outlining the possible costs and benefits of participating in the research, but nonetheless it had to be utilized as it is legislated by the federal government. In the part on risk, it read, "I do not feel that there is any medical risk involved in being part of this study although it is likely to stir up certain emotions related to these memories." In one instance, a therapist was reading the informed consent sheet before our interview was to begin and got to the part on risk when she suddenly exclaimed, "This is bullshit!" She felt that it understated the possible detrimental effects of participating in the interview. As a therapist and a former hidden child herself, she was amply aware of the potential after-effects of dredging up traumatic memories. Indeed, she later explained that she had scheduled our interview on a Sunday rather than a weeknight so that she would have some time to recover before going back to work the next day. With her guidance, I then amended the above sentence by adding, "although it is likely to stir up certain emotions related to these memories *and to the past*" as well as, "In that sense, it could be upsetting for some." I did not go back to the IRB with that particular change since it simply strengthened what had been there previously. But without a doubt, the interviews were emotionally disruptive to many of those with whom I spoke. While these were not easy memories to access and share, interviewees expressed satisfaction about being asked about this particular time in their lives and about telling their stories.

Having one's subjects "talk back" and proclaim one's approach is "bullshit" is unnerving and constitutes one effect on researchers when they are studying laterally or up. Due to their age difference, interviewing children would be "studying down," but I can imagine situations where, for example, teenagers talk back and challenge the researcher. Should this happen, I would encourage researchers to engage them by turning around their challenge, asking them why they think the research or the research question is wrong or stupid and then asking them what they think is the best way to approach to the topic. Being defensive in these situations rarely helps.

My interview style reflects a more feminist approach although clearly feminists do not have a monopoly on such methods. I attempted to engage with my research subjects empathically and sensitively, focusing on the particulars of each case while asking certain similar questions of all respondents. The interview often felt more like a guided therapy session as I gently probed into deep and usually painful memories. In two instances, I interviewed individuals who were emotionally frail and seemed to have, or to have had, clinically diagnosed mental illnesses. One had been in and out of hospitals for much of her life, suffering from depression; during our interview in New York, the other flipped mercurially from anger, accusations, and bitterness to singing and light-heartedness. In both cases, I abbreviated the interview so as to end it quickly and inquired multiple times about the individual's access to a therapist if she felt the need to talk with someone after we finished. Both said they had someone they could call.

During the interview, I tried to proceed in a chronological manner, talking through each hiding experience and the family relationships, the end of the war, postwar family relations, and the like. A few people I interviewed were unable to stay focused in this particular way and made substantial leaps back and forth in time with their stories despite my attempts to move along step by step. These interviewees had particular stories they wanted me to know about but without the context, they were difficult to follow. The result was usually a confusing interview that was difficult for me to understand or use significantly in my writing.

Several of those I interviewed felt that their story was nothing special and that it wasn't worth my time. Inevitably, after convincing them that it would interest me, the interview was always worthwhile and often surprisingly so in light of their protests. Many I interviewed referred to their age in terms of their relationship to Anne Frank—e.g., "I'm as old as Anne Frank"; "I'm a year younger/older than Anne Frank"—as though their position vis-à-vis the poster child of hidden children gave them more legitimacy. Indeed, these survivors who were hidden away from their families as children represent the norm, while Anne Frank, hiding with her intact family, represents an anomaly.

Those who had processed their history in some manner or another were better able to recount their past in a clear and thoughtful manner and tended to be more self-reflexive. This processing often included having had some education and/or therapy. Those who had not had much education or therapy, or those who dismissed the therapy they had had, demonstrated more "cluttered" thinking in that they were less able to organize their thoughts or memories. However, what appears to me as cluttered thinking may work fine for those who engage in it; I am simply commenting from the perspective of the interviewer/researcher trying to make sense of the narrative rather than judging it. In the end, I privileged those who were able to recount their history in a chronological, methodical manner since I could not decipher very much from the more jumbled interviews.

In some of the narratives, we find what Bakhtin (1981) called polyphony—several different voices working together without harmonizing inherent tensions or contradictions. For example, there usually is a modified and sometimes thoughtful perspective of the adult, filtered through decades of experience, history, knowledge, and retrospection. Often, when interviewees spoke about seeing their child or grandchild at the age they were when they went into hiding or thinking about their parents' predicament when they were the parents of young children, they spoke reflectively as adults.

At times, I heard the child's perspective, particularly in reference to certain memories of strong feelings such as fears during hiding, likes, dislikes, or feelings of unfairness. Those feelings tend not to be as filtered by an adult perspective, and parts of the narrative sound young. Interviewees sometimes lowered their voice when transmitting these feelings, as though they felt no one else should hear them. These were the raw feelings I was seeking. They surfaced when I sought out memories of their feelings about particularly dramatic events such as leaving their parents for hiding or postwar reunions with parents since certain pivotal moments are likely to conjure up the emotions one felt as a child. I provide some examples below.

As mentioned earlier, five-year-old Peter related that the police raided his apartment and dragged his grandmother away. He wept as he recounted "the shouting, the yelling, the crying and my mother's helplessness" (1997: 128). When he was sent into hiding, he recalls,

> I remember the first night. When they took me to bed and I started to cry, "I want to go home!" But I couldn't go home. I cried the whole night. And then I got out of bed and was lying on a rug. And then I remember that I was still feeling very strange. . . . I realized that you can go on crying, but it doesn't help. So you'd better stop and go to sleep. (138)

Peter's recollection of crying "I want to go home" as well as the feeling he had lying on the rug may have been revised by the fifty-plus years since those events; however, they sound very present in his mind, as though he can fully reconnect with his five-year-old-child self. Perhaps the fact that he is a therapist allowed him to connect with those feelings unashamedly.

I approached this research assuming that everyone I interviewed had been through trauma when separating from his or her parents as a child. This, however, was incorrect. A few saw this change in their lives not as terror but as a change of pace, an adventure. From the perspective of a six-year-old boy, Josef was able to recall all the details of the separation from his parents: "I remember the car, even. . . . [It] was black with yellow . . . and I also remember it was a two-door car." Josef did not cry at the separation as did his sister because to him, "it felt like an adventure" (1997: 137). Five-year-old Henny was also "excited to go on an adventure" (137). Within the context of increasingly constrained movements for Jews, a trip to a new place in a new car became an unusual and somewhat exciting event for these children. They also may have been somewhat more independent than the others quoted earlier.

Some of the most heart-wrenching narratives, however, were about hidden children's reunions with their parents at the war's end. More interviewees were able to recall this event than going into hiding because they were two years older at the war's end. A few narrative examples will demonstrate how that traumatic event is recounted. The first is from Wiesje, who was seven when the war ended:

> I was standing in front of the window and looking outside and seeing Germans with their hands held over their heads. And then I saw a couple, a man and a woman, on bicycles, . . . with wooden wheels . . . because there were no normal tires. And I looked at them because there was nothing else to look at and no one was supposed to be outside, and how could they be cycling? That was very dangerous and it was also forbidden. And I looked at them, and looked at them and looked at them and they looked at me. And the woman fell off her bicycle. And then I knew that horrible things were going to happen, dramatic things. And I hated drama. And I hated tears and screams and cries. And I ran away to the only place where I could lock a door, and it was the lavatory. And very soon, people knocked on the door telling me I had to come out and I didn't want to and I said that I didn't want to.

Five-year-old Lore recounts hearing the news that her parents were coming for her: "[I said,] 'I don't want to go!' I had no interest in leaving them [her hiding family]. I had made friends, I had a family, I had a school, I had everything I wanted, what did I want those people for? They left ME! I didn't want to go back with them." That part of her narrative revealed the raw emotions of a child who had felt abandoned by parents who had "left" her. However, at that point in the interview, Lore switched to an adult perspective; she became tearful and stated, "And when I think, if I try to reverse the situation, I mean just the horror of it, can you imagine, it's probably all they lived for. They came back and found out that I didn't want to go with them" (Wolf 2007: 172). Thus, after vividly recounting the terror and anger she felt as a child reunited with strangers who were called her "parents," she then, due to her ability to empathize as a mother, considered how her parents must have felt. This reflection allowed her to disengage somewhat from her older, very strong, angry feelings toward her parents. Perhaps reoccupying an adult perspective was more comfortable than feeling the horror about how as a child, she was sent off to live with strangers and "abandoned" by her parents.

Even when former hidden children could not recall being separated from their parents and sent to strangers, many remained close to strong early child memories of their parents' abandonment of them. Hidden children like Lore often never trusted their parents again because they were never sure if/when the parents might lie to them and leave again. An adult analysis of their feelings about abandonment would have led to an understanding that the parents were trying to save their children's lives and were forced to do the unspeakable. These decisions were motivated by love and fear, and can be seen as unselfish acts since most parents would have preferred to have their children close to them rather than give their children to complete strangers. However, no one I interviewed was able to acknowledge the courage and selflessness it took for parents to separate from them and send them into hiding. Despite knowing more about the history of that period and the dangers that lurked everywhere for Dutch Jews, former hidden children remained judgmental of, if not angry at, their parents for what they still felt was abandonment.

Some of those who were orphaned because their parents were killed in concentration camps were not able to take their parents' decisions one step further to integrate what "nonabandonment" could have led to, namely, their own death. In other words, the wish that their parents had not abandoned them to strangers did not seem to have been matched by a deeper understanding that they might have been killed instead. Or, if this connection was acknowledged, perhaps some felt that it would have been better for them to have been killed with their parents rather than left to live without them. This was never expressed to me directly, but it is the only possible explanation for their inability to acknowledge the only possible alternative to their having been sent into hiding.

For example, one man who was orphaned and lives in Israel retired early so that he could take care of his grandchildren after school. He stated that he did not want "strangers caring for them" and wanted to do it himself. This impulse was clearly motivated by his opposition to what had been done to him by his parents. Thus being given away into hiding was not experienced as something parents did "for" their children, but as more of a punishment done "to" them. This is understandable from a child's perspective. But this separation was clearly a deep trauma because former hidden children remain angry and judgmental about that decision as adults who are parents and grandparents themselves. It seems that some of their feeling is connected with a fantasy about family—"what could have been" or "what should have been"—particularly among those who were orphaned. Thus these feelings may partly express a yearning for the parents they never knew and may not even remember. Initially, I was surprised to hear these older adults express negative feelings about their parents' "abandonment" of them and posed more questions to try to get at their more adult reasoning about this decision. That adult perspective never showed up, and I quickly stopped trying to get them to view the situation differently.

In other words, both the interviewees and I had a range of access to their childhood memories. Some had left them behind and described the past as the adults they now are. However, most of those I interviewed remained at least partly rooted in their perspective as a child, unable to take an adult's perspective on their younger, intense emotions. Some, like Lore, were able to both be present in the childhood memories and be present in seeing them as her current adult self; however, many others were not able to step outside of their younger feelings.

Religious Affiliations: Before, during, and after the War

Changing their religion from Jewish to Christian did not seem to be problematic for younger children; indeed, many recounted how they enjoyed going to church. However the later discovery that they were Jewish sometimes created trauma or led to a traumatic interaction with parents. Children hidden at younger ages were made to forget that they were Jewish because it was an extremely dangerous piece of knowledge. One boy was harshly reprimanded by his hiding mother for using a Yiddish word, for which she apologized profusely after the war, explaining why she had to stop that behavior. Another little girl with a suitcase noted that one nice dress was her "*shabbos dress*"; that dress never reappeared. Many went to church on Sundays along with their foster family and enjoyed reciting their prayers.

Some Jewish children lived with orthodox Calvinist families who took them in for religious reasons and were somewhat anti-Semitic. In these cases, Jewish hidden children adopted the anti-Semitic views of their hiding parents and were shocked to find out after the war not only that their biological parents were Jews but also that they too were members of that despicable group. Margot was ten when her mother returned and by then felt very Catholic and anti-Semitic. She described her reaction to their reunion: "So here comes my mother—a Jew! What am I going to do with her? I was embarrassed to death. . . . Who wants to be involved with Jews?" (2007: 221-22).

This sentiment was echoed in a film about hidden children, *Secret Lives*. In this film, a Polish Jewish mother, probably in her seventies, explains to the filmmaker that she gave her baby to a non-Jewish neighbor hoping to save her daughter's life before she and her husband were sent on a transport to concentration camps. After the war, the parents came to claim their child. Their middle-aged daughter explains that her father was hospitalized right after the war and so "at least he looked human," implying that her mother did not. The mother said that she didn't care that her daughter had been baptized; she was simply grateful that the child had survived. At their reunion, lice were crawling all over the little girl and her mother began to pick them off her arm. The little girl, having been brought up as a Catholic in an anti-Semitic environment, said to her mother, "Get your Jewish hands off me!" Thus for some children, finding out that they were part of a detested minority was shocking indeed.

After the war, some Jewish children continued to kneel and say their bedtime Christian prayers until they were forced to stop by a parent, thus engaging their agency to keep life as it was before. Margot continued to pray twice daily with her rosary back at home with her mother and a new stepfather. She returned one day from school to find that he had thrown out her prayer book, her rosary, and her two saint medals. Margot was devastated; she felt that the medals of the saints had saved her life during the war. "So here my whole life is shattered again. It was such a terrible thing that these things that saved my life were thrown away, just demolished" (2007: 222). On top of that, even though her stepfather stated that "[t]his is a Jewish home!" she noted that they never did anything Jewish. Thus her Catholicism was not replaced by any alternative.

Those hidden children who remained with their hiding parents after the war and grew up with a non-Jewish family varied in terms of church-going, but none of them got a Jewish education or went to a synagogue during that time. Because Dutch Jews tended to be more cultural in their Jewish identification and more secular in their practices, former hidden children did not usually receive a formal Jewish education after the war unless they lived in Jewish orphanages. However, many adults stated to me that despite having a strong Jewish identity, they still feel more comfortable in a church than in a synagogue.

When those who had stayed with their hiding family after the war gained more of a Jewish identity, usually at the university, more than one was told by his or her foster parent, "We didn't save you for that!" Foster parents did not attend the Jewish weddings of these former hidden children because they disapproved and/or felt snubbed that their foster child, whom they had saved and loved, did not choose their religion. They did not remain aloof, however, and were involved as grandparents when their foster child had children. Not all foster parents told the former hidden child that he or she was Jewish after the war, and some Jewish children grew up in the church, married in the church, and, in one case, taught in a church school until he found out late in life that he was Jewish. Another who had a similar trajectory only found out about his background in the late 1990s when his foster mother died and he acquired her papers. This came as a shock to him and a jolt to his marriage because his Protestant wife did not feel comfortable with his exploration of his Jewish identity.

Thus, a switch in religious identity was traumatic for some former hidden children, depending upon the context within which they were hidden, and the age at which they found out the truth. One well-known case concerns historian Saul Friedlander, who was hidden in a monastery and only told by a priest that he was Jewish when he declared his intention to become a priest. However, we can substitute many other possible aspects of identity in this same process, such as someone finding out that he or she was adopted, or that a parent was something other than he or she had been portrayed to be, extending the relevance of such identity shifts to contemporary situations. In such contexts, the interviewer should try to uncover how the person felt when he or she realized the discrepancy between his or her assumed identity and his or her actual identity, although this is likely to have been a highly traumatic time (see Fremont 1999). In terms of a focus on childhood and religion, this case demonstrates the fluidity of religious affiliation during and after childhood, which may occur within modern contexts.

Working with Trauma

Scholars writing about the Holocaust have focused on how people remember, what they remember, and if they remember. Author Primo Levi argued that with the passing of time, memories go through a sieve, with the most painful memories fading away (1986: 136). Others do not believe that the worst memories are the ones that necessarily fade away over time (Delbo 1995). Contrary to Primo Levi, anthropologist Pamela Ballinger asserts that for those who survived genocide, the issue is not so much an inability to remember but *an inability to forget* (1998: 117). However, despite tremendous scholarly attention to memory and its different forms (Langer 1993), it is impossible to generalize about individual memory, whether formed by adults or by children.

For my interviews, I met with people only once but for an extended period. We went from the initial general questions that broke the ice ("Where were you born?" "Who was in your family?" "Were you brought up with Jewish traditions?") to discussion of their more personal circumstances in 1942. As the person being interviewed delved deeper into his or her memory and his or her past, I had to try to imagine this person (or even myself) in the situation being described so that I could follow details and probe further, asking questions about the event being described, for example, "How did you feel when your mother said good-bye?" Interviews were like a guided journey; I would shine a light on a particular pathway and the interviewee would then continue walking in that direction. This probing always took us deeper and deeper into the interviewees' past and inevitably circled around their traumas, sometimes dipping in. As the topic became more emotional, as it almost always did, these memories brought up tears for almost everyone I interviewed and outright crying for many. A few men sobbed so much that I had to turn off the tape recorder.

Our training and human subjects reviews rightly focus on protecting the subjects of our inquiry; however, nothing prepares the interviewer for how the research might affect her. The first ten or so interviews were devastating experiences for me. I often joined the interviewee in his or her tears and at the end, left in a state of numbness. Over time, the intensity of my feelings lessened, which made interviewing easier. However, during the analysis and writing stages, I revisited these emotions and was overwhelmed again many times by the tragedy of some of the lives I was privileged to document. Unlike therapists, most academics are not trained to be distant enough so that we do not end up drowning in emotions. When I was coding the interviews or writing them up, sometimes I simply would have to stop, call a friend, or take a walk. However, I do not see this emotional immersion as negative, as something to avoid. To the contrary, it may help the researcher experience some of what her subjects feel, perhaps being "transference," albeit on a smaller scale. I certainly never became detached from the "data," and I always attempted to conduct a kind of "compassionate sociology."

In terms of reciprocity, however, as with most research projects, I believe the benefits of being a part of the study were unequal in the researcher's favor. Several former hidden children expressed that it felt like an accomplishment to have done an interview with me, because they were finally able to talk about their pasts. Some clearly appreciated the focus on and attention to their particular past as hidden children, particularly what occurred after the war. I must admit that I was thrilled when one therapist thanked me for a comment I made that she considered insightful; this was the same person who proclaimed that my informed consent form was "bullshit," so I was especially relieved. But I do not assume that everyone felt similarly.

Although at least one of my informants was offended by a mistake in her transcript, another woman wrote the following to me in a letter after receiving two copies of her interview:

> Reading this back, I realize how tremendously difficult your job is. So many not really relevant stories. . . . And I am not capable of sorting it out before telling it. You must believe that reading this is very helpful for me even though it must be difficult for you. That's part of the reason why I could not do this [the interview] earlier. I really am grateful to you, thank you.

This particular person never was able to fully function in the world and remained emotionally crippled by her history. She and the few others who were in a similar situation seemed stuck in their childhood experiences, unable to move on. The majority of those I interviewed, however, were able to put together a meaningful life despite their permanent scars.

The error that offended my interviewee stands as a lesson in taking the time to carefully proofread transcripts before sending them to those featured in them. Despite the time that may take, I strongly urge researchers to try to think about ways of reciprocating even if we can never succeed in giving back as much as we have taken. Some of those I interviewed gave their transcript to their children to read, in order to perhaps fill in some of the blanks that they hadn't known. My sense was that a number of individuals, especially those with less education, were proud to have been interviewed and to have the transcript to show for it.

Conclusions

What can be culled from this foray into childhood trauma? How might it inform contemporary research on children and religion? Interviewing adults about their childhood past, whether it was traumatic or not, will result in a modified, revised history that has eroded some memories while embellishing or even creating others. As researchers, we cannot control for those shifts in memory or ever be fully sure that we are obtaining some verifiable truth. Yet if we are seeking the emotional texture of a childhood past, it may be possible to ease people back to a particular context and to stay there in order to try to evoke those feelings. Furthermore, understanding the ways in which religious identification can shift during childhood and even across the life course involves posing questions about identity rather than assuming it.

Children are still caught in wars, in natural disasters, in epidemics such as AIDS, and in dire poverty and are forced to deal with loss and trauma at an early age—the Occupation in Gaza, the earthquake in Haiti, the Hmong in refugee camps, and starvation in parts of Africa. Children have been abandoned, forced to fend for themselves, taken as near slave labor, trafficked, raped, and used as soldiers. There is no dearth of events that are currently causing trauma among children, some of which is connected to religion. Clearly, we can only understand this trauma within the context of state and global structures that affect children's lives. Working for a just world where children are protected and cared for would be the best solution, eliminating these traumas and our ability to study them altogether. Until that time, engaging in a self-reflexive and cautious approach to these painful topics can further the cause of compassionate and engaged scholarship, something well worth striving for.

Bibliography

Acland, Charles R. 1994. *Youth, Murder, Spectacle: The Cultural Politics of "Youth in Crisis."* Boulder, CO: Westview.

Adiga, Aravind. 2010. *Between the Assassinations.* London: Atlantic Books.

Agarwal, V. 2005. Awakening Latent Spirituality: Nurturing Children in the Hindu Tradition. In Karen Marie Yust, Aostre N. Johnson, Sandy E. Sasso, and Eugene Roehlkepartain (eds.), *Nurturing Child and Adolescent Spirituality.* Lanham, MD: Rowman & Littlefield, 19-32.

Alcott, A. Bronson. 1991/1936-37. *How Like an Angel Came I Down: Conversations with Children on the Gospels.* Hudson, NY: Lindisfarne Books.

Alderson, Priscilla. 2004. *Young Children's Rights.* London: Jessica Kingsley/Save the Children.

———. 2008. Children as Researchers: Participation Rights and Research Methods. In Alison James and Pia Christensen (eds.), *Researching with Children: Perspectives and Practices.* New York: Routledge, 276-90.

Alderson, Priscilla, and V. Morrow. 2010. *The Ethics of Research with Children and Young People: A Practical Handbook.* London: Sage.

Alderson, Priscilla, Katy Sutcliffe, and Katherine Curtis. 2006. "Children's Competence to Consent to Medical Treatment." *Hastings Center Report* 36: 25-34.

Alibašić, Ahmet. 2009. "Religious Education in Public Schools in Bosnia Herzegovina: Towards a Model Supporting Coexistence and Mutual Understanding." Retrieved 7/10, from http://www.soros.org.ba/images_vijesti/stipendisti_2009/eng_ahmet_alibasic_full.pdf.

Allen, Holly Catterton, ed. 2008. *Nurturing Children's Spirituality: Christian Perspectives and Best Practices.* Eugene, OR: Cascade.

Anderson, Sally. 2000. *I en klasse for sig* [In a Class of Their Own]. Copenhagen: Gyldendal.

———. 2003. Kategorisering. Fællesmængder og særpræg hos børn [Categorization: Common Sets and Remainders among Children]. In K. Hastrup (ed.), *Viden om Verden. En grundbog i antropologisk analyse* [Knowledge of the World: A Reader in Anthropological Analysis]. Copenhagen: Hans Reitzels Forlag.

Apfel, Roberta J., and Bennett Simon, eds. 1996. *Minefields in Their Hearts: The Mental Health of Children in War and Communal Violence.* New Haven, CT: Yale University Press.

Aris, Michael. 1989. *Hidden Treasures and Secret Lives: A Study of Pemalingpa (1450-1521) and the Sixth Dalai Lama (1683-1706).* London: Kegan Paul.

Armstrong, Karen. 1993. *A History of God.* New York: Ballantyne Books.

————. 2009. *The Case for God.* London: Bodley Head.

Arnett, Jeffrey Jenson. 2004. *Emerging Adulthood: The Winding Road from the Late Teens through the Twenties.* New York: Oxford University Press.

Auerbach, Carl, and Louise Silverstein. 2003. *Qualitative Data: An Introduction to Coding and Analysis.* New York: New York University Press.

Bado-Fralick, Nikki, and Rebecca S. Norris. 2010. *Toying with God: The World of Religious Games and Dolls.* Waco, TX: Baylor University Press.

Bagley, Stephen, William Reynolds, and Robert Nelson. 2007. "Is a 'Wage-Payment' Model for Research Participation Appropriate for Children?" *Pediatrics* 119: 26-51.

Bailey, Beth L. 1988. *From Front Porch to Back Seat: Courtship in Twentieth-Century America.* Baltimore: Johns Hopkins University Press.

Bakhtin, Mikhail M. 1981. *The Dialogic Imagination: Four Essays.* Ed. Michael Holquist. Trans. Caryl Emerson and Michael Holquist. Austin: University of Texas Press.

Bales, Susan Ridgely. 2005. *When I Was a Child: Children's Interpretations of First Communion.* Chapel Hill: University of North Carolina Press

Ballinger, Pamela. 1998. "The Culture of Survivors: Post-Traumatic Stress Disorder and Traumatic Memory." *History and Memory* 10, no. 1: 99-132.

Barraclough, K. 1999. "Soundings." *British Medical Journal* 319: 929.

"Battle for the Toybox." 2007. Retrieved 1/5/10, from http://one2believe.com/battlefly.bmp.

Beah, I. 2007. *A Long Way Gone: Memoirs of a Child Soldier.* London: Farrar, Straus, and Giroux.

Beck, U. 1992. *Risk Society.* London: Sage.

Beder, S. 2009. *This Little Kiddy Went to Market: The Corporate Capture of Childhood.* New York: Pluto.

Beh, Hazel. 2002. "The Role of Institutional Review Boards in Protecting Human Subjects: Are We Really Ready to Fix a Broken System?" *Law and Psychology Review* 26: 1-47.

Bell, Catherine. 1992. *Ritual Theory, Ritual Practice.* Oxford: Oxford University Press.

Benson, Peter L., Eugene C. Roehlkepartain, and Katherine Hong, eds. 2008. "Spiritual Development." Special issue, *New Directions for Youth Development* 118.

Benson, Peter L., Eugene C. Roehlkepartain, and S. P. Rude. 2003. "Spiritual Development in Childhood and Adolescence: Toward a Field of Inquiry." *Applied Developmental Science* 7: 204-12.

Bent, Geoge. 1968. *A Life of George Bent.* Norman: University of Oklahoma Press.

Berliner, David, and Ramon Sarro. 2007/1968. *Learning Religion: Anthropological Approaches.* New York: Berhahn Books.

Best, Wallace. 2005. *Passionately Human, No Less Divine: Religion and Culture in Black Chicago, 1915-1952.* Princeton, NJ: Princeton University Press.

Bhaskar, R. 2008. *Dialectic: The Pulse of Freedom.* London: Routledge.

Blanchfield, Luisa. 2009. "The United Nations Convention on the Rights of the Child: Background and Policy Issues" (Congressional Research Service, 2 December). Retrieved 3/14/11, from http://fpc.state.gov/documents/organization/134266/pdf.

Bloustien, Gerry. 2003. *Girl Making: A Cross-Cultural Ethnography on the Process of Growing up Female.* New York: Berghahn Books.

Bluebond-Langner, M. 1978. *The Private Worlds of Dying Children.* Princeton, NJ: Princeton University Press.

Bluebond-Langner, M., A. DeCicco, and J. Belasco. 2005. Involving Children with Life-Shortening Illnesses in Decisions about Participation in Clinical Research: A Proposal for Shuttle Diplomacy and Negotiation. In E. Kodish (ed.), *Ethics and Research with Children*. Oxford: Oxford University Press, 323-44.

Boyatzis, Chris J. 2003a. "Religious and Spiritual Development: An Introduction." *Review of Religious Research* 44, no. 3: 213-19.

———. 2003b. "Religious and Spiritual Development." *Review of Religious Research* 44, no. 3: 271-84.

———. 2004. The Co-construction of Spiritual Meaning in Parent-Child Communication. In Donald Radcliff (ed.), *Children's Spirituality: Christian Perspectives, Research, and Applications*. Eugene, OR: Wipf & Stock, 182-200.

———. 2005. Children's Religious and Spiritual Development. In R. F. Paloutzian and C. L. Park (eds.), *Handbook of the Psychology of Religion and Spirituality*. New York: Guilford, 123-43.

———, ed. 2006. "Unraveling the Dynamics of Religion in the Family and Parent-Child Relationships." Special issue, *International Journal for the Psychology of Religion* 16, no. 4.

Boyatzis, Chris J., D. C. Dollahite, and L. D. Marks. 2005. The Family as a Context for Religious and Spiritual Development in Children and Youth. In Eugene C. Roehlkepartain, Pamela E. King, Linda Wagener, and Peter L. Benson (eds.), *The Handbook of Spiritual Development in Childhood and Adolescence*. Thousand Oaks, CA: Sage, 297-309.

Boyatzis, Chris J., and D. Janicki. 2003. "Parent-Child Communication about Religion: Survey and Diary Data on Unilateral Transmission and Bi-Directional Reciprocity Styles." *Review of Religious Research* 44: 252-70.

Boyer, Pascal. 1994. *The Naturalness of Religious Ideas: A Cognitive Theory of Religion*. Berkeley: University of California Press.

Brading, D. A. 2001. *Mexican Phoenix: Our Lady of Guadalupe, Image and Tradition across Five Centuries*. New York: Cambridge University Press.

Bradley, Matt. 2007. "Silenced for Their Own Protection: How the IRB Marginalizes Those It Feigns to Protect." *ACME: An International E-Journal for Critical Geographies* 6, no. 3: 339-49.

Bray, Lucy. 2007. "Developing an Activity to Aid Informed Assent When Interviewing Children and Young People." *Journal of Research in Nursing* 12: 447-57.

Brighouse, H. 2002. What Rights (If Any) Do Children Have? In D. Archard and C. MacLeod, (eds.), *The Moral and Political Status of Children*. Oxford: Oxford University Press, 31-52.

Bromley, David G., and Lewis F. Carter, eds. 2001. *Toward Reflexive Ethnography: Participating, Observing, Narrating*. Oxford: Elsevier Science.

Bromley, David G., and Phillip E. Hammond, eds. 1987. *The Future of New Religious Movements*. Macon, GA: Mercer University Press.

Browning, Don S., and Marcia J. Bunge, eds. 2009. *Children and Childhood in World Religions*. New Brunswick, NJ: Rutgers University Press.

Buckser, Andrew. 1999. "Keeping Kosher and Jewish Identity among the Jews of Denmark." *Ethnology* 38, no. 3: 191-210.

———. 2003. *After the Rescue: Jewish Identity and Community in Contemporary Denmark*. New York: Palgrave Macmillan.

Bunge, Marcia, ed. 2001. *The Child in Christian Thought*. Grand Rapids, MI: Eerdmans.

Burke, Georgine. 2005. "Looking into the Institutional Review Board: Observations from Both Sides of the Table." *Journal of Nutrition* 135: 921-24.

Cahan, Emily, et al. 1993. The Elusive Historical Child: Ways of Knowing the Child of History and Psychology. In Glen Elder, John Modell, Ross Parke (eds.), *Children in Time and Place: Developmental and Historical Insights*. New York: Cambridge University Press, 192-220.

Campbell, Michelle. 1992. "Girls in Gangs." *State Press: Arizona State University's Summer Weekly*. August 6, p. 7.

Carsten, Janet. 2000. Introduction. In J. Carsten (ed.), *Cultures of Relatedness*. Cambridge: Cambridge University Press.

Cavalletti, Sofia. 1992. *The Religious Potential of the Child*. Chicago: Liturgy Training Publications.

Cernea, Ruth F. 1995. *The Passover Seder: An Anthropological Perspective on Jewish Culture*. Lanham, MD: University Press of America.

Christensen, Pia Haudrup. 2004. "Children's Participation in Ethnographic Research: Issues of Power and Representation." *Children & Society* 18, no. 2: 165-76.

Christensen, Pia Haudrup, and Allison James, eds. 2008. *Research with Children*. London: Routledge.

Clark, Cindy Dell. 1995. *Flights of Fancy, Leaps of Faith: Children's Myths in Contemporary America*. Chicago: University of Chicago Press.

———. 1998. Youth, Advertising, and Symbolic Meaning. In C. Macklin and L. Carlson (eds.), *Advertising to Children*. Thousand Oaks CA: Sage, 77-93.

———. 2003. *In Sickness and in Play: Children Coping with Chronic Illness*. New Brunswick, NJ: Rutgers University Press.

———. 2005. "Tricks of Festival: Children, Enculturation, and American Halloween." *Ethos* 33: 180-205.

———. 2010. *In a Younger Voice: Doing Children's Qualitative Research*. New York: Oxford University Press.

Clark, A., and B. Percy-Smith. 2006. "Beyond Consultation: Participatory Practices in Everyday Spaces." *Children, Youth, and Environments* 16, no. 2: 1-9.

Clayton, M., and A. Stanton. 2008. "The Changing World's View of Christian Youth Work." *Youth & Policy* 100: 109-18.

Coffin, Morse H. 1965. *The Battle of Sand Creek*. Waco, TX: W.M. Morrison.

Coles, Robert. 1990. *The Spiritual Life of Children*. Boston: Houghton Mifflin.

Collins, Peter, and Anselma Gallinat, eds. 2010. *The Ethnographic Self as Resource: Writing Memory and Experience into Ethnography*. New York: Berghahn.

Connolly, P., A. Smith, and B. Kelly. 2002. *Too Young to Notice? The Cultural and Political Awareness of 3-6-Year-Olds in Northern Ireland*. Belfast: Community Relations Council.

Corsaro, William A. 1997. *The Sociology of Childhood*. Thousand Oaks, CA: Pine Forage Press.

Crawford, Rev. W. 1865. "Public Estimate of Indians." *The Home Missionary* 37 (January).

Csordas, Thomas. 2009. "Growing Up Charismatic: Morality and Spirituality among Children in a Religious Community." *Ethos* 37: 414-40.

Daniel, William Andrew. 1925. "Negro Theological Seminary Survey." Ph.D. diss., University of Chicago.

Davin, Anna. 1999. "What Is a Child?" In *Childhood in Question: Children, Parents, and the State*. Manchester: Manchester University Press.

Davis, Andrew Jackson. 1867. *The Children's Progressive Lyceum*. 6th ed. Boston: Bela Marsh.

Dawson, K., and S.-K. Park. 2005. Reformed Spirits: Christian Practices in Presbyterian Preschools in South Korea and the United States. In Karen Marie Yust, Aostre N. Johnson, Sandy E. Sasso, and Eugene Roehlkepartain (eds.), *Nurturing Child and Adolescent Spirituality*. Lanham, MD: Rowman & Littlefield, 236-48.

Dehli, Karl. 1994. "They Rule by Sympathy: The Feminization of Pedagogy." *Canadian Journal of Sociology* 19, no. 2: 195-216.

Delbo, Charlotte. 1995. *After Auschwitz*. New Haven, CT: Yale University Press.

Deloria, Phillip J. 1998. *Playing Indian*. New Haven, CT: Yale University Press.

"Do 'Educational Toys' Really Teach?" 2009. Podcast retrieved 1/27/10, from http://www.tvo.org/cfmx/tvoorg/tvoparents/index.cfm?page_id=483&event_id=1965&sitefolder=tvoparents.

Doctor, Andreas. 2005. *Tibetan Treasure Literature: Revelation, Tradition, and Accomplishment in Visionary Buddhism*. Ithaca, NY: Snow Lion Publications.

Dollahite, D. C., and J. Y. Thatcher. 2003. "Talking about Religion: How Religious Youth and Parents Discuss Their Faith." *Journal of Adolescent Research* 23: 611-41.

Dowling, E., and W. G. Scarlett, eds. 2006. *Encyclopedia of Spiritual Development in Childhood and Adolescence*. Thousand Oaks, CA: Sage.

Downs, T. S. 1943. Research Notes, March 27, 1943, Allison Davis Papers, Box 39, Folder 2, Special Collections Research Center, University of Chicago Library, Chicago.

Drake, St. Clair, and Horace Cayton. 1970. *Black Metropolis: A Study of Negro Life in a Northern City*. New York: Harcourt, Brace, and World.

Driver, Tom E. 1998. *Liberating Rites: Understanding the Transformative Power of Ritual*. Boulder, CO: Westview.

Duque-Páramo, Maria Claudia, and Cindy Dell Clark. 2007. "Beyond Regulation: Ethical Questions for Research with Children." *Anthropology News* (April): 5.

Dyck, Noel. 2010. Remembering and the Ethnography of Children's Sports. In P. Collins and David A. Elkind (eds.), *The Power of Play: Learning What Comes Naturally*. Philadelphia: Da Capo/Perseus Books.

Elkind, D. 1970. "The Origins of Religion in the Child." *Review of Religious Research* 12: 35-42.

———. 2007. *The Power of Play: Learning What Comes Naturally*. Philadelphia: Da Capo/Perseus Books.

Erikson, Kai. 1966. *Wayward Puritans*. New York: Wiley.

Evans, E. Margaret. 2000. Beyond Scopes: Why Creationism Is Here to Stay. In Karl S. Rosengren, Carl N. Johnson, and Paul L. Harris (eds.), *Imagining the Impossible: Magical, Scientific, and Religious Thinking in Children*. New York: Cambridge University Press, 305-33.

Fabian, James. 1990. *Power and Performance: Ethnographic Explorations through Proverbial Wisdom and Theater in Shaba*. Madison: University of Wisconsin Press.

"FBI: Eco-Terrorism Remains No. 1 Domestic Terror Threat." 2008. Fox News, Monday, March 31, retrieved 3/29/10, from http://www.foxnews.com/story/0,2933,343768,00.html.

Feldman, S. Shirley, and Glen R. Elliott, eds. 1990. *At the Threshold: The Developing Adolescent.* Cambridge, MA: Harvard University Press.

Ferraro, F. R., L. L. Orvedal, and J. J. Plaud. 1998. "Institutional Review Board (IRB) Issues Related to Special Populations: Developmentally Disabled Individuals." *Journal of General Psychology* 125: 156-64.

Fowler, James. 1981. *Stages of Faith: The Psychology of Human Development and the Quest for Meaning.* New York: HarperCollins.

Francis, M., and R. Lorenzo. 2005. Children and City Design: Proactive Process and the "Renewal" of Childhood. In C. Spencer and M. Blades (eds.), *Children and Their Environment: Learning, Using, and Designing Spaces.* Cambridge: Cambridge University Press.

Franklin, B., ed. 2001. *The New Handbook of Children's Rights.* London: Routledge.

Freeman, Melissa, and Sandra Mathison. 2009. *Researching Children's Experiences.* New York: Guilford Press.

Fremont, Helen. 1999. *After a Long Silence: A Woman's Search for Her Family's Secret Identity.* London: Piatkus Books.

French, J., with Joshua Holly, Eva Holly, and Lucy Holly. 2007. Little Angels Here Below. *Something Understood.* BBC Radio 4, May 20.

Gable, Eric. 2002. "Beyond Belief? Play, Skepticism, and Religion in a West African Village." *Social Anthropology* 10, no. 1 (February): 41-56.

Gardner, Alexander Patten. 2006. "The Twenty-Five Great Sites of Khams: Religious Geography, Revelation, and Nonsectarianism in Nineteenth-Century Eastern Tibet." Ph.D. diss., University of Michigan.

Garrido, Ann. 2004. *Mustard Seed Preaching.* Chicago: Liturgy Training Publications.

Germano, David. 1998. Re-membering the Dismembered Body of Tibet: Contemporary Tibetan Visionary Movements in the People's Republic of China. In Melvyn C. Goldstein and Matthew T. Kapstein (eds.), *Buddhism in Contemporary Tibet: Religious Revival and Cultural Identity.* Berkeley: University of California Press, 53-94.

Ghartsang, Chodak Tashi. Interview, Toronto, 3/16/2007.

Gillis, John R. 2008. Epilogue: The Islanding of Children; Reshaping the Mythical Landscapes of Childhood. In Marta Gutman and Ning de Coninck-Smith (eds.), *Designing Modern Childhoods: History, Space, and the Material Culture of Children.* New Brunswick, NJ: Rutgers University Press, 316-30.

Giroux, Henry A. 1997. *Channel Surfing: Race Talk and the Destruction of Today's Youth.* New York: St. Martin's Press.

Glenn, Charles L. 1988. *The Myth of the Common School,* Amherst: University of Massachusetts Press.

———. 2003. "Fanatical Secularism." *Education Next: A Journal of Opinion and Research* 1: 60-65.

Goldman, R. G. 1964. *Religious Thinking from Childhood to Adolescence.* London: Routledge and Kegan Paul.

Goodenough, Trudy. 2007. "Review: Developing an Activity to Aid Informed Assent When Interviewing Children and Young People." *Journal of Research in Nursing* 12: 459-60.

Gordon, Devin, Anne Underwood, Tara Weingarten, and Ana Figueroa. 1999. "The Secret Life of Teens: Sex, Drugs, and Rock Have Worried Parents for Decades, but Now the Net, Videogames, and No-Holds-Barred Music Are Creating New Worlds That Many Adults Can't Enter." May 10. Retrieved 3/14/11, from http://www.newsweek.com/id/88252/page/1.

Gordon, Elisa, Amy Harris Yamokoski, and Eric Kodish. 2006. "Children, Research, and Guinea Pigs: Reflections on a Metaphor." *IRB: Ethics and Human Research* 28: 12-19.

Gottlieb, Alma. 2004. *The Afterlife Is Where We Come From: The Culture of Infancy in West Africa*. Chicago: University of Chicago Press.

Griffin, J. 2002. Do Children Have Rights? In D. Archard and C. MacLeod (eds.), *The Moral and Political Status of Children*. Oxford: Oxford University Press, 19-30.

Grodin, M., and L. Glantz. 1994. *Children as Research Subjects: Science, Ethics, and the Law*. New York: Oxford University Press.

Gross, Gary. *The Cute and the Cool: Wondrous Innocence and Modern American Children's Culture*. New York: Oxford University Press, 2004.

Grossman, James. 1989. *Land of Hope: Chicago, Black Southerners, and the Great Migration*. Chicago: University of Chicago Press.

Gyatso, Janet. 1986. "Signs, Memory, and History: A Tantric Buddhist Theory of Scriptual Transmission." *Journal of the International Association of Buddhist Studies* 9, no. 2: 7- 35.

———. 1993. "The Logic of Legitimation in the Tibetan Treasure Tradition." *History of Religions* 33, no. 1: 97- 134.

———. 1996. "Drawn from the Tibetan Treasury: The *gTer ma* Literature." In Joze Cabezon and Roger Jackson (eds.), *Tibetan Literature Studies in Genre*. Ithaca, NY: Snow Lion Publications, 147-69.

———. 1998. *Apparitions of the Self*. Princeton, NJ: Princeton University Press.

Haight, Wendy L. 1998. "'Gathering the Spirit' at First Baptist Church: Spirituality as a Protective Factor in the Lives of African American Children." *Social Work* 43: 213-21.

Halkias, Georgios. 2006. Pure-Lands and Other Visions in Seventeenth-Century Tibet: A Gnam-chos sādhana for the Pure-land Sukhāvatī Revealed in 1658 by Gnam-chos Mi-'gyur-rdo-rje (1645-1667). In B. Cuevas et al. (eds.), *Power, Politics, and the Reinvention of Tradition: Tibet in the Seventeenth and Eighteenth Century*. Leiden: Brill, 121-51.

Hartfield, Ronne. 2004. *Another Way Home: The Tangled Roots of Race in One American Family*. Chicago: University of Chicago Press.

Hay, David, and Rebecca Nye. 1998. *The Spirit of the Child*. London: Fount.

Hebdige, Dick. 1982/1983. "Posing . . . Threats, Striking . . . Poses: Youth, Surveillances, and Display" in Sub-Stance, Vol. 11/12 Issue 37/38 (Madison: University of Wisconsin Press).

Heilbroner, Oded. "From a Culture *for* Youth to a Culture *of* Youth: Recent Trends in the Historiography of Western Youth Cultures." *Contemporary European History* 17 (2008): 575-91.

Heller, David. 1986. *The Children's God*. Chicago: University of Chicago Press.

Hendrick, Harry. 2008. The Child as a Social Actor in Historical Sources: Problems of Identification and Interpretation. In Alison James and Pia Christensen (eds.), *Research with Children: Perspectives and Practices*. New York: Routledge, 36-61.

Hersch, Patricia. 1999. *A Tribe Apart: A Journey into the Heart of American Adolescence*. New York: Ballantine Books.

Hirschfeld, Lawrence A. 2002. "Why Don't Anthropologists Like Children?" *American Anthropologist* 104, no. 2: 611-27.

Hochschild, A. 2005. "Bush's Empathy Shortage." *American Prospect* 16, no. 7.

Hoig, Stan. 1974. *The Western Odyssey of John Simpson Smith*. Glendale, CA: Clark.

Holmes, Amy. 2008. "Mapping Constellations of Power in Himalayan Buddhism: The Life and Lineage of Rtogs ldan Sha' kya shri' (1853-1919)." Ph.D. diss., Australian National University.

Holmes-Tagchungdarpa, Amy. The Social Element of Visionary Revelation: Public Rites as a Means of Negotiating Authenticity in Tibetan Buddhist Visionary Lineages. In Ute Huesken and Frank Neubert (eds.), *Negotiating Rites*. New York: Oxford University Press, forthcoming 2011.

Hoover, Stewart M., Lynn Schofield Clark, and Diane F. Alters. 2004. *Media, Home, and Family*. New York: Routledge.

Hufford, David. 1995. "The Scholarly Voice and the Personal Voice: Reflexivity in Belief Studies." *Western Folklore* 54: 57-76.

Hutchinson, William. 1976. *The Modernist Impulse in American Protestantism*. Cambridge, MA: Harvard University Press.

Hyde, Kenneth E. 1990. *Religion in Childhood and Adolescence*. Birmingham, AL: Religious Education Press.

"Instruction of the Propaganda Fide concerning Catholic Children in American Public Schools." In Mark Massa and Catherine Osbeorne (eds.), *American Catholic History: A Documentary Reader*. New York: New York University Press, 2008, 54-57.

Jackson, Robert, and Ursula McKenna, eds. 2005. *Intercultural Education and Religious Plurality*. University of Oslo: Oslo Coalition on Freedom of Religion or Belief.

Jacobson, Lisa. 2005. *Raising Consumers: Children and the American Mass Market in the Early Twentieth Century*. New York: Columbia University Press.

Jacoby, Sarah. 2007. "Consorts and Revelation in Eastern Tibet: The Auto/ Biographical Writings of Sera Khandro (1892-1940)." Ph.D. diss., University of Virginia.

James, Allison. 2004. Understanding Childhood from an Interdisciplinary Perspective: Problems and Potentials. In Peter B. Pufall and Richard P. Unsworth (eds.), *Rethinking Childhood*. New Brunswick, NJ: Rutgers University Press, 25-37.

James, Allison, and Pia Christensen. 2008. Researching Children and Childhood Cultures of Communication. In Alison James and Pia Christensen (eds.), *Research with Children: Perspectives and Practices*. New York: Routledge, 1-9.

James, Allison, and Alan Prout. 1997. *Constructing and Reconstructing Childhood: Contemporary Issues in the Sociological Study of Childhood*. London: Falmer Press.

Jenkins, Henry, ed. 1998. *The Children's Culture Reader*. New York: New York University Press.

Jennings, Francis. 1976. *The Invasion of America: Indians, Colonialism, and the Cant of Conquest*. New York: Norton.

Johnson, C. N., and C. J. Boyatzis. 2005. Cognitive-Cultural Foundations of Spiritual Development. In Eugene C. Roehlkepartain, Pamela E. King, Linda Wagener, and Peter L. Benson (eds.), *The Handbook of Spiritual Development in Childhood and Adolescence*. Thousand Oaks, CA: Sage.

Jones Notes. 1944. March 21, 1944, Allison Davis Papers, Box 40, Folder 1, Special Collections Research Center, University of Chicago Library, Chicago.

Judge, Harry. 2002. *Faith-Based Schools and the State: Catholics in America, France, and England*. Oxford Studies in Comparative Education, vol. 11, no. 2. Oxford: Symposium Books.

Kanter, Rosabeth Moss. 1972. *Commitment and Community*. Cambridge, MA: Harvard University Press.

Kar ma chags med. 1983. Sprul sku mi 'gyur rdo rje'i phyi'i rnam thar kun khyab snyan pa'i 'brug sgra (phyi'i rnam thar). In Mi 'gyur rdo rje, et. al. (eds.), *Gnam chos thugs kyi gter kha snyan brgyud zab mo'i skor* [Collection des Tresors par gNam-chös Mi-'gyur rDo-rje]. Vol. 10. Paro: Dilgo Khyentsey Rinpoche, 6-533.

Karma Chagme. 2008. *The All-Pervading Sound of Thunder: The Outer Liberation Story of Terton Migyur Dorje*. Translated by Lopon Sonam Tsewang and Judith Amtzis. Taiwan: Palri Parkhang.

Katz, C. 2004. *Growing Up Global*. Minneapolis: University of Minnesota Press.

Kawin, Ethel. 1938. *The Wise Choice of Toys*. 2nd ed. Chicago: University of Chicago Press.

Kehily, Mary Jane, ed. 2004. *An Introduction to Childhood Studies*. New York: Open University Press.

Kertzer, David. I. 1988. *Ritual, Politics, and Power*. New Haven, CT: Yale University Press.

Khan, R. Y. 2005. The Child on Loan: The Pathway from Infancy through Adolescence in Islamic Studies. In Karen Marie Yust, Aostre N. Johnson, Sandy E. Sasso, and Eugene Roehlkepartain (eds.), *Nurturing Child and Adolescent Spirituality*. Lanham, MD: Rowman & Littlefield, 132-42.

King, Pamela E., and Chris J. Boyatzis. 2004." Exploring Adolescent Religious and Spiritual Development: Current and Future Theoretical and Empirical Perspectives." *Applied Developmental Science* 8: 2-6.

Klein, N. 2000. *No Logo*. London: Flamingo.

Kline, Stephen. 1993. *Out of the Garden: Toys, TV, and Children's Culture in the Age of Marketing*. London: Verso.

Klinkowitz, Jerome, ed. 1979. *The Diaries of Willard Motley*. Ames: Iowa State University Press.

Kon, Alexander. 2006. "Assent in Pediatric Research." *Pediatrics* 117: 1806-10.

Kuczynski, L. 2003. Beyond Bidirectionality: Bi-lateral Conceptual Frameworks for Understanding Dynamics. In L. Kuczynski (ed.), *Handbook of Dynamics in Parent-Child Relations*. Thousand Oaks, CA: Sage, 1-24.

Kuipers, Joel C. 1989. "Medical Discourse in Anthropological Context: Views of Language and Power." *Medical Anthropological Quarterly* 3: 99-123.

La Fontaine, Jean. 1997. Are Children People? Paper presented at *The Invisibility of Children: A Symposium on Children and Anthropology*. Department of Child Studies. Linkøping University, Sweden. 5-6 May.

Lamont, Michele, and Virag Molnar. 2002. "The Study of Boundaries in the Social Sciences." *Annual Review of Sociology* 28: 167-95.

Langer, Lawrence L. 1993. *Holocaust Testimonies: The Ruins of Memory*. New Haven, CT: Yale University Press.

Larmondin, Leanne. 2009. "Book Finds That Religious Toys Are More Than Child's Play." Dec. 18. Retrieved 1/26/10, from http://www.religionnews.com/index.php?/rnstext/book_explores_impact_significance_of_religious_toys/.

Latham, Rob. 2002. *Consuming Youth: Vampires, Cyborgs, and the Culture of Consumption*. Chicago: University of Chicago Press.

Lesko, Nancy. 2001. *Act Your Age! A Cultural Construction of Adolescence*. New York: Routledge Farmer.

Levi, Primo. 1986. *If Not Now, When?* New York: Penguin Press.

Levinson, Bradley A., and Dorothy Holland. 1996. The Cultural Production of the Educated Person: An Introduction. In Levinson et al. (eds.), *The Cultural Production of the Educated Person: Critical Ethnographies of Schooling and Local Practice*. Albany: State University of New York Press.

Lewis, V., M. Kellett, C. Robinson, S. Fraser, and S. Ding. 2004. *The Reality of Research with Children and Young People*. London: Sage.

Lillig, Tina, ed. 2004. *Catechesis of the Good Shepherd: Essential Realities*. Chicago: Liturgy Training Publications.

Lipper, Joanna. 2005. *The Road to Whatever: Middle-Class Culture and the Crisis of Adolescence*. New York: Picador.

Lofland, John. 1987. Social Movement Culture and the Unification Church. In David G. Bromley and Phillip Hammond (eds.), *The Future of New Religious Movements*. Macon, GA: Mercer University Press, 91-108.

Long, David, Diane Elkind, and Bernard Spilka. 1967. "The Child's Conception of Prayer." *Journal for the Scientific Study of Religion* 6: 101-9.

Longfellow, Henry Wadsworth. 1898. *The Song of Hiawatha*. New York: Hurst.

Lowdin, Per. 1998. *Food, Ritual, and Society: A Study of Social Structure and Food Symbolism among the Newars*. Kathmandu: Mandala Point Books.

Luhr, Eileen. 2009. *Witnessing Suburbia: Conservatives and Christian Youth Culture*. Berkeley: University of California Press.

Lundskow, G. 2008. *The Sociology of Religion*. London: Sage.

Manse, Ruby. 1934. Notes, 1934, Ernest Burgess Papers, Box 89, Folder 5, Special Collections Research Center, University of Chicago.

Marsden, George. 1980. *Fundamentalism and American Culture: The Shaping of Twentieth-Century Evangelicalism, 1870-1925*. New York: Oxford University Press.

Mattis, J., M. K. Ahluwalia, S.-A. E. Cowie, and A. M. Kirkland-Harris. 2005. Ethnicity, Culture, and Spiritual Development. In Eugene C. Roehlkepartain, Pamela E. King, Linda Wagener, and Peter L. Benson (eds.), *The Handbook of Spiritual Development in Childhood and Adolescence*. Thousand Oaks, CA: Sage, 283-96.

Maynes, Mary Jo, Jennifer L. Pierce, and Barbara Laslett. 2008. *Telling Stories: The Use of Personal Narratives in the Social Sciences and History*. Ithaca, NY: Cornell University Press.

McDannell, Colleen. 1995. *Material Christianity: Religion and Popular Culture in America*. New Haven, CT: Yale University Press.

McGreevy, John. 1996. *Parish Boundaries: The Catholic Encounter with Race in the Twentieth-Century Urban North*. Chicago: University of Chicago Press.

McMahon, Eileen. 1995. *What Parish Are You From? A Chicago Irish Community and Race Relations*. Lexington: University Press of Kentucky.

Meacham, J. A. 2004. Action, Voice, and Identity in Children's Lives. In P. B. Pufall and R. P. Unsworth (eds.), *Rethinking Childhood*. New Brunswick, NJ: Rutgers University Press, 69-84.

Mercer, J. A., D. L. Matthews, and S. Walz. 2004. Children in Congregations: Congregations as Contexts for Children's Spiritual Growth. In Donald Ratcliff (ed.), *Children's Spirituality: Christian Perspectives, Research, and Applications*. Eugene, OR: Cascade, 249-65.

Mi 'gyur rdo rje, et al., eds., 1983. *Gnam chos thugs kyi gter kha snyan brgyud zab mo'i skor* [Collection des Tresors par gNam-chös Mi-'gyur rDo-rje]. Paro: Dilgo Khyentsey Rinpoche.

Miller-McLemore, Bonnie J. 2003. *Let the Children Come: Re-imagining Childhood from a Christian Perspective*. San Francisco: Jossey Bass.

Miller-McLemore, Bonnie J., and Don S. Browning. 2009. *Children and Childhood in American Religion*. New Brunswick, NJ: Rutgers University Press.

Mintz, Steven. 2004. *Huck's Raft: A History of American Childhood*. Cambridge, MA: Harvard University Press.

Molloy, R. B. 1959. "On Educational Toys and Fun with a Purpose." *Saturday Evening Post*. June 27, p. 231.

Morrison, Theodore. 1974. *Chautauqua: A Center for Education, Religion, and the Arts in America*. Chicago: University of Chicago Press.

Nasaw, David. 1985. *Children of the City: At Work and at Play*. Garden City, NY: Anchor Press/Doubleday.

"New 'Holy Huggables' Plush Dolls Pack Fun and Faith into One Lovable Kid-Sized Package." 2007. Retrieved 1/14/10, from http://www.wdcmedia.com/newsArticle. php?ID=176.

Nisbet, R. 1967. *The Sociological Tradition*. London: Heinemann.

Norris, Rebecca Sachs. 2005. "Examining the Structure and Role of Emotion: Contributions of Neurobiology to the Study of Embodied Religious Experience." *Zygon: Journal of Religion & Science* 40, no. 1: 181-99.

Olwig, Karen Fog. 2000. Generations in the Making: The Role of Children. Paper presented at the European Association of Social Anthropologists session "Generational Boundaries and Beyond: Reexamining the Anthropology of Children and Childhood," Krakow, Poland, July.

Orsi, Robert A., ed. 1999. *Gods of the City* Bloomington: Indiana University Press.

———. 2005. *Between Heaven and Earth: The Religious Worlds People Make and the Scholars Who Study Them*. Princeton, NJ: Princeton University Press.

———. 2007a. "When 2 + 2 = 5: Can We Begin to Think about Unexplained Religious Experiences in Ways That Acknowledge Their Existence?" *American Scholar* 76, no. 2: 34-43.

———. 2007b. "A Crisis about the Theology of Children." *Harvard Divinity School Bulletin*. 6 November. Retrieved 3/13/11, from http://www.hds.harvard.edu/news/bulletin/ articles/orsi.html.

Oser, F., G. W. Scarlett, and A. Bucher. 2006. Religious and Spiritual Development throughout the Life Span. In W. Damon and R. M. Lerner (eds.), *Handbook of Child Psychology*. Vol. 1, *Theoretical Models of Development*. 6th ed. New York: Wiley, 942-97.

Palladino, Grace. 1996. *Teenagers: An American History*. New York: Basic Books.

Parish Register of St. Paul's Episcopal Church of Central City, Colorado. 1866. Diocesan Archive, Episcopal Diocese of Colorado. Pp. 475-76.

Paul, Pamela. 2008. *Parenting, Inc*. New York: Henry Holt.

Percy-Smith, B., and N. Thomas. 2010. *A Handbook of Children's and Young People's Participation*. London: Routledge.

Peshkin, Alan. 1988. *God's Choice: The Total World of a Fundamentalist Christian School*. Chicago: University of Chicago Press.

Petersen, Carsten Hjorth. 2002. *Pædagogik i Kristent Perspektiv* [Pedagogy in a Christian Perspective]. Fredericia: Credo Forlag.

———. 2007. *Påvirkning med Respekt. Skoleliv fra Intimisering til Desertering* [Influence with Respect: School Life from Intimacizing to Deserting]. Copenhagen: Gyldendal.

Pike, Sarah M. 2001. *Earthly Bodies, Magical Selves: Contemporary Pagans and the Search for Community*. Berkeley: University of California Press.

Pinson, H., M. Arnot, and M. Candappa. 2010. *Education, Asylum, and the "Non-Citizen" Child: The Politics of Compassion and Belonging.* Basingstoke: Palgrave Macmillan.

Porpora, D. 2001. *Landscapes of the Soul: Loss of Moral Meaning in American Life.* New York: Oxford University Press.

Post, Stephen G. 2005. "The IRB, Ethics, and the Objective Study of Religion in Health." *IRB: Ethics and Human Research* 17: 349-59.

Pritchard, Ivor. 2002. "Travelers and Trolls: Practitioner Research and Institutional Review Boards." *Educational Research* 31: 3-13.

Protestant Episcopal Church. 1864. *The Book of Common Prayer, and Administration of the Sacraments.* New York: Nelson.

Prothero, Stephen. 2003. *American Jesus: How the Son of God Became a National Icon.* New York: Farrar, Strauss, and Giroux.

Qvortrup, Jens. 1994. Childhood Matters: An Introduction. In J. Qvortrup, M. Bardy, G. Sgritta, and and H. Wintersberger (eds.), *Childhood Matters: Social Theory, Practice, and Politics.* Aldershot, England: Avebury, 1-23.

Raj, Selva, and Corinne G. Dempsey, eds. 2010. *Sacred Play, Ritual Levity, and Humor in South Asian Religions.* Albany: State University of New York Press.

Ratcliff, Donald, ed. 2004. *Children's Spirituality: Christian Perspectives, Research, and Applications.* Eugene, OR: Cascade.

Ratcliff, Donald and R. Nye. 2006. Childhood Spirituality: Strengthening the Research Foundation. In E. Roehlkepartain, P. Ebsteyne King, L. Wagener, and P. Benson (eds.), *The Handbook of Spiritual Development in Childhood and Adolescence.* Thousand Oaks, CA: Sage Publications.

"Read with Me Bible." 2009. Retrieved 1/14/10, from http://www.tbnwebstore.org/product.asp?sku=0310920086.

Reese, William J. 1995. *The Origins of the American High School.* New Haven, CT: Yale University Press.

Regnerus, Mark D. 2007. *Forbidden Fruit: Sex and Religion in the Lives of American Teenagers.* New York: Oxford University Press.

Reynolds, M. 2005. "Rendering unto God." *Mother Jones* 30:7. In G. Lundskow. *The Sociology of Religion.* London: Sage, 2008.

Richardson, James T., and Massimo Introvigne. 2007. New Religious Movements, Countermovements, Moral Panics, and the Media. In David G. Bromley (ed.), *Teaching New Religious Movements.* New York: Oxford University Press, 91-111.

Ridgely, Susan B. See Bales, Susan Ridgely.

Rinpoche, T. D. P. 2005. Young Minds, Youthful Buddhas: Developmental Rituals and Practices in Tibetan Buddhism. In Karen Marie Yust, Aostre N. Johnson, Sandy E. Sasso, and Eugene Roehlkepartain (eds.), *Nurturing Child and Adolescent Spirituality.* Lanham, MD: Rowman & Littlefield, 175-90.

Rochford, E. Burke. Jr. 1985. *Hare Krishna in America.* New Brunswick, NJ: Rutgers University Press, 1985.

———. 1992. On the Politics of Member Validation: Taking Findings Back to Hare Krishna. In Gale Miller and James Holstein (eds.), *Perspectives of Social Problems.* Vol. 3. Greenwich, CT: JAI Press, 99-116.

———. 2000. "Demons, Karmies, and Non-devotees: Culture, Group Boundaries, and the Development of the Hare Krishna in North America and Europe." *Social Compass* 47 (2): 169-86.

———. 2001. Accounting for Child Abuse in the Hare Krishna: Ethnographic Dilemmas and Reflections. In David G. Bromley (ed.), *Toward Reflexive Ethnography: Participating, Observing, Narrating*. Oxford: Elsevier Science, 157-79.

———. 2006. The Hare Krishna Movement: Beginnings, Change, and Transformation. In Eugene V. Gallagher and W. Michael Ashcraft (eds.), *Introduction to New and Alternative Religions*. Vol. 4. Westport, CT: Greenwood Press, 21-46.

———. 2007a. *Hare Krishna Transformed*. New York: New York University Press.

———. 2007b. The Sociology of New Religious Movements. In Anthony J. Blasi (ed.), *American Sociology of Religion*. Boston: Brill, 253-90.

Rochford, E. Burke Jr., and Kendra Bailey. 2006. "Almost Heaven: Leadership, Decline, and the Transformation of New Vrindaban." *Nova Religio* 9, no. 3: 6-23.

Roehlkepartain, Eugene C., Pamela E. King, Linda Wagener, and Peter L. Benson, eds. 2005. *The Handbook of Spiritual Development in Childhood and Adolescence*. Thousand Oaks, CA: Sage.

Roehlkepartain, Eugene, and E. Patel. 2005. Congregations: Unexamined Crucibles for Spiritual Development. In Eugene C. Roehlkepartain, Pamela E. King, Linda Wagener, and Peter L. Benson (eds.), *The Handbook of Spiritual Development in Childhood and Adolescence*. Thousand Oaks, CA: Sage, 324-36.

Roof, W. 1993. *A Generation of Seekers*. San Francisco: HarperCollins.

Rosen, M. 1994. *The Penguin Book of Childhood*. Harmondsworth, England: Penguin.

Ross, L. F. 2006. *Children in Medical Research: Access versus Protection*. New York: Oxford University Press.

Samuels, Jeffrey. 2004. "Breaking the Ethnographer's Frame: Reflections on the Use of Photo Elicitation in Understanding Sri Lankan Monastic Culture." *American Behavioral Scientist* 47, no. 12: 1528-50.

Savage, Jon. 2007. *Teenage: The Creation of Youth Culture*. New York: Viking.

Schieffelin, Edward L. 1998. Problematizing Performance. In F. Hughes-Freeland (ed.). *Ritual, Performance, Media*. London: Routledge, 194-207.

Scott, Jacqueline. 2008. Children as Respondents: The Challenge for Quantitative Methods. In Pia Christensen and Alison James (eds.), *Research with Children: Perspectives and Practices*. 2nd ed. New York: Routledge, 87-108.

Selcuk, Sirin R., and Michelle Fine. 2008. *Muslim American Youth: Understanding Hyphenated Identities through Multiple Methods*. New York: New York University Press.

Senate Report No. 142. 1865. 38th Congress, 2nd session, *Report of the Joint Committee on the Conduct of the War: Massacre of Cheyenne Indians*. Washington, DC: Government Printing Office.

Sheper-Hughes, N. 1992. *Death without Violence*. Berkeley: University of California Press.

Shinn, Larry. 1987. *The Dark Lord: Cult Images and the Hare Krishnas in America*. Philadelphia: Westminster Press.

Shire, M. 2005. Learning to Be Righteous: A Jewish Theology of Childhood. In Karen Marie Yust, Aostre N. Johnson, Sandy E. Sasso, and Eugene Roehlkepartain (eds.), *Nurturing Child and Adolescent Spirituality*. Lanham, MD: Rowman & Littlefield, 43-52.

Simmel, G. 1908/1959. *Sociology of Religion*. Translated by C. Rosenthal. New York: Philosophical Library.

Sivan, Emmanuel. 1995. The Enclave Culture. In Martin Marty and R. Scott Appleby (eds.), *Fundamentalisms Comprehended*. Chicago: University of Chicago Press, 11-68.

Smith, Christian, with Melissa Lundquist Denton. 2005. *Soul-Searching: The Religious and Spiritual Lives of American Teenagers*. Oxford: Oxford University Press.

Smith, Johnathan Z. 1978. *Map Is Not Territory: Studies in the History of Religions*. Leiden: Brill.

———. 1988. *Imagining Religion: From Babylon to Jonestown*. Chicago: University of Chicago Press.

Squarcini, Federico, and Eugenio Fizzotti. 2004. *Hare Krishna*. Salt Lake City, UT: Signature Books.

Stafford, Charles. 2007. What Is Interesting about Chinese Religion. In Ramon Sarro and David Berliner (eds.), *Learning Religion: Anthropological Approaches*. New York: Berghahn Books, 177-90.

Stambach, Amy. 2009. *Faith in Schools: Religion, Education, and American Evangelicals in East Africa*. Stanford: Stanford University Press.

Stark, Rodney. 1996. "Why Religious Movements Succeed or Fail: A Revised General Model." *Journal of Contemporary Religion* 11: 133-46.

Stensvold, Anne. 2009. Introduction to the West Balkans' Religious Scene. In A. Stensvold (ed.), *Western Balkans: The Religious Dimension*. Norway: Sypress Forlag.

Sternheimer, Karen. 2006. *Kids These Days: Facts and Fictions about Today's Youth*. Lanham, MD: Rowman & Littlefield.

Subbotsky, E. 1993. *Foundations of the Mind: Children's Understanding of Reality*. Cambridge, MA: Harvard University Press.

Sugarman, Jeremy, Kenneth Getz, Jeanne Speckman, Margaret Byrne, Jason Gerson, and Ezekiel Emanuel. 2005. "The Cost of Institutional Review Boards in Academic Medical Centers." *New England Journal of Medicine* 352: 1825-27.

Sutton-Smith, Brian. 1986. *Toys as Culture*. New York: Gardner Press.

Sutton-Smith, B. Foreword. 2004. In J. Goldstein, D. Buckingham, and G. Brougère (eds.), *Toys, Games, and Media*. Mahwah, NJ: Erlbaum, vii-x.

Swindler, Ann. 1986. "Culture in Action: Symbols and Strategies." *American Sociological Review* 51: 273-86.

"Talking Esther Doll." 2009. Retrieved 1/14/10, from http://www.spiritofthebible.com/site/1627494/product/773-7992347.

Tisdall, E. Kay, John M. Davis, and Michael Gallagher, eds. 2009. *Researching with Children and Young People: Research Design, Methods, and Analysis*. Washington, DC: Sage Press.

Tocqueville, A.1945. *Democracy in America (1830-45)*. New York: Knopf,

Toren, Christina. 1993. "Making History: The Significance of Childhood Cognition for a Comparative Anthropology of the Mind." *MAN* 28, no. 3: 461-78.

———. 2004. "Becoming a Christian in Fiji: An Ethnographic Study of Ontogeny." *Journal of the Royal Anthropological Institute* (n.s.) 10: 222-40.

———. 2006. The Effectiveness of Ritual. In F. Cannell (ed.), *The Anthropology of Christianity*. Durham, NC: Duke University Press, 185-210.

Toy Industry Association Annual Report 2008. 2009. Retrieved 8/11/10, from http://www.toyassociation.org/AM/PDFs/AnnualReport2008/TIA08.pdf.

Travis, Dempsey. 1981. *An Autobiography of Black Chicago*. Chicago: Urban Research Institute.

Trigg, Roger. 1985. Review of *Experience, Explanation, and Faith: An Introduction to the Philosophy of Religion* by Anthony O'Hear. *Philosophy* 60 (233): 413-14.

Tsering Lama Jampal Zangpo. 1988. *A Garland of Immortal Wish-Fulfilling Trees: The Palyul Tradition of Nyingmapa*. Ithaca, NY: Snow Lion Publications.

Tulku Thondup. 1986. *Hidden Teachings of Tibet: An Explanation of the Terma Tradition of the Nyingma School of Tibetan Buddhism*. London: Wisdom Publications.

Turner, Victor. 1967. *The Forest of Symbols*. Ithaca, NY: Cornell University Press.

———. 1982. *From Ritual to Theatre: The Human Seriousness of Play*. New York: Performing Arts Journal Press.

"252 Backpack Bible-NIV." 2009. Retrieved 1/14/10, from http://www.tbnwebstore.org/product.asp?sku=0310710138.

"2:52 Basics." 2009. Retrieved 1/14/10, from http://www.252basics.org/about.php.

Tyson, Ruel. 1988. Introduction: Method and Spirit; Studying Diversity of Gestures in Religion. In Ruel W. Tyson, James L. Peacock, and Daniel W. Patterson (eds.), *Diversities of Gifts: Field Studies in Southern Religion*. Chicago: University of Illinois Press, 3-20.

Verhey, Emay. 1991. *Om Het Joodse Kind* [About a Jewish Child]. Amsterdam: Nijgh & Van Ditmar.

Warner, Marina. 1994. *Managing Monsters: Six Myths of Our Time*. London: Vintage.

Warner, R. Stephen. 1997. "Religion, Boundaries, and Bridges." *Sociology of Religion* 58, no. 3: 217-38.

Weber, M. 1978. *Economy and Society*. Berkeley: University of California Press.

West, Andy. 2007. "Power Relationships and Adult Resistance to Children's Participation." *Children, Youth, and Environments* 17: 123-35.

Westerhoff, J. W. III. 2000. *Will Our Children Have Faith?* Rev. ed. Toronto: Anglican Book Centre.

Westhill Friends. 2010. Retrieved 3/14/11, from http://www.westhillsfriends.org/QVWchildren.html.

Williams, Nancy, and Elizabeth Lindsey. 2005. "Spirituality and Religion in the Lives of Runaway and Homeless Youth: Coping with Adversity." *Journal of Religion and Spirituality in Social Work* 24, no. 4: 19-38.

Williams, Roman R. 2009. "Picturing Religion in Everyday Life." *ASA Sociology of Religion Section Newsletter* 11, no. 1: 4-5.

Winter, K. 2010. *Building Relationships and Communicating with Young Children: A Practice Guide for Social Workers*. Abingdon: Routledge.

Wolf, Diane L. 1997. "Family Secrets: Transnational Struggles among Children of Filipino Immigrants" *Sociological Perspectives* 40, no. 3: 457-82.

———. 2007. *Beyond Anne Frank: Hidden Children and Postwar Families in Holland*. Berkeley: University of California Press.

Woodiwiss, A. 2005. *Human Rights*. London: Routledge.

Woolley, J. D. 2000. The Development of Beliefs about Mental-Physical Causality in Imagination, Magic, and Religion. In K. Rosengren, C. Johnson, and P. L. Harris (eds.), *Imagining the Impossible: Magical, Scientific, and Religious Thinking in Children*. Cambridge: Cambridge University Press, 99-129.

Wright, Stuart A. 1997. The Dynamics of Movement Membership: Joining and Leaving NRMs. In David G. Bromley (ed.), *Teaching New Religious Movements*. New York: Oxford University Press, 187-210.

Wuthnow, R. 1999. *Growing Up Religious: Christians and Jews and Their Journeys of Faith.* Boston: Beacon.

Yildirim, Y. 2005. Filling the Heart with the Love of God: Islamic Perspectives on Spirituality in Childhood and Adolescence. In Karen Marie Yust, Aostre N. Johnson, Sandy E. Sasso, and Eugene Roehlkepartain (eds.), *Nurturing Child and Adolescent Spirituality.* Lanham, MD: Rowman & Littlefield, 69-80.

Yust, Karen Marie, Aostre N. Johnson, Sandy E. Sasso, and Eugene Roehlkepartain, eds. 2005. *Nurturing Child and Adolescent Spirituality: Perspectives from the World's Religious Traditions.* Lanham, MD: Rowman & Littlefield.

Yust, Karen Marie, and Eugene C. Roehlkepartain. 2004. *Real Kids, Real Faith: Practices for Nurturing Children's Spiritual Lives.* San Francisco: Jossey-Bass, 2004.

Zimmerman, L. D., and G. Calovini. 1971. "Toys as Learning Materials for Preschool Children." *Exceptional Children* 37, no. 9: 642-54.

Zinnbower, B., K. Pargament, B. Cole, M. Rye, E. Butter, and T. Belavich. 1997. "Religion and Spirituality." *Journal for the Scientific Study of Religion* 36: 549-64.

About the Contributors

PRISCILLA ALDERSON is Emerita Professor of Childhood Studies, Social Science Research Unit, Institute of Education, University of London, and a member of the Westminster Quaker Meeting, London.

SALLY ANDERSON is Associate Professor in the Danish School of Education at Aarhus University. She is the author of *Civil Sociality: Children, Sport, and Cultural Policy in Denmark*.

JENNIFER BESTE is Associate Professor of Theological Ethics at Xavier University in Cincinnati, Ohio, and the author of *God and the Victim: Traumatic Intrusions on Grace and Freedom*.

CHRIS J. BOYATZIS is Professor of Psychology at Bucknell University in Lewisburg, Pennsylvania.

ANNE BRAUDE is Director of the Women's Studies in Religion Program and Senior Lecturer on American Religious History at Harvard Divinity School in Cambridge, Massachusetts. She is the author of *Radical Spirits: Spiritualism and Women's Rights in Nineteenth-Century America* and *Sisters and Saints: Women and Religion in America* and editor of *Transforming the Faiths of Our Fathers: The Women Who Changed American Religion*.

PIA CHRISTENSEN is Professor of Anthropology and Childhood Studies and Director of Research at the Institute of Education of the University of Warwick. She is coeditor (with Allison James) of *Research with Children: Perspectives and Practices* and *Children in the City: Home, Neighborhood, and Community* (with Margaret O'Brien).

CINDY DELL CLARK is Visiting Associate Professor at Rutgers University in Camden, New Jersey. She is the author of *In a Different Voice: Doing Children's Qualitative Research*; *In Sickness and in Play: Children Coping with Chronic Illness*; and *Flights of Fancy, Leaps of Faith*.

MOIRA HINDERER is Visiting Faculty in the Center for Africana Studies of John Hopkins University in Baltimore, Maryland.

AMY HOLMES-TAGCHUNGDARPA is Assistant Professor of History at the University of Alabama in Tuscaloosa.

ZOHREH KERMANI is currently adjunct faculty in the department of Religious Studies at Youngstown State University in Ohio.

RUQAYYA YASMINE KHAN is Assistant Professor of Islamc Studies in the department of Religion at Trinity University in San Antonio, Texas. She is the author of *Self and Secrecy in Early Islam*.

PHILIPPA KOCH is a doctoral student in the history of Christianity at the University of Chicago Divinity School.

KRISTY NABHAN-WARREN is Associate Professor of American Religions at Augustana College in Rock Island, Illinois. She is the author of *The Virgin of El Barrio: Marian Apparitions, Catholic Evangelizing, and Mexican American Activism* and *DeColores! American Catholic and Protestant Cursillas and the "Fourth Day" Movement*.

REBECCA SACHS NORRIS is Chair and Associate Professor in the department of Religious and Theological Studies at Merrimack College in North Andover, Massachusetts. She is coauthor (with Nikki Bado-Fralick) of *Toying with God: The World of Religious Games and Dolls*.

SARAH PIKE is Professor of Religious Studies at California State University–Chico. She is the author of *Earthly Bodies, Magical Selves: Contemporary Pagans and the Search for Community* and *New Age and Neopagan Religions in America*.

SUSAN B. RIDGELY is Assistant Professor at the University of Wisconsin at Oshkosh and the author, under the name Susan Ridgely Bales, of *When I Was a Child: Children's Interpretations of First Communion*.

E. BURKE ROCHFORD JR. is Professor of Sociology and Religion at Middlebury College in Vermont. He is the author of *Hare Krishna in America* and *Hare Krishna Transformed*.

DIANE WOLF is Professor of Sociology and Director of the Jewish Studies Program at the University of California–Davis. She is the author of *Beyond Anne Frank: Hidden Children and Jewish Families in Postwar Holland* and *Factory Daughters: Gender, Household Dynamics, and Rural Industrialization in Java* and coeditor (with Judith Gerson) of *Sociology Confronts the Holocaust: Memories and Identites in Jewish Diasporas*.

Index

gang members, 121–22, 124–28, 130–33
God, 19, 30–31, 59, 127–28, 146–47, 157–60,
    162–70, 178, 185, 208–14; children's con-
    ceptions of, 25, 30, 159, 169, 195
Great Migration, 9, 12, 223

Hall, Stanley G., 38
Hare Krishna, 7, 95, 98–99, 105–6
hidden child, 5, 10, 269–71, 274, 277–79;
    former, 269–73, 277, 279–81
high schools, 37
Hinderer, Moira, 9, 12
Hirschfield, Lawrence, 108
historical sources, children's perspectives
    in, 9–10, 15, 223, 225, 254, 291

identity. *See* religious identities
incarnations, 253, 255–56, 261; children as,
    252–53
Indians, 242, 244–45, 247–48. *See also*
    Cheyenne
Internet, 42, 45
interviews (*see also* methodology, eth-
    nography), 27, 85, 94, 127, 152, 158, 273,
    281; engaging children in, 75, 90, 92,
    109, 166; impact of place on, 8, 272; the
    impact of the setting, 8; intergenera-
    tional, 92, 109; with teenagers, 273
IRB (Institutional Review Board), 7, 10,
    67–68, 70–79, 88, 273
ISKCON (International Society for
    Krishna Consciousness), 7, 95–97, 99,
    101, 104–7
Islam, 44–45, 173–74, 177–79, 184–85, 197

James, Alison, 20, 85
James, William, 39
Janeway, James, 202
Jesus, 19, 30, 58, 104, 122, 126–27, 160,
    162–64, 197, 230
joy, 13, 158, 167, 228–29, 258
Judaism, 29, 145, 154, 190, 193, 267, 269,
    271, 278–80

Karma Chagme, 254–55, 257–64
Kermani, Zohreh, 7, 108

Koch, Philippal 204, 206, 210, 216
Kohlberg, Lawrence, 26

labyrinth walk, 113, 115
literature, children's, 202, 206
Little Book, 206–8, 210–13, 216

magical, 108, 114–15, 119
marketing, 190–91, 196, 199–200
marketplace, 1, 13, 195, 223
Mars Hill Church, 40
martyrologies, 202, 211, 213, 216
Mary, 30, 122, 130
maturity, 5–6, 19–20, 27, 31–2, 110
memoirs, 9, 228, 233
memories, 115, 270–73, 275, 280–82; as
    child-centered source, 10, 92, 227, 240,
    261, 270, 275; childhood, 3, 10, 233, 268,
    278; in childhood, 268; of childhood
    trauma, 268, 271; eliciting, 10, 248, 268;
    emotions in, 273, 275
methodologies, adult-centered, 173, 179
methodology: access children's perspectives,
    157, 169; accessing the historical child,
    9–11, 208, 222, 237, 249, 252–54, 257, 264;
    child-centered, 1–2, 5–10, 22, 24, 84–85,
    157–58, 169, 176–77, 179, 182; child's assent
    to, 68, 72, 75–76, 88–89, 157; ethnogra-
    phy, xi, 7, 9, 22, 67, 78–79, 81, 90, 92, 111;
    research with children, xi–xii, 7, 63, 67,
    75–78, 82, 90, 106, 170, 232; surveys with
    teenagers, 8, 27, 29, 34, 173, 182–83, 186
Minnehaha, 9, 238–39, 243–49
Minnie. *See* Minnehaha
Mintz, Steven, 46
Motley, Willard, 227, 233
movies, 12, 223–24, 227
Muslim, 6, 29, 51, 172–73, 177–79, 185, 190,
    221

Nabhan-Warren, Kristy, 8, 10, 12–13
Namchö Mingyur Dorje, 253–65; biogra-
    phy of, 264–65
National Study of Youth and Religion, 3, 15
new religions, 2–3, 40, 95, 102, 106, 108,
    110, 115

Smith, Jonathan Z., 117, 133
socialization, x, 28, 37, 106, 108, 139;
    through conversation, 2, 11, 22, 28–31, 75,
    109, 118, 166, 204, 285
spiritual development, 3, 19, 22–23, 166,
    190, 198–99
spiritualism, 247–48
spirituality, children's, ix, 27, 114
stage theories, 19, 26–7, 32, 60. *See also*
    Piaget, Jean
suffering. *See* violence
Sunday School, 20, 223–24, 247
synagogue, 143, 147, 279

tattoos, 121–22, 125–26
teenager, definition of, 35–36, 38–39, 46
teenagers, 6, 27, 29, 34–46, 77, 109, 173–74,
    286–87; assumptions about, 34–35, 124;
    definition of, 44; fears of, 34–36, 39–40,
    42; hybrid religious identities, 6, 8, 10;
    interviews with, 89–90, 273; liminal
    phase, 35, 38; minority, 44–45; religios-
    ity of, 34, 45; religious creativity of, 40;
    research with, 13–14, 131–32, 176–78, 182
toys, 9–10, 91–92, 165, 189–92, 195–96, 200;
    adult views of, 191–92, 200; educational,
    165, 190–93, 199; parents' influence in,
    199; relationship to children's culture,
    199; religious, 191, 199–200

traditional Catholic religious (TCR), 158,
    160–61, 168

United Nations Convention on the Rights
    of the Child (UNCRC), 52–53
U.S. government, 49, 239, 245

violence, 12, 60, 62, 122–24, 126, 130,
    132–43, 239, 249
Virgin of Guadalupe, 121–23, 125–28,
    130–34
Visions, 34, 169, 253, 255, 257–60,
    262–63

war, 182, 267, 269–72, 274, 276, 278–81, 283;
    Bosnian, 177, 182–83
Weber, Max, 55
White, Thomas, 207–15
Wicca. *See* Paganism
Wolf, Diane, 5, 10
World War II, 12, 34, 36–37, 68, 143, 267–68,
    270–72, 274, 276, 278–81
Wuthnow, Robert, 3

youth, 3, 29, 34–41, 44, 123, 130–32, 173–74,
    176–78, 182–83, 185; Bosnian, 172, 174,
    178–81. *See also* teenagers
youth culture, x, 34–35, 37–38, 45
youth identity, 172, 175, 183, 185